P9-DHT-561

LONE STAR JUSTICE

BOOKS BY THE AUTHOR

The Last Days of the Sioux Nation
1963

Frontiersmen in Blue:
The United States Army and the Indian, 1846–1865
1967

Frontier Regulars:
The United States Army and the Indian, 1865–1890
1974

The Indian Frontier of the American West, 1846–1890
1984

High Noon in Lincoln: Violence on the Western Frontier
1987

Cavalier in Buckskin:
George Armstrong Custer and the Western Military Frontier
1988; 2001

Billy the Kid: A Short and Violent Life
1989

The Lance and the Shield:
The Life and Times of Sitting Bull
1993

A Life Wild and Perilous:
Mountain Men and the Paths to the Pacific
1997

Lone Star Justice

THE FIRST CENTURY OF THE TEXAS RANGERS

Robert M. Utley

OXFORD
UNIVERSITY PRESS

2002

OXFORD
UNIVERSITY PRESS

Oxford   New York

Auckland Bangkok Buenos Aires Cape Town Chennai
Dar es Salaam Delhi Hong Kong Istanbul Karachi Kolkata
Kuala Lumpur Madrid Melbourne Mexico City Mumbai Nairobi
São Paulo Shanghai Singapore Taipei Tokyo Toronto

and an associated company in Berlin

Copyright © 2002 by Robert M. Utley

Published by Oxford University Press, Inc.,
198 Madison Avenue, New York, New York 10016

Oxford is a registered trademark of Oxford University Press

All rights reserved. No part of this publication may be reproduced,
stored in a retrieval system, or transmitted in any form or by any means,
electronic, mechanical, photocopying, recording, or otherwise,
without the prior permission of Oxford University Press.

Library of Congress Cataloging-in-Publication Data
Utley, Robert Marshall, 1929–
Lone Star justice: the first century of the Texas Rangers /
by Robert M. Utley.
p. cm.
Includes bibliographical references and index.
ISBN 0-19-512742-0
1. Texas Rangers–History–19th century.
2. Frontier and pioneer life–Texas.   3. Texas–History–1846–1950.
4. Texas–History–Republic, 1836–1846.   I. Title.
F391 .U9 2002
976.4–dc21   2001036405

Book design by Charles B. Hames

1 3 5 7 9 8 6 4 2

Printed in the United States of America
on acid-free paper

For George J. Minnucci Jr.

My favorite Old West aficionado

CONTENTS

MAPS

Illustrations follow pages 114 and 242.

PREFACE

A s I RESEARCHED this book, I thought it appropriate to see how filmdom has treated the Texas Rangers. I taped *Lone Ranger* (1956), a full-length feature drawn from the television series launched in 1949 and starring Clayton Moore and Jay Silverheels. In the first five minutes, the film exposed something drastically wrong. The Rangers played out their drama amid a forest of saguaro cactus. I have yet to see a saguaro growing in Texas. Moreover, no Ranger of record could boast the dazzling exploits of the lone survivor of that ambushed squad. Also, they wore the wagon wheel star badge that Texas Rangers did not adopt until the twentieth century.

This depiction, representative of hundreds in narrative, verse, song, audio, film, and even cyberspace, left me with no doubt that the Texas Rangers still flourish as legend. Not surprisingly, the true Rangers of then and now come across as real people with their share of talents and shortcomings—people, furthermore, who sometimes lived up to the legend. In any event, the strength and endurance of the legend mean people still care, perhaps enough to justify an effort to recapture the Texas Rangers as they were.

The history of the Rangers divides conveniently at 1910. Before 1910, the Rangers were volunteer fighting units contending with Indians and Mexicans who then turned themselves into lawmen of the Old West. By 1910, the Rangers were closing out the era of the Old West and verging on another incarnation altogether. After 1910, their story features a new cast of characters, new themes, and new kinds of adventure. That story is reserved for volume 2, which will cover the rest of the twentieth century.

For the years 1823 to 1910, the designation "Texas Ranger" encompassed two very different kinds of men. The term itself came into common usage over time and reflected a tradition taking shape over time. Until 1874, Texas Rangers were citizen soldiers, intermittently mobilized for temporary duty to fight Indians or Mexicans. Regardless of formal designation—mounted volunteers, mounted riflemen, minutemen—they adhered to a pattern of character, organization, and operation that defined a tradition rather than an institution.

For nearly half a century, the citizen soldiers confronted Indians who raided the settlements of the Texas frontier. Kiowas and Comanches struck south through Texas into Mexico, stealing stock and killing Texans as they went. Local Texas tribes occasionally joined in the marauding, as did Kickapoos, Lipan Apaches, and other Indians based in Mexico. The Indian threat was the central and lasting purpose of the Ranger units of citizen soldiers. During the years of the Texas Republic, moreover, 1836–1845, citizen soldiers gathered to fend off military incursions from Mexico, which had not conceded the independence of Texas. After statehood men volunteered to fight as U.S. troops in the Mexican War. They bore federal military designations, but they called themselves Texas Rangers. Finally, for both republic and state, the international border traced by the Rio Grande periodically drew companies of citizen soldiers to confront both Mexican bandits and raiding Indians.

An act of the Texas legislature in 1874 established what administratively came to be known as the Frontier Battalion. The authors of the law meant to create a permanent or semipermanent military force to do what the citizen soldiers had done, only better. The Rangers of this outfit displayed many of the defining features of their predecessors, but they were no longer citizen soldiers. Although created to fight Indians, the Frontier Battalion recast itself as a corps of lawmen when the Indian menace subsided. For the next three decades, therefore, Texas Ranger meant lawman rather than Indian fighter. Unlike the citizen soldier, he enjoyed institutional continuity. Unlike the citizen soldier, he contended with offenders against the laws of Texas.

The modern stereotype casts Texas Rangers solely as lawmen, and the title of this book tends to reinforce that stereotype. The citizen soldiers who preceded the lawmen, however, pursued justice as rigorously as the lawmen. It was a different concept of justice, one hardly shared by their Indian and Mexican foes. But it was justice as understood by the Anglo Texans who dominated the republic and then the state. Rooted in the white people's frontier ethos, it was unforgiving and lethal. Both as citizen soldiers and as lawmen, Texas Rangers would have proudly identified with the idea of "Lone Star Justice."

LIKE ALL MULTIETHNIC studies, this one confronts challenges of nomenclature. Indian poses no confusion of identity, even to those who insist on Native American or Amerindian. Blacks, mostly former slaves, will be called blacks, not African Americans.

Not so readily resolved is the labeling of people of Spanish-Mexican heritage and people of diverse European heritage. The former almost dictate a somewhat artificial nomenclature. They called themselves Mexican, they spoke Spanish, their loyalties ran to Mexico, and their culture was largely Mexican, adapted only as much as necessary to the culture of the dominant non-Mexicans. In the border zone on both sides of the Rio Grande, these people regarded themselves as Mexicans, whether they lived in Mexico or Texas. Many moved back and forth as family or economic circumstances decreed. The country of citizenship seemed of little consequence, although in terms of law it could be critically consequential. In any event, distinguishing Mexican Mexicans from Mexican Americans in the border zone is all but impossible. I shall call all these people Mexicans. Only in referring to Texas citizens

residing distant from the border do I employ the term "Mexican American." To me, Hispanic carries connotations untrue to the distinctly
Mexican culture that had evolved by the nineteenth century.

Border Mexicans tended to call everyone with white skin Americans.
These people immigrated from the American South and from Europe,
including French, Germans, Poles, Russians, and other nationalities
besides English, Irish, and Scottish. Nevertheless "Anglo" or "Anglo
Texan" has attained wide acceptance as the term for the white people
who dominated Texas politically, economically, and socially throughout
the nineteenth century. Although Anglo hardly describes the large
German population of Texas, I shall use it nonetheless. But the reader
should bear in mind the multinational character of Anglo Texans.

In recent decades, two contrasting views of the Texas Rangers have
taken shape in the public mind, including the academic mind. In the
first, the Rangers were fearless men of sterling character and unswerving
dedication to mission. Often compared with another elite constabulary,
the Royal Canadian Mounted Police, they made up a crack outfit—
paragons of virtue who were uniformly successful in carrying out their
duties and served as shining examples for the young. As citizen soldiers,
they fought as stalwart yeomen defending their homes against bar-
barous Indians and vicious Mexicans. As lawmen, they dispensed even-
handed justice to Anglo and Mexican alike.

In the opposing view, the Texas Rangers were ruthless, brutal, and
more lawless than the criminals they pursued. As citizen soldiers, they
indiscriminately killed men, women, and children of enemy Indian
tribes. Retaliating for supposed Mexican atrocities, they inflicted on
Mexicans atrocities of their own. As lawmen, they tortured prisoners to
extract information, shot first and asked questions later, executed many
a captive "attempting to escape," and looked on all Mexicans as bandits
deserving the swift justice of the six-shooter.

As usual, both stereotypes contain elements of truth and falsity.
Examples of confirming exploits undergird each interpretation. Most
Anglo Texans still embrace the first, Mexicans and Mexican Americans

the second. Not surprisingly, the historical reality lies somewhere between the extremes.

Ranger experts will readily identify many episodes omitted from this book. I wanted to include them. The "Horse Marines" of the Texas Revolution, certain Mexican War exploits, more of Rip Ford's Indian battles, the numerous county feuds that wracked all parts of Texas, the Fort Griffin vigilante mob, train robberies, Tascosa, and the cowboy strike in the Panhandle—all and more are contained in my notes, and some are chronicled in parts of the manuscript that fell casualty to the delete button. I hope, however, that I have identified the main themes and narrated enough adventures to convey the flavor and significance of the Texas Rangers of yesteryear.

Nearly everyone in Texas describes location by county, of which there are 254. For this reason I have tried to include on some of the maps counties that play a role in the narrative. The reader who is still confused will need to resort to a highway map.

I owe a large debt of gratitude to the people who helped guide me through four years of labor on this work. Three in particular played vital roles in shaping the manuscript: my wife, Melody Webb; my editor at Oxford, Peter Ginna; and my agent, Carl D. Brandt. The staff at the Archives Division of the Texas State Library could not have been more helpful. In particular, I single out Donaly Brice, who knows the collections thoroughly and is ever anxious to guide one to the proper destination. He is a true professional whom one soon calls friend. Photo archivist John Anderson also merits thanks. The Center for American History at the University of Texas–Austin is one of the nation's leading repositories of western American material. It is user-friendly, and the staff all accommodating. Near my home in Georgetown, Texas, is Southwestern University. The special collections there contain the Edward Clark Collection of Texana, a prime resource that saved me hours of commuting. Kathryn Stallard and Sheran Johle merit my gratitude for their solicitous support of my research. The library's Joan Parks and Lisa Anderson also played important roles in helping integrate me into the library system and expeditiously handling interlibrary loans. Finally, but for Dr. William Jones, now retired professor of history, I would not have enjoyed my valued special relationship with Southwestern.

Mike Koury of the Old Army Press in Fort Collins, Colorado, let me borrow his microfilm copy of ten years of the *Telegraph and Texas Register*. Michael Musick and William Dobak at the National Archives and Records Administration in Washington, D.C., kept their eyes alert for Texas Ranger material in the federal archives, as did the Smithsonian Institution's James S. Hutchings. John Lovett, assistant curator of Western History Collections, University of Oklahoma Library, helped with the Ranger photos in the N. H. Rose Collection.

Texans who have been helpful in one way or another include Mike Cox of Austin; Leon Metz of El Paso; Harold Weiss, Jr., of Leander; Dean Jerry D. Thompson of Texas A&M International University at Laredo; Chuck Parsons of Luling; Rick Miller of Harker Heights; Jeff Jackson of Lampasas; Prof. John Miller Morris of the University of Texas at San Antonio; Melissa Baldridge, curator of the Torch Collection in Houston; Byron A. Johnson, director, and Christina Stopka, librarian/archivist, Texas Ranger Hall of Fame, Waco; Chris Floerke at the Institute of Texan Cultures in San Antonio; and of course Peter Dana of Georgetown, who once again collaborated with me to produce fine shaded-relief maps.

In addition, I appreciate the aid and continuing interest of Prof. Paul A. Hutton of the University of New Mexico; Mark Gardner of Cascade, Colorado; and David A. Clary of Roswell, New Mexico.

LONE STAR JUSTICE

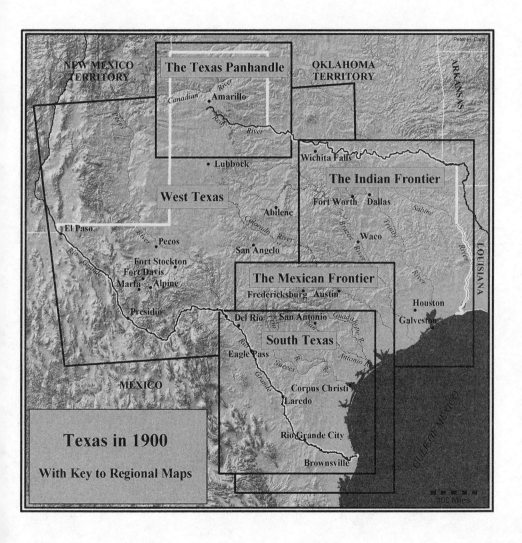

Peter H. Dana

NEW MEXICO TERRITORY

OKLAHOMA TERRITORY

ARKANSAS

The Texas Panhandle

Canadian River

Amarillo

Red River

Pecos

Lubbock

West Texas

Wichita Falls

The Indian Frontier

Fort Worth Dallas

Sabine

Abilene

Colorado River

Brazos River

Trinity

El Paso

River

Pecos

Waco

San Angelo

Rio Grande

River

LOUISIANA

Fort Stockton
Fort Davis
Marfa Alpine

The Mexican Frontier

Fredericksburg Austin

Houston

Presidio

Del Rio San Antonio

Guadalupe R.

Galveston

San

South Texas

Eagle Pass

Nueces R.

Antonio R.

MÉXICO

Rio Grande

Corpus Christi

Laredo

Texas in 1900

With Key to Regional Maps

Rio Grande City

Brownsville

GULF OF MEXICO

100 Miles

[1]

The Tradition Established:
Jack Hays and Walker Creek

For Anglo Texans, June 8, 1844, was a defining moment, if not *the* defining moment, in the transformation of their mounted volunteers performing "ranging service" into Texas Rangers. On this day, on an obscure stream named Walker Creek in the hills north of San Antonio, the qualities that would give singular character to the Texas Rangers came together in an extraordinary and dramatic way to crystallize a tradition evolving loosely and sporadically since 1823. Three of these qualities had brought the tradition to life; the fourth gave it powerful momentum.

The first and most important quality was leadership. Texan fighting men could be led but not commanded. Time and again, pitted against Mexicans and Indians, they had demonstrated a fierce personal independence that shattered subordination and discipline and sacrificed the chance of military gain. The revolutionary armies of 1835–1836, quarrelsome, fractious, and unruly, won Texas her shaky independence from Mexico not by strategy, tactics, or even the uncertain command of the legendary Sam Houston. They won by rare good fortune. Only a gifted leader, one who led by example and understood the Texan makeup, could mold such mulish freemen into a cohesive team.

3

The second quality lay within the personal characteristics of the men themselves. They were fighters, seasoned by the campaigns of the Texas Revolution and the constant struggle against Indian raiders. Most were young, hardy, physically fit, courageous, fearless, bold, endowed with fortitude and endurance, and ever ready for a fight. The most adventurous of the Anglo Texans, they had edged up the Trinity, the Brazos, the Colorado, and the Guadalupe, leaving the less adventurous to live contentedly on their plantations closer to the Gulf of Mexico. In the black soil of the stream bottoms and open prairies, the frontiersmen planted corn and cotton, kept a few horses and cows, and saw their families butchered by the Indians whose lands they invaded. Periodically they gathered informally to retaliate or, whenever the bankrupt government of the republic would sanction, to "range" the frontiers in volunteer companies looking for a fight. Such a life produced individualists impatient with restraint who were superb fighters, unlike pioneers elsewhere, who dealt with human and environmental enemies only sporadically.

The third quality brought together the specialized skills of the frontier fighter: marksmanship with rifle and pistol, horsemanship, mastery of outdoor life, and knowledge of the foe—how they fought and how to fight them. These were skills honed by experience; the more experience, the sharper the skills.

Captain Jack Hays's San Antonio–based company of mounted volunteers combined these qualities in a fighting unit of uncommon talent. In 1844 they gained a new quality: revolutionary combat tactics drawn from a new weapon. In the hands of Texas Rangers, Samuel Colt's revolving pistol would gain renown.

John Coffee Hays resonated through history as the ideal Texas Ranger, the one above all others every Ranger strove to emulate. Hays and his older brother William probably arrived in Texas early in 1838. Texas appealed to their restless, adventurous spirits and evoked family heritage as well. In 1814 their father, Harmon Hays, had fought Creek Indians and British regulars with Andrew Jackson and Sam Houston. When Harmon's second son was born on his Tennessee plantation on

4

January 28, 1817, he named him in honor of Jackson's able lieutenant, General John Coffee. Jack's mother and father both died when he was fifteen, in 1832. He and two of the other children went to live with their uncle on a Mississippi plantation. Here, still an adolescent, Jack learned surveying.

Seeking opportunity and adventure, Jack and William headed for newly independent Texas. They presented themselves to Texas President Sam Houston and handed him a letter from another uncle. It recalled old friendships and introduced them as "practicable surveyors" who believed that Texas offered "a fairer place for the exercise of their energies, industry and abilities."[1]

Jack Hays hardly looked the part of frontier fighter, or even outdoorsman. Slim, only five-eight in height, with wavy brown hair, brushy eyebrows, and smooth-shaven face, he impressed one observer as a "delicate-looking young man." Outdoor life turned his fair complexion to tawny and weather beaten, while the demands of leadership in an environment fraught with danger gave him "a thoughtful and care-worn expression" and a "habitual frown." Unprepossessing in appearance, he exhibited a like temperament. Modest, quiet, soft-spoken, thoughtful, a man of few words either spoken or written, he had no need to boast: his actions told all.[2]

The frontiers of Texas drew scores of surveyors, for land was the infant republic's only tangible asset. Hays worked out of San Antonio.

More than a century old, San Antonio lay west of the geographical and cultural border of the Anglo Texas founded by Stephen F. Austin. Only a handful of enterprising Anglos had settled there. The olive-skinned townspeople, numbering less than one thousand in 1844, clung to their Spanish language and Mexican culture and dressed in serapes, sombreros, rebozos, and other garb characteristic of communities south of the Rio Grande. In layout and architecture, the city itself evoked the Spanish heritage of Texas. Five old missions, once Franciscan, rose from the banks of the San Antonio River. Churches, government buildings, commercial structures, and dwellings of stone and adobe crowded narrow streets opening on spacious plazas.

South and west of San Antonio stretched South Texas, the vast chaparral plains extending beyond the Nueces to the Rio Grande, a harsh land roiled by Mexican and American bandits and disputed by Texas and Mexico. To the north, however, lay lands more inviting to the colonist and therefore to the surveyor. This was the Texas Hill Country, where rivers and creeks heading on the elevated Edwards Plateau gouged through beds of limestone to water fertile lowlands on their course to the Gulf. Stands of oak and cedar mixed with open prairies, rugged hills, and rocky cliffs to define the Balcones Escarpment.

For surveyor and settler, the Hill Country presented dangers as well as attractions. Beyond, great herds of bison ranged the Edwards Plateau northward across the immense, unbroken table of the Staked Plain and on to the central Great Plains. Tribes of Comanche Indians chased the herds from the Arkansas River south to the edge of the Balcones Escarpment. For decades they had also ridden over the chaparral wastes to plunder Mexican settlements on the Rio Grande and beyond. As Anglo Texans pushed up the Colorado and the Brazos to the base of the scarp in the 1830s, Comanche raiders slipped down from the highlands to join with resident Indians in raiding them too.

Comanches knew what surveyors portended, and so the surveyors had to become Indian fighters as well. In a remarkably short period, Jack Hays transformed himself into a canny Indian fighter.

Surveying and fighting produced a hardened outdoorsman. As one who rode with him recalled, Hays was "wiry and active and gifted with such an iron constitution that he was enabled to undergo hardship and exposure without perceptible effect. . . . I have frequently seen him sitting by his camp fire at night in some exposed locality, when the rain was falling in torrents, or a cold norther with sleet or snow was whistling about his ears, apparently as unconscious of all discomfort as if he had been seated in some cozy room of a first-class city hotel; and this, perhaps, when all he had eaten for supper was a hand full of pecans or a piece of hard tack."[3]

Hays also displayed the leadership skills that marked him as the greatest Ranger captain. They must have been instinctive; they materialized almost at once. The surveying parties had frequent brushes with Comanches, noted the wife of Samuel Maverick, one of the town's leading Anglos. "It was on these occasions that Hays displayed such rare military skill and daring, that very soon by consent of all, he was looked upon as the leader and his orders were obeyed and he himself loved by all. In a fight he was utterly fearless and invincible." Moreover, as one of his followers noted, "he was extremely cautious where the safety of his men was concerned, but when it was a mere question of personal danger his bravery bordered closely on rashness."[4]

By 1839, San Antonians had organized a volunteer company of "minutemen," ready in horse, arms, equipment, and provisions to respond within fifteen minutes once the alarm had been raised. By acclamation, Hays captained the minute men. "They were a noble and gallant set of 'boys,' as they styled each other," noted Mary Maverick, and the Comanches began to keep their distance.[5]

Like all ranging companies, Hays's unit lacked institutional continuity, which was somewhat ameliorated by its focus on San Antonio, where even a destitute republic had to provide at least a token military presence. Comanches rode down from the high plains to the north, while a Mexico that had never accepted Texan independence constantly threatened from the south. Hays had emerged as the guardian of this turbulent frontier. His followers, variously styled, formed units that came and went and fluctuated in size according to the magnitude of the threat and the whims of the Texas Congress. By 1844 many men had served several enlistments with Hays and were veterans.

They traveled swiftly and lightly, unencumbered by anything that could not be carried on horseback. They subsisted on wild game (or horse meat in lean times) and slept in the open under a blanket with the saddle for a pillow. Like all ranging companies, they bore no flag and sported no uniform. The Ranger's "usual habiliments," noted one, "were buckskin moccasins and overhauls, a roundabout and red shirt, a cap manufactured by his own hands from the skin of the coon or wildcat, two or three revolvers and a bowie knife in his belt, and a short rifle on his arm." Tied to his saddle was a Mexican blanket, as well as a small wallet containing salt, ammunition, tobacco, and parched corn.[6]

When they were not in the field, Hays kept his veterans occupied improving their marksmanship and horsemanship. He wanted his men to ride like Comanches, and he borrowed some techniques and equipment from Mexican *vaqueros*. In particular, the heavy Mexican bit gave a rider better control in a fight, when his hands also had to manage weapons. The Rangers also carried a hair rope called *cabrista* and a rawhide *riata* (or lariat) used to rope horses. They sat a Mexican saddle enhanced with their own improvements.[7]

In horsemanship Rangers drew inspiration from the Comanche warrior. "After practising for three or four months," wrote Jim Nichols in his phonetic rendering, "we became so purfect that we would run our horses half or full speede and pick up a hat, a coat, a blanket, or rope, or even a silver dollar, stand up in the saddle, throw ourselves on the side of our horses with only a foot and a hand to be seen, and shoot our pistols under the horses neck, rise up and reverse, etc."[8]

Nichols noted how the men combined practice at shooting and riding. "We put up a post about the size of a common man," he wrote, "then put up another 40 yards farther on. We would run our horses full speed and discharge our rifles at the first post, draw our pistles and fire at the second. At first thare was some wild shooting but we had not practised two months until thare was not many men that would not put his balls in the center of the posts."[9]

The rifles and "pistles" with which Nichols and his comrades practiced and fought in 1843 formed a diverse armory. Rangers furnished their own horses and arms. Usually the government provided powder, lead, provisions, and sometimes the promise of pay, but the men relied on their own arms. Aside from a few shotguns, most were flintlock rifles, kept more for hunting game than fighting. The Kentucky long rifle and its heavier, shorter counterpart, the Tennessee rifle, had evolved into a piece more suited to the mountains and plains of the West. Bison and other large game called for larger calibers, and use on horseback called for shorter barrels. Known both as mountain rifles and plains rifles, these shoulder arms featured barrels between thirty-six and forty-two inches in length and calibers from .49 to .55, and they weighed ten to eleven pounds. In Texas as in the Rocky Mountains and on the Great Plains, these rifles predominated. In addition, most Rangers had one or more single-shot flintlock pistols of varied design and manufacture. These were carried in saddle holsters or jammed under the belt.

Gunsmiths easily converted firearms from flintlock ignition to percussion cap, which became available in the 1820s. But in Texas the flintlock persisted because of the unreliable supply of caps.[10] (In a flintlock, a hammer gripping a piece of flint struck a metal shield and ignited powder poured into a priming pan; the flash carried through a vent hole and set off the main charge in the barrel. The self-contained percussion cap held mercury or another detonator that, fitted on a nipple and struck by the hammer, exploded and fired the main charge.)

Against the smoothbore trade muskets of the Comanches, obtained from traders on the Arkansas River, and against the smoothbore military muskets of the Mexicans, the flintlock rifles proved deadly. Their only drawback was the longer time they took to load properly—up to a minute. The powder charge and the ball and patch had to be rammed separately down the tight-fitting barrel and the pan primed with powder. Most smoothbore muskets, by contrast, received a paper cartridge containing both powder and ball. Loading time therefore decreed that in combat Texans fired in relays, half the men always carrying charged rifles to prevent being overrun. The rifle also decreed that, despite the expert mounted marksmanship Nichols described, in most combat situations Texans dismounted and fought on foot.

When they could be provoked into a fight or caught at all, Comanche warriors proved formidable foes, even for expert riflemen. In mounted combat their prime weapons were bow and arrow and lance rather than the awkward and uncertain trade musket. At close range a Comanche warrior employed the bow and arrow as a highly effective repeating weapon. He could discharge a stream of accurately aimed arrows while a Ranger laboriously reloaded his rifle. What the Ranger needed was his own repeater.

He got it early in 1844. In 1839 the Texas navy had purchased 130 of Samuel Colt's revolving pistols, manufactured at his plant in Paterson, New Jersey. When President Sam Houston disbanded the navy in 1843, Jack Hays equipped his Rangers from the surplus navy stocks.

These "Paterson Colts" held five .36-caliber paper charges containing powder and ball in a revolving cylinder. Cocking the weapon turned the cylinder to line up a new chamber with the barrel and a hammer-activated percussion cap and also to expose a recessed trigger.

The Paterson Colt was a fragile piece, demanding constant care. To mount a new cylinder, the nine-inch barrel had to be detached from the frame, then refastened by means of a wedge. Absent or improperly positioned, the wedge could cause malfunction. To replace a cylinder on horseback in the heat of battle required uncommon skill.

For all their delicacy, the Paterson Colts provided unprecedented firepower. A Ranger armed with a Paterson and an extra cylinder could fire ten rounds in forty seconds, and Hays's Rangers frequently carried two pistols and spare cylinders. At last they had the firepower to stand up to Comanches in mounted combat and more than match their rapidity of fire with bow and arrow.[11]

The new weapons and the new tactics they prompted received their first combat test on June 8, 1844, at Walker Creek. Never had Hays commanded a more efficient unit, including names that would resonate in Ranger lore. His lieutenant was Ben McCulloch, and the fourteen men Hays led out of San Antonio on June 1 included Richard A. Gillespie and Samuel H. Walker.

Hays intended to scout the Hill Country for Indian sign while McCulloch remained in San Antonio with the balance of the company. The little detachment examined the upper waters of the Pedernales and Llano Rivers (in Texas pronounced Purdanális and Lano, as in land), discovered ample sign, and turned back toward San Antonio. On June 8 they paused to draw honey from a bee tree on Walker Creek, a tributary of the Guadalupe about fifty miles north of San Antonio.

Ever cautious, Hays had left several men as rear guard. They dashed in to report ten Comanches following the Ranger trail. Hastily saddling, the men at once came in view of the Indians, whose leisurely retreat toward a timber thicket gave notice of their role as decoys. When Hays made plain that he could not be drawn into an ambush, some seventy whooping warriors galloped from the timber to confront him. Although outnumbered five to one, Hays deployed his horsemen and advanced slowly to the attack. The Indians fell back, across a shallow ravine and up a gentle rocky slope mottled with scrub oak and underbrush. At the crest they dismounted, formed a line, and in Spanish taunted the Rangers to charge.

Hays led his men down into the shallow ravine, which momentarily hid them from the view of the Comanches. There he signaled an abrupt wheel and a race two to three hundred yards down the ravine to the point of the ridge. Spurring their horses swiftly up the hillside, the Rangers burst into the open on the enemy's flank and charged into their midst. As the startled foe leaped on their mounts in confusion, the Texans discharged their rifles, threw them to the ground, and drew their five-shooters.

Rallying quickly, the warriors counterattacked in force enough to overrun the little band of whites. In a display of extraordinary discipline and horsemanship, however, the Rangers maneuvered their mounts into a circle, rump to rump, and received the charge. For fifteen minutes the two sides struggled at close range, the Indians with lances and arrows, the whites with blazing five-shooters. Both Ad Gillespie and Sam Walker took severe lance wounds, but the revolvers brought down so many of the Comanches that they fell back.

Reloading their pistols, the Rangers pursued. Exhorted by a daring chief with a powerful voice, the Indians made repeated stands, only to be broken by the determined horsemen whose pistols flashed time and again. For nearly an hour, the chase tumbled over two miles of broken plain, with the Rangers scattering as some paused to reload and others dashed forward.

Still the chief held his men against panicked flight, and still he greatly outnumbered his attackers. With one man dead and four wounded, and with ammunition all but exhausted, Hays knew his men could neither continue the pursuit nor fend off another Comanche assault. Sensing the shift in initiative, the chief gathered his decimated band for a charge.

"Any man who has a load, kill that chief," shouted Hays. Ad Gillespie retained a charged rifle. "I'll do it," he replied. Despite his lance wound, Gillespie dismounted, took careful aim with his rifle, and fired.

The ball hit its mark. The chief reeled in the saddle and fell to the ground. The warriors broke and fled from the battleground.

With fourteen men, Hays had routed seventy Comanche warriors—the West's finest horsemen and among its finest fighters, truly the "lords of the plains." They left behind, dead on the field, twenty-three of their number and carried off, in Hays's estimate, thirty more wounded. Less than twenty Comanches left the battleground unhurt.

Hays attributed his victory to the courage and discipline of his men and especially to the new five-shooters. They wrought fearful execution and came as a demoralizing shock to an enemy who had never encountered them. Predictably, Hays left unsaid the other explanation of the victory—superior leadership.[12]

At Walker Creek in 1844 the qualities that in two years would make Texas Rangers famous throughout the United States and even in Europe fused supremely. Daring, intrepid, well-trained men armed with repeating weapons functioned as a highly disciplined team under an outstanding leader.

[2]

The Tradition Evolves: Indians

Both before and during Jack Hays's time, other Texans displayed similar gifts of leadership and contributed to a Ranger tradition that took shape and gathered strength for two decades before Hays cemented it on Walker Creek. The tradition found its origins and defining character in the conflict between Anglo Texan settlers and Indians. With an intensity and persistence rivaled by no other frontier of America's westward movement, the conflict in Texas lasted for sixty years.

The advent of the first Anglo settlers coincided roughly with Mexico's independence from Spain in 1821. Taking up his dead father's mission of colonizing Americans in Mexican Texas, Stephen F. Austin became the first of a series of *empresarios* to contract with Mexico for land grants on which to settle colonists.

The vanguard of the Old Three Hundred, Austin's immigrants of 1821–1824, ran into Indian trouble even as their able young leader negotiated the conditions of their residence with authorities in Mexico City. Along the coast, immigrants encountered Karankawas. Beyond the coast, they encroached on Tonkawas, Wacos, Tawakonis, and other tribes that tilled the soil and hunted game. All these tribes greeted their new neighbors ambiguously, sometimes as friends, sometimes as thieves, and sometimes as killers.

Part of Mexico's rationale for opening Texas to Americans was the hope that they would form a buffer against aggressive Indians. That did not happen, for a geographical and cultural divide created an Anglo Texas distinct from a Mexican Texas, and the residents of each had to contend with Indians.

Mexicans concentrated in and around San Antonio and spread down the San Antonio River to La Bahía (Goliad) and beyond. South and west to the Rio Grande, a scattering of Mexican *rancheros* herded cattle and sheep on the chaparral plains, their lives oriented to the towns strung up the Rio Grande from Matamoros to Laredo. Virtually no Anglos lived west of the Guadalupe River, and to the north no Anglo buffer spread across the Hill Country and the Edwards Plateau to turn back the Comanche marauders.

To the east lay Anglo Texas, settled by Austin's Old Three Hundred and the colonists imported by other empresarios. It encompassed the coastal plain and the black-soil prairies and woodlands drained by the Trinity, Brazos, and Colorado Rivers. The Anglo Texans who peopled the coastal plain were mainly large-scale cotton planters, most with slaves. Originating primarily in Alabama, Mississippi, and Louisiana, they brought with them the culture of the Lower South, of which the new lands required only minor adaptations.

The people who would become Texas frontiersmen settled north of the plantations and established modest farms of corn, cotton, and a few head of stock. They came, mostly overland, from Tennessee, Kentucky, Arkansas, and Missouri, and they brought with them the culture of the Upper South, likewise requiring only minor adaptations.

As specified by their contracts with the Mexican government, Austin and other empresarios sought solid, productive citizens, the "better" class. Texas also attracted less substantial immigrants, however, either under cover of an empresario contract or as illegal squatters. There were adventurers, speculators, scoundrels, thieves, and refugees from debt, the sheriff, or a shrewish wife. Geographer Donald Meinig characterized Anglo Texans as "rural, egalitarian, independent, individual-istic, aggressive, and adaptable," and in places "volatile and conspirato-rial as well."[1]

Until the colony could be regularly organized, Mexican authorities granted Stephen Austin both civil and military power over the settlers, including the rank of lieutenant colonel of militia. Already the governor had authorized the enlistment of paid volunteers to serve as militia until harvest called them to their fields. On May 5, 1823, Lieutenant Moses Morrison had mustered a force of ten men. With escalating Indian trou-bles, Austin believed these too few. In August 1823 he gave thought to issuing a call for ten more men to "act as rangers for the common defence." He would pay them $15 a month in land he owned personally, and they would augment Morrison's company. There is no evidence that Austin actually followed through on these musings.[2]

Austin clearly knew the historical roots of rangers in the English colonial experience—units that operated apart from regular or militia units and "ranged" the frontiers as partisan fighters. Whether these ten men were ever raised and incorporated into Morrison's little company is undocumented, but Austin probably regarded the unit as rangers. Unpaid and unsupplied by Mexican authorities, however, they dis-banded in the autumn.

That the ranger idea was no fleeting fancy Austin disclosed three years later. The colony had grown speedily and Indian disturbances pro-portionately. To screen the settlements, he favored a permanent mounted force, constantly in the saddle patrolling the frontier. By now the Austin colony consisted of six militia districts, and when represen-tatives of each met with their colonel in August 1826 they drew up a plan for a Ranger company of twenty to thirty mounted men. Each landowner would serve for a month, or furnish a substitute, for every half league of land owned.[3]

In the absence of evidence that either summons produced a Ranger unit, both documents probably represent unrealized hopes. Neverthe-less, the Texas Rangers insistently trace their birth to Austin's call of 1823. Whether or not Lieutenant Morrison's little force can be regarded

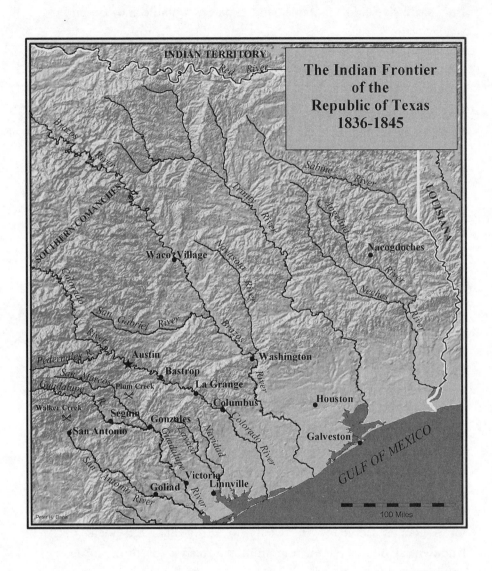

The Indian Frontier
of the
Republic of Texas
1836-1845

INDIAN TERRITORY

Red River

Brazos River

Sabine River

LOUISIANA

SOUTHERN COMANCHES

Trinity River

Angelina River

Nacogdoches

Waco Village

Navasota River

Neches River

Colorado River

San Gabriel River

Brazos River

Pedernales R.

Austin

Washington

San Marcos

Bastrop

Guadalupe

Plum Creek

La Grange

River

Walker Creek

Seguin

Columbus

Houston

San Antonio

Gonzales

Galveston

Guadalupe River

Lavaca

Navidad

Colorado River

GULF OF MEXICO

San Antonio River

Victoria

Goliad

Linnville

River

Peter H. Dana

100 Miles

as the first Texas Rangers, here is the first introduction of the word and the concept in Texas, and here lies the beginning of the Texas Ranger tradition.[4]

The Ranger tradition drew heavily on the citizen-soldier tradition, which had sustained the American Revolution and followed frontier settlers across the Appalachians and down to the Mississippi. In Texas, Anglos contended with Indians as citizens called from their fields for temporary service. Indians slipped into the settlements, stole stock, and sometimes killed settlers who got in their way. Men gathered as quickly as possible and rode in pursuit. Sometimes they overtook the culprits, recovered their animals, and killed some of the thieves. As often, their horses gave out in stifling heat and humidity or drenching rains that turned prairies into quagmires, and they returned to their homes fortunate if they mourned no more than the loss of horses and mules.

These citizen soldiers peopled the edges of settlement, north and west of the coastal plantations. The rough frontiersmen who sowed the seeds of the Ranger tradition came to Texas knowing they would have to fight Indians. By heritage and temperament, they were fighters. They made up a society that prized virility, valor, and fortitude, and they stood ready to take up arms when called. They fought because they wanted to, because their neighbors expected them to, and because, as among the Indians, society honored the brave and skilled warrior.

The ranging companies drew a mixed lot of men. Many were footloose young fellows in their twenties who drifted from job to job, including rangering. Many were young men with families who responded in times of particular need, shouldering their rifles and leaving their families to tend the homestead. Among these were frontier farmers whose wives and children had to defend themselves against Indian marauders as well as townsmen with a variety of occupations. Jack Hays himself was a surveyor by profession, and his company was a combination of San Antonio businessmen and volunteers who served full-time. Throughout the years of the citizen soldier, this pattern prevailed.

Another ingredient went into the making of the Texan citizen sol-dier—the values of the plantation aristocracy of the coastal plain. Although few in number and rarely in the field against Indians, the planters transmitted their hot-blooded code of the Old South to the rude frontiersmen who shielded them. Their readiness to take up arms against the Indians found counterpart in readiness to take up arms against one another, either as individuals or factions, when honor was infringed or injustice perceived. In frontiersman and planter alike, both personal honor and Texas chauvinism flourished throughout the nine-teenth century.[5]

Anglo Texas never fit comfortably into the Mexican Federal Republic, although the federalist constitution of 1824 drew its inspiration from the U.S. Constitution. The swelling tide of Anglo immigration, indiscreet talk of an eventual union with the mother country, and treasonous incidents such as the Fredonian Rebellion of 1826 fueled constant debate in Mexico City over the wisdom of the immigration policy. Political turmoil heightened Anglo uncertainties as federalists and cen-tralists struggled for domination of Mexico. The centralists prevailed in 1834 with the ascendancy of the wily and opportunistic Antonio López de Santa Anna, whose abolition of the constitution of 1824 exasperated Anglos and liberal Mexicans alike. Aggravating the rising political ten-sions, Anglos condescended to Mexicans as both racially and culturally inferior—attitudes already ingrained when they arrived in Texas.[6]

Anglo Texans held Indians in even greater contempt than Mexicans. Anglos regarded any Indian within the line of settlements as bent on mischief and a fair target for their rifles. Beyond the line of settlements, when "ranging" in punitive expeditions, they attacked any Indians they could find. And in truth, no matter how vigorous their protests of peace and friendship, tribal leaders could not restrain their young men from an occasional plundering foray into the settlements. Thrust and counter thrust fed on themselves and, for whites and Indians alike, made the frontier a dangerous place.

In the summer of 1835, even as Anglo Texas verged on rebellion against Mexico, the northern frontier rocked with violence. Indian marauders and vengeful Texans struck at each other. In these conflicts Stephen Austin's notion of a Ranger corps finally took a form tangible enough to fix the origins of the Texas Rangers to a time and a person.

Unwittingly, Captain Robert M. Coleman became the first Ranger captain sanctioned by law. A volatile man, courageous and impetuous, thirty-six in 1835, he had moved his wife and growing family from Kentucky four years earlier and settled near Bastrop. Early in July 1835, Coleman led a company of twenty-five men up the Brazos River. They fought a battle with Tawakonis, fell back to reinforce and regroup, and took the field again under John H. Moore.

The Moore expedition turned into an exhausting march into futility. Its significance, however, lies not in its outcome; such was the result of most attempts to bring Indians to a decisive battle. The significance lies rather in subsequent events growing out of the Texas Revolution, which broke out within weeks of the Coleman-Moore campaigns. Prominent in the deliberations of the provisional government that took form at San Felipe was the exposed frontier. From the debates emerged enactments that provided for a "Corps of Rangers" to screen the settlements while the revolution ran its course. What entitles Coleman to precedence in Ranger history, however, took place after independence had been won and the Republic of Texas established. In an act of December 10, 1836, defining the pay of mounted riflemen in the ranging service on the frontier, the new Congress provided that "all officers and soldiers, who have actually been engaged in the ranging service since July, 1835, shall be included in this act, and shall receive pay for the time he is in the service."[7]

Thus this law established the formal beginning of the Texas Rangers as July 1835, and as the first captain to take the field in that month Robert M. Coleman gained distinction as the first captain of the Texas Rangers.[8]

In 1835–1836, Indian aggressions took second priority to the rebellion against Mexico. As rebels surrounded San Antonio and seized Goliad in the autumn of 1835, political leaders struggled over what course to adopt. A "Permanent Council" met at San Felipe for two weeks in

October and established a "Consultation," which for two weeks in November wrangled over what to do and how. On the thirteenth, the Consultation adopted an Organic Law establishing a provisional government consisting of a governor and a General Council and also provided for a regular army, militia, and mounted rangers. The governor and council dithered and bickered all winter while the revolutionary army, ignoring this self-proclaimed authority, dithered and bickered in equal ineffectiveness. Only after Santa Anna seized San Antonio did delegates gather at Washington-on-the-Brazos and on March 2, 1836, even as Santa Anna prepared to storm the Alamo, declare independence from Mexico.

The representative bodies at San Felipe worried about Indians as well as Mexicans. On November 24, 1835, the General Council gathered all the previous resolutions and enactments into an "Ordinance and Decree to establish and organize a Corps of Rangers." This measure laid the legislative foundations for the ranging service. The Corps would consist of three companies of fifty-six men each. They would serve for one year and, in return for $1.25 per day, provide their own rations, clothing, horses, arms, and ammunition. Each company was authorized a captain and two lieutenants and when operating together as a battalion would report to a major. On November 29 the Council named Isaac Burton, William A. Arrington, and John J. Tumlinson as captains of the three companies and Robert M. Williamson as major. Williamson, an expansive and eloquent character destined for distinguished military and political service, suffered a deformity that bent his right leg to the rear. He had fashioned a wooden leg to attach at the knee, and as "Three-Legged Willie" he swashbuckled through Texas history.[9]

Of Major Williamson's Ranger Corps, only the company of John J. Tumlinson organized and took the field against Indians. In January 1836 Tumlinson and his thirty men marched up the Colorado River and, at the head of Brushy Creek (present Leander), erected a blockhouse as a bastion against Comanche depredations. They garrisoned it for only a few weeks, however, before swept up in the crisis precipitated by Santa

Anna's invading army. In late February 1836, as the Mexican dictator laid siege to the Alamo, Major Williamson ordered the company to fall back on Bastrop and await orders. Thereafter the company covered the rear of the "Runaway Scrape," the panicked flight of Texans eastward as General Sam Houston's army likewise retreated eastward in the face of Santa Anna's advance. Many of the Rangers, including Tumlinson, left to look for their families, while others followed Houston's army, in which Williamson served as a private. They caught up on April 22, the day after Houston destroyed the Mexican army at San Jacinto and, taking Santa Anna prisoner, gained independence for Texas.[10]

A revolution originating in demands for restoration of constitutional government within the Mexican Republic had ended in an independent Republic of Texas. Volunteers from the United States had flocked to the Lone Star banner, and their sentiments helped shift the cause away from Mexican reform to independence and annexation to the United States. Annexation did not happen, however, for reasons rooted in the slavery controversy. Northerners saw annexation as a southern plot to extend slavery and barred Texas from the Union. Precariously, the Republic of Texas endured for a decade.

Houston, "Old Sam Jacinto," easily won election as the first president of the Republic of Texas. He believed that Indian troubles should be addressed by treaties of peace and friendship and mutually beneficial trading relations. Even so, he recognized the need for a force to defend the frontier. By an act of December 5, 1836, the new Congress of the republic provided for a "battalion of mounted riflemen," 280 strong. Five days later the Congress set pay scales for "all mounted riflemen in ranging service." As with the earlier Corps of Rangers, these riflemen were expected to provide their own horses, arms, clothing, and other necessities.[11]

President Houston's peace emissaries concluded treaties with the Tonkawas, Lipan Apaches, Keechis, Wacos, Tawakonis, and Toweashes. They even succeeded in bringing Comanches to the table. In Houston on May 29, 1838, three chiefs put their marks to a treaty of peace and friendship.[12]

What even Houston failed to appreciate fully, however, was that "the Comanches" implied a unity that did not exist. The signatory chiefs came from a tribe of Southern Comanches (Penatekas) most exposed to Texan encroachment. They could not bind their Northern Comanche brethren, and they could not even ensure that their own young men abided by their promises. A loose political structure and the weak authority of Comanche leaders made the treaty an almost farcical instrument for regulating relations with Texas. Moreover, the Comanches insisted on a clear boundary line separating their territory from Texan territory. That the Republic of Texas contained any Indian land could not be conceded. Full of platitudes, the Comanche treaty said nothing about boundaries.

Texans had yet to penetrate the buffalo ranges of the Comanches and confront them with a direct threat, although they knew what the surveyors on the Pedernales River portended. Already, however, Comanche raiders, especially around San Antonio, gave notice that no other tribe in Texas remotely resembled them in deadly fighting prowess.

The Comanches differed in many fundamental ways from the other Plains tribes. They were universally acknowledged the finest horsemen of all Indians. They hunted the buffalo, but not according to the ritualized communal process of Sioux and Cheyennes. The Comanches acknowledged no government and only the law of custom. Civil and war chiefs exerted influence but, except in rigidly limited contexts, ruled no one. Only the most rudimentary spiritual beliefs qualified personal autonomy. The elaborate sacred dogmas, ceremonies, rites, obligations, and taboos of more highly organized tribes troubled no Comanche's sense of individual sovereignty. No yearly sun dance brought the bands together for social and spiritual purposes.

Numbering less than five thousand, the Comanches dominated the South Plains from the Arkansas River to the Balcones Escarpment. Although widely dispersed in family bands of varying size and shifting composition, they warred so ruthlessly and effectively that no tribe dared challenge their supremacy. And as Texans and Mexicans learned, their masterful horsemanship combined with expert use of bow and arrow, lance, and tomahawk made them mighty warriors. War was the tribe's greatest obsession and constant pursuit. For enemies, it was made the more terrible by indiscriminately falling on everyone, from infants to old people of both sexes, by rape, pillage, torture, brutal treatment of captives, and frightful butchery of the dead.[13]

Within weeks after the Comanche treaty of 1838, Comanche raiders struck near San Antonio, and their aggressions mounted throughout the rest of the year. Keechis, Tawakonis, and Wacos likewise continued to spar with Texas settlers despite the pious treaty sentiments. Only the treaties with the Tonkawas and Lipans held steady, confirming an alliance with whites against predatory Comanches that already existed and needed no treaty to cement.

Houston's peace policy expired with advent of his truculent successor. Poet, painter, newspaperman, historian, hero of San Jacinto, and vice president under Houston, Mirabeau Buonaparte Lamar took office as president of Texas on December 1, 1838. He detested Houston's policies as much as he detested Houston. Scorning union with the United States, Lamar dreamed of an independent republic extending to the Pacific Ocean. He relocated the capital from Houston far up the Colorado, at the foot of the escarpment, beyond even the line of settlement. Named Austin, the capital, Lamar believed, would stand at the intersection of two great trade routes, one from Santa Fe to Houston, the other from the Red River to the mouth of the Rio Grande.[14]

Such grandiose purpose demanded firmness toward Mexico and an end to temporizing with Indians. It also demanded a strong military force. Applauded by frontier settlers and backed by a new Congress, Lamar proposed to revive the regular army and mobilize still more mounted riflemen for the ranging service. Congress responded enthusiastically.

Exasperated by the quarrelsome, insubordinate, and mutinous regulars, Houston had furloughed two-thirds of them in 1837. Now Lamar discharged the remnant and gained legislation to create a new army of regulars—a regiment of infantry that would blaze a road along the frontier from Red River to the Nueces and build and garrison forts to keep the Indians on their side of the line. Backing them would be eight companies of mounted volunteers for the ranging service, to which Congress, responding to local constituencies, added still more.[15]

Again, legislative intent proved wildly optimistic. An empty treasury, weak currency, and the uncertainties of pay and provisions discouraged men from enlisting in the regular force, styled the Frontier Regiment. Never did its strength exceed two-thirds of the authorization.[16]

The ranging service held greater appeal: short-term service, land bounties, and an incentive to offset the pay that probably would never be forthcoming. By custom that would become firmly embedded, Rangers divided the spoils of combat among themselves. Plunder, especially horses, appealed to prospective recruits. Even so, captains had difficulty filling their ranks, and many of the companies authorized by the Texas Congress never materialized.

In his inaugural address, Lamar had called for a war against the Indians "that will admit of no compromise and have no termination except in their total extinction or total expulsion." With the Frontier Regiment expanding so slowly that recruiting stations finally had to be closed, the task fell to Ranger companies. The military buildup provoked a rash of collisions between Rangers and Indians, especially Comanches.

Most celebrated was Colonel John H. Moore's smashing Ranger attack on a Comanche camp near the mouth of the San Saba River in February 1839. The Rangers killed thirty to forty Indians, but warriors seized their horse herd and forced them to walk ninety miles back to the settlements.[17]

"Extermination or expulsion" had been Lamar's war cry. Even with a fledgling regular army and a large corps of ranging companies (although many on paper only), he could not even defend the frontier settlements, much less exterminate the tribes. The one clear success of his policy was expulsion—expulsion of the Cherokees from eastern Texas. In July 1839 some five hundred militia and regulars moved against the Cherokees, defeated them in battle, and drove them out of Texas.[18]

Although all the northern tribes continued to plague exposed Texas settlements, they were more a thieving nuisance than a serious threat. Far more dangerous and destructive were the Comanches on the high plains to the west. All Comanches, Northern and Southern, raided in Texas and Mexico. But among the Southern Comanches, some of the Penateka chiefs favored accommodation. They were more exposed to Texan retaliation, and they had been weakened by smallpox. This peace sentiment had prompted the meaningless treaty with the Houston administration in 1838.

Early in 1840, the Penateka Comanches made another bid for peace. Its progress and climax involved no Texas Rangers. But its consequences for the Texas frontier, and for the Rangers who strove to guard it, were profound.

On March 19, 1840, sixty-five Penateka Comanches, men, women, and children, straggled into San Antonio for a peace conference. Twelve were chiefs or headmen. They surrendered Matilda Lockhart, captured more than a year earlier. Mary Maverick described her condition: "Her head, arms, and face were full of bruises, and sores, and her nose actually burnt off to the bone—all the fleshy end gone, and a great scab formed on the end of the bone. Both nostrils were wide open and denuded of flesh. She told a piteous tale of how dreadfully the Indians had beaten her, and how they would wake her from sleep by sticking a chunk of fire to her flesh, especially to her nose, and how they would shout and laugh like fiends when she cried. Her body had many scars from fire."[19]

Matilda Lockhart's appearance was enough to outrage the Texas officials. But she also described her ordeal and told of other captives she had seen within the past few days. The chiefs, she said, intended to demand a high ransom for her and then bring in the other captives one at a time for ransom.

Thus alerted, the two commissioners, acting secretary of war William G. Cooke and Adjutant General Hugh McLeod, instructed the regular army's Lieutenant Colonel William S. Fisher to move two companies to the vicinity of Government House, a large flat-roofed stone building used for meetings. The twelve chiefs were then invited inside. "Where are the prisoners you promised to bring into this talk?" the commissioners asked through an interpreter. Muguara, the chief who had made the promise, answered: "We have brought in the only one we had, the others are with other tribes." After a long and tense pause, he added: "How do you like the answer?"

Ignoring the question, Cooke and McLeod had Colonel Fisher post one of his companies in the compound behind the building, where the warriors waited, and begin moving the other company into the council room. As they filed in, the commissioners had the interpreter explain item by item the treaty they had been prepared to sign but could not now because of the failure to deliver all the captives. With a soldier at each door and the rest in line from wall to wall, the officials announced that the chiefs would be held hostage until the warriors returned to their villages and brought in the rest of the captives.

As the whites descended from the platform, the chiefs followed. One suddenly dashed for the backdoor but was barred by a sentinel. The Indian drew his knife and stabbed the soldier as all the other Comanches rushed toward the door. Captain George T. Howard, the company commander, blocked one and received a severe knife wound in the side. As he fell, he ordered the sentinel to fire. He did, killing the chief. All the Indians at once drew their knives. "Fire if they resist," shouted Colonel Fisher. They resisted and within moments had all been shot down.

Outside, pandemonium erupted. In the rear yard, warriors and soldiers piled into each other. The troops drove the Indians into a stone house and exchanged fire with them. A few broke free and gained the opposite bank of the river but were run down and killed. The streets boiled with frightened people, both Indian and citizen, equally stunned by the unexpected blowup. When the firing subsided, thirty-five Comanches lay dead, including three women and two children, and twenty-seven women and children and two old men had been made prisoners. An officer and two soldiers had been killed, together with four civilians, and three officers, one private, and four civilians wounded.[20]

The "Council House fight," as it came to be known, enraged the Comanches of all tribes as far north as the Arkansas River. Twelve chiefs and twenty warriors had been slain in a deliberate act of treachery. They had come to talk peace. They had released captives, several Mexicans in addition to Matilda Lockhart. Other captives were not theirs to liberate—or so they claimed, perhaps truthfully, perhaps not. They stood ready to sign any treaty placed in front of them—or so they said, probably truthfully. Their pacific overtures had been encouraged by Texans and then met with betrayal, entrapment, and slaughter.

Texans felt just as grievously betrayed. Twice the Comanches had promised to bring in all their captives and sign a peace treaty. When they came, they brought but one (Mexicans did not count), and she told of others in the same camp where she had been held. Plainly, the Indians were acting in bad faith. They caused their own demise by fighting instead of yielding themselves as hostages for the fulfillment of their promises.

Viewed through their respective cultural lenses, both Comanches and Texans were right. But the Comanches never forgave or forgot, and memory of the Council House fight fueled decades of bitter hostility. Not that a treaty containing the Texan terms would have avoided such hostility. Whether he signed or not, no Comanche leader could have taken them seriously or enforced them on his people. Texans and Comanches were fated to fight to the end for possession of Texas.

As ordained by Comanche culture, the Council House outrage provoked a retaliation commensurate with the offense. On August 4, 1840, six hundred Comanches—warriors, old men, women and children—descended from the Hill Country at the head of the San Marcos River and swept southeast along the low divide between the Guadalupe and Lavaca Rivers. This was unsettled country, and the Comanches rode all the way to Victoria, one hundred miles, without any warning reaching the citizens. For two days they shot up the edges of Victoria and terrorized the townspeople.[21]

Instead of turning back to the Hill Country, the war expedition proceeded southeast another twenty miles to Lavaca Bay. On the morning of August 8 they fell on the port town of Linnville, seat of a custom house and warehouses full of merchandise consigned to inland communities. Again, citizens fell victim to the Comanches, but most found safety aboard vessels offshore. The Indians passed the day plundering and burning the warehouses. Sporting top hats and waving umbrellas, they cavorted among the burning structures with their horses trailing bolts of cloth and fluttering ribbons from manes, ears, and tails. Feathers from torn mattresses drifted on the smoke-laden sea breeze while warriors corralled cattle into pens to butcher some and incinerate others. Late in the afternoon, with two hundred horses and mules laden with booty, the Comanches abandoned the town and turned toward home.[22]

Upcountry, the passage of the Comanches did not long escape notice. Except for a few regulars in Austin and San Antonio, no organized military force stood ready to take the field. But the Comanche thrust left a trail of such size as to reveal the gravity of the danger, and the response demonstrated how swiftly and effectively Texan citizen soldiers could rise to an emergency. Many had been or would be Texas Rangers, and they mobilized under veteran leaders who had seen service as Ranger captains. If not Ranger companies formally in government service, they acted in all respects as Rangers and contributed their full share to the Ranger tradition.

Best known and most respected of the former captains was Mathew Caldwell of Gonzales. "Old Paint," people called him, because of his mottled complexion and dark beard splotched with white, which nicely complemented the coloration of his paint horse. Forty-two in 1840, brave and cool under fire, a man who inspired confidence in those he led, Caldwell had fought valiantly in the Texas Revolution and captained ranger companies against both Mexicans and Comanches.[23]

Less experienced than Matt Caldwell but also highly esteemed was Ben McCulloch, who with his younger brother Henry practiced surveying out of Gonzales. A Tennessean born in 1811, Ben's most prominent trait was mastery of outdoor skills, attained under no less a mentor than David Crockett. One of McCulloch's Rangers recalled him as "a brave fellow, a tall, straight man, over six feet high, rawboned, light, sandy hair, extremely reserved in manner, with keen black eyes which shone like diamonds." He was an active, energetic, quick-thinking man but quiet, rigidly self-contained, and not inclined to gregarious sociability. At San Jacinto he had handled the famed "Twin Sisters" artillery pieces, and he and Henry had both fought Comanches with "Old Paint" Caldwell.[24]

Other former Ranger captains included John J. Tumlinson, Adam Zumwalt, and Clark Owen. Jack Hays showed up from San Antonio as a volunteer fighter. Old General Ed Burleson, probably the most experienced Indian fighter in Texas, also heeded the summons. Rarely had an Indian threat called forth such an array of talent.

McCulloch, Tumlinson, and Zumwalt tried to head off the Comanches as they rode back from Linnville, but so clumsily as to anger Ben McCulloch. He turned his company over to his lieutenant and with three comrades rode around the Indians and headed for Gonzales.[25]

McCulloch found that in his absence other companies had formed. Caldwell had raised thirty-nine men in Gonzales and united them with twenty-two from Lavaca under Lafayette Ward. Wrongly guessing that the Comanches would bear farther to the west on their return, Caldwell took his unit up the Guadalupe River to Seguin. Here a messenger overtook him with McCulloch's report, and Caldwell made a forced march northeast to Plum Creek.

Meantime, McCulloch had sent one of his companions to the Colorado River settlements to alert Ed Burleson. As Caldwell approached the rendezvous from the southwest, Burleson and eighty-seven volunteers bore in from the north, accompanied by Chief Placido and twelve Tonkawa Indians on foot.

By the night of August 11, Caldwell had reached Plum Creek. Here he met another Gonzales company, thirty men under Captain James Bird, including Ben and Henry McCulloch, now serving in the ranks. Here too, from Austin, was Major General Felix Huston, the hot-tempered political and military opportunist who commanded the phantom Texas militia.

Early the next morning, August 12, pickets rode in with word of the Comanches approaching. Swiftly Caldwell mounted his hundred men and drew them up for battle. He then rode to their front and proposed that General Huston assume command. "A few responded aye and none said nay," recalled John Henry Brown, "but in fact the men wanted the old Indian fighter Caldwell to lead."[26]

Huston divided the command into three companies under Caldwell, Ward, and Bird and pushed forward to a ravine on the edge of the prairie. At this moment, with the Comanches in sight, a courier dashed in with word that Burleson and his men were only three miles away, coming on at the gallop. Huston decided to wait, and the men agonizingly watched the Indian procession pass by unchallenged.

When Burleson arrived, Huston formed the command, now two hundred strong, into three elements: Burleson on the right, Caldwell on the left, and Ward and Bird, under the regular army's Major Thomas M. Hardiman, as reserve to the rear. Thus formed, the volunteers ascended to the plain and advanced on the rear of the Indian cavalcade. Not until this moment had the Comanches been aware of the enemy presence.

Warriors formed to screen the slow-moving herd of stolen stock, the animals packed with the Linnville loot, and the women and children. Anchored in a point of oak timber, their line extended three-fourths of a mile into the open. About two hundred yards from this line, Huston halted and dismounted his formation to exchange fire with the Indians.

To buy time, several gaudily adorned chiefs performed feats of brilliant horsemanship between the lines. As Jim Nichols marveled in his expressive prose, "Lying flat on the side of their horse with nothing to be seen but a foot and a hand, they would shoot their arrows under the horses neck, run to one end of the space, straighten up, whelle their horses, and reverse themselves, allways keeping on the opisit side from us."[27] The warriors held their formation but fired steadily at the Texans, some with ineffective trade muskets but others with rifles taken at Linnville.

About thirty of the Texans had remained on horseback and dashed to and fro among the chiefs, exhibiting horsemanship as daring and skilled as the Indians' own. Henry McCulloch dismounted at a mesquite tree near where the chiefs performed and attempted, as he later said, "to git a fair pop at one of those fine dressed gentlemen." Nichols alerted Ben McCulloch to his brother's peril. As he mounted and galloped toward Henry, a chief with a buffalo-horn head gear bore down on Ben. Nichols took aim, but a ball hit his hand and buried itself in his wrist. The impact caused Nichols to squeeze his trigger finger, setting off the rifle. The ball killed the chief's horse and drove into his thigh. He rolled from under his horse and rose to hop a few paces before another Texan shot and killed him.[28]

One chief in particular caught everyone's eye, as described by the fighting Baptist parson, Zachariah Morrell: "He was riding a very fine horse, held in by a fine American bridle, with a red ribbon eight or ten feet long tied to the tail of the horse. He was dressed in elegant style, from the goods stolen at Linnville, with a high-top silk hat, fine pair of boots and leather gloves, an elegant broadcloth coat, hind part before, with brass bottons shining brightly right up and down his back. When he first made his appearance he was carrying a large umbrella stretched."[29]

A Texan sharpshooter brought this chief down, and several warriors galloped from the line to bear him from the field. Burleson, Caldwell, and McCulloch, all fretting over Huston's failure to launch a mounted charge, saw this as the right moment. "Now, General, is your time to charge them!" shouted Caldwell. "They are whipped!" Huston responded by ordering Burleson's right wing to swing around the point of timber against the Indian line and Caldwell's left wing to charge into the timber itself. The assault broke the Indian lines and sent the warriors up the valley in flight.

All pretense at command evaporated as knots of Texans pursued knots of Indians, who fought desperately even as they withdrew. Hugging the timber bordering the plain, the Indians could conceal their dead and wounded. Moreover, the dry prairie grass had recently been burned over, and thick clouds of dust and ash drifted with the action. Even so, many Comanches fell as the whites bore down on them, calmly

31

dismounted, fired, reloaded, then resumed the chase, which continued for fifteen miles.

"The Indians lost everything," recorded John Henry Brown. "The defeat was unexpected—a surprise, complete and crushing." Participants could only guess how many Comanches had been killed. Huston first reported more than forty, but a month later doubled the figure. Brown, later quizzing liberated captives, tallied eighty-six killed on the battlefield and fifty-two who died later.[30]

Whatever the exact casualties, the battle of Plum Creek was a disaster for the Comanches. In their drive to the Gulf they had slain twenty citizens, but at Plum Creek they had lost, besides human casualties, all the stock scooped up at Victoria and most of the merchandise taken from the Linnville warehouses. The Texans came out of the fight with one killed and seven wounded.[31]

Left entirely to General Huston, who had never fought Indians, Plum Creek would probably have ended with the pursuers never catching up. The experienced Ranger captains, however, saved the day. Burleson, McCulloch, and Caldwell all recognized that the only hope of victory lay in an aggressive mounted charge. Despite his vanity, Huston heeded Caldwell's shout to seize the psychological moment of a prominent chief's fall to order a mounted charge. Even though they were not officially Rangers, Plum Creek showed Rangers at their best.

It also revealed a common flaw. "The immense amount of spoils taken from the enemy has been returned to the owners when identifiable," reported the *Austin City Gazette* on August 26. "The destruction and waste that occurred in the fight, however, made much impossible to identify, and it was divided among participants in the battle." Linnville's John J. Linn had a different perspective. "'To the victors belong the spoils,'" he conceded, "and the 'Colorado men' appropriated everything to themselves." Merchant William G. Ewing recognized much that belonged to him but could get nothing back. Stockman J. O. Wheeler found 150 of the recaptured horses bearing his brand but only with great difficulty obtained a single horse to ride home.[32]

John H. Moore and his La Grange volunteers had reached the Plum Creek battlefield too late to participate in the fight. At once he set about raising a volunteer force to pursue farther and quickly recruited two companies, about ninety men. On the cold, wet morning of October 24, 1840, Moore struck a Comanche village high on the Colorado River and all but wiped it out. As usual in surprise attacks on villages, men, women, and children fell victim to the deadly fire. Found in the lodges were items taken at Linnville, which branded these Indians some of those who had escaped Plum Creek.[33]

Together with Plum Creek, Moore's victory dealt a staggering blow to the Southern Comanches. The losses, both material and psychological, were crippling but by no means lasting. Comanche raids continued, and volunteers and Rangers continued to confront them. From their setbacks, the Comanches seem to have drawn two lessons. One was to treat Texan fighters more warily. The other was to follow their own instincts rather than the urgings of Mexican officials, who almost certainly had prodded them to target Victoria and Linnville, far to the east of their accustomed trails. From these two victories the Texans drew at least one important lesson. If Comanches could be brought to battle at all, a sudden charge on horseback offered better chances of success than dismounting to fight on foot.[34]

Lamar's war policy proved no more successful than Houston's peace policy, and at enormously greater expense. As directed by the Texas Congress, the regular army's Colonel William G. Cook opened a primitive road from Red River to Austin and established garrisoned blockhouses at intervals. But the regulars turned out to be so ravaged by desertions and so undisciplined and even mutinous as to bring disrepute on themselves. Without repealing the authorizing legislation of December 1838, Congress adjourned in February 1841 without appropriating funds for the regulars. This left Lamar no choice but to disband the regular army.[35]

At the same time, the Congress moved to provide frontier protection in another way. An act of February 4, 1841, empowered each of twenty named counties to organize a company of between twenty and fifty-six minutemen. They would furnish their own horses, arms, ammunition, and provisions; elect their own officers; and be ready to mobilize on call. Up to five men could be designated spies to patrol the county frontiers constantly. When actually in service, minute men would receive recompense of one dollar a day.[36]

The law did not call the minutemen Rangers nor refer to "ranging service." But Rangers they were, and range they did, even though enjoined by law from taking the field unless their communities confronted "extraordinary danger." County chief justices decided what constituted extraordinary danger. Roving tribesmen provided ample pretext for declaring an emergency, but Indian plunder also provided an inducement for ranging. Often volunteers augmented the enrolled strength of the minutemen.

In December 1841 Sam Houston began his second term as president of the Republic of Texas with a full-bore assault on Lamar's hawkish policies and with a vow to bring peace to the frontier through diplomacy for one-fourth the amount Lamar had spent. As in his first term, Houston sought treaties with all the tribes, government-regulated trading houses protected by twenty-five or thirty men spaced along the frontier, and mutually profitable commercial relations that would quiet the Indians with self-interest.[37]

Houston ridiculed the minuteman system as inefficient and expensive. It had overrun its appropriation. All control of the companies had been ceded to county chief justices, who hardly qualified as military experts and whose oversight opened the treasury to all manner of fraud. Like all other of Lamar's military measures, it had failed in its purpose.[38]

Although distracted by Mexican aggressions and intrigues throughout much of his term, Houston persevered in his peace policy. His emissaries treated with all the northern tribes and even made contact with the Comanches. They proved balky negotiators because of the Council House legacy. Less reluctant were the agricultural tribes strung across northern Texas. On September 29, 1843, chiefs of ten of these groups scratched their marks on a treaty that the Texas Senate ratified the following January.

Not for another year could any Comanche chiefs be coaxed into attending a council. Finally, early in October 1844, three Comanche chiefs responded to Houston's invitation to a grand council of all tribal leaders near Torrey's trading house (south of present Waco). One was the Penateka war chief Buffalo Hump, who had led the Linnville raid and fought at Plum Creek. He proved a forceful negotiator, standing up to the blandishments of Houston. The treaty contained all the platitudes of the 1843 treaty but also defined a line to separate Comanches from Texans. Buffalo Hump and Houston argued at length over its placement. If Houston had his way, the Indians could not follow the buffalo south of the San Saba River. If Buffalo Hump had his way, the line would run through the heights overlooking Austin and San Antonio. Finally Houston proposed a compromise: "we will sign all but that part, which we will rub out and go on as before."

And so three Comanche chiefs signed another treaty that stipulated no boundary line. This was probably the best outcome, since no chief could prevent men of his or any other Comanche tribe from crossing such a line and since Houston probably could not have won ratification of a treaty that even hinted at Indian ownership of any part of Texas. Houston's successor, President Anson Jones, proclaimed the treaty in January 1845.[39]

Indian depredations declined somewhat during Houston's second term, although San Antonio and environs never for long escaped the attention of Comanche raiding parties, as the operations of Jack Hays's Rangers disclosed. On April 17, 1844, the *Telegraph and Texas Register* carried a tribute to the Hays Rangers: "The company of Western Rangers, under the command of the gallant Capt. Hays, has now its full complement of men, and is now in active service on the western frontier. The main station of Capt. Hays is some distance west of Bexar [San Antonio]. The soldiers are sent out by turns to scour the country in every direction. The men are well armed, and are probably the most happy, jovial and hearty set of men in all Texas. They have several full blooded race horses, remarkable for their fleetness, and with them they can attack, pursue, or escape from Indian or Mexican enemies at their pleasure."

Less than two months later, Jack Hays and this "jovial and hearty set of men" demonstrated their mettle to the Comanches at Walker Creek.

[3]

The Tradition Evolves: Mexicans

"REMEMBER THE ALAMO!" "Remember Goliad!" So shouted Sam Houston's men as they rolled over the startled army of General Antonio López de Santa Anna at San Jacinto on April 21, 1836.

On March 6, 1836, the Mexican dictator's assault columns, commanded to give no quarter, had stormed the Alamo in San Antonio. William B. Travis, Jim Bowie, David Crockett—names already honored in Texas—had perished with every defender, nearly two hundred men. The few who fell captive were promptly put to death on Santa Anna's order.

The Alamo garrison had died in battle. Not so the Goliad victims. Outgunned on the battlefield, Colonel James W. Fannin had surrendered his command as prisoners of war. They had been marched to confinement in the old Spanish presidio at Goliad. On March 27, three weeks after the Alamo slaughter, reluctant subordinates had carried out Santa Anna's orders to execute the prisoners. Firing squads shot down some 350 men.

San Jacinto did not even the score. For a decade Texans and Mexicans struck at each other in a flurry of clashes that intensified the hatred. The legacy of the Alamo and Goliad, combined with the violent history of the decade of the Texas Republic, solidly planted in the Anglo Texan psyche a deadly malice toward Mexicans.

Anglos brought their racial and cultural prejudices to Texas with them. Not until after the Texas Revolution, when they began to move to San Antonio and scatter down the San Antonio River to Goliad and Victoria, did significant mingling occur. This only confirmed the stereotype, by now laden with the rage fired by the Alamo and Goliad. Even though Ranger rolls during the republic bore Hispanic and even Indian names, Ranger attitudes expressed the attitudes of the Anglo community, as they would for generations to come. For Rangers, these attitudes attained sharp definition in the conflicts between Mexico and Texas that agitated the republic throughout its decade of independence. While Rangers contended with Indians on the northern and western frontiers of settlement, they (and other citizen soldiers) faced Mexicans in South Texas.[1]

A semiarid, nearly treeless land of hardy grass and thorny tangles of chaparral, alternately drenched by flooding rains and scorched by merciless sun, South Texas stretched from the San Antonio River to the Rio Grande. One major river, the Nueces, dropped off the Balcones Escarpment to bisect this region and empty into Corpus Christi Bay. A substantial population occupied the lower Rio Grande, placed there by Spain in the eighteenth century as a buffer against the *indios bárbaros* from the north. *Las Villas del Norte*–Reynosa, Camargo, Mier, Guerrero, Laredo–anchored this *frontera*, but a robust breed of *rancheros*, bearing royal land grants, extended the defenses as far north as the Nueces. Sheep and longhorn cattle by the thousands mingled with wild mustang horses by the thousands. Periodically these ranch families had to abandon their fortress-like *ranchos* in the face of Indian raiders or the chaos that followed the Texas Revolution, but they usually came back. Whether branded or not, the stock belonged to them; it was not, like the mustangs, "wild" and thus to be had for the taking, as Texans believed.[2]

From 1836 to 1846, South Texas seethed with anarchy. Cattle, sheep, and mustangs attracted Comanche raiders, Mexican *bandidos*, and

Texan "cowboys." All preyed ruthlessly on the stock, no matter how clear the ownership, on the few resident rancheros who had not fled south of the Rio Grande, and on the trading caravans plying between San Antonio and the Rio Grande towns.

Adding to the mix were two burning issues of jurisdiction. First was Texas itself. Santa Anna had abdicated without carrying out his promise to Sam Houston at San Jacinto. His centralist successors, and he himself when he returned to power in 1841, refused to recognize Texan independence and vowed to recover the lost province. The second issue, contained within the first, centered on the Nueces River. Under both Spain and Mexico, the Nueces had defined the southern boundary of Texas; even if Texas maintained its independence, the territory south of the Nueces belonged to Mexico. In 1836, however, the Texas Congress declared the southern and western boundary of the Republic of Texas to follow the Rio Grande all the way from its mouth to its source and then even beyond to the forty-second parallel. Mexican troops, both regular and irregular, roamed this Nueces Strip, while Texas Rangers and volunteers occasionally carried the Lone Star flag as far as the Rio Grande simply to assert Texan sovereignty.

Bandit depredations reached far north of the Nueces, even to the western edges of Anglo settlement. Both Mexican and Texan gangs were active, with Texan gangs inflicting as much damage as Mexican. From San Antonio to Goliad and Victoria, stockmen suffered Texan aggressions. "Band of Brothers," these Anglo Texans called themselves, and intimidated or even murdered citizens who protested. One observer estimated their number at two hundred. At the same time, no fewer than four separate parties of Texan marauders were said to be operating west of the Nueces, preying mainly on Mexicans.[3]

President Mirabeau Buonaparte Lamar's token efforts to suppress banditry dimmed in the shadow of extravagant imperial ambitions. He had always looked longingly on the commerce that flowed between Santa Fe and Missouri. He dreamed of diverting it from the Santa Fe Trail southeast to Houston via the new capital of Austin; and if not that, at least diverting the customs fees into the empty Texas treasury. The

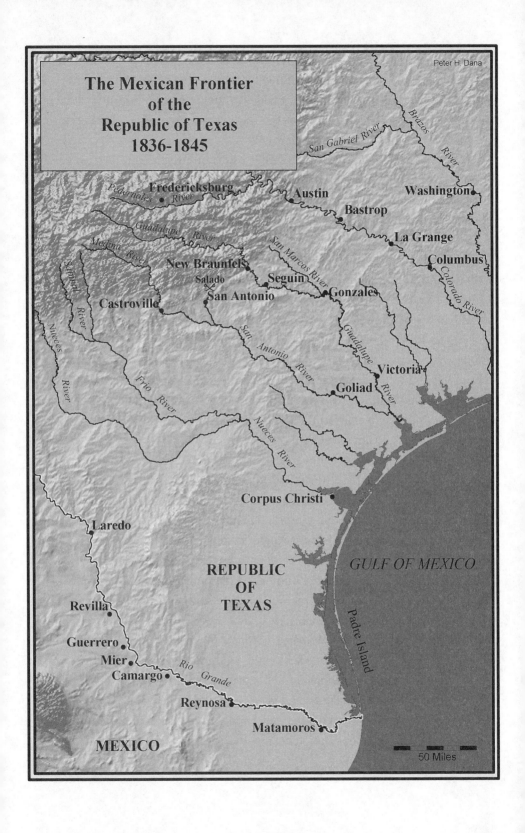

The Mexican Frontier
of the
Republic of Texas
1836-1845

Peter H. Dana

Brazos River

San Gabriel River

Pedernales River

Fredericksburg

Austin

Washington

Bastrop

Guadalupe River

La Grange

Medina River

New Braunfels

San Marcos River

Columbus

Salado

Seguin

Colorado River

San Antonio

Gonzales

Castroville

Sabinal River

Nueces River

San Antonio River

Guadalupe River

Victoria

Frio River

Goliad

Nueces River

Corpus Christi

Laredo

REPUBLIC

GULF OF MEXICO

OF

Revilla

TEXAS

Guerrero

Padre Island

Mier

Camargo

Rio Grande

Reynosa

Matamoros

MEXICO

50 Miles

Texas Congress had proclaimed the Rio Grande the boundary of Texas, which meant that Santa Fe rested on Texas soil. Deluding himself that Santa Feans would welcome a new allegiance, Lamar dispatched an expedition to open trade and assert the republic's authority over its distant appendage.

The Santa Fe expedition of 1841 was not a Ranger operation but was carried out by a corps of volunteers who shared Lamar's vision. A trading caravan of fifty-one men, a military contingent of 270 men, and three commissioners to treat with New Mexican officials made up the column. Veterans of the ranging service participated, most notably Mathew Caldwell, who served as captain of one of the companies. Poorly led, poorly equipped, poorly guided, riven by dissension and finally betrayal, the expedition fell apart even before reaching Santa Fe.

No matter where the Texas Congress chose to draw a boundary line, New Mexicans considered themselves citizens of a Mexican province and the Texans as foreign invaders. Easily taken captive, the Texans were marched to imprisonment in Perote Castle, an old Spanish fortress east of Mexico City that served as the nation's forbidding dungeon. A sadistic officer conducted the trek down the Rio Grande to El Paso. The men endured terrible suffering. Those who fell behind were shot and their ears cut off and strung on a leather thong. From El Paso to Mexico City they fared better, but Perote Prison brought them months of torment.[4]

Although the U.S. minister persuaded Santa Anna to parole the prisoners in April 1842, the Santa Fe expedition left festering sores in both Texas and Mexico. The cruelties of the captives' march and imprisonment reinforced Texan hatreds—one more battle cry to add to Alamo and Goliad. For Santa Anna, it prompted moves to throw Texas off balance and keep the prospect of a major invasion alive until Mexico could gain the strength to organize one.

In January 1842, months before release of the Santa Fe prisoners, San Antonio residents knew a Mexican invasion was imminent, but not when or in what strength. As volunteer units gathered, Ranger captain Jack Hays kept spies out seeking information. With a Mexican offensive no longer in doubt, citizens fled east in the "Runaway of '42," while the defenders elected Hays their commander.

Early in March Ben McCulloch arrived with his company from Gonzales. Hays dispatched him and a comrade to learn what they could of the enemy force. They rode as far west as the Hondo, then concealed themselves in chaparral and counted the column of General Ráfael Vásquez as it marched by–a ragtag collection of about seven hundred regular cavalry and infantry, *defensores* (militia), and even Caddo Indians. To ensure that no larger invasion army followed, the two rode on to the Nueces before turning back. From the hills overlooking San Antonio, they saw the Mexican flag floating from the dome of San Fernando cathedral.[5]

McCulloch returned on the very day, March 5, that Vásquez reached San Antonio and demanded its surrender. Ignorant of his strength, counting only 107 riflemen, Hays's officers voted to withdraw from the city rather than fight or surrender. They fell back to the Guadalupe as the alarm spread and veterans sprang to arms.

They were not needed. After one night in San Antonio, on March 6 Vásquez evacuated the city and, heavily laden with plunder, withdrew to the south. Hays and his men followed as far as the Rio Grande but forbore to attack because of Vásquez's superior numbers.

The Vásquez "invasion" had been no more than a quick raid. It was designed to test Texan defenses, disorganize any foray against Mexico that might be forming, exact a measure of vengeance for the Santa Fe expedition, and dramatize that the central government still regarded Texas as part of Mexico. It also occasioned service for Ranger captains and for volunteers who were Rangers in all but name.[6]

Except for Hays's handful of men, the southwestern frontier lay open to further Mexican incursions. Late in July 1842 President Houston promoted Hays to major and empowered him to augment his company to 150 Rangers. Recruiting efforts, however, proved disappointing. Veterans of two years' intermittent service had impoverished themselves supplying horses and provisions without reimbursement, and others willing to sign up lacked the means to equip themselves without the help that the government could not provide. To range the entire frontier from San Antonio to the Rio Grande, as Houston directed, Hays could muster no more than fifty to sixty men.[7]

Throughout the first days of September 1842, warnings of some sort of Mexican move on Texas reached Austin and San Antonio. Citizens debated whether they confronted an invading army or simply another band of freebooters. At San Antonio the men organized in a defense force of two divisions, a hundred Mexicans and seventy-five Anglos, and elected Jack Hays colonel. On the night of September 10, Hays took five men to scout the roads leading from the west. Finding nothing, they returned to the city the next morning, only to discover it occupied by a Mexican military force. For once, Hays had been fooled. The invaders had left the main road and circled through the hills to the north; then at daybreak on the eleventh, aided by a dense fog, they swiftly seized the town. In the plaza, the defenders fired on the advance guard but quickly surrendered when they learned how formidable a force they faced.[8]

The occupying army consisted of a division of Mexican regulars numbering nearly one thousand infantry, cavalry, and artillery, together with another two or three hundred irregulars and militia. There was even a contingent of Cherokee Indians under Vicente Córdova, a special villain to Texans as the Mexican officer who attempted to foment an uprising of Texas Indians in 1838–1839. Brigadier General Adrián Woll, a Frenchman in Mexican service, commanded.[9]

Mathew Caldwell, imprisoned for months in Mexico with other men of the ill-fated Santa Fe expedition of 1841, had returned to his Gonzales home only a few weeks earlier. Ignoring the terms of his parole from Perote Prison, he quickly raised a group of volunteers and on September 13 moved to Seguin to unite with Hays and a handful of Rangers. From the Cibolo, east of San Antonio, he called for more men; when he had 250, he vowed, he would attack Woll. "Hurry on! Hurry on! and lose no time, we fear nothing but God and through him we fight our battles. Huzza! huzza for Texas!"[10]

By September 17, 1842, Caldwell had 202 men on the Cibolo. They fell into line and elected him major by acclamation. He divided them into five companies, including forty of the best mounted drawn from all the companies to serve as spies "under the worthy Capt. John C. Hays." Following Hays were some of his ablest men—Henry McCulloch as lieutenant, Ad Gillespie, Sam Walker, and William A. A. Wallace (a bulky scrapper destined for legend as "Big Foot" Wallace). Ben McCulloch had been visiting friends on the Colorado but was hurrying for the rendezvous site.[11]

On the night of September 17 Caldwell and Hays posted their little force on Salado Creek, six miles east of San Antonio. The creek, about forty feet wide and eight to twelve deep, bore generally southeast, but the position lay along a stretch that flowed from west to east before again turning south. To discourage a cavalry attack on their rear, the officers established the line on the north side of the creek, with the creek behind them. A brushy bottom shaded by large pecan and elm trees, about forty yards wide, afforded cover for the horses. A low bank at the edge of the timber provided cover for the riflemen. In their front, an open prairie reached north to a slope rising to an elevated mesquite flat. Two ravines, five hundred yards apart, opened into the Salado to anchor the flanks of the thin Texan line.[12]

Considering his force too weak to risk an attack on San Antonio, Caldwell hoped to decoy Woll into an assault on this strong defensive position. Hays would lead the decoy party, thirty-eight men on the only horses deemed strong enough for the mission. Early on the eighteenth, the horsemen rode out and shortly reached the edge of San Antonio. With six men, the captain rode almost to the Alamo and taunted the Mexicans to come out and fight. They did, quickly, well mounted on fresh horses, and several hundred strong. Taken by surprise, Hays fell back to his men, and all spurred their horses for the Salado, the brightly uniformed cavalry in close pursuit. Covered by a rear guard under McCulloch, the Texans reached the safety of Caldwell's position with hardly a moment to spare.

Although nearly a disaster, Hays's decoy mission succeeded admirably. By late morning, Woll had his entire command, nearly a thousand men, posted on the slope some four hundred yards in front of the Texan position. The cavalry took station to the northeast, presumably to block the approach of reinforcements and cut off a retreat toward Seguin. Caldwell made an inspirational speech, pointing out that he could not surrender because the Mexicans would execute him for breaking his parole, and Reverend Zachariah Morrell delivered suitable remarks, concluding: "Let us shoot low, and my impression before God is, that we shall win this fight."[13]

Throughout the afternoon, the two sides skirmished indecisively. Careful to conceal his true strength, Caldwell had parties of fifteen to twenty men sally forth to engage both infantry and cavalry, and then hastily fall back to the timber. Only with great difficulty could the Texans be restrained from responding to the Mexican taunts with a full-scale attack, but under Caldwell's stern eye they held to the defensive. Without taking any casualties themselves, they brought down many a Mexican.

By late afternoon Woll had determined on his own full-scale assault. The two cannons opened with grapeshot and canister, which harmlessly shredded the trees as drums rolled to signal the assault. In massed formation, the Reverend Morrell recorded, "The Mexicans now advanced upon us, under a splendid puff of music, the ornaments, guns, spears and swords glistening in plain view."[14]

Ranger Jim Nichols recalled the tactics of the assault: "Then formeing an oblong circul covering our intire line and traveled around that circul by platoons. As they would come round in a run nearest our lines, they would fire by platoons and keepe on in a run round the circul. When they would arrive on the back line furthest from us they would reload, still traveling around the circul." The Texans, all dead shots, returned the fire from the cover of the embankment, "and it was seldom a Texas rifle fired that thare was not one seen to bit the dust."[15]

One assault column made for the Texan left, intending to direct an enfilading fire down the flank. Hays sent ten men, including Pastor Morrell, to confront this threat with double-barreled shotguns. At thirty paces, a volley of buckshot sent every Mexican to the ground, and they advanced no farther.

45

On the right flank, Vicente Córdova with forty Cherokees and a few Mexicans worked down the brushy ravine to attempt a similar tactic. Part of Ewen Cameron's company had been posted to prevent such a move. They charged into the ravine and fought hand to hand until the Indians retreated, leaving eleven dead on the ground. Córdova, cheering on his men from the edge of the ravine, caught the eye of a marksman fully ninety yards distant and fell with a ball through the heart.[16]

Woll's assault, doomed from the start, lasted hardly twenty minutes. It was launched, recalled a participant, "with that hideous and wolfish yell which characterizes the savage." Texan rifles barked, "and then that high and manly patriotic *huzza! Huzza!!* resounded from every Texian heart with such vehemence that one would have supposed himself at an American barbeque." Everywhere he could see "wretches tumble down like beeves." In language that reflected common Texan attitudes, he described what Woll himself could plainly see.[17]

By sunset Woll had withdrawn his battalions to San Antonio. They carried their wounded and many of their dead, reported Caldwell, and left on the ground sixty dead or mortally wounded, "of which the wounded mostly died that night." The Texan loss was one man killed and about a dozen wounded.

Once again, the Texan citizen soldier had demonstrated his courage and fighting prowess. He had also shown that, led by a respected commander such as "Old Paint," he could fight as a disciplined team and restrain his impulse to throw himself suicidally on the enemy. The battle of Salado testified to the Texan fighting potential when led by a man who knew how to harness it.

Tempering the elation was a disaster that gave Texans still another reason to despise Mexicans. Hardly had they repulsed Woll's attack than Caldwell's men heard firing to the northeast, behind the Mexican positions, and knew that other Texans were fighting. They were a company of fifty-three men under Captain Nicholas Dawson, hurrying to join Caldwell. Even then on the point of withdrawing to San Antonio, Woll sent two cavalry squadrons and a cannon to confront Dawson.

The LaGrange men had ridden close enough to the battlefield to hear the firing when two scouts returned to report a fight in progress. Dawson knew that Captain Jesse Billingsley and a company of about eighty men followed in his rear and thought prudence counseled a delay so that all could charge into the fray together. An old man with more zeal than judgment, however, made an impassioned speech urging an immediate advance. With true Texan democracy, Dawson put the question to a vote, and the men overwhelmingly backed the venerable orator.[18]

Confronted by four hundred Mexican cavalry, Dawson dismounted his men and took position in a mesquite mott about two acres in area. An officer bearing a white flag demanded surrender, but Dawson, a seasoned soldier and veteran of San Jacinto, waved him off. As the horsemen advanced in fine order, Dawson cooly took aim and shot an officer from his saddle. "That's the way I used to do it," he remarked.

The short-range carbines of the cavalry could not reach the Texans, but the cannons could. When the artillerymen found the range, they sent grape and canister tearing into Dawson's position, shredding the mesquite and dropping horses and men. Even at long range, however, the riflemen occasionally hit one of the soldiers. Dawson strode up and down the lines, urging the Texans to keep cool and take careful aim. But the storm of shrapnel signaled defeat.

After the artillery had done its execution, the cavalry again charged to the edge of the mott and dismounted. Some opened fire while others ran into the thicket with slashing sabers. With half his men down and his own hip shattered, Dawson tied a blanket to his rifle and limped into the open to surrender. The enemy kept firing. Again he exposed himself to wave the improvised flag, to no avail. "Sell your lives as dearly as possible," Dawson exhorted, "let victory be purchased with blood." He then sank to the ground and died.[19]

Alsey Miller seized the surrender flag, mounted one of the few remaining horses, and rode into the open shouting, "We surrender!" The surviving Texans echoed the refrain. Mexican balls riddled the surrender flag, so Miller simply spurred through the enemy lines and kept going.

As five soldiers gave chase, his horse began to falter. He glanced to his rear. A "fine American horse" playfully galloped behind him. Quickly remounting, he pulled away from his pursuers and made good his escape.[20]

In the thicket the surviving Texans fought hand to hand, with knives and clubbed muskets. Some tried to surrender, but others fought on. The Mexicans continued the slaughter.

Samuel Maverick's slave, "a negro of Hurculean powers," had joined Dawson in hopes of reaching San Antonio and, passing himself off as a runaway, trying to liberate his master. Offered quarter by the Mexicans, Joe Griffin refused and fought ferociously. Ammunition exhausted, he swung his rifle, and when the stock broke, he seized a mesquite limb and continued to battle until felled by multiple wounds. The Mexican cavalry commander later described for Sam Maverick the feats of "that valiant black man."[21]

Early in the fighting Henry Woods had been wounded in the shoulder. He saw his seventy-year-old father killed and his brother severely wounded (he would later die in a Mexican prison). Henry stepped from the thicket and dropped his rifle and shot pouch on the ground, signaling to an officer his wish to surrender. The officer merely nodded and rode on. Behind him four mounted soldiers bore down on him. Two shot at him and missed. Two, whose pieces misfired, clubbed him with their muskets. One slashed him across the head with a sword. Another charged with a lance. Henry seized the lance, unhorsed his assailant, ran him through the chest with his own weapon, threw himself on the horse, and, brandishing the lance, galloped from the field. Cavalrymen looked on in stunned silence. Then one gave chase. Woods pulled a pistol from the saddle holster and pointed it at his pursuer, who dropped back while Henry made good his escape.[22]

In the mesquite mott, the fighting finally ended. Thirty-six Texans lay dead. Fifteen had succeeded in surrendering. Both the dead and the captives were stripped of clothing, arms, and everything else of value. The living were led to San Antonio and later confined in Mexico with the Anglo citizens seized by Woll as prisoners of war after the first exchange of fire in the city plaza on the morning of September 11.

The Dawson massacre was a needless sacrifice of life. Had Dawson not yielded his judgment to the clamor of his men, the company would have fallen back to unite with Billingsley's stronger force. Yet the unequal battle again highlighted the courage and fighting skill of the individual citizen soldier. It was another dramatic instance of the citizen soldier's fatal proclivity for self-destruction. The Dawson massacre took rank with other Mexican atrocities inflaming the Texan loathing for Mexicans.

On the evening of September 18, an elated Matt Caldwell again called for help. "We have a glorious band of Texian patriots," he exulted in describing the battle of Salado. "Come on and help me, it is the most favorable opportunity I ever saw. There are 1100 of the enemy. I can whip them on my own ground without any help, but I cannot take prisoners. Why don't you come on! Huzza! Huzza for Texas!"[23]

Men were coming on. Before daybreak on September 19 the companies of Jesse Billingsley and William I. Wallace, one hundred men, joined Caldwell. They elected James S. Mayfield as their major. Another hundred from the Colorado and Lavaca were hurrying forward, Colonel John H. Moore among their number. Others gathered and took up the march. "Arouse the country," Mayfield wrote to General Ed Burleson, "let's chastise the enemy and defend and save our families and friends. More depends on the lively patriotism of the people than all the Government can give."[24]

Heavy rains fell throughout September 19 as Caldwell's victorious men held their positions on the Salado. Ben McCulloch had come in during the night and joined with Hays and brother Henry in reconnoitering toward San Antonio. On the morning of the twentieth, Caldwell learned that Woll had evacuated San Antonio and was withdrawing toward the Rio Grande. At once his strengthened command, now numbering more than three hundred, took up the trail, Hays's Rangers in advance. By midnight, they reached the rain-swollen Medina and camped.

On September 21 Caldwell moved slowly up the Medina, tarrying to give Moore and his hundred men time to come up. Hays and the two McCullochs scouted ahead, locating Woll's army camped on the other side of the Medina about eight miles above Caldwell (about six miles north of present Castroville). Moore's arrival late in the afternoon brought the Texan force to nearly five hundred. They agreed to operate as two battalions, with Caldwell as colonel, Moore as lieutenant colonel, and Mayfield as major. Caldwell now felt himself strong enough to take on Woll.[25]

The next morning the Texans pushed the pursuit, Hays's Rangers in advance. Woll had broken camp and moved on to the west. About midafternoon, after a forced march of twenty miles, Hays came on Woll's rear guard and exchanged shots. Hoping to lure the Mexicans into an attack, Hays dismounted and formed line while the rest of the force filed into position. But the foe did not take the bait.

Two miles ahead, Woll reached the Arroyo Hondo and began crossing his army to the west bank. To cover the crossing, he posted an artillery piece with infantry support on a ridge overlooking the road. Hays halted beyond cannon range and sent a courier back to Caldwell, who hurried forward.

At the head of some fifty men, Hays shouted "Charge!" The cannon fired but overshot. Again the Reverend Morrell was one of the soldiers: "The Texan yell followed the cannon's thunder, and so excited the Mexican infantry, placed in position to pour a fire down our lines, that they overshot us; and by the time the artillery hurled its canister the second time, shot-guns and pistols were freely used by the Texans. Every man at the cannon was killed, as the company passed it."[26]

Five artillerymen were slain, the infantry routed, and the cannon captured. Four of Hays's men were wounded. Woll had reacted quickly to the threat, however, recrossing the Hondo with his other cannon and enough soldiers to force Hays to call off the attack and fall back.

Meantime, with the sun setting, the Texan command structure had fallen apart. Both Moore and Mayfield claimed the command, and their men supported them. At the same time, Caldwell seems to have determined that nightfall, together with boggy ground, made further offensive action unwise. Amid angry shouts of dissent and widespread grumbling over the failure to follow up on Hays's success, the army went into camp. Next morning, Woll was found to have slipped away at midnight. The bickering among Caldwell, Moore, and Mayfield continued, the issue whether to resume the pursuit or return to San Antonio. Tired horses and tired men furnished a pretext for giving up, although the petty jealousies stirred by Moore and Mayfield operated more decisively. The pursuers turned back, as one recorded, "feeling about like Jack did when he let the bird go."[27]

Caldwell took full responsibility for the failure of the pursuit, and many willingly threw all the blame on him. Moore and Mayfield, displaying a vainglory all too common among Texan leaders, were at least equally culpable. Whether Caldwell, backed by them, would have supported Hays on the night of the twenty-second or resumed the chase the next morning can only be speculated. Woll's army had been reduced by detachments to escort prisoners, wounded, and baggage to Mexico. With no more men than Caldwell, Woll could almost certainly have been defeated on either occasion by resolute, united Texans. A Mexican officer remarked that the Texans on the Hondo "were not fit to stand in the shoes of those who fought at the Salado."[28] Yet many were the same Texans, and the others were cut from the same mold. What they lacked on the Hondo was the brand of leadership they had on the Salado.

Mortified, humiliated, guilt-ridden, Matt Caldwell relinquished his command and, noted the *Telegraph and Texas Register*, "went off by himself as a private soldier, and on the bank of the Medina he was seen sitting alone by a little camp fire that he had built with his own hands, roasting a piece of meat on the end of a stick." He returned to his Gonzales home and within three months died, some said of a broken heart although more likely of a lifetime of exposure and hardship.[29]

Withdrawing from the Hondo, Caldwell's dispirited followers met a force led by Edward Burleson, now vice president of the Texas Republic. A fiery patriot who had tried to organize an invasion of Mexico after the Vásquez raid, Burleson brought new energy to the fray. On September

25, standing in a window of the Alamo, he delivered a ringing call to retaliate for the Woll outrage, urging the men to go home, get fresh horses and more ammunition, and rendezvous in San Antonio on October 25.[30]

Meantime, unaware of Woll's withdrawal, President Houston had roused the country to meet the aggression, and hundreds of militiamen and volunteers hurried toward San Antonio. Although the immediate threat had receded, once again, as after the Vásquez raid, Houston confronted a public demand for an offensive into Mexico and the men already mobilized to carry it out. His own vice president had requested authority to lead it and was issuing appeals for volunteers to gather in San Antonio.[31]

Houston knew that the government could not sustain such an operation, that the volunteers were stirred not only by war ardor but by visions of plunder, but that he could not defy the public clamor. The wily old politician devised a cunning stratagem: instead of naming Burleson to the command, he sent militia general Alexander Somervell to take charge of the troops assembling in San Antonio. Somervell's orders directed him to move south if and when he judged success attainable, thus freeing Houston of responsibility for whatever happened.[32]

Houston could have selected no one better qualified to ensure failure. A short, plump, amiable fellow, Somervell was weak, indecisive, inept, militarily incompetent, and temperamentally unfitted to win over men who wanted Burleson as their leader. By the time he reached San Antonio on November 4, the army had begun to fall apart, with men slipping away to return to their homes; those who remained were unruly, quarrelsome, and occasionally drunken. Somervell made matters worse by distancing himself from the men, squandering three weeks in attending to details of organization and logistics that could have been accomplished speedily and in waiting for a cannon that he would send back after six miles of mud on the first day's march.

By November 25, when Somervell broke camp on the Medina and took up the march for Laredo, his "army" numbered scarcely seven hundred, both militia and volunteers. They were organized in a skeleton brigade hardly deserving to be called even a regiment. The only efficient units were the Ranger companies of Jack Hays and Samuel Bogart, numbering about sixty men each. Even they made trouble by constantly bickering over precedence.

Short tempers were unsurprising. Besides all the other frustrations, the men had endured days of soaking rain in San Antonio and still more on the march. They arrived in Laredo on December 8 to find it abandoned by the military force they had hoped to fight. Instead, on December 9 two hundred men, nearly one-third of Somervell's force, descended on the town. All morning and into the afternoon, knots of men roamed the streets battering down doors and looting homes, stores, and warehouses. Not until 2:00 P.M. did Somervell send his officers to herd the pillagers back to camp. Somervell ordered all the spoils deposited for return to the owners. Some obeyed wholly or partly, others not at all.

Leading the army down the Rio Grande, Somervell suddenly veered east into dense chaparral. Officers and men alike grumbled that he was feeling his way toward the San Antonio road and would abandon the expedition. He himself probably did not know what he intended. Except for the Ranger companies of Hays and Bogart, Somervell led an undisciplined rabble, his horses broken down, his provisions all but exhausted, and at any moment vulnerable to a concentration of Mexican forces that might destroy him. On the morning of the tenth he called together his captains and asked what should be done. Eleven of the fourteen pressed for crossing the Rio Grande and seeking battle with the Mexican army. Not satisfied, Somervell put the issue to a vote of the army. All who wanted to go home should fall out and form on a nearby hill. One hundred, mostly conscripted militia, accepted the invitation, to be joined by another eighty-seven the next day. They went home.

With Hays's Rangers scouting well in advance, the shrunken army headed for Guerrero, sixty miles below Laredo on the west side of the Rio Grande. On December 14 the command reached the river. Hays and Bogart found a small dugout canoe and began crossing their companies to the west bank, six or seven men at a time, the horses swimming.[33]

As the troops shivered in drenching rain and sleet, they demanded that Somervell march them six miles inland to Guerrero and allow them to take what they wanted. Instead, fearing another Laredo, he ordered them back across the Rio Grande. Fretting that Mexican forces might at any moment concentrate against him, he had probably already decided that further prosecution of the campaign could only end in disaster. On December 19, therefore, he issued orders to begin the return march. Most of the men were furious over abjectly turning back without having struck a blow in Mexico and gathered the promised plunder.

Five captains, supported by most of their companies, flatly refused to obey Somervell's order. Bolstered by officers and men from other units, the mutineers numbered more than three hundred. With only 189 men, mostly militia, Somervell took up the march for home.

Sam Houston had chosen his scapegoat wisely. Somervell lacked the special qualities of leadership, so conspicuous in Matt Caldwell, needed to fuse intractable citizen soldiers into a disciplined military command. At least he had the good sense, by December 19, 1842, to understand that his army was out of control, weakened by the defections after Laredo, destitute of horses, rations, and clothing, and the objective of strong Mexican forces concentrating for the kill.

The mutineers elected one of their captains, William S. Fisher, as colonel and struck out for Mier, the next town down the Rio Grande from Guerrero. Theirs is not a story of Texas Rangers, although many former Rangers took part. Both Hays and Bogart obeyed Somervell's order, but some of their men went over to Fisher. Without forming part of Fisher's command, Ben and Henry McCulloch agreed to head about a dozen Rangers to act as scouts.

As Fisher's three hundred descended the river, part in boats and part on the east bank, the McCullochs' little band scouted the west bank to the edge of Mier. Sighting numerous Mexican scouting parties, they recrossed the river and reported their findings to Fisher on December 22. Fisher vowed to cross the next day and seize Mier. Ben McCulloch persuaded him to delay until he made a reconnaissance in force. The next day, while one hundred men held the river crossing, McCulloch and twenty-five rode into the plaza of Mier and received the town's sur-render from the alcalde. Here an American told him that General Pedro Ampudia and fifteen hundred infantry were marching from Matamoros, and from a nearby hill McCulloch himself could see militia riding in from the north.

Reporting the Mexican buildup, McCulloch urged Fisher to call off the offensive and return to Texas. Fisher refused. He and his followers regarded themselves as a match for any Mexican force that could be assembled, and no more than Somervell could Fisher prevent the men from seizing and plundering Mier. Wanting no part of a suicidal mission, Ben and Henry, accompanied by Ad Gillespie and a few others, headed for home.

Disaster overtook Fisher. On Christmas Day 1842, he led 261 Texans in a rash attack on Mier. McCulloch was right. Ampudia was there with a large force. The Texans fought valiantly until the afternoon of December 26, when they surrendered. Thirty Texans were killed or wounded, while their deadly fire dropped hundreds of Mexican soldiers. The prisoners were marched to Matamoros and thence toward Mexico City. En route, Ewen Cameron engineered a mass escape. In a fatal move, the fugitives left the roads and took to the wintry mountains, which proved bereft of water. Thirst destroyed organization and resolve. Only three men made their way to safety. The balance, 176, were recaptured. Santa Anna ordered them all executed, but in the end every tenth man, the unlucky ones who drew the seventeen black beans from an earthen jar of white beans, stood before the firing squad. Ewen Cameron drew a white bean, but later, by Santa Anna's personal order, he was executed too.

The Mier prisoners endured the miseries of Perote Castle. Some escaped. Some died. The last were released and returned to Texas in September 1844.[34]

The black bean episode enraged Anglo Texans. In their memory, the executions would rank with the Alamo and Goliad in powering a compulsive loathing of Mexicans. That Fisher's men invaded a foreign nation without the sanction of their own government, and indeed even technically as deserters from its military service, excused the Mexican act only in the minds of Sam Houston and a few of his associates. In the war soon to break out between the United States and Mexico, the Texas Rangers would draw from Mexican atrocities inspiration and justification for atrocities of their own against the foe, combatant and noncombatant alike.

The animosities generated by the Alamo, Goliad, Perote Castle, the Dawson massacre, and the black beans are crucial to understanding the evolving traditions of the Texas Rangers and their attitudes and actions.

[4]

The Tradition Nationalized:
War with Mexico

THE REPUBLIC OF TEXAS endured for almost a decade, from 1836 to 1845. By hardly any measure of nationhood could it be judged a success. By 1845, Mexico stood no more ready than it was in 1836 to acknowledge Texan independence. Neither the Texas Congress nor the three presidents—Houston, Lamar, and Anson Jones—governed effectively, largely because of partisan rivalries and an empty treasury. Drawn by liberal land laws, seven thousand immigrants a year boosted the population to 100,000 (plus nearly thirty-eight thousand slaves); but the economy remained essentially cashless and subsistence-based. People could not pay taxes. Although assiduously cultivated by Texan diplomats, foreign nations discovered no incentive to grant loans.

Declaring independence in 1836, the citizenry expected prompt annexation to the mother country. Not until December 1845, however, could the political obstacles in the United States be shouldered aside and Texas added to the American union.

With Texas, the United States acquired a huge new state populated by a rowdy frontier people, individualists to the core. "Texians," as they called themselves, boasted a pride and sense of unique identity found nowhere else in the nation. Of all the states, Texas alone gloried in its heritage of independent nationhood. The Lone Star, although now one of the galaxy of American stars, for Texans remained a Lone Star that would forever crown them with special singularity.

With Texas, moreover, the United States inherited a decade-long war with Mexico. President James K. Polk did not want war, but he meant to acquire Texas and California, and he was prepared to pay handsomely for them. But Mexico, weak and politically riven as ever, rebuffed Polk. In June 1845, anticipating annexation, Polk ordered General Zachary Taylor to concentrate one-fourth of the U.S. Army, two thousand regulars, in Louisiana as an "army of observation." Two months later, after the Texas Congress voted overwhelmingly for annexation, Polk had Taylor take station on the shores of Corpus Christi Bay. In February 1846, with annexation formally accomplished, Taylor received orders to march to a new position near the mouth of the Rio Grande, a move that asserted the river as the southern boundary of the United States. Polk's provocative act thrust the two nations to the brink of war.[1]

The Mexican War was fought by the U.S. regular army augmented by state volunteer regiments called into federal service. The Texas units resembled no others—in appearance, fighting technique, or discipline. Whether in camp, on campaign, or in battle, they contrasted so vividly with the rest of the army that newspaper correspondents and military letter writers penned graphic descriptions of these outfits that, regardless of the designation under which mustered, called themselves Texas Rangers. Until 1846, hardly anyone outside Texas had heard of Texas Rangers. The Mexican War nationalized the Texas Ranger tradition and earned it an enduring place in the imagination of Americans.

On the Rio Grande in April 1846, Zachary Taylor's army of thirty-five hundred men counted no volunteers as it threw up an earthen fort across the river from Matamoros and faced much larger Mexican forces. Thickset, with stubby legs, Taylor rarely donned a uniform and affected no military airs. Nor did he display much grasp of strategy, tactics, or logistics. But "Old Rough and Ready" could be counted on to fight.

Texans saw in Taylor many of the egalitarian qualities they admired. And by the middle of April, Taylor had decided that he needed some of the qualities that Texans offered. His supply base lay on Point Isabel, thirty miles northeast across tangled chaparral flats spotted with shallow lagoons. Vessels from New Orleans slipped around the southern tip of Padre Island into Laguna Madre and deposited their cargos at Point Isabel. A Mexican force, Taylor saw, could easily ford the Rio Grande and sever the supply line. He wanted Texans to replace the dragoons in keeping open the road. Fortuitously, at this very time he met Samuel H. Walker.[2]

Although not so well known, Walker rivaled Jack Hays in Ranger qualities. Thirty years old, smooth-shaven, with bright blue eyes, a head of thick hair, and a muscular physique hardened by outdoor life, he arrived in Texas early in 1842 after volunteer service in the Creek and Seminole wars. He began his Ranger service in Captain Jesse Billingsley's company during the Woll invasion. He went with Fisher to Mier and, drawing a white bean, ended in the Molino del Rey prison, from which he escaped in August 1843. Back in Texas, Walker enlisted in Hays's Ranger company, took a lance wound at Walker Creek, and emerged as one of the best of Hays's men. Like Hays, Walker was daring and brave but modest about his exploits, serious, cool and deliberate, and popular with his comrades. Observed one, "War was his element, the bivouac his delight, and the battlefield his playground." Walker's one passion was a loathing of Mexicans and a determination to exact revenge for his months in prison.[3]

Walker showed up at Taylor's headquarters early in April 1846. With the general's blessing, he rounded up twenty-six men from among the herders and other hangers-on who had followed the army down from Corpus Christi. On April 21, at Point Isabel, they were sworn into federal service and at once began to range the chaparral. Even before the muster, Walker rummaged through the depot at Point Isabel and found thirty-two Paterson Colt revolvers, which he instantly requisitioned for his men. As a veteran of Walker Creek, he knew their value.[4]

On April 23 sixteen hundred Mexican lancers crossed the Rio Grande upstream from Matamoros and Taylor's camp. Taylor sent Captain Seth Thornton and sixty-three dragoons to investigate. The next day Thornton allowed himself to be ambushed, had sixteen of his men cut down, and surrendered the rest. "Hostilities may now be considered as commenced," Taylor reported to army headquarters on April 26, "and I have this day deemed it necessary to call on the governor of Texas for four regiments of volunteers, two to be mounted and two to serve as foot."[5]

As the call went forth for more Texans, Captain Walker established himself about halfway between Point Isabel and Taylor's camp. With small squads he and his lieutenant, Joseph P. Wells, ranged a land suddenly swarming with lancers and partisans led by Antonio Canales, the "Chaparral Fox." Taylor's supply line lay exposed to this peril as well as the main Mexican army even then crossing the Rio Grande.

Walker's base camp lay exposed also. In the absence of Walker and Wells, Sergeant Edward Radcliffe and twelve men held the position, a makeshift little fort of mesquite limbs about 120 feet square, enclosing horses, men, and equipment. It lay near the edge of Palo Alto Lagoon, surrounded by heavy chaparral. Walker left strict instructions for posting security, but these were not the Rangers he had soldiered with under Hays. As their nighttime pickets ambled in at first light of April 28, hundreds of Canales's guerrillas overran the camp, killed and mutilated six Rangers, captured four, and spent hours searching for the three who had scampered to safety amid the mesquite and prickly pear. Among the plunder seized at the camp were one-third of the Colt five-shooters.[6]

The debacle embarrassed Walker and alarmed the troops at Point Isabel, but the commander, Major John Munroe, believed he could withstand any attack the Mexicans might mount. He wanted Taylor to know that. On the evening of April 29, therefore, Walker and four Rangers set forth with a dispatch for Taylor. They wended their way through the concealing chaparral, had several narrow escapes, and once had to cut their way through a startled body of Mexican lancers, but by morning they delivered the dispatch to Taylor.[7]

At once Walker gained even more praise. On May 1, leaving a garrison under Major Jacob Brown to man the new earthwork, Taylor marched the army back to Point Isabel for resupply. Before reveille on the third, the sound of cannon fire drifted over Point Isabel. Major Brown was clearly in an artillery duel with Mexican batteries in Matamoros. Anxious over the fate of Brown, Taylor asked Walker if he could get through once more. A squadron of dragoons under Captain Charles May escorted Walker and a handful of men to a lagoon at the edge of the chaparral and promised to await their return. When they failed to appear the next morning, May hurried back to Point Isabel. As the cannonade continued, all agonized for both Brown and Walker. At last, at nine o'clock on the morning of the fifth, Walker rode in with word that Major Brown could hold his own. "Captain Walker ran a great many risks making his way to the fort," recalled an officer, "and deserves great credit for the fearless manner in which he effected the communication."[8]

Sam Walker was the first authentic hero of the Mexican War. He scouted further for Taylor and then, with the remnant of his Ranger company, fought with Captain May's dragoons in the two decisive battles of Palo Alto and Resaca de la Palma, May 8 and May 9. But it was Walker's bold deeds in twice cutting his way through enemy-infested country as a dispatch bearer that gained him the adulation of Americans. Newspapers extolled his adventures. President Polk appointed him a captain in the regular army. New Orleans admirers purchased a "fine-blooded war steed" for him and later followed with "a very elegant and serviceable sword."[9]

Meantime, Governor J. Pinckney Henderson broadcast Taylor's call for two mounted and two foot regiments. Henderson doubted that many Texans would volunteer as infantrymen. "There would be no difficulty in raising forty companies provided they were mounted," he wrote Taylor on May 3, 1846. "The Texians are generally good horsemen and prefer to be employed in that way and I am sure they could & would do good service."[10]

The governor knew his citizens. From all over Texas mounted companies sufficient for two regiments converged on the lower Rio Grande,

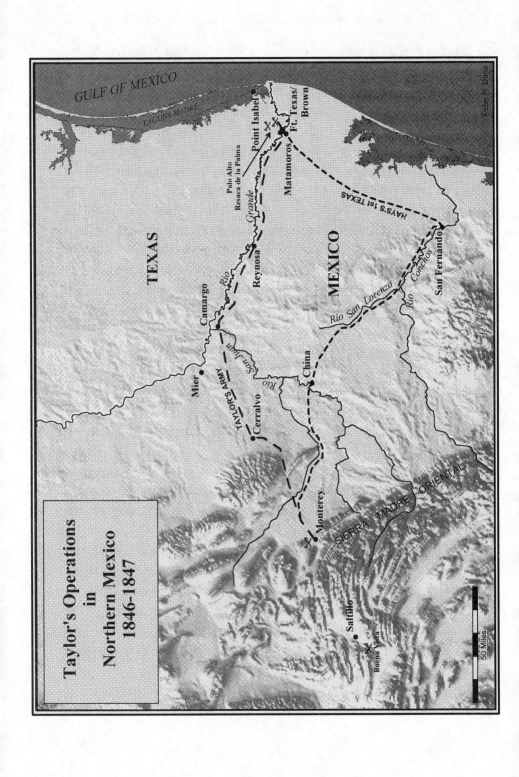

Taylor's Operations
in
Northern Mexico
1846-1847

GULF OF MEXICO

LAGUNA MADRE

TEXAS

MEXICO

Point Isabel

Palo Alto
Resaca de la Palma

Rio Grande

Matamoros

Ft. Texas/Brown

HAYS'S 1st TEXAS

San Fernando

Rio Conchos

Rio San Lorenzo

Reynosa

Camargo

Rio San Juan

Mier

TAYLOR'S ARMY

Cerralvo

China

Monterey

SIERRA MADRE ORIENTAL

Saltillo

Buena Vista

Peter H. Dana

50 Miles

while only enough men volunteered for foot service to fill out a single regiment. Even so, the governor counted four regiments as composing a division, a major general's command, turned his office over to the lieutenant governor, and showed up at Taylor's headquarters to be mustered as a major general. Never overly concerned with protocol, Taylor, who had been breveted major general in June, let Henderson have his way. On July 30, at Matamoros, Henderson was sworn into the federal service, together with a staff that included former president Mirabeau B. Lamar and former vice president Edward Burleson.[11]

At once the Texans exhibited themselves to the Mexicans as ruffians and to the army command as troublemakers. As a regular soldier observed, "The Mexicans dread the Texians more than they do the devil, and they have good reason for it." And General Taylor declared, "If they could be made subordinate they would be the best, at any rate as good as any volunteer corps in the service, but I fear they are & will continue too licentious to do much good." As the Rangers rarely took sexual liberties with the Mexican women, Taylor undoubtedly meant the word in its other connotations: unrestrained by law or general morality, going beyond customary bounds or limits, disregarding rules. Judged by those definitions, the Rangers compiled a conspicuous record of licentiousness.[12]

With Jack Hays not yet in service, the most helpful Texan to join Taylor was Captain Ben McCulloch with his Gonzales Rangers. McCulloch's talents as a scout, honed to perfection against Indians and Mexicans, caused Taylor to withhold the company from the regiments organizing under General Henderson and attach it to his own headquarters. McCulloch's men proved their value as scouts and partisan fighters and lived up to their reputation as terrors to Mexicans.[13]

After abandoning Matamoros, the Mexican army fell back to the plateau city of Monterey, capital of Nuevo Leon, home to more than twelve thousand people, and guardian of the passes through the Sierra Madre that bore the "high road" to Mexico City. (The modern spelling is Monterrey, but during the Mexican War it was Monterey.) General Taylor had no illusions about taking Mexico City by this route; a supply line of one thousand miles could not be maintained through rugged country swarming with guerrillas. Monterey and its army of defenders, however, offered an immediate objective. Throughout the summer, as volunteer regiments from the States poured through Point Isabel, the general employed McCulloch's Rangers to scout the best approaches to the city and contend with the roving bands of partisans under the detested Canales. By late July Captain Richard Gillespie and his Ranger company had reached Camargo, after a march from San Antonio by way of Laredo, and Taylor kept him there to operate with McCulloch.[14]

The other Texas units used up most of the summer trying to get organized. With McCulloch and Gillespie intended as part of the First Texas Mounted Volunteers, the other eight companies gathered at the Point Isabel rendezvous and late in June elected Jack Hays their colonel, Sam Walker lieutenant colonel, and Mike Chevallie major. Thus Walker put aside, for the time being, his captain's commission in the regular army to help lead the Texans. The Second Texas Mounted Volunteers counted ten companies by early July and elected state senator George T. Wood colonel. As the governor had foreseen, Texans responded reluctantly to the call for footmen. Not until a spare company of Mississippians agreed to reconstitute themselves as Texans could the First Texas Foot Rifles be completed, with the veteran Albert Sidney Johnston as colonel.

A vast confusion dogged the organization of the Texas regiments. Some of the companies had been enlisted for three months under the militia laws even though a recent act of Congress decreed twelve months or the duration of the war. Early in August, disgruntled over a requirement to sign for another nine months, the Texas foot regiment voted to go home, leaving Johnston an angry colonel without a command. The two mounted regiments consented to another three months, which Taylor, heeding expediency instead of law, reluctantly agreed to. Johnston took service on the staff of the division of volunteers.[15]

For Taylor, the two Texas regiments proved indispensable. Except for four companies of the Second Dragoons, they were his only mounted troops. The First consisted entirely of men recruited on the frontier, mostly Ranger veterans seasoned by Indian campaigns and outdoor life, tough fighters spoiling for a fight with Mexicans. The companies of the Second Regiment were raised in the settled areas but still were intrepid, aggressive Texans. The men called themselves the Western Regiment and the Eastern Regiment. Both, however, boasted splendid horsemen equipped with rifles, pistols (some the Colt five-shooters), knives, and even swords. No uniform, insignia of rank, or battle flag marked the Texans. Nor did they pay much attention to regulations or other military proprieties. Officers and men mingled as comrades, shared equally in privation and plenitude, and called one another by their first names.

By early September, Taylor had concentrated an army of more than six thousand at Camargo, ready to launch an offensive against Monterey by way of Cerralvo and Marín. Of three approaches investigated by McCulloch, this offered the best road for wagons and artillery as well as adequate water. The army consisted of three divisions, two of regulars under Brigadier Generals David E. Twiggs and William J. Worth and one of volunteers under Major General William O. Butler. The roster also listed a Texas division under Major General Henderson, but it consisted of only the First and Second Texas Regiments.[16]

Although part of Hays's First Texas, the companies of McCulloch and Gillespie had never joined it. Indeed, Hays and the balance of the regiment had never joined Taylor. Wood's Second Texas had made its way to Camargo, but Hays's Rangers were off doing what they liked best—acting independently in a swing south from Matamoros and then west as far as the town of China.

Early in September Taylor and his three divisions began to move by stages to Cerralvo and on toward Monterey. McCulloch and Gillespie, still kept by the general, rode advance and rear guard, escort, and express. Hays continued to occupy his position at China. Wood's Second Texas, Henderson and his staff of celebrities accompanying, followed a parallel route up the San Juan and on the fourteenth joined Hays near China. Finally, Henderson could assume command of his "division." He bore orders from Taylor to push it rapidly cross country and join the main army at Marín.[17]

65

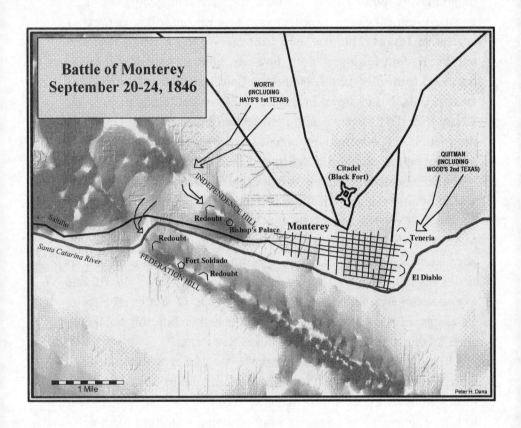

Battle of Monterey
September 20-24, 1846

After a forced march through mountainous terrain, the Texans reached Marín on the morning of September 18, just after the army had moved out. By afternoon they had overtaken Taylor. That night, for the first time, the companies of McCulloch and Gillespie joined their regiment, bringing Henderson's command to about a thousand rifles. That same night Taylor decreed that the Texans would take the advance on the morrow. At first light on September 19 the army marched. As Lieutenant James K. Holland of Wood's regiment recorded: "Texas went ahead today—now that danger is expected old Taylor has put us in front—Every man in glorious spirits."[18]

Taylor faced a formidable foe. General Pedro Ampudia commanded seven thousand regulars and three thousand irregulars. He had heavily fortified the city, a dense concentration of stone houses strung for a mile along the Santa Catarina River, a tributary of the San Juan. High, rugged hills, spurs of the Sierra Madre, guarded the western end of town and the vital road that linked Monterey with Saltillo. The hills had been fortified and armed with artillery. On the east edge of the city engineers had thrown up two earthworks mounting cannon that commanded the roads from the northeast. Half a mile to the north, dominating the broad plain by which Taylor had to approach, stood a huge fortification called the Citadel but dubbed the "Black Fort" by the Americans.

By nine o'clock on the morning of September 19, Taylor and his staff, riding with Hays's First Texas as the divisions of blue-clad infantry followed, reached the edge of the plain and glimpsed Monterey's cathedral spire rising from the mist less than three miles to the south. Corn fields, grazing cattle, and an occasional *jacale* spread across the foreground. The Citadel rose ominously in their front. A body of brightly uniformed lancers tried to entice the Texans to charge, but when the fort's cannon opened fire Taylor restrained them. In a magnificent grove of oak and pecan trees, watered by a bubbling spring, he established his headquarters and sent his engineers forward to reconnoiter.

Detachments of Rangers escorted the engineers, but the rest of the Texans emerged to make their own sportive reconnaissance. "Like boys at play," wrote an officer of an Ohio regiment, "those fearless horsemen, in a spirit of boastful rivalry, vied with each other in approaching the very edge of danger. Riding singly and rapidly, they swept around the plain under the walls, each one in a wider and more perilous circle than his predecessor. Their proximity occasionally provoked the enemy's fire, but the Mexicans might as well have attempted to bring down skimming swallows as those racing dare-devils."[19]

The engineers confirmed that, despite the fortified hills, the western end of the city might be seized at less cost than the eastern. Success in that quarter would also sever the Saltillo road, Ampudia's sole line of supply, reinforcement, and retreat, and gain heights that commanded the city. This mission Taylor assigned to Worth's Second Division, bolstered by Hays's Texas Rangers, about two thousand men. Twiggs's First Division, with Wood's Second Texas, would support Worth by creating a diversion on the east end of Monterey.

In full view of the enemy, the Rangers in advance, Worth's division made its way in an arc to the west during the afternoon of September 20. Nearing the Saltillo road, the Americans could plainly see Mexican forces moving through the city to strengthen the hilltop defenses.

The nearest eminence, Loma Independencia, sloped from west to east, the high western edge crowned by a sandbag redoubt, the lower marked by the "Bishop's Palace," an abandoned ecclesiastical structure. Partly masked to the south lay Loma Federación, likewise guarded by redoubts on the craggy western end and a fort, El Soldado, in a depression to the east. The Saltillo road and the Santa Catarina River ran through the narrow valley between these two steep ridges.

Under low-hanging clouds, after a miserably rainy night, the Texans again took the lead early on September 21. Within three hundred yards of the Saltillo road, they rounded a mountain spur to confront a force of Mexican cavalry and infantry estimated at fifteen hundred, three-fourths the strength of Worth's entire division. The cannon on Independence Hill opened fire. Two crack squadrons of lancers, about two hundred men, formed to charge.

Quickly, Worth dismounted Hays's Texans and deployed them with two infantry companies behind a hedge fence at the roadside. On the extreme right, to cover his flank, Hays kept McCulloch's company in the roadway on horseback. As the brightly uniformed troopers galloped down the road, thudding musketry mingled with the sharp crack of the Texan rifles to sweep their ranks. Still mounted, McCulloch's men loosed a storm of rifle, shotgun, and pistol fire, then met the Mexican charge head-on. The big American horses slammed against the smaller Mexican mounts and blunted the rush. In a hand-to-hand melee, lance contended with five-shooter. Their colonel down and dozens of saddles emptied, the lancers turned to retreat. McCulloch and part of his Rangers found themselves at the very center of the enemy force, borne to the rear by the retreat. Desperately, they fought their way against the tide back to safety. Seven took lance wounds, but not one lost his life.

The rout was complete. All the Mexican cavalry and infantry fell back toward the Bishop's Palace on Independence Hill. One hundred dead and wounded lancers littered the road. At the cost of one Texan killed by friendly fire, Worth had control of the Saltillo road.[20]

Worth now resolved to storm the redoubts on Federation Hill, which would command the Soldado fort lower to the east, the Bishop's Palace across the valley on Independence Hill, and the western approach to the city. The sound of gunfire from the east, moreover, told that Taylor had launched a diversion in Worth's favor. The assault party, led by Captain Charles F. Smith of the regulars, consisted of about three hundred men, half artillery acting as footmen ("red-legged infantry") and half dismounted Texas Rangers. Mike Chevallie commanded the Rangers, who assured Worth they did not mind their major serving under his captain.[21]

Federation Hill presented a rocky slope covered with chaparral rising about four hundred feet above the valley. The Mexican artillery pieces could not be lowered enough to bring the Americans under fire, so infantry began to scramble down the hillside to meet the attack. Observing reinforcements hastening to bolster the defenders, Worth dispatched the Seventh and Fifth Infantry to Smith's support. Colonel Hays gathered another hundred Rangers and hurried to catch up.

Up the slope the regulars and Rangers rushed, pausing to fire and reload but with a sustained momentum that drove the Mexicans back to the top and then down the slope toward the Soldado fortification. At the redoubt, the victors righted an overturned nine-pounder and opened on the Soldado, luckily disabling the cannon there, then poured down the ridge spine toward the fort. Grape shot from the Bishop's Palace across the valley swept the ridge. First over the Soldado parapet was Captain Gillespie of the Rangers, followed by the color sergeant of the Fifth Infantry, who rammed the staff of the banner into a breastwork.

As the Mexicans fled precipitately toward the city, regulars and Rangers filled the fort's compound. A lieutenant of the regulars strode over to a captured cannon. "Well, boys," he said to the Rangers, "we liked to have beaten you." With a piece of chalk, he then scrawled on the gun barrel: "Texas Rangers and 5th Infantry."[22]

For the next day, September 22, Worth planned an even more daunting mission—the seizure of Independence Hill and Bishop's Palace. He entrusted the task to Captain Thomas Childs of the artillery footmen. The force consisted of about five hundred men, half regulars and half Rangers.

A cold downpour drenched the men as they moved into position at the base of Independence during the night. The ascent would be even harder than Federation, for the incline was almost vertical and jumbled with outcroppings of rock and thorny brush. The Mexicans judged their redoubt unassailable, and this, together with the rain, dulled their watchfulness. At 3:00 A.M., as the rain slackened and a mist set in, the attackers began the climb, Hays and part of the Rangers with Childs on the southwestern approach, Walker and the rest with Captain John R. Vinton on the northwestern. Slowly and silently they made their way up, as rainwater cascaded down the slope, stones broke free and tumbled around them, and vertical rock ledges forced them to find sturdy enough brush by which to pull themselves up. About a hundred yards from the crest, a Mexican picket guard raised the alarm, fired blindly, and ran back to the top. On came the climbers, without firing a shot, until some sixty feet from the objective. Then, rifles and muskets erupting, they poured over the breastworks into the redoubt.

First to mount the parapet, Ad Gillespie urged his company forward. A Mexican took aim and brought him down. Some of his men stopped to help him, but he ordered them on. A surgeon bent over him and confirmed the wound as mortal. "Boys," Gillespie shouted, "place me behind that ledge of rock and give me my revolver, I will do some executing on them yet before I die." He died the next day.[23]

After a brief struggle in the redoubt, the Mexicans fled down the reverse grade to the safety of the Bishop's Palace. Exhausted, the victors halted while reinforcements came up. More than 250 Mexicans barricaded in the palace kept them under artillery and musket fire all morning. By noon, a twelve-pounder howitzer had been taken apart and dragged piece by piece to the hilltop, to be reassembled and directed at the palace.

Captain Childs conceived a stratagem for meeting the expected counterattack. The Rangers crept into positions on both sides of the ridge spine, hidden from the view from the palace, Hays on the right, Walker on the left. Farther up the slope to the west, Childs placed companies on both sides of the ridge, out of sight of the Mexicans. The company of Louisiana infantry played decoy, advancing as skirmishers to lure out the enemy, then falling back as Mexican bugles summoned both infantry and cavalry to the charge.

Galloping lancers had almost overrun the rock wall when the American infantry sprang to their feet, swung their flanks into a solid line across the ridge top, and fired their muskets at point-blank range. Horsemen reared and fell back, disorganizing the infantry following them. At this juncture, the Texas Rangers rose from their concealed positions and poured volleys of rifle and pistol fire into both flanks of the Mexican formation.

"Charge!" someone shouted, and the Americans rushed forward. Most of the retreating Mexicans flowed around the palace and descended to the city, but some crowded into the palace and slammed shut the massive gate. The American howitzer came forward and blew it down. In poured regulars and Texans to fight fiercely in hand-to-hand combat. "Throw yourselves flat," cried an officer, and almost at once the howitzer loosed a double charge of canister. The surviving Mexicans fled the palace into the streets of Monterey.

By 4:00 P.M., the American flag flew over the Bishop's Palace. General Worth controlled the western approaches to Monterey, and his guns commanded the city itself. In two days of fighting, he had lost only thirty-two killed and wounded.[24]

Worth's triumph on September 21 found antithesis in calamity at the other end of Monterey. General Taylor issued such vague and ambiguous orders that the demonstration in Worth's favor turned into a murderous battle for the fortifications blocking the eastern and northern approaches to the city. The result was a brave but bloody offensive, ending with the Americans in precarious possession of one small fort and with a casualty list nearing four hundred. By dawn of September 23, Brigadier General John A. Quitman's volunteer brigade, probing the eastern margin of Monterey, discovered that the enemy had abandoned the forts and pulled back toward the central plaza. He pushed skirmishers into the streets until running into resistance. Taylor sent two regular regiments and Wood's Texans, dismounted, to Quitman's support. Block by block, they fought toward the central plaza. The objective within grasp, however, General Taylor called off the offensive. He later explained that Quitman's operation had shown that the city could be taken. He pulled back, therefore, to arrange with Worth for a simultaneous attack from east and west the next day. What he seems not to have known until too late was that Worth had already launched his own attack from the west.[25]

At the Bishop's Palace, Worth and his men had heard the firing in the city below. No orders had come from Taylor, and in fact none had been sent. Worth therefore decided to assume that attack orders had miscarried and early in the afternoon sent his division into the western streets of Monterey. On foot, Hays and half the Rangers accompanied the right assault column, Walker and the rest the left, as the two advanced on parallel streets. The fighting developed in the same pattern as on the east—house to house, room to room, roof to roof. Now, because Taylor had canceled the advance from the east, Worth's men confronted all the Mexican defenders. By nightfall, however, his troops held positions within one block of the central plaza. During the night they placed artillery on the rooftops and prepared for a final onslaught the next morning.

But next morning General Ampudia signaled a truce and asked to confer with Taylor. Hays and Walker impatiently held their positions, anxious to make the dash on the cathedral in the plaza. By noon, however, Taylor had a panel of officers negotiating with Ampudia's representatives. By evening the armistice had been arranged. The Mexican army could evacuate the city under arms, with banners flying, and without giving parole. Taylor promised not to move beyond Monterey for eight weeks.

Although the general had some valid reasons for such generosity, he had a hard time explaining them to a furious President Polk. The Texans, even more furious, were in no mood for explanations. "A burst of indignation and angry discontent was manifested on every side," wrote Reid. "The Texians were maddened with disappointment." Or as a less sympathetic observer noted, "unsated with slaughter, they but waited for morning to avenge signally the hoarded wrongs suffered during their long war for independence. The capitulation of the 24th, of course, disappointed all their sweet and long cherished hopes of vengeance."[26]

With their three-month enlistment due to expire, the disgruntled Texans said they wanted to go home. Taylor lost no time in granting their wish, for in the days after the battle they reverted to some of their old bad habits. "With their departure we may look for a restoration of quiet and order in Monterey," Taylor wrote on October 6, "for I regret to report that some shameful atrocities have been perpetrated by them since the capitulation of the town." Appalled by their "lawless and vindictive spirit," Ohio's Major Luther Giddings conceded that they made "excellent light troops" but watched them depart only with "the hope that all honest Mexicans were at a safe distance from their path."[27]

Except for the Texans, Taylor's officers and men felt relief that he had struck a deal. The army was battered, bloodied, and exhausted, short on ammunition and supplies, and, they thought, not strong enough to overwhelm Ampudia's superior numbers. A final push on September 24, however, would almost certainly have gained the city and the enemy's unconditional surrender. The two Texas regiments alone, thrusting from east and west, could probably have won the victory. As it was, the Mexican army had been allowed to march away to fight another day, and the battle of Monterey, while a strategic gain of some importance, fell far short of the decisive victory it might have been.

In the Monterey campaign and culminating battle, the Texas Rangers played a role of major significance. Ben McCulloch's scouting had been vital in revealing the best route of approach. In the battle itself, both the First and Second Texas, whether on foot or horseback, had consistently excelled as tough combat soldiers. Hays's men proved critical in the storming of Federation and Independence hills and in seizing the western half of Monterey. Wood's regiment fully matched the prowess of the Western Rangers, as exhibited by the street fighting in the eastern half of the city. The rifles and five-shooters of the Rangers gave them a firepower superior to any other elements of the army. Of the volunteers, only Colonel Jefferson Davis's red-shirted Mississippians came close to the Texans in combat effectiveness, and they too carried rifles instead of muskets. Graphically reported by several newsmen, Monterey further nationalized the fame of the Texas Rangers. It fully sustained their fighting reputation but also their darker reputation for insubordination and excess.

ON OCTOBER 1, 1846, Lieutenant Colonel Walker of the Texas Rangers became Captain Walker of the U.S. Regiment of Mounted Riflemen, directed to proceed at once to the East and recruit his company. Walker and Jack Hays traveled together as far as New Orleans, where the citizens lionized them as war heroes. In Washington, Baltimore, and New York, Walker received the same enthusiastic welcome. Hays returned to Texas to begin organizing the new Ranger regiment expected to be called into federal service.

Although now an officer of the regular army, Sam Walker cherished the Texas Rangers. Desperately seeking to interest a hidebound ordnance department in his revolving pistol, Samuel Colt approached

Walker for an endorsement. Responding enthusiastically, the captain described how a handful of Rangers armed with the Paterson Colt had bested five times their number of Comanches at Walker Creek in 1844. The Colt five-shooters had given the Rangers the confidence to undertake daring adventures. "With improvements," Walker asserted, "I think they can be rendered the most perfect weapon in the World for light mounted troops."[28]

Appealing directly to President Polk and the secretary of war, Walker helped Colt circumvent the ordnance department's opposition to repeating arms and gain a contract. Walker also worked with the gun maker on the improvements. The result was the first six-shooter, which the inventor named the "Walker Colt." It was a heavy, powerful handgun, weighing four and one-half pounds, .44-caliber, with a nine-inch barrel and a large cylinder to accommodate six rounds backed by hefty powder charges. It was sturdier than the old Paterson and easier to load. In striking power, it rivaled the regulation army musket and at one hundred yards even the rifle. The first Walker Colts were to be sent to Walker's company in Mexico and to arm the new Ranger regiment Jack Hays was raising in Texas.[29]

The regiment took shape slowly because the War Department wanted it enlisted for the duration of the war. Texans would sign on for twelve months and no more. Back in the capital after his service with Taylor, Governor Henderson in February 1847 sent Hays to Washington to talk with the president and secretary of war and see if the obstacles could be set aside. They were, but continued bumbling and confusion prevented the muster of a full regiment for combat duty until July 1847.[30]

As the regiment took up the march for Mexico, its colonel proudly bore two Walker Colts, presented by Samuel Colt. The cylinders displayed an engraving, as Colt explained, "representing as near as I can the engagement you had with the Camanches in which you & your little band so Brilliantly distinguished yourselves."[31]

AFTER MONTEREY, TAYLOR watched the Texans go home without regret. Idle Texans made constant trouble. From one unit, however, he extracted a promise to return if hostilities resumed: Ben McCulloch, the sinewy, reserved captain whose unsurpassed scouting talents had proved so critical in the Monterey campaign. When President Polk canceled Taylor's armistice in November 1846, McCulloch raised another Gonzales company. On January 31, 1847, he reported his little band of twenty-seven to Taylor in Monterey, to be mustered for six months as McCulloch's Company, Texas Mounted Volunteers (Spies).[32]

Since Monterey, Taylor's situation had changed drastically. The administration had decided to take Mexico City by the direct route, from the Gulf port of Vera Cruz over the mountains to the capital. The army's general in chief, Winfield Scott, had been entrusted with this mission. He had withdrawn almost all of Taylor's seasoned regulars and replaced them with untested volunteer units. Santa Anna gathered an army of more than twenty thousand and struck north to destroy the weakened Taylor before turning to confront Scott. McCulloch had arrived just in time to tell Taylor what he needed to know.

The general had posted his army of 4,650 men at Agua Nueva, a broad plain surrounded by mountains seventeen miles south of Saltillo. He needed accurate intelligence of the strength and position of the enemy forces he knew to be operating to the south. On February 20, with Lieutenant Fielding Alston, four Rangers, and a volunteer Kentucky lieutenant, McCulloch took the road south. It ran through a narrow valley shouldered by steep rocky ridges on either side. Apprehensive of advance cavalry pickets, the Rangers crept as silently as possible to a ridge top and looked out over a broad valley. It blazed with camp fires that lit the night sky. The mountains on all sides twinkled with the fires of picket guards.

McCulloch had found Santa Anna's army. Taylor had to be informed as quickly as possible. Lieutenant Alston, the Kentucky officer, and three Rangers would carry the word. McCulloch and Ranger William Phillips would wait for daylight to reveal the enemy in more detail—a rash if not foolhardy course.

Discovered by pickets before dawn, McCulloch and Phillips escaped only by skill and good luck. At daylight they watched the army come to life, gained a better estimate of its strength in infantry, cavalry, and artillery, and heard hundreds of bugles call it to the advance on Agua Nueva. Getting there themselves proved a harrowing ordeal, as they eluded some pickets and outran or outmaneuvered others. Exhausted and maddened with thirst, they rode into Agua Nueva late in the afternoon of February 21. No exploit of his career more keenly tested Ben McCulloch's every faculty as partisan fighter or more dramatically confirmed his reputation as the king of them all.[33]

Alston and his companions had reached Agua Nueva safely early on September 21 and reported to Taylor. At once the general ordered his army to fall back to previously selected defensive positions just south of Buena Vista. On February 22–23 Santa Anna hurled fifteen thousand troops against those positions. He nearly overwhelmed the green volunteers, but the regular army artillery so battered his army that he dared not order a final assault. His withdrawal left the Americans in possession of the field and thus the victors. The battle of Buena Vista, to which Ben McCulloch had contributed so significantly, launched Zachary Taylor on an easy road to the White House.

As TAYLOR GRAPPLED with Santa Anna at Buena Vista, an event took place near Ramos that forecast the character of the rest of the war in the northern theater. Ramos lay on Taylor's supply route to Monterey. On February 22, 1847, Mexican lancers and irregulars captured an American wagon train, killed and mutilated a hundred teamsters, and took prisoner the infantry escort.[34]

To secure the supply line, more Rangers were sent for. The first company came from Corpus Christi under Captain Mabry B. Gray. A veteran of San Jacinto, "Mustang" Gray had already attained fame as one of the "cowboys" who ravaged the Nueces Strip during the early years of the Republic, preying on Anglo and Mexican alike. He was destined for a secure niche in Texas folklore. For now, he took revenge for Ramos by putting to death the entire male population of a village near Ramos, twenty-four men. Fearful of a like fate, no Mexican witness would identify the perpetrators.[35]

In April and May 1847 a San Antonio battalion of five companies under Major Michael Chevallie reported for duty. McCulloch's company had already gone home, and Gray's was mustered out in July. Chevallie and his Rangers fought a dirty guerrilla war that went on month after month. In August he had a dispute with General John E. Wool and resigned. Captain Walter P. Lane succeeded to the command. The battalion never operated as a unit, but as separate companies. They chased partisan groups that easily dispersed and fought dozens of indecisive skirmishes when they could corner the adversary.[36]

The record of the Rangers in northern Mexico after Buena Vista is thus one of hard service against a wily foe that could rarely be pinned down. Their record of excess is less easily assessed. Except for Gray's slaughter of civilians, few specific atrocities found their way into the record. Yet enough generalities were set to paper to leave little doubt of their harsh treatment of a populace in which partisan could rarely be distinguished from noncombatant. Rangers tended to console themselves that all able-bodied men were partisans. After paying tribute to the Rangers of Hays and Wood, Surgeon S. Compton Smith declared that "some of the so-called Texas Rangers, who came into the country at a later period, were mostly made up of adventurers and vagabonds, whose whole object was plunder," adding that "the gang of miscreants under the leadership of 'Mustang Grey' were of this description."[37]

Gray's atrocities may have tainted the record of the companies later deployed against the guerrillas under Chevallie and Lane. Zachary Taylor did not think so. On June 16 he reported from Monterey that "the mounted men from Texas have scarcely made one expedition without unwarrantably killing a Mexican. I have in consequence ordered Major Chevallie's command to Saltillo where it can do less mischief than here and where its services moreover are wanted. The constant recurrence of such atrocities which I have been reluctant to report to the Department is my motive for requesting that no more troops may be sent to this column from the State of Texas."[38]

Two aspects of Taylor's censure are revealing. First, whatever the indiscretions of his Rangers, Chevallie's services were needed at Saltillo.

Second, while he received no more troops from Texas, Taylor did not send Chevallie's battalion home but rather kept it in constant field service. Not until June 30, 1848, did the companies, now under Walter Lane, receive their discharge. Never did Zachary Taylor succeed in resolving his ambivalence about Texas Rangers.

JACK HAYS'S TEXANS missed out altogether on Winfield Scott's brilliant campaign that culminated in the fall of Mexico City on September 14, 1847. "Old Fuss and Feathers" was the antithesis of "Old Rough and Ready" in almost every way, including generalship. Scott was the greatest American general before the Civil War, and his masterful drive on Mexico City excited the admiration England's Duke of Wellington, the conqueror of Napoleon.

Scott's biggest challenge lay not in fighting hard-contested battles but in keeping his army supplied. The National Road, linking the port of Vera Cruz with Mexico City, wound its way for 250 miles across three mountain ranges, from the tropics to the great central plateau of Mexico. Guerrillas and lancers infested the entire length, and only heavily guarded trains could get through. The surrender of Mexico City did not end the affliction, for Santa Anna took his army to the countryside to join with the guerrillas and continue the war.

Texas Rangers knew guerrilla warfare. They operated as guerrillas themselves, fully as brutal and unforgiving as their opponents. Jack Hays's Rangers did not reach Vera Cruz until the middle of October 1847, but in the four months remaining until the conclusion of the Treaty of Guadalupe Hidalgo, they showed General Scott what General Taylor already knew: Texas Rangers were unsurpassed both as fighters and as troublemakers.

Hays commanded a strange outfit. Five of the ten companies had been detained in Texas to protect the frontier against Indians. Yet Hays's five companies numbered between 110 and 130 each, which yielded a force as strong as the one he had fielded at Monterey.[39]

Of special importance, before leaving for the Mexican interior Hays drew 394 Model 1847 Colt revolvers–the Walker Colt six-shooter. Many of the Rangers already had the Paterson five-shooter, and the issue of Walkers probably equipped everyone with at least one revolver. Men accustomed to the light Paterson had difficulty adjusting to the heavy Walker. In a painful irony, most of the Walkers were stamped for the U.S. Mounted Rifles, Captain Walker's outfit. But an offended ordnance department had made certain that Walker's men received single-shot pistols. Although Walker knew his Colts had arrived at Vera Cruz, he could not get them sent forward. "If I only had my Revolving Pistols," he wrote his brother as early as June 6, "I could soon clear the Road of all these bands between this and Vera Cruz." The disappointment was all the more acute because Walker had just received a presentation pair sent him by Samuel Colt. "There is not an officer who has seen them but what speaks in the highest terms of them," he declared, "and all of the Cavalry officers are determined to get them if possible."[40]

Four days later, Walker Colts blazing, Samuel H. Walker was killed at the battle of Huamantla. Even at the time, writers tended to identify him as a Texas Ranger rather than a U.S. regular. And such he remained in the imagination of a nation for which he was the first to popularize the Texas Ranger. For his exploits on the Indian frontier and in the Mexican War, and for his role in the production of the first six-shooter, Sam Walker made a large contribution to the Texas Ranger tradition.

Hays's regiment had been assigned to the brigade of Brigadier General Joseph Lane, a vigorous, hot-tempered political general from Indiana. As unorthodox in his soldiering as Hays himself, Lane had emerged as Scott's chief of antiguerrilla operations. Hays's regiment arrived in Puebla, Lane's headquarters, in the middle of November 1847.

"They certainly were an odd-looking set of fellows," observed one of Lane's officers, "and it seemed to be their aim to dress as outlandishly as possible." Dust coated their bushy beards and their mélange of garb and headgear, lending them a "savage appearance." They rode every variety of mount from little mustangs to big American horses. Each carried a rifle, a pair of pistols, and one or two Colt revolvers. "A hundred of them could discharge a thousand shots in two minutes, and with what precision the Mexicans alone can tell."[41]

The Mexicans found out in less than a week, when Lane's Texans and a unit of Louisiana dragoons, 135 horsemen, tangled with lancers. On November 23 the Americans had liberated some prisoners at Izúcar de Matamoros, fifty miles south of Puebla, and were returning next day. Threading a mountain pass, the column strung out. Captain Jacob Roberts's Ranger company, about thirty men, rode advance guard. Suddenly they confronted two hundred lancers driving in the pickets. Hays rushed to Roberts's side. Flashing Colts turned the charge into a retreat. Hays and his men galloped in pursuit. Over the summit the race continued. On the reverse slope, however, the little band of Rangers encountered another five hundred lancers. With revolvers now emptied, Hays turned his men back, reloading as they went. Pressed too closely, Hays himself reined his horse about and coolly shot two from their saddles, then alone covered the withdrawal to the main command. Here the Ranger firepower easily repulsed the lancers. Lane estimated enemy casualties at not less than fifty.

It had been a singular fight, at times thirty against five hundred, but as at Walker Creek against the Comanches in 1844, the deciding factors were leadership, seasoned and intrepid soldiers, and the firepower of repeating pistols. "Never did any officer act with more gallantry than did Colonel Hays in this affair of the 24th," General Lane reported. In each other Lane and Hays had found kindred souls.[42]

After this clash, Lane moved his headquarters to Mexico City, where he could be close to General Scott. Thus did Mexico City, like Monterey, experience the Texas Rangers. "Hays's Rangers have come," recorded Scott's inspector general on December 6, "their appearance never to be forgotten." Despite their motley aspect, "they are strong athletic fellows. The Mexicans are terribly afraid of them."[43]

With good reason. Rangers did not calibrate offenses. The butchery of one of their own in a back alley, an insult, or the theft of a handkerchief all earned the same response—a slug from a heavy Walker Colt. The

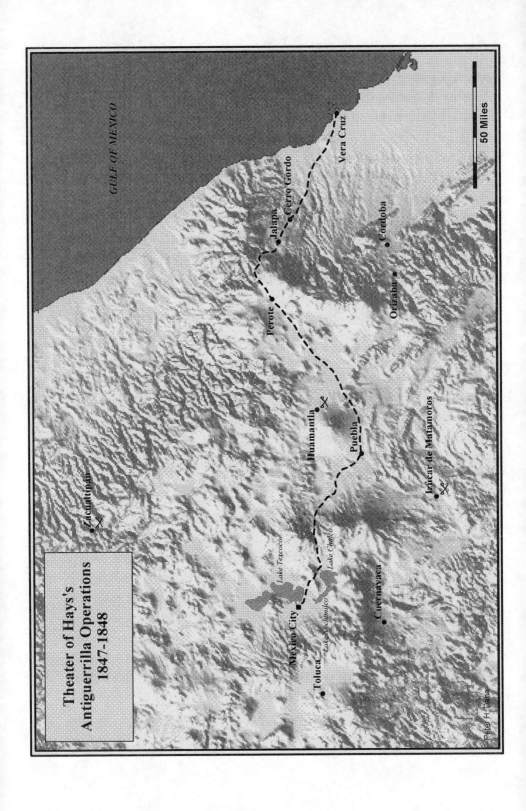

Theater of Hays's
Antiguerrilla Operations
1847-1848

GULF OF MEXICO

Vera Cruz

Cerro Gordo

Jalapa

Córdoba

Orizaba

Perote

Huamantla

Puebla

Izúcar de Matamoros

Zacualtipan

Lake Texcoco

Lake Chalco

Lake Xochimilco

Cuernavaca

Mexico City

Toluca

50 Miles

Peter H. Dana

city's residents did not take kindly to the American occupation, and soldiers who let their guard down could be suddenly stoned from above or shouldered into the gutter. As Adjutant John S. Ford recorded, "some gringo lost his life every night."

One afternoon a Ranger unwisely strayed into a section of the city labeled "Cutthroat." Recalled Ford: "He was assailed by a murderous crowd and almost literally cut to pieces." His horse brought him out, but he died the next day. Cutthroat paid the penalty. Through a long night the streets echoed with the distinctive thud of heavy Colts. By the next afternoon the morgue contained eighty corpses picked up from the streets of Cutthroat, a number that represented only those victims who had no relative to retrieve the remains. Although General Scott reprimanded Hays for other, lesser offenses, no hint of Cutthroat found its way into the official record.[44]

Not without justification, the people of Mexico City remembered the Texas Rangers as *Los Diablos Tejanos*. It was an epithet that would resonate among Mexicans for generations to come.

Jack Hays's special target was Padre Celestino Jarauta, an elusive guerrilla chief who had confounded efforts to trap him ever since the Americans landed at Vera Cruz. Early in January 1848 Hays accompanied a Ranger company in a probe of the mountains south of Mexico City. In the village of San Juan Teotihuacán, exhausted Rangers dropped into a deep sleep on the floor of a large building fronting the plaza. Uncharacteristically, they failed to post security. During the night seventy-five mounted lancers charged across the plaza and nearly breached the building before the Rangers roused themselves. Blazing revolvers threw the horsemen back. Padre Jarauta rallied them and charged again. Lieutenant Ephriam Daggett took aim with his pistol and brought him down. Demoralized, the attackers bore Jarauta to cover and withdrew from San Juan. "One thing that contributed to save our command in this affair," Daggett wrote, "was the holy awe and superstition entertained by the untutored greaser in regard to the 'revolver.'"[45]

The treaty signed on February 2, 1848, at Guadalupe Hidalgo did not end the Mexican War. It still had to be ratified by both nations, which would take many more months. For Joe Lane and Jack Hays, the war did not end because for Jarauta, recovered from his wound, it did not end. By now, moreover, Lane and Hays had forged a winning team, with Lane hardly distinguishable from a Ranger either in appearance or fighting technique. Joe Lane's fiery backwoods persona not only commanded the respect and affection of the Texas Rangers—they called him Old Gritter Face—but would promote his political ambitions after the war.[46]

Again in February 1848 Lane set forth against Jarauta, reported with his entire force of about 450 men in the mountain town of Zacualtipán. After a forced march, Lane's horsemen—250 Rangers under Hays and 130 dragoons and riflemen under Major William H. Polk (brother of the president)—struck Zacualtipán shortly after daybreak on February 25. At last they had brought Jarauta to battle. "General Lane announced no plan of battle," related Adjutant Ford. "We were to find where the guerrilla bands were located and fight them."

In vicious street combat reminiscent of Monterey, Rangers and regulars swept the town, charged into buildings full of enemy defenders, battered down gates, and converged on the plaza. It was a "running and mixed fight," Hays reported, against four hundred lancers and fifty infantrymen. At every point, the Mexicans fell back before the deadly volleys from the six-shooters. In separate parties, the Rangers and regulars went after the enemy wherever he appeared—in the streets, in buildings and behind walls, in the plaza, and in the cathedral. Polk's regulars seized the cathedral only moments after Jarauta made his escape.

Zacualtipán shattered guerrilla power. General Lane reported 150 Mexicans killed, many wounded, and 50 taken prisoner, at a loss to his command of five wounded, one mortally. The Mexicans had fought desperately, but revolving pistols in the hands of well-led and equally desperate Americans had made the difference—a stunning difference in casualties. Zacualtipán was the last battle of the Mexican War, fought more than three weeks after conclusion of the Treaty of Guadalupe Hidalgo.[47]

Padre Jarauta still lived, but not to fight Americans. He joined in a revolt against the government that had signed the peace treaty with the

United States. In July 1848 government forces achieved what Americans could not. They captured Jarauta. Convicted of treason, he fell before a firing squad.[48]

In four months of operations against guerrillas, Jack Hays's second regiment of mounted Texans had matched his first for combat effectiveness. At Izúcar de Matamoros and Zacualtipán, they had exhibited the same aggressive prowess as their counterparts at Monterey. In a standup fight with Mexicans, regular or partisan, the Texans consistently excelled, employing mobility, firepower, and shock action with stunning effect. With extraordinarily slight loss, they repeatedly drove the enemy from the field with great loss. At the same time, in the idleness of Mexico City, the Texans displayed the same undisciplined rowdiness and brutal treatment of civilians as their counterparts from Camargo to Monterey.[49]

Thus the Texas Rangers ended the Mexican War with the twin legacy of combat excellence and vengeful excess. They also ended the war with a secure place in the imagination of Americans everywhere. The Texans went home with a new pride and an identity now lastingly planted in the perceptions of all Anglo Texans. Significantly, John C. Hays signed his official report of the battle of Zacualtipán not as commander of the First Regiment Texas Cavalry but as "Colonel Texas Rangers."

ONE DRAMA REMAINED to the Texas Rangers before they went home from Mexico. About April 25, 1848, en route to Vera Cruz, they bivouacked beside the National Road two miles west of Jalapa. Word reached them that Santa Anna, on his way into another exile, would travel the road later in the day. They resolved to kill him. Adjutant Ford argued vehemently against such an act and finally commanded: "Reflect a moment. General Santa Anna dishonored himself by murdering prisoners of war; will you not dishonor Texas and ourselves by killing him?" All conceded that they could not dishonor Texas.

As Santa Anna's cavalcade neared, the Rangers lounged on rock walls on both sides of the road. The open carriage bore the general, his wife, and daughter. Riding escort were gaudily uniformed Mexican lancers as well as three mounted companies of Americans commanded by Major John R. Kenly. The major had left nothing to chance. Placing a company on each side of the carriage and a third bringing up the rear, he posted a color sergeant at the head of each of the flanking companies. The United States flag rippled above the carriage doors on both sides.

"As we approached the camp of the Texans, they were seen on the stone fences on either side which separated their camp from the road," related Kenly. "There were several hundred of them, and apparently as quiet as if at a camp-meeting, listening to a sermon." To Kenly's vast relief, not a man moved or uttered a sound. They disdained to offer any insult "to one under safeguard and honor of our flag."[50]

Afterward, according to Adjutant Ford, "The Texans broke ranks and returned to camp. Not a murmur of disappointed feeling at the failure to wreak a bloody revenge was uttered; not an unseemly bravado was heard. The memories of the bloody past were buried, and no one cared to disturb their repose."[51]

[5]

"Give Us Rangers in Texas"

S ENATOR SAM HOUSTON spoke for all Texans on February 11, 1858, when he implored of the U.S. Senate: "Give us Rangers in Texas." The plea sounded repeatedly in Washington from the day of annexation until the outbreak of the Civil War.

By admitting Texas to the Union, the United States assumed responsibility for defending Texans. It failed—failed to keep marauding Indians out of the frontier settlements and failed to bring security to a Mexican borderland in constant turmoil. The solution, Texans agreed, was to call Texas Rangers into federal service and turn them loose against Indians and troublesome Mexicans. For fifteen years, every governor, every legislature, and every member of the state's congressional delegation bombarded the Congress, the president, and the War Department with demands for Texas Rangers.

Throughout the 1850s, Texas Rangers campaigned against Indians and on occasion Mexicans. Successive governors called Rangers into temporary state service in hopes that the legislature if not the Congress would pay the bill. Prodded by the Texas delegation, sometimes the Congress did, more often not. At times, hard-pressed federal commanders gained authority to muster Rangers into the federal service, a measure of last resort because Rangers usually did things their own way instead of the army way. Whether in state or federal service, the Rangers compiled a record that sustained the reputation they had won in the Mexican War–good fighters under good leadership, bad fighters under bad leadership, troublemakers under any leadership.

The territorial acquisitions of the Mexican War confronted the little regular army with an impossible mission. Nowhere was it more daunting than Texas. A frontier of settlement extended four hundred miles from the Red River to the Rio Grande and an international frontier a thousand miles from El Paso to the Gulf of Mexico. Yet in 1850 the army could spare scarcely more than fifteen hundred regulars to guard these frontiers, and 80 percent of them were foot soldiers, useless except to defend their own parade ground.

What Texas wanted, Houston explained to the Senate, was not a larger federal force but a more efficient force. "You may withdraw every regular soldier . . . from the border of Texas," he declared, "if you will give her a single regiment, one thousand or even eight hundred men, of Texas rangers to protect her frontier. . . . They are men who are acquainted with action; they are efficient; they are athletic; they are inured to toil, to enterprise, to danger; and they carry with them a spirit that is not to be found in the troops that are generally collected in the regular Army."[1]

While championing federalized Rangers, Houston spoke more often to senators in behalf of the policies he had pursued as president of the Texas Republic: treaties of peace and friendship with the tribes, fortified by trading posts to build mutual self-interest. In fact, federal officials negotiated such treaties in May 1846 and again in December 1850.[2] Even the principal chiefs of the Southern Comanches signed. But these treaties proved as meaningless as those concluded during the republic. The Indians could be guaranteed no territory of their own, and chiefs could not control the actions of their young men.

The territorial issue hung over every Indian council. The Texas Republic had acknowledged no Indian title to any land in Texas. On joining the union in 1845, Texas reserved all vacant lands, leaving no federal public domain to be set aside for Indians. Like their predecessors during the republic, therefore, federal negotiators had to settle for a line that supposedly separated Indians and whites. It fell on an east–west axis roughly drawn by the Llano River, a western tributary of the Colorado. But all land north of the line, since it belonged exclusively to Texas, remained open to white settlement, and surveyors with their transits and chains kept the Comanches constantly upset. At the same time, the line failed to discourage the southward movement of Comanches following the buffalo, seeking mustangs on the Nueces Plain, or bent on plundering raids in Mexico.

The Texas treaties, moreover, did not bind the Northern Comanches or the Kiowas. In 1853 they signed treaties with federal officials on the Arkansas River but continued to raid in Texas and Mexico. They never understood that Americans and Texans were the same people. These Indians drew federal annuities on the Arkansas River and traded the stock and other plunder seized in Mexico and Texas with American traders on the Arkansas River and, on the Canadian River in the Texas Panhandle, with Comanchero traders out of Santa Fe. Robert S. Neighbors, the able federal Indian agent for Texas, pointed out the anomaly in 1855. Each fall on the Arkansas, the Northern Comanches and Kiowas drew $10,000 in presents from the United States, a sum that would not pay for the property they had stolen from Texans during the summer.[3]

When called out by the governor, Ranger units operated within a federal defense system erected by the army in the decade following annexation. Brevet Major General George M. Brooke laid the groundwork in 1849 with four posts on the Rio Grande frontier, three overseeing the favorite Indian raiding trails across the Nueces Plain, and a curving line of five slightly in advance of the frontier of settlement in 1849. Within two years, however, settlers had moved up the Trinity, the Brazos, and the Colorado beyond Brooke's shield. His successor, Brevet Major General Persifor F. Smith, therefore drew another line in 1851—seven forts tracing the western limit of reliable water flow in the rivers heading on the Staked Plain and the Edwards Plateau. With an inner and outer ring enclosing the frontier of settlement and a third chain policing the international boundary, Smith turned in 1854 to a system to guard the road from San Antonio to El Paso. By the end of the decade six forts watched over this vital travel link.

By 1860 the fifteen hundred regulars of 1850 had doubled, but they still remained woefully weak even to garrison the forts, much less undertake serious field operations. Little wonder that citizens ridiculed the regulars and demanded that their governor call out the Rangers.[4]

JACK HAYS JOINED the gold rush to California, where he made a bright name for himself as sheriff of San Francisco, U.S. surveyor general for the state, and a founder of the city of Oakland. Ben McCulloch went to California too but returned to Texas. He sought high rank in one of the two cavalry regiments Congress added to the regular army in 1855, but Jefferson Davis, Secretary of War, favored West Point professionals. If Congress had given Sam Houston the Ranger regiment he advocated in 1858, McCulloch would probably have been named its colonel. Although Henry McCulloch periodically added luster to the Ranger record, after Buena Vista Ben McCulloch never again devoted his considerable talents to the Ranger tradition.[5]

With Hays and McCulloch gone, and Walker and Gillespie dead, the Rangers of the "1850s needed a new exemplar. They found him in John Salmon Ford–"Old Rip" Ford, as his men called him for obscure reasons.[6]

Unlike Jack Hays, Rip Ford looked and acted like a Ranger. More than six feet tall, lean and blue-eyed, voluble and fun-loving, he had led an active and varied life since immigrating to Texas from Tennessee in 1836. He practiced medicine, studied law and passed the bar exam, dabbled in surveying and politics, and by 1845 edited an Austin newspaper. As individualistic and outspoken as any Ranger, he served ably as Hays's adjutant in the final months of the Mexican War. In August 1849 he launched his career as a Ranger captain. He was thirty-four, and during more than a decade of intermittent service he would replace Jack Hays as the model Texas Ranger.[7]

"Whip them and then talk of treaties." That was Ford's creed, and from 1849 through 1851 he carried it out with rare success. In later years he looked back on the exploits of "Ford's Old Company" with a nostalgia that may have contained some embellishment, but the contemporary record confirms the essentials. Ford's Rangers trained rigorously in horsemanship, marksmanship, teamwork, and the special techniques of Comanche warfare, and they performed with unit discipline that testified to leadership in the tradition of Hays and McCulloch.[8]

General Brooke deplored having to call on Governor George T. Wood for Rangers. "Their feeling, and, you may say, general and natural hostility to Indians," he complained to army headquarters, "would be very apt to bring about what we wish to avoid—a general war."[9]

South Texans would have indignantly replied that "a general war" already existed. Comanches began raiding in Mexico in the eighteenth century, but in the 1830s the incursions took on new intensity. This reflected several factors. First, in the mid-1830s American traders appeared on the Arkansas River and in the Indian Territory, offering a ready market for the fruits of Mexican raids. Second, an increasing competition for subsistence and other resources in the traditional Comanche and Kiowa ranges occurred as the United States deposited large numbers of eastern Indians on their borders, and in partial compensation they turned more and more to the stock and plunder of Mexico. And finally, the market for Mexican stock and plunder expanded as these immigrant Indians developed trade relationships with the Comanches and Kiowas. With South Texas gaining population after the Mexican War, the raiders also began to take a frightful toll in lives and property around Corpus Christi, Goliad, and especially Laredo. General Brooke's handful of regulars, mostly infantry, could do little to still the anguished complaints.[10]

Still, General Brooke's emphasis on the "natural hostility" of Rangers to Indians identified one reason the U.S. government repeatedly resisted federalized Rangers. The Mexican War filled the postwar Ranger companies both with seasoned combat veterans and with recruits proud of what the men of Hays and McCulloch had accomplished. Many were

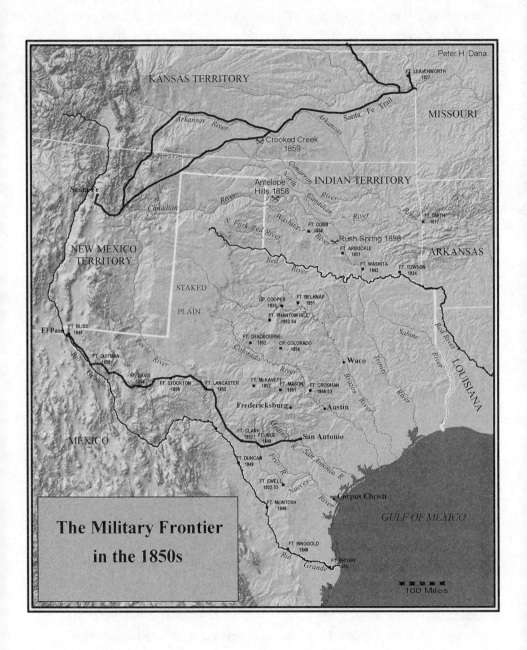

Peter H. Dana

KANSAS TERRITORY

FT. LEAVENWORTH
1827

MISSOURI

Arkansas River

Santa Fe Trail

Arkansas

Crooked Creek
1859

Cimarron

INDIAN TERRITORY

Santa Fe

Canadian
River

North
Canadian
River

Antelope
Hills 1858

River

River

FT. SMITH
1817

ARKANSAS

NEW MEXICO
TERRITORY

N. Fork Red River

Washita
River

FT. COBB
1858

Rush Spring 1858

FT. ARBUCKLE
1851

Red River

FT. WASHITA
1842

FT. TOWSON
1824

STAKED

PLAIN

CP. COOPER
1855

FT. BELKNAP
1851

FT. PHANTOM HILL
1852-54

Sabine

Red River

El Paso

FT. BLISS
1849

FT. QUITMAN
1856

Pecos River

Rio Grande

FT. CHADBOURNE
1852

CP. COLORADO
1856

Colorado
River

Waco

Trinity
River

LOUISIANA

FT. DAVIS
1854

FT. STOCKTON
1859

FT. LANCASTER
1855

FT. McKAVETT
1852

FT. MASON
1851

FT. CROGHAN
1849-53

Brazos River

River

MÉXICO

Fredericksburg

Austin

Medina R.

FT. CLARK
1852

FT. INGE
1849

San Antonio

FT. DUNCAN
1849

Frio R.

San Antonio R.

FT. EWELL
1852-55

Nueces

Corpus Christi

FT. McINTOSH
1849

River

GULF OF MEXICO

The Military Frontier

in the 1850s

FT. RINGGOLD
1848

FT. BROWN
1846

Rio

Grande

100 Miles

still frontier farmers or ranchers intent on punishing the aggressors from the north. More, however, appear to have been footloose young men seeking a job and adventure, and they gained experience with each enlistment. The Rangers of Ford's time looked diligently for a fight, and when they could bring one on they battled with a lethal ferocity that subsided only when the enemy had scattered or been wiped out. This of course is what combat soldiers were supposed to do and what Texans expected their Rangers to do.

As Brooke and all the generals who followed recognized, however, Ranger victories demanded Indian retaliation, which brought even greater destruction to the settlements and hampered federal efforts to make peace with the raiding tribes. So of course did the infrequent successes of U.S. troops, an inconsistency that the generals conveniently overlooked when they lauded achievements of their own units.

Despite his reservations, in September 1849 Brooke federalized three companies of Rangers, one under Rip Ford. In March 1850 the general called for a fourth, mobilized under the legendary Indian fighter William A. A. (Big Foot) Wallace. As eight other companies in state service ranged farther north, these federalized companies, remustered when their terms expired, policed the sandy deserts and chaparral plains between the Frio, Nueces, and Rio Grande for two years. Although the army's adjutant general complained of the "great negligence" of the Rangers in providing the muster rolls and returns required by regulations, General Brooke paid tribute to their "energy and perseverance in the most active scouting and pursuit of the savages, with a perfect obedience in the execution of all orders."[11]

All the companies saw hard and effective service in interdicting the raiding trails, but Ford's men excelled in the difficult art of actually bringing Comanches to battle. It required constant scouting, trail cutting, vigorous pursuit, and a cunning matching that of the Comanches. These were small-unit combats, involving fifteen or twenty men on each side and usually culminating in close-order fighting with arrows and lances against firearms.

Laced by patrols that marched and countermarched and occasionally met and routed the enemy, the Nueces Strip took on new danger for southward ranging Comanche raiders. Rip Ford and his fellow captains remained in federal service until the fall of 1851, carrying out exactly this sort of demanding operation. They and their successors, regulars and Rangers, never shut down the Comanche raiding pattern. But beginning in 1850, the threat receded somewhat as Comanches increasingly moved their war trails to Mexico farther west and turned their attention elsewhere.[12]

FOR ALL THEIR preoccupation with Indians, Rangers never freed themselves of the old animosities toward Mexicans. The Alamo and Goliad dimmed somewhat in the Anglo Texan memory, but racial and cultural prejudice remained as strong as ever. Stephen Austin's immigrants had brought intolerance with them nearly three decades earlier. People of color, whether Indian or Mexican, were inferior, their lives of less worth. The Rangers embodied the values of Anglo Texans, and when they encountered Indians or Mexicans they carried them into effect.

Volatile conditions along the Rio Grande frontier periodically drew the Rangers from their Indian duties and sometimes involved them in escapades that blotted their record both ethically and legally. Such was the character of the Callahan expedition of 1855, which victimized Mexicans in the name of slavery.

War's aftermath attracted American traders, merchants, and speculators to the Rio Grande. American towns sprang up opposite their Mexican counterparts—Brownsville, Rio Grande City, Roma, Eagle Pass. Mexican rancheros reclaimed land grants between the Rio Grande and the Nueces but fought a losing battle to retain them against avaricious newcomers wielding unfamiliar legal and political weapons combined with intimidation and violence. The Anglo elite oppressed the overwhelming Mexican majority in ways both subtle and direct. Smuggling flourished, encouraged by capriciously applied Mexican tariffs. Mexico's continuing struggle between conservatives (centrists) and liberals (federalists) kept the nation's border states in constant political and military turmoil. Mexican and American bandits, many leading double lives as respectable citizens, preyed on victims on both sides of the river without much regard for nationality or ethnicity.[13]

The regular army garrisons of Forts Brown, Ringgold, McIntosh, and Duncan lacked either authority or power to contend with this chaos. Most of the offenses north of the river violated the laws of Texas, not the United States. Sheriffs and prosecuting attorneys, if not actually smuggling or rustling stock themselves, lacked the means to contend with such massive disorder.

Another border irritant was the wholesale escape of slaves from Texas into Mexico. Slavery had undergird the Texas economy ever since the Old Three Hundred of Austin's time. As a journalist and prominent citizen, Rip Ford agitated the issue, proposing that the runaways be recovered by negotiation or, that failing, force. Santa Anna had returned to the Mexican presidency, and his harshly centralist reign stirred up another revolution in the northern states. The political turmoil of 1855 invited incursions by filibusters—adventurers seeking gain by stirring revolutionary ferment—who justified their enterprises as aid to Mexican patriots in a war against tyranny, recovery of fugitive slaves, and punishment of Mexican Indians raiding in Texas. The most vociferous of these warriors was William R. Henry of San Antonio, who enjoyed the support of nearly all his fellow citizens of Anglo heritage and who, bankrolled by Brazos River planters, recruited several hundred followers for a foray into Mexico.

As Henry and Ford inflamed the slavery issue in the summer of 1855, Indian depredations fell with mounting frequency on the settlers of the Guadalupe and Blanco Rivers in the Hill Country north of San Antonio. When General Smith could not promptly dispatch mounted regulars, Governor Elisha M. Pease called a Ranger company into state service. It was commanded by James H. Callahan, a tough, highly regarded veteran of the revolution and ranging service under the Texas Republic. He was an experienced Indian fighter, and through August and September 1855 his company made the Hill Country a dangerous place for marauders.[14]

Late in September 1855, Callahan decided to pursue the raiders into Mexico. Under the doctrine of hot pursuit, this was consistent with international law. But as General Smith later observed, the Rio Grande Valley was so overrun with small parties of Indians that anyone could claim to be following the trail of marauders.[15] Almost certainly, Callahan's resolve followed a meeting with William R. Henry, fresh from an abortive foray into Mexico. They agreed to join forces and use hot pursuit of Indians as a cover for a slave-hunting thrust into Mexico, one that if successful might be parleyed into a permanent occupation.[16]

On the night of October 1, 1855, with 111 men, Callahan and Henry forded the Rio Grande three miles below Eagle Pass, thus quietly bypassing the federal garrison at Fort McIntosh. About midday of October 3, the Texans ran into a superior force of soldiers and Indians. The two sides exchanged fire until nightfall, when the Mexicans withdrew, having lost four killed and three wounded. Claiming victory, Callahan also withdrew with four killed and seven wounded and the conviction that his men had slain sixty to seventy of their opponents.

By the morning of October 4, the Texans had occupied the town of Piedras Negras, on the Rio Grande opposite Eagle Pass and Fort Duncan. Certain that an overwhelming Mexican force closed on them, they sent repeated appeals to Fort Duncan to protect their crossing. Captain Sidney Burbank rolled several artillery pieces into position aimed at the crossing site, but no Texans appeared. The river had risen too high to get their horses across, they explained, and they set about fortifying the town for a fight. They seem also to have sent a call for reinforcements, for in San Antonio General Smith marveled at the bustle of preparations. "It has struck me as extraordinary," he observed, "that while complaining that they are left without protection from Indian incursions, they can yet afford to send away three times the number of the regular mounted force in the whole state, from the very portion of the State where assistance is said to be so much needed."[17]

Although fortifying Piedras Negras and apparently preparing for its defense, Callahan and Henry began crossing their horses on the sixth. Late in the afternoon, however, the Mexican force arrived. At first sight, the Texans fired and looted the town and sent repeated appeals for help to Burbank, which met with his "decided refusal." The Mexicans never attacked, however, and by the next morning all the Texans had reached the safety of the American shore.

Viewed from any perspective, the Callahan expedition was a fiasco. Even the most liberal interpretation of the doctrine of hot pursuit could not justify what in fact was a filbustering expedition aimed principally at recovery of runaway slaves, carried out by a captain and sixty Rangers in the service of the state of Texas, joined by nearly as many buccaneers in the service of Texas cotton planters. While the U.S. State Department struggled with the diplomatic fallout, Governor Pease defended Callahan's crossing but rebuked him for the destruction of Piedras Negras. Texans applauded the exploit and lionized Callahan, and the legislature promptly voted funds to pay not only Callahan's expenses but those of Henry's "volunteers who went to his aid."[18]

For its part, after twenty years the United States finally conceded that Mexico had been wronged. As part of a comprehensive adjudication of the claims of Americans and Mexicans against each other, a commission awarded a paltry $50,000 to be divided among 150 claimants for losses sustained in the burning and sacking of Piedras Negras.[19]

Callahan and Rip Ford tried to mobilize another incursion into Mexico. Within six months, however, Callahan had been killed in a feud with a neighbor, whom irate citizens dragged from jail and filled with lead—shot to death, decided a grand jury, "by a company of men unknown to the jury." Hunter of slaves and persecutor of Mexicans, Callahan remained a hero to Anglo Texans. In 1858 the legislature created Callahan County in his honor, and in 1931, as a further tribute "to this man who contributed so much to the state in its infancy," the remains of Callahan and his wife were exhumed from their Blanco graves and reburied in the Texas State Cemetery in Austin.[20]

No man more keenly felt the want of territory that could be guaranteed to the Indians than Robert Simpson Neighbors, federal agent for the Indians of Texas. A big, powerful man of uncommon talents, thoroughly dedicated to his charges, Neighbors bore an impeccable Texas lineage: veteran of the Texas army, a ranger under Jack Hays, a prisoner in Perote Castle following the Woll invasion of 1842, Indian agent for the Texas Republic and for the United States. Ranging far beyond the frontier, he sat in council with most of the tribal leaders, even the Comanche chiefs, and gained their trust and respect.[21]

In Neighbors's view, backed by high officials in Washington, Texas must relinquish some of its public domain for reservations on which the Texas tribes could be settled, taught to farm, and benefit from the protection of the federal intercourse laws. The army supported this measure too, for once reservations had been laid out any Indian caught outside their limits could be regarded as hostile. Prodded by Governor Peter H. Bell, the legislature in February 1854 authorized the transfer of twelve leagues of land to the federal government for Indian reservations. During the summer of 1854, Neighbors and the army's Captain Randolph B. Marcy explored the northwestern frontier, conferred with the Indians, and surveyed two reservations. One, for the Southern Comanches, lay on the Clear Fork of the Brazos River about forty miles west of Fort Belknap. The other, on the Brazos itself twelve miles below Fort Belknap, was for the "remnant tribes" of Caddo, Anadarko, Waco, Ioni, Keechi, Tonkawa, and Tawakoni. The reservations were not large—18,576 acres for the Upper or Comanche Reserve, twice that for the Lower or Brazos Reserve.[22]

The notion that reservations would reduce Indian raiding proved more logical than workable. The Brazos Reserve achieved some success, for its tenants were tillers of the soil who did not have to be taught, and they had an exceptionally able agent in Shapley P. Ross, a former Ranger captain well versed in Indian ways. By the fall of 1856, they numbered nearly a thousand. On the Comanche Reserve, by contrast, the people had no experience or interest in farming. Their number ultimately grew to around five hundred.[23]

Other influences converged to leave frontier settlers more exposed and devastated than ever. For one, the frontier itself continued to advance up the Brazos and the Colorado, beyond the outer ring of forts

and surrounding both reservations. For another, the principal aggressors were not the Southern Comanches, ravaged by cholera and
whiskey, but Northern Comanches and Kiowas from north of Red River.
The Texas frontier did not threaten these tribes, who saw it simply as a
source of plunder. With their raiding trails across South Texas to Mexico
increasingly interdicted by regulars and Rangers, these Comanches and
Kiowas turned more and more to the newcomers on the northwestern
frontier, which included not only whites but the confederated tribes of
the Brazos Reserve. Cannily, the war parties made certain that their
trails led toward the reservations, thus sowing suspicion of the reservation Indians in the minds of the white victims. The suspicions, moreover, were not entirely unfounded, for reserve Comanches sometimes
joined their northern kin in their depredations.

After the lull of 1856, the frontier exploded, exposing the Texas reservations as no solution for aggressions launched from north of Texas.
Neighbors repeatedly protested the issue of annuities, arms, and ammunition to the very Indians despoiling the Texas frontier. Brevet Major
General David E. Twiggs, who assumed command in Texas in May 1857,
confessed similar bafflement. He did not understand a government
policy that armed Indians known to be raiding Texans, he wrote. "I do
not complain of it, but think it strange that such things are."[24]

Neighbors and Twiggs agreed on the solution: address the problem at
its source. As early as 1855, Neighbors had proposed that all the "prairie
bands" north of Red River be settled on a reservation in the Indian Territory, leased from the Choctaw and Chickasaw owners, and kept under
control (and out of Texas) by a strong mounted force. By 1857 the Leased
District had been established, but no fort had been erected and no military action taken to bring the Kiowas and Comanches under submis-
sion. By June 1857 Twiggs was urging army headquarters to send
mounted expeditions summer and winter into their hunting grounds,
"where their families are."[25]

If an offensive force were to seek out the offenders where their families were, it would have to come from Texas. Twiggs could not undertake such a mission without stripping the frontier of its defenses. He and

Governor Pease worked to have Congress authorize a full regiment of federalized Texas Rangers. Twiggs even drafted the legislation for Pease to forward to the Texas congressional delegation. The state legislature weighed in with a joint resolution of support.[26]

Supplanting Pease as governor at the end of 1857, Hardin R. Runnels pressed even sterner measures on the legislature. He knew that the Texas Regiment bill would require months of debate in the Congress. Meantime, his constituents on the frontier bombarded him with pleas for aid. With four Ranger companies already in the field, in January 1858 Runnels asked for more Rangers, "to follow the Indians to their retreats, break up their lodges, and execute summary vengeance." Four days later the legislature directed the governor to call up an additional hundred Rangers and appropriated $70,000 for their support. As an Austin newspaper editorialized, "The United States fails to afford Texas the protection to save the scalps of our citizens. Let us, therefore, protect ourselves and charge the bill to Uncle Sam."[27]

The day after the legislature acted, Governor Runnels appointed a "senior captain commanding Texas frontier," gave him command of the companies already in service, instructed him to recruit the additional hundred Rangers authorized by the legislature, and turned him loose to war on the guilty Indians, wherever they might be found. The senior captain was John Salmon Ford.[28]

By March 1858, Ford was advancing toward the northwestern frontier, combing a broad swath of country in four columns. He felt himself too weak, however, to mount an offensive into the Comanche homeland. The Rangers called up under the Pease administration had reached the end of their terms and were being replaced. That left Ford with only a few more than a hundred men, including his seventy-three-year-old father. At the Brazos Agency, however, Agent Shapley Ross solved Ford's problem; more than a hundred Caddos, Anadarkos, Wacos, Tawakonis, and Tonkawas placed themselves under Ross's command to take the warpath with Ford's Rangers.[29]

Striking northwest from his base near Fort Belknap, Ford crossed Red River and bore north into the Comanche ranges west of the Wichita

Mountains. The Indian auxiliaries not only doubled Ford's firepower but proved their worth as guides and trackers. The Rangers were superior fighters, well drilled by Ford. All they needed was to find the elusive Comanches, which they achieved by falling on a broad trail that led to the Canadian River opposite the landmark Antelope Hills.

Early on May 12, 1858, the Rangers and their allies splashed across the Canadian and raced headlong toward the village of the Comanche chief Iron Jacket. The Brazos Indians took the lead, bore to the left, between the village and the river, and poured a deadly fire into surprised warriors bolting from their lodges. Iron Jacket, brightly painted and armored in a coat of Spanish mail, mounted and charged the Brazos line. "The sharp crack of five or six rifles brought his horse to the ground," recalled Ford, "and in a few moments the Chief fell riddled with balls." The auxiliaries shot down all the Comanches attacking toward the river. Meanwhile, in two wings the Rangers stormed into the village itself. The fight then became a free-for-all, with knots of Rangers and their allies chasing fleeing Comanches. Here and there warriors paused to make a stand and give their families time to escape. But the Rangers, their six-shooters popping, broke up every such attempt. Shortly after noon, the winded pursuers returned to the village. Warriors from another camp a few miles up the Canadian attempted a counterattack but were driven off.

In the battle of Antelope Hills, Ford's Rangers and their invaluable allies had won a striking victory. Iron Jacket's Kotsoteka Comanche village numbered seventy lodges with a fighting force, when reinforced from the second village, of about three hundred. The victors counted seventy-six bodies on the battleground, gender unspecified, wounded many who got away, and took eighteen captives, mostly women and children. All this cost the attackers two killed and three wounded. Ford heaped lavish praise on Shapley Ross and the Brazos auxiliaries. As for his own men, it was enough to declare that "they have fully vindicated their right to be recognized as Texas Rangers of the old stamp."[30]

Two curiosities went unremarked. Of the three hundred captured horses, most of which went to the Indian allies, few were "American" horses. Clearly, these Comanches had not recently raided in Texas. Not that it mattered; every Comanche had at one time or another raided in Texas. Equally damning in Ford's mind, the village brimmed with rifles, powder, and lead of American manufacture, which testified to the brisk trade the Comanches carried on with American traders. As another anomaly, the victory had been won by Texas Rangers in state service operating beyond the borders of Texas. That did not matter either, for at last a band of Comanches had been destroyed in their own homeland, "where their families are."[31]

Governor Runnels instructed Ford to keep his men in service, recruit more if necessary, and strike another blow if he could. This was not enough for Ford. Call out the Texas Regiment immediately, he urged. It had been authorized by Congress in April but no money appropriated for its support. In state service it could undertake another invasion of the Comanche domain (implicitly with Ford as colonel). Congress could not avoid footing the bill, Ford believed. If it did, Texas would be justified in seceding from the Union.[32]

Appropriations for the Ranger act failed in the Congress. With the Second U.S. Cavalry concentrated at Fort Belknap, General Twiggs decided to use part of it for an operation on the Ford model. Brevet Major Earl Van Dorn would lead four companies across Red River into the Comanche homeland and, as Twiggs put it, give the Indians something to do at home in taking care of their families, which might cause them to leave Texas alone. Twice Van Dorn scored victories comparable to Ford's. At the battle of Rush Springs on October 1, 1858, and the battle of Crooked Creek (far north in Kansas) on May 13, 1859, the regular cavalrymen dealt costly blows to the Comanches.[33]

But the new strategy did not cause the Comanches to leave Texas alone. Buffalo Hump was furious over Ford's triumph. Although a Penateka, he had refused to settle on the Comanche Reserve and had emerged as a leading chief among the northern bands of Nokonis and Kotsotekas. In July he showed up on the Arkansas River to draw his annuities, robbed two Mexican trading caravans while the federal issuing agent watched, and boasted that as soon as he had received his goods he intended to lead a large war party against "the white man of the south." In this he was delayed, for it was Buffalo Hump's village that Van Dorn surprised and destroyed at Rush Springs. Even so, Comanche depredations fell repeatedly on settlers along the entire length of the frontier. As one beleaguered stockman expressed it in November 1858, "I think ever since Van Dorn routed them and dismounted so maney they have bin down to get more horses and I think he will drive them down on us." Which is exactly what happened.[34]

Neither Rangers nor regulars seemed able to stem the loss of life, horses, and property. Some pioneers "forted up" for mutual protection. Others gave up and fell back to less exposed areas. Agitators stirred hostility toward all Indians, including those on both Texas reserves. Even as warriors of the Brazos Reserve rode with Ford and Van Dorn, their families bore the unreasoning rage of nearby whites. Neighbors, Ross, and the Comanche agent defended their charges, only to find themselves excoriated by the citizens.

Enough evidence surfaced to link the reservation Comanches to occasional horse thievery, but none ever implicated the Brazos tribes. That their stock grazed and they hunted beyond the reservation boundaries, however, exasperated the whites. John R. Baylor, former Comanche agent fired by Neighbors, kept them stirred up against all Indians. In this explosive climate, on December 23, 1858, a band of whites fell on a sleeping party of Caddo hunters, killing three women and five men. The survivors fled back to the reservation. Civil authorities hastened to assure the enraged Indians that justice would be done.[35]

Justice was not done. Rip Ford, in the area with another call-up of Rangers, refused to counter public sentiment by serving arrest warrants issued by a state judge in Waco, even when ordered by Governor Runnels. No one was ever arrested or indicted.[36]

Everyone, including the Indians themselves, agreed that the reservation experiment had failed and that the only solution lay in moving the residents to the Leased District north of Red River. In March 1859 Neighbors received authority to prepare the Indians to move in the fall or early winter. The Texans would not wait. Baylor continued his fulminations and exhorted men to organize and hasten the process. For their own protection, Neighbors declared, the Indians must be moved at once.[37]

Neighbors did not exaggerate. On May 23 Baylor forced the issue by leading 250 "rangers" against the Brazos Agency. Agent Ross had taken the precaution of appealing for federal troops, and two infantry companies had been sent to his aid. Captain Joseph B. Plummer ordered Baylor to clear out, but that defender of the frontier served notice that if the regulars sided with the Indians he would fight them too. As Plummer formed his riflemen for battle, Baylor's resolution wavered. Withdrawing, however, his men killed an old man and an old woman. Infuriated warriors chased the would-be rangers for eight miles and killed two and wounded three before they scattered.[38]

The pioneers did not again try to bully the regulars, but they continued to run down any Indians found off the reservation, to confiscate their stock, and to indulge in much noisy and belligerent talk. Early in July Neighbors received authority to move the Indians. In the haste of departure, they had to leave nearly all their possessions, but Major George H. Thomas formed a cavalry screen to protect their march. A force of Texas Rangers under John Henry Brown, dispatched by Governor Runnels to make certain the Indians got out of Texas without committing any mischief, followed the regulars.

On July 8, 1859, Neighbors sat in his tent on the north bank of Red River and wrote a letter to his wife. "I have this day crossed all the Indians out of the heathen land of 'Texas' and am now 'out of the land of the Philistines,'" he wrote. "If you want to hear a full description of our Exodus out of Texas, read the 'Bible' where the children of Israel crossed the Red Sea."[39]

Returning to Texas, Robert S. Neighbors spent the night in the little town of Fort Belknap. The next morning a man stepped from behind a building and unloaded the contents of a double-barreled shotgun into the agent's back.

[6]

Last Days of the Old Lion: Mexicans and Indians

FOR TEXAS, STATEHOOD gave rise to prosperity. Nascent industry, business, and cotton cultivation expanded as trade flowed through Houston and the port cities of Galveston and Indianola. The U.S. Army contributed powerfully to the economy, with department headquarters, arsenal, and quartermaster depot in San Antonio and some twenty frontier forts stoking local agriculture and commerce. During the 1850s, immigration from the other states and Europe boosted population fourfold, to more than 600,000, about one-third of whom were slaves. Especially notable was the continuing influx of Germans, which began in the 1830s. By 1860, twenty thousand Germans peopled Texas from Houston to the Hill Country outpost of Fredericksburg.

San Antonio recovered from the setbacks of the Texas Republic, when the Woll invasion of 1842 drove its population down to eight hundred. By 1860, as Anglos and Germans combined with and even outnumbered Mexicans, eighty-two hundred residents lived in the old city, which now mingled American architecture of brick and wood with the traditional structures of Spanish and Mexican design.

Austin, in 1845 a bleak collection of rundown log buildings occupied by hardly two hundred people, gained stability when named the capital of the new state. A Greek Revival capitol and adjacent governor's mansion, completed in 1853 and 1856, mingled with other government buildings and fine homes, churches, and commercial structures to support a population of thirty-five hundred in 1860.

Texas had evolved as a state with two starkly contrasting identities, western and southern: a frontier people struggling in an environment of open prairies, rugged hills, and chaparral plains; and a planter and business elite content in humid lowlands resembling Louisiana and Mississippi.

SAM HOUSTON COULD not claim a successful career in the U.S. Senate. His role in the slavery controversy cast him as an inflexible defender of the federal union, a foe of states' rights and slavery, a traitor to the South. Yet he remained a national hero, the victor at San Jacinto, twice president of the Republic of Texas. He looked and acted like a senator. His speeches and debates stamped him a master of grand oratory and biting wit and commanded the attention of most senators—but not their votes.

Houston's senatorial fortunes went into steep decline in 1855, when the Texas legislature formally censured him. In 1857 he ran against his own party's nominee for governor, Hardin R. Runnels, and lost. The legislature took revenge for such apostasy by naming another to replace Houston in the Senate. Ignoring demands that he resign, the Old Lion served out his term. He came home in 1859 to challenge Runnels again for the governorship. This time he won.[1]

Between his electoral victory in July and inauguration in December, Houston watched the lame duck Runnels contend with daunting emergencies. The removal of the reserve Indians out of Texas had not dampened the Comanche flames on the northwestern frontier, where Ranger companies bled the treasury without bringing relief to the settlers.

Worse yet, the Rio Grande frontier blew up again. This time the troubles could be personalized in a swashbuckling rogue named Juan Nepomuceno Cortina, whose offenses along the river between Brownsville and Rio Grande City magnified exponentially as the news swept northward. General David E. Twiggs had withdrawn all the federal troops from Forts Brown, Ringgold, and McIntosh to mount offensives into the Comanche homeland to the north. Now he regarded every wild rumor from the Rio Grande as fact and tried desperately to reconcentrate his forces while beseeching army headquarters for more. While Twiggs dithered, Governor Runnels sent Rangers.

Houston's accession to the governorship in December 1859 framed the Cortina disturbance in larger dimensions than simply another outburst of border banditry. In his last two years in the Senate, Houston had forcefully advocated a U.S. protectorate over Mexico, imposed if necessary by a military force. His urgings got nowhere in the Congress. But the administration of President James Buchanan embraced the notion and for three consecutive years, 1858–1860, declared it to be U.S. policy.[2]

Mexico had writhed in revolutionary ferment ever since winning independence from Spain in 1821. Mexico could not pay its debts, could not maintain order in the nation, and could not police its boundary against Indians and bandits who plagued Texas from foreign sanctuary. In Houston's mind, the solution lay in a protectorate. Many Americans believed that he saw this scheme as a means of distracting his countrymen, drawing them back from the precipice of disunion, and incidentally elevating the governor of Texas to the executive mansion in Washington City. Historians have argued the issue ever since.[3]

Such were the terms, both in the United States and Mexico, that gave more than local significance to the Cortina affair of 1859–1860. Juan Nepomuceno Cortina was a thug and a patriot rolled into one. Thirty-five in 1859, illiterate yet smart and cunning, he used his mother's ranch nine miles up the river from Brownsville as base for a variety of nefarious schemes. He readily joined with Anglos in stealing cattle and horses on both sides of the boundary and disposing of them on the other side. Nor was he troubled by working with the minority Anglo political establishment to attain their ends, so long as he benefited. As

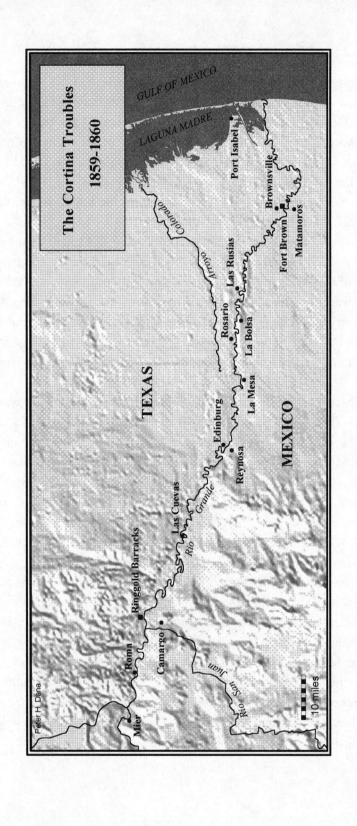

The Cortina Troubles
1859-1860

GULF OF MEXICO

LAGUNA MADRE

Port Isabel

Brownsville

Fort Brown

Matamoros

Las Rusias

Rosario

La Bolsa

La Mesa

Edinburg

Reynosa

TEXAS

MEXICO

Las Cuevas

Rio Grande

Ringgold Barracks

Roma

Camargo

Rio San Juan

Mier

Colorado

Arroyo

10 miles

Peter H. Dana

Brownsville's newspaper conceded of the Mexican American citizens: "An hour before the election they are fast friends, 'Mexicans my very good friends'—an hour after the election, they are a 'crowd of greasers.'" At election time, Cortina could deliver the votes of forty or fifty "very good friends," which explains why for a decade arrest warrants sworn against him for cattle theft and even murder went unserved.[4]

Despite his thuggish side, Cortina was a patriot, proud of his Mexican heritage and deeply offended by the discrimination, injustice, and casual violence and death inflicted by the handful of Anglo rulers on the "crowd of greasers." Mexicans of every station on both sides of the border hated the gringos for the Mexican War and for the oppression that followed. Cortina shared their feelings. When some of his criminal escapades turned up Anglo enemies he thought needed killing, he risked his life and fortunes in behalf of the persecuted.[5]

The origins of the Cortina "war" revealed both faces of Cortina. His patriotic face appeared on the streets of Brownsville on July 13, 1859, when the city marshal pistol-whipped an intoxicated Mexican who had once worked on the Cortina ranch. Cortina intervened. The dispute ended with Cortina firing a ball from his six-shooter into the marshal's shoulder, hoisting the liberated prisoner behind his saddle, and riding defiantly out of town. From sanctuary in Matamoros, Cortina tried to make amends with a monetary offering, but a satisfactory amount could not be agreed on.

Cortina's other face, the knavish, showed itself in Brownsville before dawn on September 28, 1859. With forty or more men he stormed into town intent on killing a list of personal enemies who had crossed him in one way or another as well as some men who had murdered Mexicans and got away with it. He indulged in no indiscriminate killing, plunder, or destruction, but he executed five men, freed all the inmates of the jail, and evacuated the terrorized community only after the veteran revolutionary, José María Carvajal, crossed the river from Matamoros and persuaded him that he had already caused enough trouble.[6]

What began as a personal vendetta swiftly turned into a rising against Anglo tyranny. Recruits drawn by the twin attractions of righteous revolt and rich plunder flocked to Cortina's barricades on his mother's ranch. Citizens organized themselves into the "Brownsville Tigers," and Matamoros officials sent a militia force across the river to help defend the town.

On September 30 the illiterate Cortina issued a *pronunciamento*, couched in grand rhetoric ringing with noble purpose. Resentment of Anglo despotism and Anglo methods of divesting rancheros of their land ran throughout the grandiose verbiage, but it disavowed any aggressive designs on Brownsville or its citizens, except for the targeted men who had escaped vengeance two days earlier. If they were delivered for their merited execution, no harm would befall Brownsville.[7]

Although Cortina hurled no more than bombast at Brownsville, the frightened citizens barricaded the streets and patrolled night and day. In fact, Cortina and two hundred followers had crossed into Mexico to receive the plaudits of the citizens of Matamoros. The Cameron County sheriff and a small posse chose this time to reconnoiter upstream. On October 12 they returned with Tomás Cabrera, Cortina's sixty-year-old lieutenant in the raid of September 28, and threw him in the Brownsville jail. Furious, Cortina sent word across the river to release Cabrera at once or he would "lay the town in ashes."[8]

The "war" might have ended here had Brownsville authorities complied. When they refused, Cortina recrossed the Rio Grande and posted several hundred men in chaparral defenses around his mother's ranch. The town's "Committee of Safety" decided to dislodge him. On October 23 twenty Brownsville Tigers rode forth, backed by forty valley Mexicans of doubtful resolve and (irony compounded) seventy-five militia from Matamoros. They hauled two small cannon. On October 25 they attacked. None did very well in the comic opera encounter with the enemy and, abandoning their artillery, flew back to Brownsville in a rout so complete the newspaper editor confessed it "painful for us to chronicle."[9]

Texas Rangers finally reached the scene on November 10. William G. Tobin commanded. Only twenty-six in 1859, he had come to San Antonio in 1853, married the mayor's daughter, and quickly made a place for himself in the city's business world. His military ambitions greatly exceeded his capability, but he had persuaded his townsmen to bankroll a company of fifty men to hasten to the relief of Brownsville. Only after they were on the march did he offer their services to Governor Runnels, who promptly accepted and authorized him to fill out the company to one hundred. Thus the Rangers arrived in Brownsville under a captain bearing a self-assumed commission ratified by an acquiescent governor.[10]

These Rangers lost no time in revealing their true character. On November 13, a "lawless mob" dragged Tomás Cabrera from his cell and lynched him in Market Square. No one ever officially charged the Rangers with complicity, but it is implicit in several credible reports and entirely consistent with their excesses so long as commanded by young Tobin. There can be little doubt that the Rangers not only participated in the mob action but actually incited it.[11]

Other volunteer companies began to reach Brownsville, spawning confusion and disputes over command. Also, a company of U.S. regulars, shipped by sea from New Orleans, reoccupied Fort Brown. Brownsville could now defend itself. Cortina had made no move to "lay the town in ashes," but his followers, exhilarated by the rout of the Tigers and the capture of two cannon, had begun to plunder and lay waste the valley's Anglo ranches as far upriver as Rio Grande City.

After hanging Cabrera, Tobin continued to exhibit his ineptitude. On November 21 thirty Rangers rode into a chaparral ambush set up by Cortina and got thrown back with three killed and three wounded. At once Tobin marched on Cortina's fortified Rancho del Carmen. The next day other companies from Brownsville joined him. On November 24, two hundred citizen soldiers advanced to within half a mile of Cortina's works. Here, as Tobin reported, "the officers consulted and determined it impracticable to attack the enemy in his fortifications." He ordered them back to Brownsville to "reinforce and organize another attack."[12]

On November 23 Cortina issued a second *pronunciamento*. It rang with the same grandiosity as the first and replayed the same themes of

Anglo land grabbing and despotism. By now Cortina flew the Mexican flag and talked loftily enough that most of his army of three to four hundred saw themselves less as a pillaging mob than as crusaders taking back what properly belonged to them. The document bristled with revolutionary rhetoric, but it called only for the overthrow of tyrants.[13]

Meantime, General Twiggs, old, ill, and anxious to depart on sick leave, had finally responded to the threat. On December 5 Major Samuel P. Heintzelman, a stolid infantry veteran of thirty-three years, marched into Brownsville with two foot companies and one mounted, 122 men. Added to the company already at Fort Brown, the major commanded 163 regulars.

At the same time, Governor Runnels had begun to worry that he had not sent enough Rangers, if not to wonder whether he had been too hasty in entrusting them to Tobin. On November 17 the governor turned to John Salmon Ford, commissioning him as major and instructing him to raise a company, proceed to Brownsville, unite with Tobin, and hold an election to determine who would command as major.[14]

Ford's company, numbering fifty-five, reached Brownsville on December 14 in time to hear gunfire from up the river. Pushing their mounts hard, they reached the battleground of El Ebonal, a dense chaparral studded with ebony trees, just as the battle ended. Before daybreak Heintzelman had marched with his entire force and Tobin's Rangers, now numbering about 150 in three companies, and confronted the *Cortinistas*. The Rangers had to be prodded into the attack, but once energized they fought well and supported the regulars in driving the enemy into the chaparral.

"I am mistified at the little we have done with near 300 men," wrote Heintzelman. He was justly "mistified," for the enemy consisted of about sixty infantry and artillery, who offered only "trifling resistance." Cortina and the main force were off to the east setting up an ambush for Rip Ford, who had the good fortune to choose another road. As for El Ebonal, "We would undoubtedly have done better without the Rangers."[15]

Heintzelman set forth again from Brownsville on December 21. His Ranger force now numbered nearly two hundred–the companies of Ford and Tobin together with three more that had responded to the call for volunteers. Tobin retained command of all the Rangers except Ford's.

Nearing Rio Grande City, Heintzelman gained intelligence that Cortina occupied Ringgold Barracks with his entire following. After midnight on December 27, the major quietly broke camp and advanced. The battle of Rio Grande City, which actually took place beyond the town and the military barracks, turned out to be exclusively a Ranger affair. Ford assailed the center of the enemy line, where Cortina had posted his artillery. Against grape, canister, and musket balls, Ford's men pressed the offense in a dense fog, seeking to capture the artillery. Sixteen men fell with wounds. Tobin belatedly appeared in Ford's rear, too late to enable him to hold the artillery that he had almost captured. The two cannon trundled off the field as Cortina's line dissolved in retreat, abandoning baggage, equipment, and half-cooked breakfast. Heintzelman rode up to Ford and declared that there could be no victory if the enemy carried off his artillery. Instantly Ford rallied his scattered men and galloped up the road. Within nine miles, he had seized both cannon.

"We made a great march & surprised them," exulted Heintzelman. "Near 50 miles and a fight is a pretty good business." It was–for Ford's Rangers. Neither Tobin's Rangers nor the regulars had contributed much to the victory. The regulars arrived on the field after the fighting ended.

The battle of Rio Grande City was a decisive victory. As an organized force, Cortina's following no longer occupied the Texas side of the Rio Grande. Cortina himself swam the river to safety in Mexico, where he held together a fluctuating number of fighters whose maneuvers served notice that the "war" had not ended. Thanks to Rip Ford and eighty Texas Rangers, however, the roots of the Cortina menace had been transplanted from Texas across the border to Mexico.[16]

Probably apprehensive that Tobin's men had little taste for Ford's discipline, Ford stalled the election for major. Heintzelman much preferred Ford. "He controls his men & Tobin is controlled by his. I would rather have Ford with 50 than Tobin with all his men." At Ringgold Barracks on January 1, however, Tobin won by a majority of six votes. Ford resigned, and his company refused to muster under Tobin.[17]

In Brownsville Ford and his officers met with Robert Taylor and Angel Navarro, commissioners dispatched by Sam Houston, newly inaugurated as governor but ignorant of the true state of affairs on the Rio Grande, to investigate and act on his behalf. They had arrived on January 10 and two days later ordered Tobin and his men to Brownsville to be mustered out. Tobin, Taylor informed the governor, "is utterly incompetent to command in the field," and some of his Rangers "who have been Burning ranches & Hanging & shooting Mexicans . . . are more dreaded than Cortinas." Taylor and Navarro quickly mustered Ford and most of his company back into state service, together with another under Captain John Littleton. With Ford as senior captain, the "Rio Grande Squadron," by direction of the commissioners, operated under Heintzelman's command.[18]

Heintzelman set the Rangers to patrolling the river. Even though based in Mexico since the battle of Rio Grande City, Cortina's men still crossed in plundering squads and returned with such stock and other spoils as they could find. The only solution lay in destroying Cortina in his home lair. As early as January 29, 1860, Major Heintzelman stated the obvious: "Complete security can only be obtained by crossing the river into Mexico, or by more active exertions on the part of the Mexican authorities in arresting these parties."[19]

Daunting political obstacles inhibited Mexican authorities. First, Mexicans of all stations universally detested the gringos and, loudly or silently, cheered Cortina's revolt. Second, although representing the shaky government of Benito Juárez in Vera Cruz, border politicians feared that the conservatives entrenched in Mexico City might prevail. Public opinion and political uncertainty prompted leaders on the distant

CITIZEN SOLDIERS. Volunteers gather to "range" the frontier seeking Comanche raiders. In the 1830s and 1840s, these "ranging companies" gave birth to the Texas Ranger tradition. Before the advent of the Colt repeating pistol in 1844, the typical "ranger" was armed with single-shot pistols, a rifle, and a Bowie knife. *Texas State Library and Archives.*

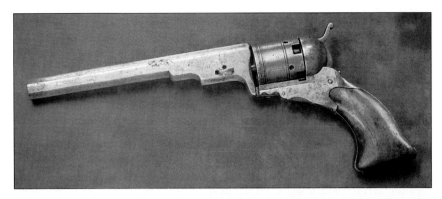

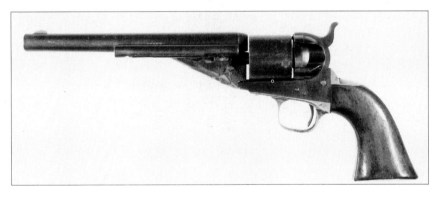

RANGER WEAPONS. The five-shot Paterson Colt, adopted by Hays's Rangers in 1844, revolutionized mounted warfare on the frontier. Now the Ranger had a repeating weapon to match the Comanche warrior's bow and arrows. The Walker Colt, developed in 1846 by Samuel Colt with the aid of former Ranger Samuel Walker, was the first six-shooter. In the hands of Hays's Rangers in the Mexican War, the Walker wrought deadly execution. The Walker was heavy and powerful, but Rangers of the 1850s preferred the lighter Colt Navy or Dragoon six-shooter, which could be handled more easily on horseback. This is a Navy. Paterson, *Texas Ranger Hall of Fame* and *National Cowboy and Western Heritage Museum*. Walker, *Texas Ranger Hall of Fame and Museum*. Colt Navy, *Panhandle Plains Historical Museum*.

SAM HOUSTON and MIRABEAU BUONAPARTE LAMAR. As presidents of the Republic of Texas (Houston twice), these men contended with both Indians and Mexicans, as well as with each other. Houston championed an Indian peace policy, Lamar a war policy. Lamar (below) is seen about 1857, Houston (above) about 1860, after he had served in the U.S. Senate and been elected governor of Texas. *Texas State Library and Archives.*

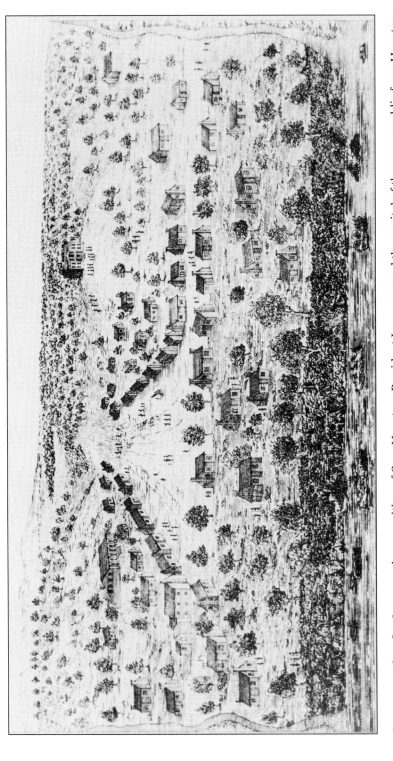

AUSTIN IN 1840. In 1839, over the opposition of Sam Houston, President Lamar moved the capital of the new republic from Houston far up the Colorado River to the frontier. This view looks up what would become Congress Avenue. The capitol of the Republic is the long log structure set back to the left from the avenue. The president's mansion stands on the hill to the right. *Texas State Library and Archives.*

SAN ANTONIO IN THE 1850S. Two centuries old when Texas gained her independence, San Antonio was the center of Spanish-Mexican culture and suffered a steep decline in population and commerce during the Republic. By the 1850s it had regained life as the military headquarters and supply depot for the U.S. Army in Texas, marked here by the American flag. *Texas State Library and Archives.*

The Battle of Plum Creek. Seeking revenge for the slaying of their chiefs in the Council House parley with Texas officers, Comanches raided all the way to the Gulf Coast. Matt Caldwell and other hastily assembled volunteers headed them off on their return and on August 12, 1840, dealt a devastating blow at Plum Creek, as depicted by artist Lee Herring. *William Adams and Institute of Texan Cultures.*

MEXICAN WAR. Austin artist Bruce Marshall captured the essence of the Texas Rangers in the Mexican War, depicting their unmilitary appearance and their mounted charges with the heavy Colt Walker six-shooter. The clash with Mexican lancers suggests Hays's battle near Izúcar de Matamoros on November 23, 1847. The street scene, entitled "The Return of Ben McCulloch," represents the second mobilization of McCulloch's Gonzales Ranger company. *Bruce Marshall and Institute of Texan Cultures.*

THE BATTLE OF MONTEREY. The Ranger regiments distinguished themselves in General Zachary Taylor's assault on the Mexican city. This lithograph by Carl Nebel (1851) looks south toward Monterey. In the foreground is the "Black Fort." In the middle distance the defenses atop Independence and Federation Hills may be dimly seen. *Texas State Library and Archives.*

NEWSPAPER CARICATURE. During the Mexican War the national press delighted in bizarre portrayals of the Texas Ranger. *Texas State Library and Archives.*

JOHN COFFEE HAYS. Observers noted how unlike a Ranger the boyish-looking Hays appeared. Yet as an Indian fighter and Mexican War officer, 1839–48, Hays won acclaim for exceptional qualities of leadership. Generations of Rangers would revere him as the ideal captain, the model for all to imitate. This drawing was made by T. J. Owen, a pseudonym for William Sydney Porter, an Austin bank teller who later wrote under the name of O. Henry. *Texas State Library and Archives.*

SAMUEL H. WALKER. A veteran Ranger wounded by Comanches at Walker Creek in 1844, Sam Walker was the first hero of the Mexican War, lionized throughout the nation. After serving as lieutenant colonel of Jack Hays's regiment, Walker worked with Samuel Colt to develop the first six-shooter, the "Walker Colt," which Hays's Rangers used against lancers and guerrillas in central Mexico in 1847–48. Walker, commissioned by the president in the regular army, was killed at the Battle of Huamantla in the Mexican War. *Texas State Library and Archives.*

BENJAMIN McCULLOCH. The captain from Gonzales served as an effective Indian fighter for the Republic of Texas and distinguished himself in the Mexican War, both as a combat leader and a scout. *Texas State Library and Archives.*

RIP FORD. After the Mexican War, Jack Hays's mantle as ideal captain fell on John Salmon ("Rip") Ford, who intermittently led Ranger companies against Indians throughout the 1850s and contended with the Cortina rebellion on the Rio Grande in 1859–60. In this portrait of about 1858, Ford is armed with two Colt six-shooters. His most notable exploit was the Battle of Antelope Hills, May 12, 1858, in which his Rangers surprised and destroyed the Comanche village of Iron Jacket. Four decades later artist Frederic Remington interviewed the old Ranger and executed the wash drawing, "We Struck Some Boggy Ground," representing the Ranger charge at Antelope Hills. Portrait, *John N. McWilliams Collection*; art, *R. W. Norton Art Gallery, Shreveport, Louisiana.*

JOHN B. JONES. Major Jones organized the Frontier Battalion, authorized by the legislature in 1874 to fight Indians. With the Indian menace subsiding, he transformed the battalion into a corps of lawmen. Ending the time of the citizen soldier, Jones laid the groundwork for the Texas Rangers to achieve institutional continuity as professional law officers with statewide powers. *Texas State Library and Archives.*

LEANDER H. MCNELLY. From 1874 to 1877, the sickly young captain headed a company of militia that later was redesignated Special State Troops. Although not part of the Frontier Battalion, his men were "McNelly's Rangers," and they gained fame by employing direct and often cruelly illegal methods against Mexican cattle thieves. Although Mexicans had good reason to despise McNelly, Anglo Texans applauded his exploits, and his men adored him. Tuberculosis killed him in 1877. *Western History Collections, University of Oklahoma Libraries.*

JOHN WESLEY HARDIN and JOHN B. ARMSTRONG. Of all the outlaw killers of the Old West, John Wesley Hardin came closest to living up to the legend. He killed at least twenty men, perhaps more than twice that many. Wanted in Texas for murder, Hardin hid in Florida. In August 1877, Ranger Lieutenant Armstrong–"McNelly's Bulldog"–traveled to Florida to seek out Hardin. In a famous encounter in a railway coach, Armstrong felled Hardin with the barrel of his Colt six-shooter. After years in the penitentiary, Hardin went to El Paso, where he was killed by an outlaw turned lawman, Constable John Sellman. *Western History Collections, University of Oklahoma Libraries.*

northern frontier to counter American protests with words of sympathy combined with empty shows of martial bluster.

Heintzelman lacked authority to cross U.S. regulars into Mexico. Rip Ford, at heart a filibuster, felt no such compunction. He would welcome a chance to carry the fight across the boundary. This was exactly what made Heintzelman skittish about any border crossing. He did not trust the Rangers to curb their destructive tendencies. "I want them on this side," he later wrote, "as I know they will be guilty of all kinds of outrages."[20]

Tobin did not march from Rio Grande City until the end of January 1860. En route, about thirty miles upstream from Brownsville, he met Ford and his company on patrol and played a final ambiguous role in the next episode of the Cortina troubles.

Tobin's men escorted the steamer *Ranchero*, bound from Rio Grande City for Brownsville with a cargo worth $200,000, including $60,000 in specie. Cortina had gathered some two hundred men at Rancho La Bolsa, cradled by a narrow, northward-sweeping bend of the Rio Grande. At noon on February 4, as the steamer reached the northern arc of the bend, it came under fire from the Mexican shore. Tobin and Ford met shortly afterward. The *Ranchero* gave Ford the pretext he wanted to cross the Rio Grande.[21]

That afternoon he did, with thirty-five of his own Rangers and Tobin with a dozen of his. Cortina had posted his men behind hastily erected palisades and among the buildings and jacales of Rancho La Bolsa. Expertly, Ford maneuvered his Rangers under cover of an old river bank and opened a deadly fire on Cortina's left flank. The Mexicans returned a heavier but harmless fire. After cutting down many defenders, Ford ordered a charge around the defensive palisade and rolled up the line. Only gathering darkness saved Cortina himself. Five balls grazed him and his horse as he sought vainly to rally his men. They fled with a loss of twenty-nine killed and forty wounded. Ford's loss: two wounded.

The sounds of battle, including the shouts of men on both sides, drifted back to the *Ranchero*. One of the women passengers nervously asked, "Is that the Mexicans shouting?" "No, madam," was the answer, "it is Texians. Mexican lungs cannot produce such a sound as that vengeful war cry." (The distinctive "Texas yell," as Ford labeled it, prefigured the famed rebel yell soon to reverberate on Civil War battlefields.)[22]

La Bolsa was a greater victory than Rio Grande City. A company of well-led Rangers routed four times their number, inflicted heavy casualties, and almost shot down Cortina himself. More important from Ford's viewpoint, the battle took place on Mexican soil, thus serving notice that the international boundary might deter U.S. regulars, but not Texas Rangers.

In Austin, Governor Houston rattled his saber loudly enough to worry federal officials in Washington. Declaring the Cortina troubles a federal responsibility, he warned Secretary of War John B. Floyd that "Texas cannot be invaded with impunity. If thrown upon her own resources she may not only resist but adopt means to prevent recurrence of the outrage."[23]

Houston's words alarmed Floyd and other high officials, not only because of his long-trumpeted ambition to establish a U.S. protectorate over Mexico but also because of other actions he had recently taken. Comanches had continued to ravage the northwestern frontier, and this longtime advocate of an Indian policy of peace and negotiation had reacted as an arrant militarist. During January he called out three Ranger companies and posted them in the affected area. In January also, the legislature authorized him to mobilize an entire Ranger regiment, ten companies, for Indian duty. When he pointed out that they had to be paid, the legislature appropriated $300,000. Lest Secretary Floyd and President Buchanan fail to grasp how these Rangers might be used, Houston also wrote his old friend Ben McCulloch, then in Washington: "There will be stirring times on the Rio Grande ere long. What are you doing? See the President and the Secretary of War."[24]

With Houston's bellicosity as background, on February 24 Floyd caused orders to be issued to Lieutenant Colonel Robert E. Lee to assume command of the Department of Texas in his brevet grade of colonel. Although phrased less bluntly, his orders directed him to confront Mexican authorities with an ultimatum to capture Cortina and his followers or Lee would do it himself. Explicitly, Floyd sanctioned the deployment of U.S. regulars "beyond the limits of the United States."[25]

Colonel Lee's freedom to pursue Cortina into Mexico, widely reported in the newspapers, emboldened Ford while it spread alarm through Matamoros and other border towns. It prompted at least an appearance of greater cooperation from the Mexican commandant, General Guadalupe García. But it did not lessen Heintzelman's qualms about unleashing Texas Rangers in Mexico.[26]

Heintzelman had more confidence in his cavalry commander. Captain George Stoneman and his company of the Second Cavalry had formed the mounted component of the Brownsville expedition from the first. Ford and Stoneman got along well and seem to have been imbued with a similar aggressiveness. The regulars had recently been strengthened by a second cavalry company. Together, Ford and Stoneman presented a formidable force of between two and three hundred horsemen.

On March 13 General García alerted Heintzelman that Cortina and forty men had been reported at Rancho La Mesa and invited a cooperative effort to seize him. Camped some forty-five miles above Brownsville, nearly opposite La Mesa, Ford hesitated to cross. He mistrusted García and suspected him of conspiring with Cortina to ambush the Rangers. When Stoneman came on the scene with permission from Heintzelman to cross the river, however, Ford eagerly threw in with him.

The Rangers and regulars forded the river before daylight on March 18 and rode toward Rancho La Mesa. Fearing that an ambush had been set up on the main road, Ford counseled a circuitous route. This brought them to the objective shortly before dawn. A Mexican picket gave the alarm. Surprisingly, drums beat the long roll, and both infantry and cavalry quickly formed line—hardly a response typical of Cortina. Stoneman's regulars charged the cavalry on the right flank, Ford's Rangers the infantry on the left, and together they rolled up the enemy line and drove it back into the village. Many fell prisoner, while others scampered for refuge in the buildings. A woman fell with mortal wounds, the only casualty, except for a wounded Mexican and a dead mule, in what had turned out to be a battle with units of the Mexican *Guardia National*.

The shouts of a Mexican officer halted the firing on both sides. Another Mexican force of some 150 guardsmen appeared on the main road. Ford parleyed with their colonel. The two testily exchanged accusations. The talk ended with a typically Fordian gesture: place the regulars on the sidelines and fight it out with the Mexicans. The colonel declined the invitation.[27]

Ford and Stoneman had a second mission. The *Ranchero* was again bound downriver. On March 19 they escorted it past La Bolsa Bend, where a courier brought a dispatch from Heintzelman, who had received their report of the fight at La Mesa the night before. Unless they had positive information of Cortina in the vicinity, the major directed, they were to return to the American side of the boundary.[28]

Rumor placed Cortina twenty-four miles south of Matamoros and a sixty-mile ride to the southeast. Although this was hardly the vicinity contemplated by Heintzelman, the Rangers and regulars took up the chase. For two days, following one rumor after another, they drove themselves and their mounts a distance of nearly 150 miles in an arc that displayed them in village after village, and to at least one military garrison. Deep in Mexico, with no chance of overhauling a quarry reported to have fled to Monterey, they recrossed the Rio Grande on December 21.[29]

Thus ended the Cortina troubles, before Colonel Robert E. Lee even reached the scene of action. During the first week of April he descended the Rio Grande from Fort Duncan to Brownsville, delivering his blunt ultimatum to Mexican municipal authorities as well as to the governor of Tamaulipas. Lee's warnings gained force from the operations of Ford and Stoneman, but it was their actions, not Lee's words, that broke the back of the Cortina revolt.

Rip Ford's Rio Grande Squadron Texas Rangers played a decisive part in the operations against Cortina and his bandit-rebels. Although typically vexing, as all Rangers were, Ford's men were more disciplined and followed a respected leader, which made them effective fighters. Virtually alone they achieved the victory at the Battle of Rio Grande City, and alone they routed Cortina at La Bolsa Bend. With Captain Stoneman they faced down Mexican guardsmen and Cortina's horsemen at La Mesa, then swept through Mexico in the lightning march that proclaimed the new American combativeness. In the final operations, George Stoneman deserves a full share of the credit. He imbued Heintzelman's orders with an extraordinary elasticity and carried his cooperation with Ford far beyond what he knew his commander would approve.

An assessment of the Rangers' role must also take account of their performance before Captain Tobin retired from the Rio Grande in early February 1860. Lacking even a shadow of leadership, the Tobin Rangers ran wild, killing, burning, and looting with all the fervor of the Cortinistas. But for Tobin, moreover, the Cortina uprising probably would not have ballooned beyond its origin as a personal feud. Only after his Rangers hanged Tomás Cabrera on November 13, 1859, did Cortina fully emerge as a warrior chief battling the oppression of the Anglo minority. More than any predecessor, William G. Tobin exemplified the dark side of Texas Rangers when captained by an ineffectual leader.

WITH CORTINA DISTANT from the boundary and his following apparently scattered, Sam Houston turned his full attention to the Indian frontier. The protective shield of Rangers, the offensives of Rangers and regulars into the Comanche homeland north of Red River, the expulsion of the reserve Indians from Texas, peace overtures—nothing had afforded more than brief respites from Kiowa and Comanche forays.

Throughout the spring and summer of 1860, Governor Houston served as commander in chief in fact as well as law. All Ranger leaders reported directly to him, and he supervised them with an oppressive oversight wholly alien to traditional Ranger independence. He specified camp locations, mode of pursuing raiders, frequency and coverage of scouting, posting of guards, administrative and reporting requirements, care of horses and property, enforcement of discipline, and even maintenance of "moral tone"—no liquor, no gambling, no horse racing. Violations would bring dishonorable discharge. Besides general regulations, Houston bombarded captains with specific directives on how and where to employ their companies. An aide traveled from camp to camp ensuring compliance and passing on new instructions from the governor.[30]

Although Houston still believed in peace treaties, his principal response to the anguished appeals from the frontier was military rather than diplomatic. As authorized by the legislature, he would form the Ranger regiment he had long sought and launch it against the Comanches.

Why Houston acted contrary to long-established principles can only be speculated. His course on the eve of the Civil War has led some to believe that the direct command of the Rangers and a military instead of a diplomatic offensive against the Comanches somehow meshed with his hope of fixing a protectorate on Mexico. Whatever swirled about his active mind fell victim to the secession of Texas.[31]

To organize and command the new Ranger regiment, Houston turned to Middleton T. Johnson, a wealthy cotton planter from Fort Worth and perennially unsuccessful candidate for state office. A Texan since 1839, fifty years old in 1860, Johnson had served in the Mexican War and led several fruitless expeditions against Indians, a record that hardly qualified him for the mission Houston assigned on March 17, 1860: assemble and organize a regiment of Rangers and conduct an offensive in the Comanche homeland such as had won laurels for Rip Ford in 1858.[32]

Middleton Johnson fell woefully short of the challenge. His optimistic reports to the governor belied confusion, logistical deficiencies, and vacillating purpose that only grew worse as the companies gathered at Fort Belknap in May and June. The heart of the regiment consisted of units raised by Johnson's cronies in the Dallas–Fort Worth area. Supply officers failed to concentrate the transportation, rations, and arms and ammunition needed for a campaign into a plains country verging on an exceptional drought. Incredibly, as the problems multiplied, the recently widowed colonel resolved that he must have a three-week leave of absence to journey to Galveston and take a new wife. "Dont scold," he reassured Houston, "all shall be well and I will make the quickest trip ever made."[33]

Throughout the summer of 1860, Johnson's units bumbled from one embarrassing failure to another. Drought-stricken plains broke down men and horses. They killed no hostile Indians, found no sign of hostile Indians, cost the state treasury a great sum of money and the governor a great sum of political capital, intruded into Indian reservations under the jurisdiction of the United States, and provoked the U.S. Army to ready units for a possible standoff with a military force operating under the authority of the governor of Texas. Worst of all, perhaps, Middleton T. Johnson made Texas Rangers look like fools. On August 4 Houston peremptorily ordered the regiment disbanded.[34]

Thus ingloriously ended Sam Houston's grand offensive of 1860 against the Comanches. And thus ingloriously did the incompetent Johnson make a mockery of all Houston's fine words about the excellence of Texas Rangers as Indian fighters.

With Johnson's regiment disbanding, raiders stepped up the pace of depredations. Pilloried by frontier settlers for the Johnson fiasco, Governor Houston turned to a youth verging on his twenty-second birthday but a veteran nonetheless. The son of Brazos agent Shapley P. Ross, Lawrence Sullivan Ross had returned home in the summer of 1858 from college in Alabama. His father had just led the Brazos Reserve Indians in Rip Ford's victory over Iron Jacket at Antelope Hills. Now Major Van Dorn wanted a similar contingent to join his autumn campaign against the Comanches. "Sul" Ross ably led the Indians, who respected him as they had respected his father. At the battle of Rush Springs on October 1, 1858, Ross plunged into the thick of the fight and fell seriously wounded by an arrow and a pistol ball. After recovery, he returned to college, graduated, and came home in 1860 in time to command a Ranger company and take part in Colonel Johnson's campaign. To maintain a Ranger presence on the exposed frontier, on September 11,

1860, Houston asked Sul Ross to raise a company of sixty Rangers and take station at Fort Belknap.[35]

Sul Ross handed Houston a victory. On December 18, 1860, as Comanches ravaged the northwestern frontier, Ross and forty Rangers, bolstered by a sergeant and twenty regular cavalrymen, discovered a Comanche village in the narrow valley of Mule Creek just above its confluence with Pease River. The surprise was complete. Warriors fell under the deadly fire of Ranger six-shooters. Others rushed down the valley and collided with a fusillade from the carbines and revolvers of the regulars. Then, as Ross recalled, "every one fled his own way, and was hotly pursued and hard pressed."

Ross himself tangled with a Comanche chief and killed him. He turned out to be Peta Nocona. His wife and child were captured. She was soon identified as Cynthia Ann Parker, seized in a Comanche raid on Parker's Fort in 1836. She was also the mother of a youth who in later decades achieved fame as Quanah Parker.[36]

The battle of Pease River restored luster to a Ranger image stained by the folly of Middleton Johnson. No more than Antelope Hills, Rush Springs, or Crooked Creek, however, did it quiet Comanche and Kiowa raids on the Texas frontier. Neither offense nor defense seemed to have more than momentary effect. Frontier citizens would find little relief for another fifteen years.

Pease River revealed Sul Ross as a superior Ranger captain. Despite his youth, he commanded the respect and therefore the disciplined teamwork of his men, a quality that set such captains as Jack Hays, Ben McCulloch, and Rip Ford apart from lesser leaders. The well-publicized victory over Peta Nocona launched Ross toward distinction in Texas history—combat-hardened Confederate brigadier, state senator, governor of Texas, and president of Texas A&M University.

Sam Houston promoted so many machinations during 1860 that direct operational management of the Texas Rangers is cause for wonder. The national electorate knew that the presidential contest of 1860 would prove crucial in a sectional conflict that had reached crisis proportions. Irreconcilable passions tore apart the national Democratic

Party and the Texas Democratic Party. Love of the Union and love of Texas warred within Sam Houston, but he stood forthrightly against secession. The election of Abraham Lincoln in November 1860 set off the rush to secession. Stubborn Unionist to the last, the governor fought desperately to prevent the secession of Texas, to no avail. On March 16, 1861, Sam Houston refused to swear fealty to the Confederacy and yielded his office.

The Old Lion died on July 26, 1863. With him ended a momentous era in the history of Texas as well as the history of the Texas Rangers.

[7]

Chaos in Frontier Defense, 1861–1874

T HE STORM THAT BURST over Texas early in 1861 inaugurated thirteen years of chaos in the defense of the frontier settlements. These years spanned four of Civil War, five of presidential and congressional Reconstruction, and another three of Radical Republican rule before conservative Democrats recaptured the state government and crafted an organized response to the cries from the frontier. Two themes ruled the period: repeated raids by Comanche and Kiowa marauders from north of Red River, and an intermittent line of defenders who, whatever the official nomenclature, bore the distinguishing marks of Texas Rangers.

Some seventy thousand Texans fought for the Confederacy, mostly beyond the bounds of Texas. The Eighth Texas Cavalry bore the sobriquet of "Terry's Texas Rangers." It achieved an outstanding combat record, but it was a conventional Confederate regiment whose only tie to Rangers lay in the name. Nonetheless, the name alone testified to the identity and reputation the of the Rangers. Texans grieved over casualty returns and endured wartime shortages, but they escaped the devastation that swept the rest of the Confederacy. No major Union invasion penetrated the state. Instead, the hardest soldiering took place along the frontier from Red River to the Rio Grande.

With Federal troops evacuating the frontier forts, state Rangers hastened to fill the void. The Committee of Public Safety, an arm of the Secession Convention, conferred colonelcies on John S. Ford and Ben and Henry McCulloch. Ford took charge of the Rio Grande line, Henry McCulloch of the frontier. Ben McCulloch, commissioned a Confederate brigadier, commanded impressively in Arkansas and Missouri but was killed at the battle of Pea Ridge, March 7, 1862.

Under the authority of the Secession Convention, Ford and Henry McCulloch immediately began to raise troops. By April 1861, the Richmond government had been persuaded that frontier defense was a responsibility of the Confederacy, and McCulloch's recruits were mustered into the Confederate service as the First Texas Mounted Rifles. Ford's regiment, organized under an act of the legislature, was later taken into Confederate service as the Second Texas Mounted Rifles. This unit operated mainly as a conventional force, concerned less with frontier defense than battling Union efforts to disrupt the vital wartime trade across the Rio Grande. Colonel Henry McCulloch's First Texas, however, faced off against Comanches and Kiowas as had their predecessors for thirty years.[1]

McCulloch's Rangers, averaging eight hundred to a thousand strong, served out their year's enlistment in dreary patrolling. McCulloch, called to Austin for other duties, relinquished direct command. The First Texas ended its enlistment in April 1862.

Governor Francis R. Lubbock and the state legislature had already taken measures to prevent any lapse in frontier defense. On December 21, 1861, in a law reviving a formula that had never worked with the U.S. government, the legislature authorized a new regiment of Texas Rangers. It would be organized under the rules and regulations of the Confederate States Army and offered for muster into the Confederate service. But it would remain under the governor's control and could not be removed from the state. Here again was the old design of fighting Indians with Texas Rangers while sending the bill to the central government. Texas representatives slipped the scheme through the Confederate Congress, only to have it vetoed by President Jefferson Davis. No Confederate unit, he decreed, would be suffered to operate outside the Confederate command structure. For two years Austin and Richmond wrangled over the issue, but when the First Texas dissolved in April 1862 the Frontier Regiment, controlled and paid for by the state, took its place.[2]

The Frontier Regiment consisted of Rangers in the classic mold. They came from the frontier counties, provided their own horses, arms, and accouterments, and wore no uniforms. Scattered in eighteen small detachments along the frontier line, they scouted for Indian sign and took up the pursuit when they found a trail. The regiment averaged between a thousand and twelve hundred men, a strength readily maintained because frontier service exempted them from Confederate conscription laws and allowed them to serve closer to their homes.

The Frontier Regiment compiled a dismal record in the winter of 1862–1863, primarily because of a rigid patrol system instituted by the unpopular Colonel James M. Norris. Raiders quickly picked up the routine and easily slipped through to the settlements. Early in 1863, in an effort to improve chances for acceptance into Confederate service, Governor Lubbock reorganized the regiment. Colonel Norris stepped down, to be succeeded by the able James E. McCord. The new colonel abandoned the patrols and launched larger units in extended sweeps of the Indian approach routes.

The man mainly responsible for the new system was the most experienced officer in the Frontier Regiment and now its lieutenant colonel. James B. "Buck" Barry had ridden with Jack Hays against Indians and Mexicans, taken a wound in the storming of Monterey, soldiered with Sul Ross in the expedition that liberated Cynthia Ann Parker, served as an officer in the First Texas Rifles and as captain and major in the Frontier Regiment. A wiry man of medium stature, weighing less than 150 pounds, he sported dark curling hair that fell over shoulders invariably clad in buckskin. Master of frontier skills, energetic, decisive, fearless, respected and well liked, Buck Barry had a proven record of leadership in the best Ranger tradition.

With headquarters at Fort Belknap, Barry commanded six companies covering the northwestern frontier. Despite acute shortages of ammunition and provisions and chronically defective gunpowder, his Rangers intercepted several raiding parties in 1863. "Victories by small squads and by companies which had been able to involve the Indians in a fight," he recalled, "came often enough to encourage us."[3]

But not enough to encourage the settlers. War parties slipped by Barry's scouts, seized horses and captives, killed anyone who got in their way, and scampered back to their home ranges without ever being glimpsed. These aggressions fell on the long-established farming communities of the black-soil Cross Timbers. Farther west, immigrant stockmen had recently begun to move cattle herds to the rolling plains rising toward the caprock, which defined the eastern edges of the Staked Plain. Late in 1863, finding that contractors for the Union Army offered a market for Texas beef, the Kiowas and Comanches began to drive off cattle too.[4]

Barry's Rangers were not the only frontier defenders. A Confederate outfit, Bourland's Border Regiment, the combative old Ranger James Bourland commanding, covered both sides of Red River eastward from Barry's right flank and northward to Fort Arbuckle, in the Indian Territory. Some of the northern counties fielded minute companies. Militia companies also sprouted, for militiamen claimed exemption from Confederate conscription. Finally, fearing a Union invasion from the Indian Territory, the Confederacy established a Northern Subdistrict, headquartered at Bonham, and forwarded Confederate units to meet the threat. Confederate and state authority overlapped in the district, creating cumbersome command relationships for Rangers, militia, and regulars. In August 1863 the command fell to Brigadier General Henry E. McCulloch.[5]

By the end of 1863, neither Union invasion nor even Kiowa and Comanche raiding headed McCulloch's list of priorities or dominated the operations of Rangers and militia. The northern counties, heavily Unionist in sentiment, had become havens for as many as a thousand Confederate deserters and draft dodgers. Many rode in pillaging bands that preyed on citizens and posted military formations to guard their hideaways. Offering amnesty, McCulloch tried to coax the fugitives out of the brush thickets where they camped. Some five hundred responded. McCulloch organized them into the Brush Battalion and sent them to bolster Colonel Bourland's frontier line in the Indian Territory.

Neither the Brush Battalion, Bourland's Borderers, nor a Ranger company at Red River Station hindered a ruinous Comanche foray in December 1863. Three hundred warriors swept through the farmlands of Montague and Cooke Counties, northwest of Fort Worth. As McCulloch acidly observed, so large a Comanche inroad "could have been discovered if there had been anyone on the watch at all."[6]

The Brush Battalion proved a bad mistake. McCulloch withdrew it from the frontier and sent it against the brush fugitives themselves. That proved a mistake too, for many went back to the brush. McCulloch disbanded the battalion in March 1864, but with the scant resources at his command he could not root out runaways in the brush. With the Confederate cause sinking toward collapse, the number of deserters and draft evaders multiplied. Even the Frontier Regiment and Bourland's Border Regiment, charged with running down deserters, lost heavily to desertion.

Meanwhile, the governor and legislature continued the effort to get the Frontier Regiment off the state payroll and into Confederate service. They succeeded only by giving in to Confederate terms. An act of December 15, 1863, coupled the transfer of the regiment to Confederate control with the creation of a new Frontier Organization. Twenty frontier counties were divided into three frontier districts, each under a major of cavalry. Each county would form a company of minutemen reporting to the district major. They would be paid and provisioned by the state, but on the Ranger pattern they would provide their own horses, arms, and accouterments. The new system took effect in March 1864.[7]

Since the Confederate government had accepted responsibility for frontier defense, legislators expected the Frontier Regiment to remain on the frontier unless imperatively required elsewhere. No sooner had the transfer been completed, however, than the Confederate commander in Texas ordered Colonel McCord and six companies of the regiment to new posts in the interior. With the remaining four, about three hundred strong, Lieutenant Colonel Buck Barry took station at Fort Belknap and reported to General McCulloch at Bonham.[8]

But not for long. In August 1864 Barry and his men were pulled off the frontier and sent to join the rest of the regiment. This left the frontier to be covered by Bourland's Border Regiment, no more than five hundred men stretched thinly from Fort Arbuckle to the Colorado River. Buck Barry and his companies of the Frontier Regiment returned to Fort Belknap after three months' absence, but too late for the most catastrophic Indian raid of the wartime years.

Although many settlers had fled the northwestern counties, a sturdy few remained. Some forted up, surrounding their homes with palisades where neighbors could gather for defense when the alarm was raised. About twelve miles west of Fort Belknap, where the Cross Timbers merged with the rolling plains, about a dozen families of farmers and stockmen lived along Elm Creek, a southern tributary of the Brazos.

On October 13, 1864, as many as six hundred Comanches and Kiowas in several parties swept down the Brazos and up Elm Creek. They butchered men in the fields and women and children in their homes. Columns of smoke from burning buildings alerted others to their peril. The settlers held out in improvised forts until the Indians drew off. Neither Borderers nor minutemen had detected the approach of the raiders or mobilized quickly or strongly enough to give effective pursuit. Even if still on the frontier, Buck Barry's Rangers would probably not have changed the outcome.[9]

A final clash of arms climaxed the Indian service of the wartime Rangers. It left an ugly blemish on their record and created a legacy of vengeance that tormented South Texas for more than a decade.

On December 9, 1864, a scouting party of militia discovered a broad Indian trail crossing the upper Clear Fork of the Brazos and pointing southwest. Militia companies mobilized in several frontier counties. At the same time, Buck Barry fielded 110 men of the Frontier Regiment, together with nearly 50 militia under Captain Henry Fossett. By late December more than three hundred militia had also assembled under Captain Silas Totten. By January 7, 1865, both forces had found the objective—a large Indian camp nestled in a ravine-scored thicket of Dove Creek, a tributary of the Concho River (southwest of present San Angelo).

The Indians were about seven hundred Kickapoos. Many Texans had lost stock and even their lives to Kickapoos, but these were striving to slip across West Texas without ever encountering a Texan. Disgusted with the chaos stirred by the Civil War in Kansas, they had resolved to join kinsmen in Coahuila, where Mexican authorities employed Kickapoos and Seminoles as frontier defenders.

To the Texans, however, any Indians might raid the frontier, and in any event their camp would yield rich spoils. Early on January 8, militia and regulars joined after a punishing nighttime march in cold, snow, and mud. Totten now led about 220 men, the rest strung out in the rear with broken-down horses. Fossett commanded some 140. The two captains agreed to strike from two directions. Totten would dismount, wade Dove Creek, and charge on foot directly into the village from the north. Fossett would cross the creek, swing south of the village and scoop up the horse herd, then turn to attack the village from the south.

Dripping from the creek crossing, Totten's men burst into the Indian camp, only to find themselves outgunned by warriors firing Enfield military rifles from ravines cloaked by timber and brush. By contrast, the "flop-eared militia," as the Rangers dubbed them, "were armed with all kinds of firearms, shot-guns, squirrel rifles, some muskets and pistols." Almost at the first fire, three captains and sixteen men fell dead. "The militia was thrown into panic," recalled one of the Rangers, "and fled like stampeded cattle out of the camp with about one hundred Indians pursuing them."[10]

Fossett's Rangers, meanwhile, seized the Indian horse herd and turned to strike the village from the south. With the militia beaten, the Kickapoos rallied to meet the new threat. Fossett deployed his men in a line along the west bank of Dove Creek. For five hours the two sides exchanged fire, the Indians enjoying the advantage of positions hidden by timber and brush. With evening approaching, Fossett broke off the battle and turned north to join Totten. Crossing Dove Creek, he got caught in a deadly fire from warriors hidden beneath the stream banks. The Rangers panicked, abandoned the captured Indian horses, and fled in disorder to join the militia.

Lying exhausted on Spring Creek, to the north, the demoralized Texans counted their losses: twenty-six killed and twenty-three wounded—worse than any suffered in Ranger memory. Most of the dead lay on the battlefield, but heavy snow and Kickapoo rifles afforded good reasons for not returning. In fact, the Kickapoos had broken camp in the night, left their dead and much camp equipage on the battleground, and hastened toward a Rio Grande crossing near Eagle Pass. The attackers consoled themselves that they had shot down a hundred Indians—not much more than the Kickapoos' own count of eleven killed and seventy-six wounded.

Dove Creek displayed a leadership so poor that it bungled a battle that should not have been fought, cost unnecessarily heavy casualties, and planted in Mexican lairs an enemy unlikely to forget or forgive. After investigating the debacle, the state militia's Brigadier General John D. McAdoo spared no feelings in setting forth the failings of Captains Fossett and Totten: "Without any council of war, without any distribution of orders, without any formation of a line of battle, without any preparation, without any inspection of the camp, without any communication with the Indians, or inquiry as to what tribe they belonged to, without any knowledge of their strength or position, the command 'Forward' was given; and a pell-mell charge was made for three miles." Buck Barry tried to present his subordinates in more favorable light, but McAdoo's blunt judgment could be phrased even more harshly without damage to the truth.[11]

For Texans, the Civil War did not end with the surrender of General Robert E. Lee at Appomattox Courthouse. Not until June 2, 1865, did the Trans-Mississippi armies surrender. On June 19, a Union army of occupation landed at Galveston. On the distant frontier, settlers anxiously looked to the day when Yankee soldiers would reoccupy the old forts and once again take up the national responsibility for frontier defense.

The men who defended the frontier during the Civil War years rode under a variety of designations—First Texas Mounted Rifles, Frontier Regiment, Bourland's Border Regiment, state militia, and minutemen. Whether they should be known as Texas Rangers has been a matter of confusion and disagreement. But they all, whether in Confederate or state service, resembled the prewar Rangers. Most came from the frontier counties, provided their own horses and arms, elected their own officers and noncommissioned officers, and followed tactics adapted to the elusive Indian enemy rather than the blue formations their brethren confronted on eastern battlefields. That they scored no memorable victories such as those of Matt Caldwell, Jack Hays, Rip Ford, and Sul Ross made them no less Rangers. Many were too young, too old, or too unfit for the big war against the Union. Many sought to avoid the war altogether, to look instead to the safety of their families, or to hide Unionist sentiment, or simply to distance themselves from the perils of the battlefield.

The wartime Rangers confronted obstacles unknown to their predecessors. Most severe was the contention between the state and Confederate governments. The two-year standoff over mustering the Frontier Regiment into the Confederate Army underscored the state's determination that the frontier have protection and the Confederacy's determination that its generals have complete control of their armies. Like the U.S. government, the Confederate government readily acknowledged its responsibility for frontier defense. But a distant frontier could not begin to compete for men and resources with bleeding gray armies. Thus the state had to have its own system in place. And whether Confederate or state, Rangers endured increasingly crippling shortages of ammunition, transportation, and other supplies.

Whether Confederate or state also, Rangers bore the secondary mission of apprehending deserters and draft dodgers. By 1863, their growing numbers seriously troubled the high command and led to intense pressure on the frontier units to round them up. During the final years of the war, Rangers devoted as much effort to this repugnant mission as to keeping watch for Indian raiders—with comparable lack of success.

Yet for all their failures and defects, the wartime Rangers did no worse than their prewar counterparts. Neither Texas Rangers nor U.S. regulars, despite successful pursuits and occasional skirmishes, prevented Indians from slipping through the lines and falling on exposed settlements. Rip Ford won acclaim for his victory at Antelope Hills, but it served only to bring wrathful Comanches down to exact revenge. In truth, no frontier defenders had ever succeeded in keeping raiders out of the settlements. Against that backdrop, Buck Barry's Rangers can no more be faulted than Rip Ford's for failing in a mission impossible.

Texas had not been ravaged by Union invasion nor its economy wrecked by the war. Even so, the postwar years stirred hardly less turmoil than in the other states of the collapsed Confederacy. Few Anglo Texans could bring themselves to face the consequences of defeat, especially the full meaning of emancipation. Texas blacks numbered twice as many as in 1861, the result of planters from elsewhere moving their slaves out of harm's way. This infusion of laborers expanded the cotton fields and strengthened the economy. But it also aggravated race relations, as constitutional amendments awarded the former slaves rights and privileges that Anglo Texans could not meekly accept. Confederate veterans—maimed, bitter, rebellious, or simply resigned—watched the old order crumble as a Union army of occupation spread across the state and Texas Unionists moved into government offices.

Adding to this explosive mix, footloose young men by the thousands rolled into Texas to join with homegrown malcontents in escalating disorder, violence, and crime. They were scourings of the Confederate Army, deserters, or simply refugees from the breakdown of law and order elsewhere. Their offenses ranged from rowdyism to larceny and murder. They congregated in the western counties, already ravaged by Indian raids, and overwhelmed county lawmen and courts.

Texas suffered little during Reconstruction from "carpetbaggers." Enough prominent Texas Unionists stepped forward to keep civil offices safely in Texan hands. Such was Andrew J. Hamilton, whom President Andrew Johnson appointed provisional governor in June 1865. Hamilton served for more than a year, until Johnson's benign presidential Reconstruction produced a new constitution and an elected government. Governor James W. Throckmorton took office on August 13, 1866. He was a Conservative Unionist, as opposed to Hamilton's Radical Unionists, and he won with the support of the old secessionists. While he displayed a Unionist facade to the North, the legislature enacted black codes, promoted the political and economic interests of the prewar establishment, and sent two rabid secessionists to the U.S. Senate (which refused to seat them). With the state government back in elected hands, however, the issue of frontier defense loomed in the volcanic politics of Reconstruction.[12]

Throckmorton had no sooner moved into the statehouse in Austin than his desk overflowed with heart-rending appeals from the frontier. Kiowas and Comanches scourged the northwestern counties, Lipans and Kickapoos from Mexico the southwestern counties. Responsibility for the frontier had once more fallen to the federal government, but violence against freedmen and Unionists in the interior, coupled with the intransigence of the new state government, preoccupied military commanders. Throckmorton turned to the legislature, which on September 21, 1866, responded with the tired old formula that had never worked with either the U.S. or the Confederate government: a regiment of one thousand "Texas Rangers" (the first use of the term in legislation), organized under the rules and regulations of the U.S. Army, deployed on the frontier under state authority, and offered for muster into the U.S. service.[13]

The governor forged ahead with the organization of the Rangers even as the United States refused to accept them. He found war-weary men reluctant to enlist, especially with such poor prospects of pay and with federal troops menacing citizens of the interior instead of taking their rightful place on the frontier. Throckmorton's most formidable obstacle, however, resided in New Orleans, where pugnacious Major General Philip H. Sheridan presided over the Department of the Gulf.

Sheridan regarded Throckmorton as "disloyal" and reports of frontier atrocities as ploys to get the troops out of the interior and posted where frontier settlers would find a market for their products with army contractors. President Johnson proved more sympathetic, and he urged that the regulars in Texas be transferred to the frontier as soon as possible. At once Sheridan ordered two cavalry regiments to the frontier and promised that all the frontier forts would be garrisoned in the spring of 1867. "Now, as I have ordered to the frontier double the number of men the legislature thought necessary," he telegraphed the governor on November 11, 1866, "I cannot see any good excuse for the employment of this volunteer force."[14]

Replacing presidential Reconstruction, congressional Reconstruction armed the generals with new military powers. On July 30, 1867, Sheridan deposed Governor Throckmorton and appointed Elisha M. Pease provisional governor. Leader of the Radical Unionists bested by Throckmorton in the election of 1866, Pease was a widely respected Texan who had served as governor in 1853–1857. He worked closely with Sheridan's successor, Brevet Major General Joseph J. Reynolds, to reconstruct Texas and strengthen frontier defenses.

Sheridan's quick dispatch of cavalry to the frontier in the winter of 1866–1867 helped defuse the Ranger issue. By the middle of 1867, 1,500 cavalrymen in three regiments garrisoned eleven frontier forts. Another 726 soldiers held the four posts on the Rio Grande border. Deployed on Reconstruction duty, 1,442 officers and enlisted men, nearly all infantry, manned twenty-two stations in the interior. The postwar regulars, however, had no better success than their prewar counterparts at keeping raiders out of the settlements.[15]

Frontier defense lay at the margins of the political struggles wracking Texas for the two years of the Pease–Reynolds regime. Not until January 1870 could General Reynolds declare a new constitution ratified and

Radical Republican Edmund J. Davis elected governor. Reynolds summoned the newly elected legislature in February to ratify the Fourteenth and Fifteenth Amendments to the U.S. Constitution and select U.S. senators. On March 30, 1870, President Ulysses S. Grant signed the act readmitting Texas to the Union.

The end of Reconstruction did not end the raging controversies that had divided Texans since 1865. The Radical Republican administration of Edmund J. Davis, a prominent Texan who had commanded Texas troops fighting for the Union, stirred as much rancor, conflict, and violence as Reconstruction. For all its immersion in the momentous issues that split Texans, however, the Davis administration did not neglect frontier defense.

BY 1870, FRONTIER SETTLERS complained of a double grievance. Not only did the federal defense line fail to safeguard settlers from Indian raids, but the federal government itself provided the Kiowas and Comanches with a base of operations. Chiefs of both tribes had made their marks on the Medicine Lodge Treaty of 1867, by which they pledged to settle their people on a reservation in the Indian Territory, accept a bounteous array of gifts from the Great Father, and learn to support themselves by farming. Under President Grant's Peace Policy, pacifist Quaker agents set forth to transform their charges into imitation whites.

For the Kiowa and Comanche tribes, however, aggressions against the Texas frontier settlements had become a cultural imperative. Aspiring young men organized war parties to sweep down the edges of settlement, killing and pillaging. If successful, they returned home not only with loot but, more importantly, with fresh war honors. Women, children, and men too old for the warpath paid them homage. The trail to stature and leadership in the tribe began on the Texas frontier. These Indians still looked on Americans and Texans as different people, and they saw no inconsistency in signing treaties with the Americans while continuing to war on the Texans. Even when they tried, chiefs could not prevent young warriors from seeking glory to the south.

Only Red River separated the Kiowa–Comanche reservation from Texas, and far from diminishing, the pace of aggressions quickened. The Peace Policy allowed troops in Texas to attack raiders in Texas but barred them from crossing Red River onto the reservation. The big garrison at Fort Sill watched over the reservation itself but could act only on application of the agent—one whose religious scruples enjoined nonviolence. Truly, as Texans charged, Fort Sill became a city of refuge, where warriors received government supplies and protection while resting between raids.[16]

As Red River shielded the Kiowas and Comanches, even more infuriatingly the Rio Grande shielded Lipans and Kickapoos. All across South Texas, to the very outskirts of San Antonio, these Indians ran off horses and cattle by the hundreds and left dead or wounded any Texan who got in their way. For U.S. troops, of course, the Rio Grande presented an even more formidable barrier than Red River.[17]

The Texas constitution of 1868 centralized government and armed it with strong powers. Edmund Davis, swept into the governorship by the black vote and polls closely watched by federal troops, made full use of his powers to impose imperious rule on Texas. A supportive legislature gave him a state police force with the muscle to combat crime and violence and a state militia that he could mobilize to clamp martial law on recalcitrant localities.

A product of the frontier himself, Davis felt a keen obligation to the anguished frontier families. At his behest, on June 13, 1870, the legislature authorized him to muster, for twelve months' service, twenty companies of Texas Rangers—the second appearance of the term in law. As usual, Rangers would provide their own horses, six-shooters, accouterments, and camp equipage. For the first time, however, the shoulder arm—breech-loading cavalry carbines—would be purchased by the state, issued to the Rangers, and the cost deducted from the first pay. And pay was promised, from $100 a month for captains to $50 for privates. The state would furnish provisions, ammunition, and forage. Although organized under the rules and regulations of the U.S. Army, the Rangers would always operate under state control, reporting to an adjutant general authorized by the militia act.[18]

The enabling legislation remained silent on how to pay for what came to be known as the Frontier Forces. However, on August 5, 1870, the legislature resorted to the novel expedient of floating $750,000 in state bonds, with interest at 7 percent, payable in gold twice a year. These Frontier Defense Bonds would be redeemable in twenty years and paid off in forty.[19]

With pay and logistical support promised, Ranger companies came together swiftly. Governor Davis appointed the captains, mostly solid Unionists with solid Ranger credentials. By the end of 1870, fourteen companies had been organized and posted at key locations on the frontier. The full twenty never took shape, but for the first time since 1865 Texas Rangers patrolled the frontier.[20]

The U.S. War Department lost little more than a month in reacting to the advent of Texas Rangers. On July 19 William W. Belknap, secretary of war, declared that the state of Texas would not be allowed to make war on the Indians, that the U.S. military authorities would preserve the peace. The U.S. military authorities, of course, had signally failed to preserve the peace. No matter what the secretary of war decreed, the state of Texas would make war on the Indians.[21]

Davis's Texas Rangers performed exceptionally well. Their record is especially impressive in view of the short time allotted them. They began to deploy in the autumn of 1870, and the last company was mustered out in June 1871. Such was the state's credit rating that the bonds that were to pay for them proved unmarketable. The state treasury could not sustain Davis's expensive programs, and frontier defense was among the first casualties. Despite their achievements, the Davis Rangers dropped from memory, buried by the fulminations of early Texas historians against the iniquities of the Davis regime.[22]

Two captains proved particularly capable and energetic: John W. Sansom, a rancher and farmer from the Hill Country north of San Antonio, and Captain H. J. Richarz, a veteran of Prussian military service who established himself as a sheep and cattle grower west of San

Antonio. Two companies stood out as distinctive if not wholly unprecedented. Composed of Mexican Americans, Captain Cesario G. Falcón's unit took station on the lower Rio Grande while Captain Gregorio García's formed around distant El Paso.

Sansom sheltered his men in the crumbling buildings of old Camp Verde, in strategic Bandera Pass, while Richarz moved into the dilapidated remains of prewar Fort Inge (present Uvalde), long used as hog and cattle pens. Thanks largely to the drive of these captains, the frontier from the mouth of the Pecos to Laredo came under closer scrutiny than ever before. Constant and thorough scouting curtailed Indian raids and gave stockmen of the Nueces and Frio ranges a new sense of security.

Still, the work was frustrating because of the sanctuary across the Rio Grande. "If it were not for this cursed international law," Richarz proclaimed, "I know very well what to do to clean out these bloody savages on the other side of the Rio Grande."[23]

Rigorous scouting for Indian trails uncovered a class of depredation the Rangers had not been formed to combat but that would increasingly preoccupy them for decades to come: cattle theft.

Cattle raising in Texas south of the Nueces dated from Spanish times and endured even after Anglo stockmen such as Richard King began to displace the descendants of the original grantees. North of the Nueces, cattlemen began moving onto the grasslands south and west of San Antonio after the Mexican War. Central to both Mexican and Anglo practice was the free-ranging longhorn, a robust and prolific beast that multiplied enormously during the wartime years when men lay down their branding irons and shouldered muskets. Returning from the war, stockmen found the ranges swarming with thousands of unbranded longhorns as well as hundreds of would-be stockmen and freebooters of less respectable intent. By 1870 cattlemen with branded herds of longhorns and squads of cowboys to handle them curved west and north from San Antonio to the headwaters of the Llano River. South of the Nueces, a land of defined though unfenced ranches, vaqueros managed branded herds in much the same fashion as they had for more than a century. Texas beef emerged as a profitable commodity, especially after trail drives north to the railroads connected the longhorns with lucrative northern markets.[24]

From the beginning of their service, the two companies stationed on the lower Rio Grande dealt almost solely with cow theft. Indian raiders seldom found their way that far down the river, but Mexican bandits constantly stole from ranchers on the Texas side. Captain Cesario Falcón in Starr County and Captain Bland Chamberlain in Zapata County campaigned tirelessly and sometimes successfully. By giving special attention to the wants of Richard King, they laid the groundwork for an enduring relationship. In 1853 King had begun to acquire Mexican land titles, and by his death in 1885 he reigned over a ranching domain of more than 600,000 acres, extending from the Nueces all the way to the Rio Grande. Richard King was a generous friend of the Texas Rangers, and the King Ranch enjoyed their grateful vigilance well into the twentieth century.

On the northwestern frontier, the Kiowas and Comanches also found the new Rangers worthy foes. Honors for the hardest fight fell to Sergeant Edward H. Cobb of Captain David P. Baker's company, posted to cover the favorite Indian crossings of Red River in Montague County. Early in February 1871 Kiowas and Comanches raided down Clear Creek, on the open prairies northwest of Denton. With ten men Cobb hit the trail at once and overtook the quarry. With superior numbers, the warriors charged time and again. At close quarters, the six-shooters and Winchester repeating carbines of the Rangers stood them off and killed both the Kiowa and the Comanche chief. The Indians abandoned the field, leaving Cobb's battered little force with several wounded but none dead. An examination of the battlefield the next morning disclosed the bodies of six slain Indians.[25]

"All the citizens say with one accord, and proudly too, they never saw Rangers like these, to contend with such great odds," Cobb's lieutenant reported. For so few, youthful, and inexperienced men to stand up to four times their number of seasoned Indian warriors was extraordinary.

The adjutant general published general orders holding up Cobb as an example for all Texas Rangers.[26]

Overshadowing Cobb's desperate fight and all other Ranger activities in the northwest was another raid, on May 18, 1871. Satanta, the leading Kiowa war chief, led a hundred warriors into Jack County. On Salt Creek Prairie, about eight miles southwest of Jacksboro and the federal post of Fort Richardson, the raiders watched the road to Fort Griffin. They let a small train escorted by soldiers pass, then fell on Henry Warren's train of ten freight wagons, butchering seven of the twelve teamsters as the rest ran to safety.

The train spared by Satanta, at the urging of a medicine man who predicted richer prey on the way, bore none other than General William Tecumseh Sherman, come to see for himself whether Texans exaggerated the Indian menace. Furious, Sherman at once fielded the Fort Richardson cavalry, under the aggressive Colonel Ranald S. Mackenzie, while he himself stormed off to Fort Sill to confront the chiefs. In a tense confrontation that almost erupted in violence, Sherman had Satanta, Satank, and Big Tree seized and packed off to Jacksboro to stand civil trial for murder. En route, Satank tried to escape and was killed, but the other two, convicted of murder, faced the hangman's noose.

The Jacksboro affair convinced Sherman and prompted some vigorous campaigning by Mackenzie, but it did not dismantle the Fort Sill city of refuge. Champions of the Peace Policy pressed Governor Davis to commute the sentences of the two Kiowas and ultimately to pardon them. Henceforth raiders would proceed more warily, but they would not quit tormenting the Texas frontier.[27]

With the termination of the Frontier Forces in June 1871, Texas Rangers no longer strove to head off Kiowas and Comanches. That mission remained with the federal troops, who did no better. As a substitute for the Rangers, in November 1871 the legislature authorized twenty-four companies of minutemen to serve for twelve months. The adjutant general convinced himself that the minutemen were more effective while less expensive.[28]

Less expensive they were, but whether more effective is arguable. Forgotten to history, the Frontier Forces of 1870–1871 played a brief but creditable role.

THE ADMINISTRATION OF Edmund J. Davis gained an infamy that embedded itself in the memory of generations of Anglo Texans. Among other transgressions, he used the state police and militia for partisan purposes. That both included blacks did not endear either to white citizens. Yet the state police made great strides in containing violence and crime in the interior counties, and the stubborn refusal of many Texans to accept the verdict of the Civil War invited heavy-handed measures.

Even with federal troops no longer acting as poll watchers and blacks increasingly intimidated, Davis hoped for a second term. As a harbinger, in 1872 the newly emergent Democrats gained control of the lower house of the legislature, and they promptly set about dismantling his programs. Among other measures, they abolished the state police and curtailed his control of the militia. The end came with the gubernatorial election of December 1873, in which Democrat Richard Coke overwhelmingly defeated Davis.

A staunch secessionist, member of the Secession Convention of 1861, and Confederate veteran, Richard Coke had altered his principles very little since the war. His election crushed Radical Republicanism, returned the state to the conservative Anglo Texan establishment, and began the process of undoing the aims of congressional Reconstruction.[29]

Whether conservative or radical, however, no governor could long ignore the appeals of the frontier settlers. In April 1874 the legislature once again dealt with this perennial issue.

[8]

Institutionalizing the Rangers, 1874

T HE MIDDLE 1870S MARKED a significant transition in the history of Texas. In trouncing Edmund Davis for the governorship in 1873, Richard Coke and his Southern Redeemers restored Texas safely to the Democratic fold for generations to come. The years of Radical Republican rule remained a bad memory. Democrats might fight among themselves, but they would never suffer their government to wield such powers as the constitution of 1869 conferred on Edmund Davis. In 1876 they adopted still another constitution, the third in a decade, which limited the state government so severely that it could hardly function. Reflecting the views of their constituents, legislators displayed an almost pathological obstinacy against levying taxes and spending money. Penury hung over every arm of government and every employee of the state.

The political resurrection of the Old South establishment failed to calm the passions of Civil War and Reconstruction. Rooted in the war, politics, financial and economic disputes, status of the freedmen, and even quarrels between families, feuds rocked Texas for a generation. Feudists and outlaws, sometimes the same, spawned violence that flamed beyond the control of local authorities. Davis's state police and militia no longer stood by to fight the flames.

Nor had the line of federal forts spared frontier citizens the continuing ravages of Indian raids. Kiowas and Comanches from the Fort Sill city of refuge stabbed at the settlements all the way from Red River to the Rio Grande, while Lipans and Kickapoos swept through South Texas from their sanctuaries in Mexico. In 1874 nearly five thousand U.S. soldiers—three regiments of cavalry and three of infantry—garrisoned fifteen posts in Texas. They campaigned energetically, scored occasional successes, but gave the frontier no greater security than their predecessors before the Civil War.[1]

Frontier defense thus stood high on the list of issues taken up by the legislature that convened in Austin early in 1874, shortly after Richard Coke established himself in the statehouse. In his first message to the legislature, the governor declared that the state must step in where the federal government had failed. He believed that the law of December 15, 1863, provided the model—the archaic formula of minute companies. Even as he spoke, minute companies called out by Governor Davis were demonstrating their inadequacy, lack of accountability, and drain on a treasury already virtually empty.[2]

The act that emerged from the legislature on April 10, 1874, went far beyond Coke's concept. It aimed not only at Indians but also at "Mexicans" and "other marauding or thieving parties." It thus reflected the rising concern of the lawmakers over the ever turbulent Rio Grande borderland and the disorder and violence rampant across the state, especially in the western counties.

In response to the governor's preference for minute companies, the first sections of the law authorized him to call out such units in any county he judged threatened. The men would furnish their own horse, accouterments, and six-shooter. The state would pay and supply the companies and issue a standard carbine whose cost would be deducted from the first pay.

Subsequent provisions of the act, however, shifted the emphasis away from minute companies. A battalion of six companies of seventy-five mounted men each would be assembled and placed under the governor's control. Like the minute companies, they would be paid and provisioned by the state but mounted and armed by the men themselves–the standard cavalry carbine to be furnished by the state and paid for by the men. The governor could do anything he wanted with this force, including disband and recall it, but clearly the legislature envisioned a permanent military force, the first line of defense. Only when the governor deemed it inadequate for frontier defense was he to call out minute companies, which would be "auxiliary and supplemental" to the battalion.

Although aimed chiefly at the Indian menace, the law provided tools to address the enlarged purpose envisioned by the legislators. It vested the officers both of the battalion and of the minute companies with all the powers of a peace officer and charged them with executing criminal process and arresting offenders against the laws of Texas.[3]

The law of 1874 thus contained two significant provisions that Governor Coke had not recommended–a permanent military force that was also a permanent law enforcement arm, under state rather than local control. Coke's subsequent pronouncements make it improbable that he urged such an expansion of scope. The initiative came from within the legislature. The record shows that the House and Senate dithered for nearly two months over minute companies. Not until the waning days of the session, in late March 1874, did Senator David B. Culberson offer the amendments that would establish a permanent military force. The House balked but in conference with the Senate agreed. Within four days the original bill had been drastically transformed, thanks, ironically, to a senator from Jefferson in far East Texas. Within a year, Culberson sat in the U.S. House of Representatives, where he represented his district for eleven terms. His son Charles later served as attorney general, governor, and U.S. senator.[4]

Unlike the acts of 1866 and 1870, the legislation did not label the new battalion "Texas Rangers," or anything else for that matter. It was simply a battalion of mounted men. Administratively, it became known as the

Frontier Battalion. Its personnel, however, called themselves Texas Rangers. So did the newspapers, and so did the people.

The Frontier Battalion institutionalized the Ranger service and ended the time of the citizen soldier. The Frontier Forces of 1870–1871 bridged the two eras, foreshadowing in law and practice the permanent unit created by the act of 1874. The second distinct period in the history of the Texas Rangers thus dates from 1874, when Texans fashioned a new organization and concept to replace the intermittent service of the citizen soldiers. As the man who laid the legislative foundation for the Frontier Battalion, David Culberson achieves high significance in the history of the Texas Rangers.

The Frontier Battalion and the minute companies fell under the jurisdiction of the state's adjutant general, who was also responsible for the militia. Coke named William Steele as his adjutant general. A West Point graduate, veteran of the Mexican War and frontier service in the prewar regular army, and successful Confederate general, Steele provided experienced and sympathetic oversight of the state's war on Indians and outlaws.

More than any other man, however, the Rangers owed their march toward institutional continuity to John B. Jones. Governor Coke had known him during the war and admired the courage, judgment, and military ability he had displayed as a Confederate officer. On May 2, 1874, Coke named Jones commander of the Frontier Battalion, with the rank of major.

Jones no more looked the part of Texas Ranger than Jack Hays. Spare of build (five-seven, 125 pounds, according to one of his Rangers), with high forehead, penetrating eyes, and drooping mustache, he dressed impeccably and sat on his horse erectly. He was forty in 1874, a bachelor, dignified and humorless, religious, a user of neither tobacco nor alcohol, soft-spoken, courteous, kindly, and determined to fashion an organization capable of carrying out its assigned mission.[5]

Indefatigable, Jones succeeded in asserting mastery over administrative, logistical, financial, and political concerns in Austin while exercising operational control of his companies and riding the frontier several times a year. Without ever assembling the battalion, he at once posted the five companies, lettered A through E, at strategic points. He then rode from one to the next making clear what he expected. Although the governor named the first captains, most turned out to be able leaders. Those found wanting did not last long.

Major Jones reshaped the Texas Ranger tradition without destroying it. Rangers still provided their own horses and arms. They still wore no uniforms. They still enjoyed an easy camaraderie with one another and with their officers. Yet they were no longer citizen soldiers springing to arms to meet a threat, then returning to their homes; they were men recruited to serve as long as the money held out, up to four years according to law, one year by administrative decision. They were, in short, a special breed of soldier, drawn not just from the frontier but from anywhere in the state and trained in the hard school of experience. Despite informal relationships within a company, moreover, they served in a plainly military organization, one in which Jones insisted on system, order, discipline, subordination, accountability, and diligent performance of the mission.

Ranger service offered a rugged outdoor life, and more excitement and adventure than it actually delivered. It also offered pay. It attracted good men and bad, though more of the former than the latter. The roster of officers bore the names of a few who failed to rise to Major Jones's standards but a surprisingly large cadre who upheld the Ranger tradition of strong leadership rather than strict command.

The men came mostly from the western counties, although few boasted frontier experience. On the whole, they were unmarried young men in search of adventure or merely a job. They turned in a commendable performance. The best, of course, developed under the best captains. Budgetary constraints produced enough reductions in the battalion that at each reorganization captains discharged everyone and reenlisted only the best. Even so, men sometimes went to town, got drunk, flourished their six-shooters, and on occasion joined with the cowboys in shooting up the place. Some men also sowed dissension and discontent within the company and resisted the discipline and subordination Jones demanded. He met such misbehavior with dishonorable discharges.

If not already proficient, recruits quickly learned horsemanship, marksmanship, how to pack mules and wagons, and how to function in the outdoors. They passed most of their days on horseback and many of their nights under the sky, with saddle for pillow and blanket to ward off the cold and the frequent drenching downpours. In camp they lived under canvas and cooked over a fire. Jones contracted for their staples, such as beef, flour, salt, and sugar; but they provided much of their own fare—deer, turkey, and other game brought down with their own arms, catfish hooked in the pools and eddies of streams, honey garnered from bee trees, pecans, wild berries, and other fruits of the land.[6]

In keeping with tradition, the Ranger dressed as he pleased. "He usually wears heavy woolen clothes of any color that strikes his fancy," explained James B. Gillett. "Some are partial to corduroy suits, while others prefer buckskin. A felt hat of any make and color completes his outfit. While riding, a ranger always wears spurs and very high-heeled boots to prevent his foot from slipping through the stirrup, for both the ranger and the cowboy ride with the stirrup in the middle of the foot." Most horsemen, including cavalrymen, used a leather-hooded stirrup in which the sole of the foot bore most of the weight. Rangers wore no badge but, as the need for identification became apparent, received a documentary "descriptive list" of features of appearance.[7]

Carbine or rifle and pistol armed the Ranger, at his own expense. At first the state insisted on the Sharps carbine, a heavy, single-shot, .50-caliber shoulder arm favored by buffalo hunters. But the lighter Winchester, a .44-caliber repeater holding twelve rounds as a carbine and fifteen as a rifle, swiftly gained such favor that the state relented and abandoned the Sharps. The standard six-shooter was still the Colt, though a great technological leap from the heavy Walker Colt of 1847. Gone from both shoulder and hand guns were the old paper cartridges ignited by a percussion cap. Rim-fire metallic cartridges replaced them in the 1860s, and the more powerful center-fire in 1873. By 1877 most Rangers carried the Winchester '73 ("the gun that won the West") and the Colt '73–the Army Colt, or "Peacemaker." A looped belt distributed cartridges around the waist and supported revolver and Bowie knife in leather scabbards.[8]

Rangers spent more time in the field than in camp. In camp they indulged a variety of amusements. They played cards, hunted and fished, read books and magazines, raced horses, and sat around campfires telling tall tales. Seldom, however, were many in camp at the same time. Captains kept details constantly on the prowl for Indian trails and evidence of criminal wrongdoing and let few leads pass unnoticed. Days of exhausting trailing more often than not ended with broken down horses or trails obliterated by rain or rocky terrain. "No pace is too quick, no task too difficult or too hazardous," recalled Ranger Gillett with a touch of hyperbole. "Night and day will the ranger trail his prey, through rain and shine." Scores of official reports document the truth of Gillett's appraisal.[9]

HARDLY TWO MONTHS after assuming command of the Frontier Battalion, Major Jones got his first taste of Indian fighting. With an escort drawn from several companies, he rode the northwestern frontier. On July 12, 1874, while he inspected the company of Captain G. W. Stevens near Fort Belknap, a scouting party turned up a broad trail of about fifty Indians heading southeast down Salt Creek. With Stevens, the lieutenant commanding the escort, and thirty-three Rangers drawn from both company and escort, Jones himself got on the trail.

Comanche raiders had made the trail. Two days earlier they had attacked the ranch of Oliver Loving and killed one of his hands. But on the western rim of Lost Valley, a grassy, mesquite-dappled basin rimmed by rocky mountains, the Comanche trail lost itself in another. A large Kiowa war party led by Mamanti and Lone Wolf had ridden south on a raid aimed at revenge for the death of Lone Wolf's son in an earlier raid. From the heights west of Lost Valley, they spotted the Rangers and threw out a decoy to lure them into the valley.

Jones and his men were new to the ways of the Plains Indians. They galloped into the valley and into the ambush Mamanti had prepared.

Jones kept his head and provided an example of courage and cool deliberation that braced his men. He ordered them to cut their way through a weak part of the Kiowa circle and take positions in a shallow, brushy gully. One man died and another was wounded in the thrust. For the rest of the afternoon, the two sides exchanged long-range fire. Thirst plagued the Rangers, but Jones would not let anyone ride to Cameron Creek, about a mile to the north. Even so, as dusk settled on the valley and no Indians could be seen, two men set forth with canteens. They fell victim to another ambush and spurred their mounts to escape. One made it, but a warrior dashed on David Bailey and unhorsed him with a lance. Lone Wolf himself exacted his revenge by smashing Bailey's skull and dismembering his body.

Major Jones portrayed the Lost Valley fight as a victory, in which the Rangers had driven the Indians from the field in disorder. He reported three Indians killed and three wounded and the raiders turned back from their plundering mission. He estimated his enemies at 150, both Kiowas and Comanches, all equipped with breech-loading arms. In the Kiowa version of the battle, by contrast, the Indians suffered no casualties, did not even know Comanches were in the area, and were on a revenge raid, not a plundering raid. In their view, they had twice outwitted the Texans, killed two, dealt the others a sound thrashing, and gained the vengeance they sought.[10]

A neophyte at Indian warfare, Jones probably believed that he had driven the enemy from the field and won a victory. Although the Kiowa account seems closer to the truth, Texans accepted Jones's interpretation, and Lost Valley helped validate the existence of the Frontier Battalion. Beyond dispute is the major's bravery and leadership once battle was joined. As one Ranger observed, "We in truth had an officer in whom we could put the utmost confidence in all cases of emergency." Moreover, he added, "ranging is a glorious thing when you learn to like it."[11]

Unknown to Jones and his comrades, Lost Valley coincided with developments that would have a significant effect on the mission of the Frontier Battalion. General Sherman finally convinced policy makers that he could not defend the Texas frontier so long as the Peace Policy barred military operations on the reservations. Eight days after Lost Valley, on July 20, 1874, Sherman telegraphed General Philip H. Sheridan to turn loose the troops. The city of refuge collapsed.

As tribal peace factions clung to their agencies, nearly five thousand Kiowas, Comanches, and Cheyennes fled west, to the upper reaches of the Washita and Red Rivers. From forts in Kansas, the Indian Territory, Texas, and New Mexico, five strong columns converged on the Texas Panhandle. In half a dozen engagements, troops clashed with warriors, most notably on September 28, when Colonel Ranald S. Mackenzie fell on a Comanche village in Palo Duro Canyon. Dispirited groups began to drift into the agencies and surrender. Others remained out. So did Colonel Nelson A. Miles, whose foot soldiers combed the snowy plains all winter, keeping the quarry on the run and tormented by constant insecurity. By the spring of 1875, the war had ended in the surrender of nearly all the holdouts. The principal leaders were shipped into exile in Florida. Satanta returned to the Texas Penitentiary in Huntsville, where in 1878 he threw himself to his death from the second floor of the prison hospital.[12]

The Red River War of 1874–1875 crushed the southern Plains tribes. Never again did they contest federal control. Texas farmers and ranchers enjoyed a security unknown for half a century. Within a year, cowmen such as Charles Goodnight had moved their herds to the vast table of the Staked Plain, flinging the Texas frontier westward into New Mexico.

The conquest of the Kiowas and Comanches greatly simplified the Indian mission of the Frontier Battalion, but it did not mark the end of ranging against Indians. For several years, thieving parties occasionally slipped across Red River, keeping the Rangers alert and providing them with trails to follow and an occasional skirmish to report for the edification of the legislature. In South Texas, the ravages of Lipans and Kickapoos had subsided, the result of a bold foray into Mexico in 1873 by Colonel Mackenzie. By 1876, however, they had resumed. In a few years, as the frontier moved to the deserts and mountains west of the Pecos

River, the Rangers would find themselves contending with Mescalero Apaches based in another "city of refuge."

THE RED RIVER WAR coincided with the rising importance of the second mission the authors of the act of 1874 had foreseen—law enforcement. Despite the explicit language of the act, Governor Coke seems never to have viewed the Frontier Battalion as lawmen. A state police, conjuring all the horrors of the Davis regime, could not even be contemplated. He seems never to have recognized that he commanded a police force with statewide powers. When appeals for state help in combating lawlessness piled up on his desk, he could think only in terms of minutemen. By the end of 1874, however, the Frontier Battalion had already begun the shift from Indian fighting to law enforcement. Major Jones made it official in March 1877 with an order to discontinue Indian scouting and concentrate on the suppression of lawlessness and crime in the frontier counties and along the cattle trails to the north.[13]

As lawmen, however, the Frontier Battalion labored under handicaps that never restrained Davis's state police. In this realm, the county sheriff remained dominant. Steele and Jones repeatedly emphasized that Rangers must act only at the behest of and in support of local authorities, a limitation that often proved crippling and that made the force reactive rather than proactive. In Governor Coke's mind, the supremacy of county authority, reflecting the minuteman concept, may have rationalized the employment of Rangers as lawmen.

Even so, in the course of reacting, the Rangers sought fugitives wanted elsewhere. Their principal tool was the Fugitive List, otherwise known as the Black Book, Bible II, or Book of Knaves. Developed by Steele and Jones in 1876, it contained information about men wanted by Texas sheriffs and lawmen in other states and territories. It named fugitives and their offenses, listed rewards, and often contained helpful personal hints, such as "knock-kneed," "a little hump-shouldered," and "laughs without expression." Each Ranger carried a copy, often bearing his own annotations in the margins. Although incomplete and in places misleading, the Fugitive List served a valuable purpose to generations of Rangers.[14]

By all odds the most formidable challenge to the Rangers was cattle theft. By 1876, herds had not only begun to range the Panhandle but grazed the headwaters of the Llano and Concho Rivers high on the Edwards Plateau. From the counties southeast of San Antonio to the Rio Grande and the Pecos, and from Fort Worth to the New Mexico boundary, the cattle industry boomed. So did cattle theft. Thieves either slaughtered the animals solely for their hides or altered the brands and slipped them into herds trailing north to the railroads for shipment east.

Jones's Rangers made little headway against cattle rustling. Not that they lacked diligence or failed to round up many a rustler. The reason lay in the almost complete absence of authority in the afflicted counties. The number of men who preyed on legitimate ranchers was huge. They intimidated sheriffs, prosecutors, judges, jurors, and witnesses. They bought off or installed their own lackeys as county officials. Sometimes they had to do neither, for frontier sheriffs, prosecutors, or judges could be incompetents, drunkards, or both.

Complicating Ranger efforts, feeble county authority led stockmen to take the law into their own hands. For more than a century, vigilantism had moved west with the frontier, from the Appalachians across the Mississippi onto the Great Plains and with the gold rush to California. It had risen in East Texas during the years of the republic. Wherever courts and local officials proved powerless, the pioneer elite took the lead in organizing to rid society of threats to life and property by the most direct means—rope or bullet. San Francisco and Montana afforded classic examples, but nearly every western state and territory gave birth to vigilante movements. Nowhere did it flourish as widely or long as in Texas, nor with such harm to the very purpose that inspired it.[15]

Rangers often encountered vigilantes, sometimes on the trail of rustlers but sometimes bent on nefarious schemes of their own. Who was and who was not a cow thief usually lay in the eye of the beholder. The "cow thief" reported by Sergeant Jacob Hand in June 1876 may have been one, or he may simply have been someone the vigilantes wished to push off the range. The man, wrote the sergeant, "had formed a connection with a limb of a tree, as he was found suspended by the neck," leading Hand to "suppose he intended to avoid the law and succeeded admirably."[16]

In short, hamstrung by vigilantes and impotent local authority, Rangers made many arrests but secured almost no convictions. If arrested, criminals might not even be received by the sheriff. If received, they might be discharged for lack of evidence. If jailed, they might be broken out by their friends or by vigilantes intent on forming connections with tree limbs. If indicted, they might never come to trial. If tried, they were likely to be found innocent for want of convincing evidence. If convicted, they might escape, usually with the aid of friends or the connivance of jailors.

The most severe setback the Frontier Battalion suffered in its war on crime (and Indians), however, sprang from the miserly legislature. The act of 1874 carried an appropriation of $300,000 for frontier defense. Coke called up several of the minute companies he so favored, paying for them from the frontier defense appropriation. By December 1874, Jones knew that the money would run out before the end of the fiscal year. Rather than disband the battalion altogether, he cut it from 470 to 200, with each company authorized one lieutenant and thirty men. Even then, the money ran out, and Jones persuaded a skeleton force to serve without pay in the expectation that the legislature, when it finally convened, would make good.

Never did the battalion escape severe blows from the budget ax, wielded mainly by representatives of the eastern counties who had little interest in the frontier. Never did the battalion achieve the strength authorized by the act of 1874. By late 1875, it had stabilized at five companies consisting of a captain and twenty men each, with one serving as Jones's personal escort.[17]

VIOLENCE AND LAWLESSNESS afflicted not only the counties springing up in the wake of the westward moving frontier. From the end of the Civil War until at least the close of the nineteenth century, Anglo Texans were an uncommonly violent people, addicted as were few other Americans to tumultuous feuding. Such clashes pitted family clan against family clan, political faction against political faction, Anglos against Mexicans, whites against blacks, haves against have-nots, cattlemen against sheepmen, vigilante mobs against the unwanted, "good people" against "desperadoes"–the last two labels of ever shifting content. "I'll die before I'll run" aptly characterizes a Texas bubbling with a volatile mix of southern honor, western independence, ethnic hostility, copious whiskey, and ample firepower readily summoned to a righteous or expedient cause. Many of the Frontier Battalion's challenges traced roots to such feuds.[18]

Ironically, in contrast to the gun-toting freedom of later generations, Texans carried arms at their peril. The constitutions of 1866, 1869, and 1875, echoing earlier charters, guaranteed the right of citizens to bear arms, "but the legislature shall have the power by law to regulate the wearing of arms with a view to prevent crime." This the legislature did, in strings of verbiage that in effect banned all weapons, including Bowie knives and even sword canes. Unmentioned were shoulder arms, and exempted were law officers and the citizens of frontier counties identified by gubernatorial proclamation as threatened by Indians. Embedded in the penal codes of 1871 and 1879, the prohibition gave peace officers a convenient pretext for arrest but scarcely cleansed Texans of their private arsenals.[19]

IN THE AUTUMN OF 1875 Jones literally rode into the first challenge to his lawman skills. He and his escort were en route to probe the little-known country west of the Pecos River. A courier from Austin overtook them with word that Mason County had blown up, showering Governor Coke with entreaties for help. Jones, then on the upper Guadalupe, canceled his plans and with twenty men of his escort headed for Mason.[20]

Mason County lay among the grassy hills cut by the upper Llano River and its tributaries, its county seat forty-two miles northwest of Fredericksburg. This was fine cattle country, and nearly everyone was a stockman. About 75 percent of the people were Germans, heavily Unionist during the Civil War. The minority "American" element truculently flaunted their Confederate heritage.

Although not entirely innocent themselves, the Germans rightly complained of widespread American tampering with their herds. With the probable complicity of their sheriff, John Clark, in February 1875 they launched a vigilante operation. A spate of killings and lynchings followed. One of the victims, Tim Williamson, had reared an orphan waif named Scott Cooley. He grew up a stocky, dark-complexioned man who served a hitch in the Rangers. Now he farmed near Menardville, on the San Saba River northwest of Mason.

Burning for revenge, Cooley rode down to Mason and compiled a list of the posse members who had arrested Williamson and then killed him. Heading the list was Deputy Sheriff John Wohrle. Cooley caught him digging a well, filled him with lead, and scalped him. At Loyal Valley (also known as Cold Spring) he recruited a small gang.

On September 28, 1875, Major Jones and his twenty Rangers passed through Loyal Valley, crossed the Llano, and approached Keller's store on the north bank. Suddenly fifteen to twenty men rose from behind a stone fence and leveled Winchesters at them. Jones quickly established his identity, and Sheriff Clark came forward to explain that his posse had gathered in response to reports that Cooley followers were riding up from Loyal Valley to "burn out the Dutch." Jones turned back to Loyal Valley to investigate. Finding the village tense but quiet, he rode into Mason the next day.

There Jones discovered that Cooley and three comrades had been in town while the sheriff and his men tarried at Keller's store. Only hours earlier, on the Mason town square, they had shotgunned another leader of the German faction. Earlier they had erased still another name from their list. They had burst into his kitchen as he set the breakfast table for his family, riddled him with bullets, then ate their own breakfast in the town's hotel dining room. There they boasted loudly that they had "made beef of Cheney and if somebody did not bury him he would stink."

For the next several weeks, Jones's patrols scoured the county for the murderers, without success. As his captains had already discovered, however, the mere presence of Rangers calmed a turbulent community even while failing to get at the root of the troubles. Rightly considering himself a marked man, Sheriff Clark resigned and vanished. Cooley and his confederates likewise left the county.

By the end of October, Jones concluded that the time had come for him to move on. He had intended to leave Dan Roberts's company to keep the peace. But Cooley had served in that company and still counted many friends in it, and they showed no enthusiasm for the chase. Instead, Jones left thirty men from his own escort company under Lieutenant Ira Long. They had only recently been recruited elsewhere and had no stake in the feud. Jones summed up the results of his month in Mason: twenty-two arrests, not a single killing since his arrival, and "a perfect quiet" reigning throughout the county.[21]

Adjutant General Steele had his own summary, a reflection less on Jones and his Rangers than on the machinery of justice in Texas. In Mason County, Steele wrote, murder committed in open day light, in the presence of numerous witnesses, was ignored by the grand jury, which explained that "they had not time to examine into the many cases." Therefore, they found no indictments, and the Rangers had to release their prisoners.[22]

JOHN B. JONES shared the beginnings of a new Ranger era with an even more improbable figure than he. As a short, lean youth of seventeen, Leander H. McNelly had joined the Confederate Army in 1861 and made such a name for himself as a scout and partisan that he emerged a battle-tested, battle-scarred captain at war's end. In 1870–1873 he left his farm and family near Brenham to serve effectively as one of the four captains of Governor Davis's hated state police. Despite the Radical Republican taint, his wartime and police record commended him to Adjutant General Steele, who probably had known him during the war. In July 1874, with the most violent feud in Texas history ravaging DeWitt County, southeast of San Antonio, Steele asked McNelly to raise a company of fifty volunteer militia in his home county, Washington, who could restore order without becoming entangled with either faction. Without legislative sanction, therefore, the governor exercised his command of the militia to create a special body of lawmen.[23]

Despite its unusual origin, McNelly's Company A, Volunteer Militia of Washington County, compared in most essentials to the companies of the Frontier "Battalion. The men regarded themselves as Rangers, and so did the public—"McNelly's Rangers."

In one respect, however, no other company resembled McNelly's Rangers—the captain himself. A full brown beard and brushy mustache failed to offset the gaunt face and frail body. Although wracked by tuberculosis, Leander McNelly possessed in full measure the ingredients of leadership that had endowed the great captains of the past. As one of his recruits recalled, "The way Captain fixed control over this bunch can't be told. I still don't know how he did it, but he did. One thing, he didn't waste a word or a move. He appeared to know exactly what he wanted to do and how to go about doing it. I got the feeling that here was a man who could tell you what to do and you'd do it and never have any suspicion that he might be wrong."[24]

In still another way McNelly's Rangers differed from Jones's. Most came from Washington County and so knew one another and their captain. They were proud of his war record, proud to serve in his company, proud that he enjoyed the confidence of the governor and the adjutant general, and instantly obedient to his every command.

The crisis that brought McNelly to DeWitt County was the Sutton–Taylor feud. By 1874 it had spun completely out of control. In the simplest view, the Sutton crowd represented the excesses of Reconstruction authorities and Davis's state police. On the other side was the sprawling Taylor clan, two generations and their kin by marriage, belligerently independent and unrepentantly southern. By 1874 terror, violence, killings, and lynchings, combined with stock theft, swept the county and reduced local authority to impotence. Governor Coke sent Adjutant General Steele to investigate in person. Within four days of his return, Coke called on Leander McNelly to organize the Washington County volunteers and ride down to DeWitt County to restore order.[25]

On August 1, 1874, McNelly led his company into Clinton, seat of DeWitt County, located on the west bank of the tree-shaded Guadalupe River. District court convened on the third, with the grand jury expected to hand down murder indictments of men of both factions. "A perfect reign of terror existed in this and adjoining counties," McNelly reported.[26]

"The men of both factions are men accustomed to righting their own wrongs," observed one of McNelly's Rangers, "and they object decidedly to any interference, even should that interference be lawful."[27] And therein lay the dilemma that confronted a generation of Rangers. McNelly could interfere lawfully only under the auspices of the local authorities, and "with the present incumbents," he concluded, "there is no hope."[28] Through the fall months, his Rangers patrolled constantly, paying special attention to the "grog shops," which kept feudists and wanted fugitives off balance and on the run. The December court term passed quietly, in part, according to McNelly, because the district attorney "is drunk most of the time & when sober is of no earthly account."[29]

McNelly did nothing to end the Sutton–Taylor feud; it had not run its course. His operations in DeWitt County restored a measure of order that only his continued presence could guarantee. The state, however, could scarcely be expected to maintain a nearly idle Ranger company indefinitely in one county. McNelly's men had been mustered for six months, and if the Sutton–Taylor feud remained dormant they could expect to go back home to Washington County early in 1875.

Another crisis saved them from discharge.

[9]

McNelly and Hall:
Border Adventures

O N MARCH 26, 1875, a gang of about thirty Mexicans cut a destructive swath through the outlying districts of Corpus Christi, robbing travelers, looting and burning stores, and killing five citizens. One
of their own, shot and left behind, told the Nueces County sheriff that
the robbers had traveled from Mexico in small parties, then ren-
dezvoused just before the raid. They had intended to sack the city
itself, but not enough men had shown up to make that possible. The
raiders swiftly disappeared into Mexico; but furious townsmen lynched
the prisoner and then set forth in a revenge raid, cloaked as a vigilante
pursuit of hide thieves, that fell indiscriminately on rural Mexican
Americans.[1]

Neither Steele nor Governor Coke could ignore the appeals from
Corpus Christi. On March 31 McNelly's company was mustered out of
the state service and on April 1 mustered back in. The next day, by command of the governor, Steele issued orders directing McNelly to march
at once to Corpus Christi "for service against the armed bands of Mexican marauders infesting the region between the Nueces and the Mexican Boundary."[2]

The border had long generated its own strife, but rarely had it roiled north as far as Corpus Christi. The political fallout of so bold a sally probably had as much to do with the new mission assigned McNelly as a compelling need on the Rio Grande. As elsewhere, the mere presence of Rangers curtailed the depredations of stock thieves, whether Mexican or Anglo. In May 1874 Governor Coke had responded to a similar plea from Corpus Christi by calling out a minute company under Captain Warren Wallace. It had accomplished its purpose but behaved so ruthlessly against Mexican residents of Texas that an officer and some men wound up in court charged with murder and robbery, and in September Steele disbanded the company. With one of the best companies of the Frontier Battalion, Captain Neal Coldwell took Wallace's place. Neither he nor aggressively scouting federal troops from Fort Brown and Ringgold Barracks could discover evidence of unusual stock theft. "If we find thieves," Coldwell declared, "we have to go to the newspapers for them."[3]

Even so, informing the governor that a state of war existed between the "Mexican banditti" and the people of Texas, Steele dispatched McNelly to the Rio Grande and returned Coldwell's company to the Frontier Battalion. It is hard to view the exchange of companies in any other light than a well-publicized response to a political urgency.[4]

Some Texas beef had always found its way into Mexico, and the reports of Captain Coldwell indicated not that the traffic had stopped altogether but that it had greatly diminished because of his own operations and those of the errant Captain Wallace before him. One "contractor" who seems not to have been intimidated was none other than Juan Nepomuceno Cortina. Since his rebellion of 1859, he had risen amid the crosswinds of Mexican revolutionary politics to the governorship of Tamaulipas and a general's commission in the Mexican army. In 1875 he reigned as alcalde of Matamoros and headed an organized band of thieves who spirited Texas cattle and hides across the Rio Grande for speedy shipment to foreign ports.[5]

McNelly applied two techniques that Captain Coldwell had not. One, developed in DeWitt County, was a network of spies. Paid informants who blended with the population on the Mexican side kept him apprised of impending stock raids and other relevant intelligence. The other was a more direct means of extracting information from suspects who fell into his hands.[6]

McNelly's inquisitor, recently enlisted as a Ranger and employed as a scout and guide, was Jesús Sandoval–"Old Casuse," as the men knew him. A ranchero with a spread fifteen miles north of Brownsville, Sandoval had incurred the enmity of his countrymen across the river. "They say I am Americanized," he explained, "and consequently criminal." Efforts to kill him, burn him out, and run off his stock had driven him to the chaparral and fueled a passion for revenge against all bandits–a term he defined as loosely as did his captain.[7]

McNelly turned his captives over to Casuse. American citizens were freed, but "bandit spies" (how so determined remains unclear) suffered the standard treatment. Casuse slipped a noose around a prisoner's neck, threw the rope over a tree limb, and repeatedly hoisted him from the ground until he told all. "As far as we knew," recalled Ranger William Callicott, "this treatment always brought out the truth." The final phase, according to Callicott, was "to make the bandit get on Casuse's old paint horse, and stand up in the saddle. Casuse would then make the loose end of the rope fast, get behind his horse, hit him a hard lick and the horse would jump from under the spy, breaking his neck instantly."[8]

Early in June 1875, McNelly learned from his own spies that Cortina had contracted to furnish a shipload of cattle to a Cuban buyer. He also learned that the vessel could hold 250 more animals and that another raid could therefore be expected. Capturing two suspected thieves, McNelly applied the Casuse treatment to coerce the when and the where.

Instead of execution Casuse style, McNelly turned these particular spies over to the sheriff of Cameron County, and it may be doubted that Casuse ended his interrogations with a rope very often, if at all. That McNelly gained intelligence by unorthodox means, however, was confirmed by Brigadier General Edward O. C. Ord, the federal commander in Texas: "The officer of the State troops in command had learned the whereabouts of this raiding party by means which I could not legally resort to, but which were the only means of getting at the actual facts. He caught one of the number and had hung him up until he was made to confess where the rest of the raiders were."[9]

On June 12 the Ranger company closed on sixteen Mexicans and about three hundred cows on Palo Alto Prairie, scene of the Mexican War battle. The thieves corralled the herd on a small island in a salt marsh and spread out in a defensive line. Without firing a shot, McNelly's men urged their mounts slowly across the marsh and then charged. In a melee of individual encounters, the Rangers shot down every raider (although one managed to crawl to safety in the tall grass). A sheriff's posse identified the slain as Matamoros policemen and several as among Cortina's "favorite bravos." McNelly had the corpses stacked in Brownsville's public square as a lesson for the denizens of Matamoros, who loudly vowed revenge. McNelly's sole fatality, a youth of sixteen, was buried with full military honors rendered by the U.S. garrison at Fort Brown.[10]

Meantime, Governor Coke had dispatched Adjutant General Steele to the Nueces and the lower Rio Grande to investigate personally. He was accompanied by state senator Joseph E. Dwyer of San Antonio, who spoke Spanish, knew the country and its people, and had gained standing on the Mexican side from the business connections of his father. His presence lent unusual credibility to Steele's report, and he submitted his own as well.[11]

Along the Rio Grande from Brownsville to Camargo, the two found that Cortina's power and role in the theft of Texas cattle had not been exaggerated. They found that Texas cattle had been spirited across the Rio Grande "almost daily" since the end of the Civil War. They found Mexican officialdom unwilling to act against their countrymen and even, like Cortina, sometimes complicit in the thievery. They found a population overwhelmingly of Mexican origin and sympathy, with Spanish the universal language. And they found "thieves and cutthroats" collected on the border who "think the killing a Texan something to be proud of."

But that was only part of the story. Farther north, approaching the Nueces, "a considerable element" of the Anglo population "think the killing of a Mexican no crime." Corpus Christi merchants encouraged the traffic in illegal hides, whether purveyed by Mexican or Anglo. As Senator Dwyer observed, "Americans have committed terrible outrages on citizens of Mexican origin." The retaliation of Anglos for the Corpus Christi raid had included such outrages. Steele conceded that Wallace's Corpus Christi minute company of 1874 had been no more than an "armed mob," with the captain exercising no restraint on "the blood-thirsty instincts of many of his company." Such was the ethnic animosity and cultural division that formed the backdrop for the operations of McNelly's Rangers, who shared the common Anglo attitude toward Mexicans.

The federal government had followed an ambivalent course toward the troubled border, with the State Department favoring diplomatic solutions and the War Department a loose construction of the doctrine of hot pursuit. No such uncertainty troubled McNelly. On Palo Alto Prairie he had caught the thieves before they crossed the river. Despite his active network of spies, he never duplicated that success. By autumn, Adjutant General Steele prepared to disband the company. The captain desperately needed to catch another band of thieves.

He got his chance, thanks to the U.S. Army. The federal garrisons on the border had not, as Texans liked to think, sat idly in their forts. Using McNelly's own method of gaining intelligence through local informants, Captain James G. Randlett learned of a band of fifteen thieves who had crossed into Texas from Rancho Las Cuevas, about twenty miles down-river from Camargo, on November 16, 1875. He telegraphed his district commander at Fort Brown that he would try to intercept them. In reply, Colonel Joseph H. Potter advised Randlett that he would order rein-forcements from Ringgold Barracks (at Rio Grande City) and Edinburg. "If you catch the thieves, hit them hard," he directed. "If you come up to them while they cross the river, follow them into Mexico."

Randlett tried to do just that. Late in the afternoon of November 17, he and his troop of the Eighth Cavalry caught the thieves herding 250 head of cattle across the river. It ran high and swift, with both banks quagmires. Already some fifty animals had become mired. The troopers opened fire, killing two of the thieves and wounding another. While the two sides shot at each other, Randlett tried to find a crossing. Mud and nightfall thwarted the effort. He dispatched a courier to the alcalde of Camargo demanding that the stolen cattle and the thieves be delivered to him at once.

Early on the eighteenth, as Randlett's cavalrymen were finishing breakfast and preparing to resume their attempt to cross the river, Major David R. Clendenin rode in with another cavalry troop from Ringgold Barracks. Since Randlett had opened communication with the alcalde, Clendenin believed that crossing now would be an act of bad faith and suspended the movement.

Meantime, McNelly's own sources had picked up word of a contract to deliver eighteen thousand head of cattle to Monterey, and he had begun to move up the Rio Grande from Brownsville. Randlett's success brought McNelly to the scene by noon of the eighteenth and his hard-riding company of thirty to the river bank that night. He informed Clendenin of his intention to cross into Mexico at once under cover of darkness.

McNelly expected the federal troops to support him. During the afternoon, Colonel Potter telegraphed Clendenin to wait until Major Andrew J. Alexander arrived with still more troops and assumed command, thus implying approval of a federal crossing. Clendenin urged McNelly to wait too, but to no avail. Clendenin seemed to think that a crossing would occur when Alexander arrived. "If you are determined to cross," the major declared, "we will cover your return, but cannot cross at present to help you."[12]

Further reinforcing McNelly's expectations, Clendenin allowed Randlett's troopers to aid in the crossing. Mud promptly immobilized the horses. When only five could make it, McNelly settled for ferrying his thirty men by relays in a small boat.

A dense fog lay on the Mexican shore. With Sandoval in the lead, the five horsemen preceded the footmen along a cattle trail through high grass, brush, and a scattering of trees. Three miles inland they closed on a small assortment of ranch buildings. A sentry fired, but McNelly dropped him with his six-shooter. The horsemen then charged among the buildings, shooting down men chopping wood for breakfast fires. McNelly later reported four killed, but other participants counted five or six times as many. A woman slapping tortillas informed the interpreter that Las Cuevas lay a mile beyond. He had struck the wrong ranch.

Untroubled by the killings, since all Mexican men could be regarded as cattle thieves, McNelly lamented the loss of surprise. The Las Cuevas defenders would be waiting. They were, some 150 footmen and 100 horsemen holding the ranch corrals, led by Juan Flores Salinas, owner of Las Cuevas and a general of the Mexican frontier police. After lively exchanges of fire in which the Rangers' Sharps carbines did deadly execution, McNelly withdrew to the river. From the cover of an embankment, the Texans met a mounted charge with a volley that brought down Flores himself and threw back his soldiers.

McNelly had not only failed in his objective but now faced as many as eight times his number of fighters. Captain Randlett ferried forty cavalrymen across to back the Texans if the Mexicans again charged. McNelly implored Randlett to join in another assault on Las Cuevas, but the captain refused to move until Major Alexander arrived. Rangers and troopers turned back several feeble Mexican attacks during the afternoon. About 5:00 P.M. a flag of truce appeared. Randlett walked out to meet messengers bearing a dispatch signed by the alcalde of Camargo. It demanded the withdrawal of U.S. forces from Mexico and promised that measures were being taken to apprehend the thieves and the stolen stock. Randlett agreed to a truce until 9:00 A.M. the next day.

By now Major Alexander had reached the scene. Randlett crossed and showed him the alcalde's message. Alexander ordered a withdrawal from the Mexican side. The cavalrymen returned, but McNelly refused to leave until the thieves and stock had been delivered to him.

The drama being played out on both sides of the river involved tiers of officialdom all the way to Washington, for the soldiers had tapped into the military telegraph line connecting Ringgold Barracks and Fort

Brown. On November 20 the wire bore a plaintive message from McNelly to Steele informing him of what was happening: "The Mexicans in my front are about four hundred. What shall I do?" The wire also brought a peremptory directive from Colonel Potter at Fort Brown: Alexander should "advise" McNelly to return at once, that if he refused federal troops would not aid him if the Mexicans attacked.

Exposed at any moment to annihilation, McNelly held his position throughout November 20. Late in the afternoon, in an apparent show of bravado, he sent word to the Mexican lines that, unless assured within one hour that the stock and the thieves would be delivered in Rio Grande City the next morning, he would attack. He received the assurance and with pride intact boated his Rangers back to Texas. As he well knew, however, the alcalde of Camargo had met with Major Alexander during the morning and promised to turn over such cattle as had been recovered the next day at Ringgold Barracks.

On the morning of November 21 Camargo officials vacillated. McNelly this time resorted to genuine bravura, crossing a dozen Rangers by ferry, flourishing carbines and six-shooters, and hurling about epithets and threats. By afternoon, sixty-five cows had been driven across the Rio Grande. No thieves had been produced and hardly one-third of the stolen stock, but the Las Cuevas affair had drawn to a close.[13]

McNelly's reputation soared. Texans admired brave men who threw aside legalities to right wrongs by direct action. That the Rangers had killed a dozen or so Mexicans of uncertain guilt, that McNelly's stubborn refusal to withdraw from Mexican soil had almost got his command obliterated, and that the return of a few score stolen cows was less a victory than a formula for backing down without losing face were unpleasant realities, but they were drowned by public applause for a handful of bold Rangers who had outfought and outfoxed overwhelming numbers of iniquitous Mexicans.

Las Cuevas did not put a stop to stock raids from Mexico. Nor did the Frontier Battalion's tireless scouting and occasional skirmish put a stop to renewed Lipan and Kickapoo raids from Mexico. Rather, incursions by Mexicans and Indians alike diminished because of developments beyond the scope of Ranger operations.

In 1876 another revolution brought Porfirio Díaz to the Mexican presidency. Early in 1877, a diplomatic standoff developed between the United States and Mexico, with the former demanding action to bring border troubles under control and the latter holding out for U.S. recognition of the new regime. To break the deadlock, on June 1, 1877, President Rutherford B. Hayes outraged Mexico by authorizing U.S. troops to cross the boundary in pursuit of Indian raiders.

Securely entrenched in power, Díaz reacted by imposing firm central authority on the border. Raiding subsided. Hayes canceled the freedom of his soldiers to cross into Mexico and also recognized the Díaz regime. Border outrages that had so long plagued Texas thus ebbed not because of Texas Rangers but because of the rise of a Mexican strongman combined with the saber-rattling diplomacy of the United States.[14]

AS BORDER TROUBLES faded, Leander McNelly's attention shifted to outlawry, and to the chaparral plains sweeping north from Laredo to the upper Nueces. Monarch of this domain, with headquarters on Pendencia Creek ten miles west of Carrizo Springs, was John King Fisher. Twenty-two in 1876, a dandy in dress and deportment, smart, engaging, and recently married, King Fisher provided sanctuary for scores of desperadoes in the Nueces Strip and commanded his own gang of cattle thieves. His ranges held hundreds of stolen cattle destined for sale in Mexico. He had shown no reluctance to enforce his will with the six-shooter. Ignoring county authority, McNelly went after him.[15]

Capturing Fisher proved the least of McNelly's problems. So stealthily did he surround the ranch headquarters on June 4 that his men were inside, pistols drawn, before the occupants knew of their presence. Without protest and in irons, Fisher and nine of his men were escorted to Eagle Pass and turned over to the Maverick County sheriff. Needing witnesses, McNelly himself rode forty miles to round them up. Returning on June 6, he met Fisher and his comrades on the way home. They had conjured so many legal technicalities that they gained almost instant release. As McNelly had observed to Steele, "County in a most deplorable condition. All civil officers helpless."[16]

Disgusted, McNelly told the witnesses to go back home. He also turned loose six to eight hundred head of stolen cattle rounded up on Fisher's range. No owner had the courage to come forth and claim them.[17]

McNelly's frustrating encounter with King Fisher led to at least one tangible result. On June 21, 1876, the captain appeared before a legislative committee and told of the impossibility of accomplishing anything in counties where a despotic brigand held sway over powerless local authorities. On July 22 the legislature responded by placing McNelly's company on a firmer footing, appropriating $40,000 for fifty-three men to operate against outlaws and Mexican bandits in South Texas. The Washington County Volunteer Militia was mustered out and mustered back in as a company of "Special State Troops." In everyone's perception, however, they remained McNelly's Rangers.[18]

Even so, change seemed forthcoming. The day after the legislature voted the new company, twenty members of the house urged Governor Coke to commission their own sergeant at arms, J. Lee Hall, a lieutenant under McNelly. The governor promptly complied. The strapping Hall, twenty-seven, with red hair and mustache, had not only smoothly captivated the politicians but written a record of steely courage and proven success as a town marshal and deputy sheriff in North Texas. A later adjutant general described Hall as "a man of daring and almost reckless courage, of fine physique and resistless energy."[19]

McNelly had always chosen his own officers and men. The naming of an outsider was in part a response to his declining health. But it also reflected an increasing irritation with McNelly's disdain of such paperwork as muster rolls and vouchers and with his habit of reporting his operations only sporadically and in scant detail. Fresh leadership could be expected to bring greater system and accountability into what had been something of a rogue company.

McNelly's Rangers at once perceived the intent and welcomed "Red" Hall coolly. They thought that if anyone replaced McNelly it should be

Sergeant John B. Armstrong, who had served his chief loyally and exceptionally. But the efficient lieutenant, deferring to McNelly and demonstrating his worth, soon earned their grudging respect if not affection.[20]

From a bed in San Antonio or Austin or from his farm in Washington County, Captain McNelly made a show of directing his Special State Troops. Twice a San Antonio doctor penned a certificate of disability. From the perspective of Austin, where McNelly's unconventional ways had never set well, the time had come for a change. Governor Coke had been elected U.S. senator, and the lieutenant governor, Richard B. Hubbard, had moved into the governor's office. "Jumbo" Hubbard, all four hundred pounds of him, continued Coke's policies. As the expiration of the six-month term of the Special State Troops approached in January 1877, Hubbard himself issued orders for Lieutenant Hall to muster out the company and reconstitute it with only twenty-four men. McNelly's health, it was explained, combined with budgetary shortfalls that mandated a company too small for a captain's command, made McNelly's termination regrettably necessary. Castigated by the press for such shabby treatment of a dying hero, Adjutant General Steele replied testily that McNelly had done virtually no duty in six months, and his medical bills for that period accounted for nearly one-third the entire amount spent on the company.[21]

With his family at his bedside, Leander McNelly died on September 4, 1877, age thirty-three. He was buried at Mount Zion Cemetery, near Burton. Among those who mourned the young captain's passing was Richard King, whose vast cattle domain McNelly had taken special care to guard. In a generous show of thanks after Las Cuevas, King had equipped McNelly's entire company with Winchester repeaters. By January 1878 he had mounted a large granite stone, suitably inscribed, over the grave of his friend.[22]

As LEANDER MCNELLY fought off tuberculosis in the autumn of 1875, Lieutenant Lee Hall took firm and efficient control of his company, now designated Special State Troops. Sergeant John B. Armstrong, seasoned as a key player in McNelly's exploits, gained promotion to second lieutenant. In contrast to McNelly, Armstrong presented a huge frame of great strength, surmounted by a full, handsome face adorned with sweeping blonde mustache and goatee. His leadership and methods, copied from his mentor, earned him the sobriquet of "McNelly's Bulldog."

Hall had no sooner taken over than the Sutton–Taylor feud blew up again in DeWitt County. Killings had resumed after McNelly's departure. On the night of September 19, 1876, a masked "posse" rousted a respected physician and his son out of bed, escorted them down the road, and executed them. Public indignation ran at fever pitch. Taking station in Clinton on November 23, Hall found himself in a familiar situation: a hostile sheriff, a terrorized community, a scarcity of witnesses to testify against men everyone knew to have been the killers. Two in fact were deputy sheriffs. Within a month, however, when the grand jury took up the murder cases, Hall had rounded up enough witnesses to produce indictments against seven men. In a dramatic scene much recounted in later years, on December 22 Hall and sixteen Rangers, armed with arrest warrants, burst in on a wedding party and escorted the accused to jail. In a courtroom cowed by grim Rangers, Judge H. Clay Pleasants refused bail and ordered the defendants to secure jails elsewhere, to be held for trial in less turbulent settings.[23]

Red Hall took proud satisfaction in having brought peace to DeWitt County, as in fact he had. As early as May 1877, a citizen of Cuero, the new county seat, could advise the governor that not a murder had occurred in DeWitt County for eight months, that the local authorities were all doing their job, and that Hall and his Rangers deserved the credit.[24]

The fate of the indicted defendants, however, traced one of the most tortuous legal courses in all Texas history. Some were tried and acquitted. So in a separate action was Bill Taylor, for his part in the Sutton murder. Others of the indicted were tried and convicted, lost on appeal, and then went free when the court records mysteriously vanished. For years the accused shuffled amid a dense thicket of legal technicalities. In the end, only one man was convicted. Sentenced to twenty-five years, he never served a day. The governor could not bear to see an old Confederate veteran committed to Huntsville Penitentiary and pardoned him. Thus, in 1899, the Sutton–Taylor feud at last drew to a close.

ONE SUTTON–TAYLOR feudist remained at liberty, and he was the one Red Hall wanted most: John Wesley Hardin, a Taylor gunman. He had not been seen since 1874, before McNelly's Rangers took station in DeWitt County. But as late as 1877 the Taylors were still popularly known as the Taylor–Hardin faction.

Of all the killers of outlaw legend, none more richly deserves the reputation than John Wesley Hardin. Slight of build, of disposition oscillating between sunny and deadly, Hardin combined a powerful drive to be always in control with an unlimited capacity for self-justification. The numbers vary, but he gunned down between twenty and fifty men, every one of whom, he truly believed, deserved to die. Some were Yankee soldiers, shot during Reconstruction while still in his teens. Others were Governor Davis's state police, especially black police. Others simply crossed him in the saloons where he drank and gambled. Still others fell during the Sutton–Taylor feud.[25]

The offense that gained Hardin widespread notoriety had nothing to do with the Sutton–Taylor feud. It occurred in Comanche, many miles north of DeWitt County, as he and some Taylorite friends trailed a cattle herd to Kansas. His mother and father (a Methodist minister) lived here, as did brother Joe, a lawyer adept at creating fraudulent bills of sale for Wes. On May 26, 1874, a drunken Wes Hardin, with Jim Taylor standing by, shot and killed Deputy Sheriff Charles Webb of neighboring Brown County.

The Webb slaying made Texas too dangerous for Wes Hardin. Late in 1874, as McNelly policed DeWitt County and searched for him, the fugitive packed up his wife and infant daughter and headed for the Florida panhandle. There, under the alias of John H. Swain, he operated saloons, butchered beef, gambled and drank obsessively, sired a son, and finally moved to Alabama to evade Pinkerton and other bounty hunters. They searched for him because on January 10, 1875, the Texas legislature had voted a reward of $4,000 for Hardin, "delivered within the jail house door of Travis County"—Austin.[26]

Early in 1877 rumors of Hardin's Florida residence reached Lee Hall. Well versed in the value of undercover operatives, he sought out John R. Duncan, a Dallas policeman with an outstanding record as a criminal investigator, and in July enlisted him as a Ranger private. Duncan's assignment was to nose around DeWitt and Gonzales Counties, where Hardin relatives lived, and try to turn up a Florida address. Pretending to be a Taylor partisan, he cultivated a friendship with Neal Bowen, Hardin's father-in-law, and succeeded in reading an address on an envelope.[27]

Duncan had been working with Lieutenant Armstrong, who in May had accidentally shot himself in the hip. He could not ride and used a cane to get about on foot. Hall had planned to go with Duncan to Florida, but the detective "worked up" the case in less than a month, before Hall could free himself from another mission. On August 18, 1877, therefore, Armstrong and Duncan boarded an eastbound train in Austin, leaving Adjutant General Steele to forward arrest warrants for both Hardin and Swain.[28]

Again Duncan demonstrated his skill at digging up critical information. While Armstrong delayed in Montgomery to await the warrants from Texas, Duncan proceeded to Pollard, Alabama, and then, on a tip, to Pensacola, Florida. Telegraphed to hasten east, Armstrong joined Duncan. The Rangers enlisted Escambia County sheriff William H. Hutchinson to aid in the arrest, although without revealing who Swain really was. On August 23, as the officers worked on plans to take Swain/Hardin, they learned that he had purchased a ticket on the afternoon train for Whiting, Alabama. Hutchinson deputized eight men, and the group set forth to secure the station and platform and seize Hardin after he had boarded the train.

Hardin and three friends settled in the smoking car. Armstrong took station in the express car next to the smoker. Six or seven of the deputies remained outside. Jack Duncan joined the sheriff. Hutchinson, a deputy, and Duncan entered one end of the car, behind Hardin, while at the same moment Armstrong entered the other end, facing Hardin. As Armstrong came through the door, he shifted his cane to his left hand and drew his pistol. Spotting the long-barreled Colt revolver, Hardin exclaimed, "Texas, by God!" The sheriff pounced. Hardin struggled furiously, trying the fend off the attack and get at his pistol, snarled in a suspender strap beneath his trousers. One of Hardin's companions dove for a window, which set off a fusillade of gunfire that catapulted him to the platform, dead. As Hutchinson, Duncan, and the deputy continued to wrestle Hardin, Armstrong limped down the aisle and smashed him over the head with his pistol barrel. That stunned Hardin long enough for the lawmen to manacle him.[29]

As the Florida officers turned back, Armstrong and Duncan hurried their prisoner to Montgomery. Here they endured an anxious two days. The arrest warrants had gone astray, and Hardin, contending he was Swain and had been kidnapped, quickly hired a lawyer to get him freed on a writ of habeas corpus. Also, Hardin's friends were known to be gathering to attempt to take him from jail. A cooperative judge stalled his decision, giving the Texans five days to legalize the arrest. Finally a telegram from Governor Hubbard to the governor of Alabama broke the legal stalemate. By August 25 Armstrong could wire Steele, "On our way. Papers OK."[30]

On the morning of August 28, 1877, Armstrong and Duncan, as commanded by the Texas legislature, delivered John Wesley Hardin "within the jail house door of Travis County." As curious crowds had dogged the journey from Alabama, so now a throng gathered at the jail to gawk at the celebrity outlaw. Duncan, Armstrong, and the Ranger guards had to lift and carry him bodily over the heads of the densely packed spectators to the jailhouse door.

Under strong guard by Lieutenant Nelson O. Reynolds and Rangers of the Frontier Battalion, Hardin stood trial in Comanche for the murder of Deputy Webb. The jury swiftly convicted him, and the judge sent him to the Huntsville Penitentiary for twenty-five years. There he resisted violently, sought to escape, endured severe punishment, and finally turned model prisoner. He studied theology and law, taught Sunday school, and penned his autobiography. Pardoned by the governor in 1894, he set up a law practice in El Paso. There his old temperament reasserted itself, and the rivalries of that violent town snared him. On August 19, 1895, as he stood unsteadily at the bar of the Acme Saloon, Constable John Selman walked in, raised his .45 revolver, and sent three bullets into John Wesley Hardin. It was an ironic ending for one of the West's most famous gunmen, for John Selman himself counted two decades as one of the West's most vicious outlaws. His motives for the slaying are still debated.[31]

Having met the terms enacted by the legislature, Lieutenant John Armstrong and Ranger Jack Duncan drew the $4,000 reward. Armstrong went on to a distinguished career as Ranger officer, U.S. marshal, and finally prosperous South Texas stockman. He died in 1913. For his part, Jack Duncan left the Rangers in November 1877 and returned to Dallas. He prospered as a detective but became entangled in the seamy underside of urban life and caught a severe chest wound from a pistol wielded by a prostitute. He continued to pursue his profession, however, until killed in an automobile accident in 1911.

How Armstrong and Duncan split the reward went unrecorded. They made an effective team, and each played a crucial role in the capture of John Wesley Hardin. They deserved the praise heaped on them by newspapers all over the nation. A fair division of the $4,000, however, would have awarded about two-thirds to Duncan and one-third to Armstrong. Without Duncan's superlative detective work in Texas, Alabama, and Florida, Armstrong would never have got the chance to smash Hardin senseless on the floor of the railroad coach in Pensacola.

Like the Frontier Battalion, Lee Hall's company of Special State Troops led a precarious existence, as expenses constantly exceeded appropriations and parsimonious legislators doubted their necessity. By the close of 1877, their well-publicized successes in suppressing the Sutton–Taylor feud and nailing John Wesley Hardin placed them on a firmer political footing. In December 1877, with McNelly in his grave for three months, Lee Hall was promoted to captain and John Armstrong to first lieutenant.[32]

Lee Hall's company covered a huge expanse: from San Antonio west to Eagle Pass and south to Corpus Christi and Brownsville. Outlaws overran all this area, especially after resistance to the Díaz regime collapsed and released hundreds of "thieves and cutthroats" from the armies contesting his revolution. In most of the thirty counties, local authorities lacked the strength or will to enforce the law, and in some they were in league with the criminals.

Cattle rustlers, hide skinners, and horse thieves, both Anglo and Mexican, remained the most formidable outlaws. Not a few murderers mixed with them. Mexican raiders still ran cattle across the Rio Grande, and Mexican officials still flouted the extradition treaty. In Nueces County, in a campaign to keep sheep off their ranges, influential cattlemen quietly sponsored a reign of terror against Mexican shepherds.

Thinly spread across a land of vast distances, thick chaparral, and scarce water, Hall's little company battled valiantly, arresting or killing scores of bad men. Except in the immediate vicinity of Rangers, however, desperadoes remained as numerous and active as ever. The Rangers were too few, the jails too insecure, and the courts too ready to acquit.[33]

Lee Hall wanted King Fisher as badly as he wanted John Wesley Hardin. The flamboyant Fisher had eluded McNelly and still reigned over the chaparral plains as the "king of the strip." But as Hall discovered, he could not bring together a combination of evidence and jury that would convict King Fisher of any crime. Hall resorted instead to a campaign of harassment by indictment. For almost four years, he tangled Fisher in a web of indictments for murder, horse theft, and other offenses for which he could not be convicted. However extralegal, the strategy worked. Trials, acquittals, dismissals, changes of venue, and even a four-month incarceration in San Antonio's "Bat Cave" lockup kept the King and his legal team preoccupied. Not until 1881 did he put the last of the twenty-one indictments behind him. He resolved to afford pretext for no more.[34]

He kept his resolve. Like several other noted western bad men, in fact, he turned lawman. In 1881 he was appointed deputy sheriff of Uvalde County, a post in which he proved both effective and popular. As he laid plans to run for sheriff in 1884, he journeyed to Austin and San Antonio, where he fell in with an equally famous gunman, Ben Thompson. In San Antonio they went to the Vaudeville Variety Theater, where Thompson had quarreled with the proprietor. They walked into an ambush, and in the gunfight that erupted both Thompson and Fisher were killed.[35]

Even as Leander McNelly slipped from the scene, Lee Hall professionalized the Special State Troops. Although an imposing figure, he lacked McNelly's flamboyance and swashbuckling independence. The public applauded McNelly, even for indiscretions that displeased his superiors. But Hall placed the Special State Troops on a sound administrative footing, gained the confidence of the adjutant general, and carried out his mission more efficiently if less theatrically. Conventional Texas history treats McNelly fondly, celebrating his direct, unorthodox methods and crediting him with exploits redolent of legend. Lee Hall, a true professional but less beloved, remains in the shadow of Leander McNelly.

[10]

The Adventures of Major Jones

A S LEE HALL professionalized the Special State Troops, so John B. Jones professionalized the Frontier Battalion and oversaw its transition from Indian fighting to law enforcement. Like his predecessors in the time of the citizen soldier, the serious little man led by example; but unlike his predecessors, he did not hesitate to enforce military discipline. He passed as much time with his units in the field as he did in his Austin office. His officers found him both strict and supportive. They communicated his spirit and professionalism to their men and weeded out those who failed to measure up.

Jones gave the appearance of a man more at ease at a banker's desk than on horseback. Yet at the Lost Valley fight with Kiowas he had won plaudits for calm courage and effective command. And in the Mason County war he had displayed a passion for resolving disputes without bloodshed, a skill at mediating between feuding factions without betraying a hint of partiality, and a determination to secure justice in the courts without resort to the six-shooter.

Almost any other commander of the Frontier Battalion would have expected his field officers to handle such ugly collisions as occurred in

Mason County. Not Major Jones. In three high-profile cases, he assumed field leadership himself.

KIMBLE COUNTY, ESTABLISHED in 1858 but not organized until 1876, embraced rugged, brush-choked canyons slashing through lofty limestone ridges peppered with stands of oak and cedar. The North and South Llano Rivers and their major tributaries beckoned immigrants with lush grass and fertile soil. Many of the settlers who began filtering in before the Civil War fell victim to Comanche or Apache raiding parties. More newcomers arrived in the early 1870s, enough to support a county government. The county seat, which sprang up at the junction of the two branches of the Llano, took the name Junction. It lay fifty miles northwest of Kerrville and sixty miles west of Fredericksburg.

By October 1876, Kimble County had become a hotbed of crime. Such complete criminal domination of an entire county deeply offended Jones's commitment to law and order. But most disturbing, the outlaws threatened to prevent Judge W. A. Blackburn from convening the state district court in Junction late in April 1877.[1]

Moving swiftly and secretly, Jones organized a sweep of Kimble County. On April 19, with Neal Coldwell's Company A and thirteen men of Pat Dolan's Company F, he advanced down the South Llano, probing every ravine with detachments and seizing every man who could not account for himself. In Junction on April 20 he added another company, already stationed there. The force now numbered about fifty. For three days, operating in five squads, they combed both Llanos and their tributaries. Every man who even looked suspicious wound up in Junction bound to a tree (Junction had no jail). Some were caught by "rounding up" their cabins or spotting their campfires in the woods at night. Rangers "were terribly tongue-lashed by the women for searching their homes and arresting their men."

A complete surprise to everyone, Jones's offensive encountered no resistance. Not a shot was fired nor a drop of blood shed. By April 23 he had twenty-three fugitives, and in the next several days he ran the number up to forty-one, all included on his wanted list. Decent citizens turned out to welcome the Rangers and promise cooperation. "We are cutting out some work for your court next week," Jones informed Judge Blackburn, "and I shall remain here to help you make it up."[2]

He did. Both the judge and the district attorney told him that no court could have been held in the absence of Rangers. And if it had, jurors and witnesses would have been terrorized into silence. The grand jury handed down twenty-five indictments, several against the sheriff and county judge, both of whom resigned. Because the young county's jury list bore only nine names, however, no trials could be held, and all cases had to be continued.[3]

Jones's cleanup of Kimble County was a masterpiece of careful planning, sound intelligence, organization, secrecy, rapid movement, and decisive action. He caught everyone by surprise and moved with such resolute purpose and in such strength that the opposition had no chance to combine or flee. His Rangers functioned with professional efficiency that did them proud. "Each man seems to take a personal interest and pride in catching every one he is ordered to arrest," the major boasted.[4]

Jones probably understood that he had not truly cleaned up Kimble County. Only a few of those indicted would be convicted or even tried. But he had smashed outlaw domination. For the next three years, the companies of Dan Roberts, Nelson O. Reynolds, and Neal Coldwell campaigned against the bad men of Kimble County and finally, with Winchesters, six-shooters, and the courts, finished what Jones had begun. As with all frontier counties, even after criminal rule had been crushed, Kimble County periodically erupted with theft and violence serious enough to call for Ranger attention. But Jones's sweep of April 1877 had given the "good citizens" the chance they needed to start building a stable government that could take care of the county with only occasional resort to the Rangers.

MAJOR JONES HAD no sooner pacified Kimble County in the spring of 1877 than he rode into the midst of another famous Texas feud. Like others, this one centered on allegations of cattle rustling and pitted against each other two factions of tough men accustomed to righting their own wrongs with Winchesters rather than lawmen and courts. The scene was Lampasas County fifty miles northwest of Austin, a land of high rolling grasslands cut by clear running streams. On the one side were the five Horrell brothers and their cronies, on the other John Calhoun Pinkney Higgins—Pink Higgins—and his cronies.[5]

The Horrels had been in trouble at least since 1873, when Mart, Tom, and several cohorts tangled with a contingent of Governor Davis's state police in a Lampasas saloon. When the smoke cleared, a captain and three policemen lay dead, and three had fled. Mart and Tom Horrell both took wounds. Mart and two friends wound up in the Williamson County jail at Georgetown, but were broken out by a crowd of their friends. All five brothers hurried with their families to New Mexico, where they got embroiled in the early stages of the Lincoln County War. Brother Ben was slain in a gun battle, and the rest went back to Lampasas County, where Tom, Mart, and Merritt stood trial for killing the state police captain and were acquitted.

The four brothers resumed running cows. Pink Higgins contended that some were his cows. After several contentious collisions, on January 22, 1877, Pink strode into the Gem Saloon in Lampasas and pumped four Winchester bullets into Merritt Horrell. That left Mart, Tom, and Sam to even the score with Pink, his brother-in-law Bob Mitchell, and their pal Bill Wren.

On March 20, 1877, with district court convening, Captain John C. Sparks led his Ranger company into Lampasas. That very morning, five miles east of town, Higgins, Wren, and several others ambushed Mart and Tom Horrell, hitting Mart in the right shoulder with a bullet and Tom in the back. The wounds did not prevent the brothers from continuing to Lampasas. Although hurt, Mart accompanied Sparks and his company in a futile search for the culprits. "Winchesters are plentiful," the captain advised Major Jones, and but for the ranger presence the two factions would be battling each other.[6]

In May Jones moved Sparks and his company elsewhere. On June 11 he himself, prostrate in a wagon with fever, arrived in Lampasas to learn that Sparks's prophecy had been fulfilled four days earlier. Men of both factions, including the three Horrell brothers and Higgins, Mitchell, and Wren, had blundered into each other in Lampasas. The battle raged from the town square through the streets and two stores, costing two killed and one wounded, until townsmen brokered a truce.[7]

"This trouble is one of the most perplexing to me that I have yet to contend with," Jones confessed. The feud had grown so violent and bloody and had so divided the populace that he foresaw little hope of ending it through conventional legal methods. Here as elsewhere witnesses shrank from testifying and jurors from serving. He felt himself on good terms with both sides, and he resolved to act "in the interest of peace and quiet, rather than in accordance with the strict dictates of the law."

Jones had brought in a squad of Rangers under Sergeant Nelson O. Reynolds. Acting on a tip, in the rainy predawn darkness of July 28, Reynolds and seven Rangers closed on Mart Horrell's ranch ten miles from Lampasas. As day broke, they burst into the house with Winchesters ready, catching rooms full of men, women, and children sleeping in beds and on floor pallets. Suddenly awakened and unaware of the identity of the intruders, the brothers started to resist. Sam Horrell grabbed the barrel of Reynolds's Winchester, which went off in the scuffle. Reynolds shouted who he was, and after a tense moment the three brothers surrendered.

In Lampasas, Jones lectured them sternly on the necessity of ending the war. He then wrote out a long, conciliatory letter addressed to Higgins, Mitchell, and Wren and dated July 30. It pledged an end to fighting and restoration of peace if the overture were reciprocated. Mart, Sam, and Tom all signed. The next day, Jones himself arrested the three addressees and drafted a similar letter, dated August 2, to the three Horrell brothers. This letter accepted the proposal and also promised an end to the quarrel and to bad feeling. Higgins, Mitchell, and Wren signed.

The exchange of letters, published in the Lampasas newspaper, established a shaky peace between the Horrell and Higgins feudists. Although bitter feelings persisted well into the twentieth century, they did not again explode in violence. Jones's unusual combination of threat and persuasion had worked. Legal process undoubtedly would have sputtered inconclusively for years as the factions popped at each other with Winchesters and Colts. Jones took pride in his pragmatism, even though prompting him to apologize for not strictly honoring the law.[8]

To clear the books, Pink Higgins stood trial for the murder of Merritt Horrell and was acquitted. He lived a long and occasionally violent life, reared a large family, prospered as a stockman, and died at the age of sixty-six in 1913. Mart and Tom Horrell did not last so long. Arrested for robbing and murdering a storekeeper, they were lodged in the Bosque County jail at Meridian. On December 15, 1878, a mob of masked men broke into the jail and, thrusting their weapons through the cell bars, blasted both men to death. Rumor numbered Pink Higgins and Bob Mitchell among the vigilantes. Sam Horrell outlived them all: he moved to California and died in bed in 1936, age ninety-nine.[9]

IN THE SPRING OF 1878, Major Jones had to shift his attention and resources away from the frontier to Dallas and the tangled timber-and-brush country of Denton County to the north. This assignment involved no feud but the apprehension of an outlaw already on his way to legendary stature–Sam Bass.

The reality differed from the mythology that would ultimately elevate Sam Bass to the temple of outlaw immortals. He came to Texas from Indiana in 1869; and in Denton County he was known as an industrious, sober, companionable youth with a flair for horse racing. By his mid-twenties, he was still boyish looking, slightly stooped, swarthy, with close-cropped black hair and a pencil mustache. He could neither read nor write, thought and talked slowly, and seemed destined for a lifetime of anonymity.

In 1875, however, Bass and some friends slipped into a life of crime. They bought a cattle herd on credit, trailed it north to the Black Hills, and sold it for $8,000. Instead of paying off their loan, they squandered the proceeds and embarked on an unprofitable career of robbing stage coaches. Their luck turned sensationally on September 18, 1877, when Bass and five comrades stopped a Union Pacific passenger train at Big

Spring, Nebraska, and netted $60,000 in newly minted twenty-dollar gold coins. The feat drew nationwide attention and healthy rewards posted by the railroad and express companies. Headed back to Texas, two of the gang ran afoul of Kansas lawmen and U.S. soldiers and lost their lives, together with $20,000 of the loot.

In Texas, Bass and a gang of shifting numbers and composition confounded Lee Hall's Rangers from San Antonio to Eagle Pass, robbed two stagecoaches west of Fort Worth, then turned to the railroads. Between late February and early April 1878, they struck four times, all near Dallas. None of the robberies gained much more than pocket change, but they aroused corporate and political Texas as no other crimes had.[10]

The Dallas area swarmed with federal and county lawmen, would-be lawmen, bounty hunters, half a dozen posses, militia units, Pinkerton detectives, and others eager for a chance at the rewards offered for the capture of Bass or any of his followers. Lee Hall even had some of his undercover Rangers working with the sheriff of Denton County. So numerous had the pursuers become that they stumbled over one another and sometimes mistook their own for the fugitives. To bring order out of this chaos and curb the political fallout from the northern counties, on April 11, 1878, Governor Hubbard turned to Major Jones.[11]

To avoid diverting units from the frontier, Jones enlisted a thirty-man company in Dallas and incorporated it into the Frontier Battalion. He commissioned Junius "June" Peak (a friend of the governor's) as second lieutenant and set him to recruiting the company. Most of Peak's men lacked experience. The company added to the confusion already dogging the manhunt and in the end proved useless.[12]

Jones's plan contrasted with his unorthodox approach to the Horrell–Higgins feud. Now he manipulated the legal system to the limit to accomplish his ends. Since the outlaws had robbed the U.S. mails, they were wanted by federal as well as state authorities. In league with the U.S. district attorney, U.S. marshal, and federal district judge, all based in Tyler, Jones succeeded in bringing about what a later generation would label a plea bargain. James Murphy, a friend of Bass's, had been caught in a general roundup of Bass gangsters and associates and charged as an accessory in the mail heists. He was more embarrassed than culpable, and he offered, in exchange for dropping the charge, to join the Bass gang and keep Jones alerted to impending crime.[13]

Murphy had undertaken a fearful task. Neither Bass nor his cohorts, Seaborn Barnes and Frank Jackson, would hesitate to kill him if they even suspected him of double dealing. And in fact doubts greeted him as soon as he presented himself to Bass in the Denton brush. Barnes demanded that Murphy be executed at once. Only some quick talking that convinced Jackson saved Murphy. As the four men drifted south looking for an easy bank to rob, Bass and Barnes continued the argument while Jackson defended Murphy. Through the first two weeks of July 1878, while the posses continued to beat the brush north of Dallas, the gang checked banks at Ennis, Waco, Belton, and finally Round Rock. At Belton and again at Georgetown, Murphy succeeded in getting off a letter identifying Round Rock as the likely target, although Bass almost caught him in the Georgetown post office.

While the four robbers rested their horses in camp near Round Rock, Jones frantically tried to round up enough Rangers to concentrate in the old Chisholm Trail town on Brushy Creek, twenty miles north of Austin. The International and Great Northern Railroad now linked the two. In the capital Jones had only a few men. The nearest were at Lampasas under Lieutenant Nelson O. Reynolds. Jones dispatched a hard-riding courier to summon Reynolds and his men to Round Rock. He then ordered the remaining three of his own detail to ride to Round Rock and stable their horses; they were Dick Ware, Chris Connor, and George Herold. Jones himself rode the train up to Round Rock on July 18, taking with him Travis County deputy sheriff and ex-Ranger Maurice B. Moore.[14]

The next day, July 19, Jones augmented his little squad with two more former Rangers: Henry Highsmith, Round Rock stable keeper, and Williamson County deputy sheriff A. W. Grimes. Also, Adjutant General Steele sent Captain Lee Hall of the Special State Troops up from Austin. Unknown to Jones, Lieutenant Reynolds had moved his command from

Lampasas west to San Saba, where the courier overtook him. With eight men Reynolds began a mad dash toward Round Rock, 110 miles distant. By the morning of July 19, they still had forty-five miles to ride.[15]

Establishing headquarters in a hotel room, Jones scattered his manpower around the town, virtually deserted on a torrid summer afternoon. Lee Hall, whom Bass knew by sight, lay on the bed in his hotel room.

About 4:00 P.M. Bass, Barnes, and Jackson rode into Round Rock to buy tobacco and make one last reconnaissance before hitting the bank the next day. Murphy managed to tarry at a store on the edge of town. The three outlaws hitched their horses in an alley and walked up a street toward a store. Lazing in the dusty street, some of Jones's men watched the strangers, apparently without recognizing their identity. The Travis deputy, Moore, spotted the bulge of a pistol and alerted the Williamson County deputy, Grimes, who had orders to ensure that all strangers check their arms while in town. With Moore behind him, Grimes followed the men into the store and asked Sam Bass if he had a pistol. "Yes," said Bass, and all three outlaws spun around and began firing. Moore fired back. The outlaws burst from the smoke-filled store into the street as Grimes fell dead on the doorstep and Moore staggered with a bullet in his lung.

Round Rock erupted in a confused battle of frantic activity, blazing six-shooters, rearing horses, and gunsmoke filling the stifling air. Lee Hall gained the street with his Winchester, and Jones rounded the corner of a building as a bullet splintered the wall above him. He emptied his pistol at the retreating bandits. Others drove them toward their horses, firing steadily. In the store Moore had shot Bass in the hand, and now, as he tried to mount his bucking horse, George Herold got close enough to send a Winchester slug slicing through Bass's back and kidney. Dick Ware took deliberate aim and put a bullet through Barnes's head, killing him instantly. Jackson gained his saddle and helped the wounded Bass into his. Together they galloped out of town, followed by the scattering of lawmen who could get themselves mounted.

Lieutenant Reynolds and his exhausted squad reached Round Rock two hours after the fight. Next morning Sergeant Charles Nevill took a detail to try to pick up the trail of the escaped bandits. Lying at the foot of an oak tree they found Sam Bass, who promptly surrendered. Conveyed to town and laid out on a cot, Bass proved remarkably talkative for a dying man, but, despite persistent grilling by Major Jones, he divulged little. Not until late afternoon of July 21, forty-eight hours after the battle, did Sam Bass finally die.

What should he do with the corpse? Jones wired Steele. "Have an inquest and have him buried" came the laconic reply.[16]

Both Sam Bass and Seaborn Barnes were buried in the Round Rock cemetery. Frank Jackson, abandoning the comrade whose wounds he knew to be mortal, vanished from history. Controversy at once broke out over who gave Bass and Barnes their mortal bullet, to be followed by another controversy over which county lawmen should share the credit. Then came a flurry of calculations dividing the reward money. Jim Murphy, rightly disgruntled by his paltry $50 share of the reward, feuded with Major Jones for a few months. On June 5, 1879, however, he accidentally swallowed a toxic eyewash and died instantly.[17]

The biggest winners of the Bass saga were Jones and his Rangers. The violent triumph over the celebrity outlaws, achieved virtually on the outskirts of the state capital, earned public acclaim that translated into solid political support—though never generous appropriations—for the Frontier Battalion of Texas Rangers.

[11]

The El Paso Salt War

L ATE IN 1877, bracketing triumphs over feudists and outlaws, Major Jones confronted the severest challenge to his leadership. It thwarted him and ended in the most humiliating failure in the annals of the Texas Rangers. The scene was five hundred miles west of Austin, where New Mexico and Old Mexico narrowed Texas to a point embracing the little town of El Paso, still known to locals as Franklin.

El Paso had more in common with neighboring New Mexico than with a Texas whose population was concentrated far to the east. The Rio Grande, the international boundary, emerged from the historic Pass of the North and turned southeast into a thirty-mile stretch of irrigated farmland that supported most of the people. In all directions sandy deserts and barren mountains, the haunt of roving bands of Apaches, isolated the valley from the rest of the world. Stagecoaches connected El Paso with San Antonio and with Mesilla, upriver in New Mexico.

Only about eighty non-Mexicans lived in the valley. Although of varied national origin, they were usually lumped together as "Americans." Some five thousand Mexicans farmed the valley, and another seven thousand made up the Mexican city of Paso del Norte, at the mouth of the pass. Opposite Paso del Norte, north of the river, lay American El Paso, or Franklin, a rundown assortment of adobe buildings lining dusty streets. It counted only eight hundred inhabitants. Other towns scattered along the valley—Ysleta, fifteen miles downriver, with fifteen hundred people; Socorro, another four, with seven hundred; and San Elizario, six miles more, with two thousand, including perhaps a dozen Americans. In 1877 Ysleta claimed the seat of El Paso County.[1]

Valley dwellers traced their heritage to the late seventeenth century, when the Pueblo Revolt of 1680 expelled Spanish colonizers from the upper Rio Grande. Loyalist Indians from the upriver pueblos of Socorro and Isleta established namesake pueblos and missions at these new locations. From the valley, beginning in 1692, Spain launched the reconquest of New Mexico. The expatriates remained in their new homes, however, and by the middle of the nineteenth century they had merged into the Mexican population, although some of the old traditions survived in muted form.[2]

Residents of Ysleta and Socorro, whatever the remnant of Pueblo blood and culture, regarded themselves as Mexicans (which is why "American" is appropriate terminology for the rest). So did the people of San Elizario, a trading center that had grown up around a Spanish presidio. Their ties to Mexico were especially strong because until the early 1830s all three towns lay on the south side of the Rio Grande. A rampaging flood gouged a new channel and created "La Isla," an island twenty miles long and two to four miles wide. Gradually the old channel dried up, leaving the new riverbed south of the towns and thus, under the treaty ending the Mexican War, the international boundary.[3]

Mexican rather than Texan the townspeople remained. A common culture as well as family, social, economic, and political bonds straddled the boundary to erase distinctions of citizenship. In their daily lives, citizenship had little meaning, and they moved their residence from one side of the river to the other whenever they wanted. Few spoke English. Few had any understanding of the laws of Texas and the United States, which caused little inconvenience since authorities lacked the power to enforce them. But as army Colonel Edward Hatch later observed, "When you touch one you touch all, and where one is hurt, all feel it."[4]

Although sparse in numbers, the American population indulged in vicious feuding. Personal ambition and bitter political rivalries spawned by the Civil War and Reconstruction created factions that pursued their aims ruthlessly and unscrupulously, even to assassination. By 1877 the leading feudists were Charles H. Howard and Don Luis Cardis.

Of formidable physique and forbidding visage, Howard was alternately arrogant and companionable. A lawyer, he had immigrated from Missouri in 1872. He enjoyed stature and respectability among many friends and supporters. He had served briefly as state district judge. But like other leading Americans, he was driven by a quest for power and money.

Stubby and plump, with black hair, mustache, and goatee, Cardis was an Italian who had mastered Spanish and emerged as political leader of the Mexican population. He could turn out the vote, regardless of citizenship, for any local election, including his own. He served as El Paso's representative in the state legislature.

Cardis's power rested largely on the sinister power of Father Antonio Borajo, formerly parish priest at San Elizario. A tall, thin old man with flowing white hair, he warred incessantly against everything gringo except dollars, which he pursued voraciously though surreptitiously. Although an ecclesiastical reorganization had forced him across the border and replaced him with Father Pierre Bourgade, he continued to manipulate people and events on the Texas side, unhesitatingly employing church canons to attain his personal ends. Although greatly beloved by the people, Cardis functioned mainly as the public face of Borajo, who kept his intrigues hidden from public scrutiny.

Powering the crisis that landed on Major Jones's desk in October 1877 was salt—saline lakes a hundred miles east of El Paso, below jagged Guadalupe Peak. In times of drought, Mexicans had long fallen back on salt to tide them over. They prodded their ox-drawn carts north to the saline lakes, then hauled their loads across the Rio Grande to peddle in towns of the Mexican interior.

After the Civil War, the issue of ownership and use of the Guadalupe salt lakes began to reverberate in local and state politics. By 1877, however, an Austin banker, Howard's father-in-law, had gained title to the lakes and appointed his daughter's husband "salt agent" on the scene. Howard gave notice that salt would no longer be free.

Mexicans regarded the salt as common property, open to anyone who wished to cart it away. That Charles Howard could wave a gringo paper over a patch of desert and exclude everyone from it rankled their sense of justice. But Cardis and Borajo assured them that laws inscribed on paper took no precedence over what the people united in believing to be right. Shared convictions had the weight of law, to be carried out by force if necessary.

The brew came to a boil on September 29, 1877. In San Elizario Howard had two men brought before the county judge for merely vowing to take salt from the lakes. One denied the charge, but the other did not. The judge had him turned over to Sheriff Charles Kerber in Ysleta. Angry Mexicans gathered in San Elizario and demanded that the justice of the peace and then the county judge issue a warrant for Howard's arrest. Both officials tried to explain the requirements of legal process.

But legal process now rested with the growing "mob," who had been told that they were the law. They "arrested" the judge and the justice of the peace and set forth to arrest Charles Howard. They found him shortly after midnight, holed up in the home of Sheriff Kerber in Ysleta. While the occupants took defensive positions on the roof, Kerber went out to confront about fifty Mexicans. They arrested him too and at daylight ordered Howard and his agent, John McBride, down from the roof. Hoisting the two men on horses, they conveyed them back to San Elizario amid jeering spectators.[5]

Held in a dwelling surrounded by several hundred armed Mexicans, for three days and nights Howard bargained his fate. The Mexican leadership numbered as many as a dozen from the three towns, but the principal chief throughout all that followed was Francisco "Chico" Barela, who was recognized as Indian as well as Mexican.[6] The junta wrangled over transforming Howard's arrest into an execution, but they sensed that Cardis and Borajo had got them into more trouble than they bargained for. Cardis, bluntly commanded by Kerber to allow no harm to come to Howard, hastened to San Elizario. He pleaded for restraint and perhaps suggested a way out that would incidentally rid Cardis of his enemy. Cardis then returned to El Paso.

Under threat of death, Howard signed a document thrust before him. Drawn up in legal language that Barela nor any of his cohorts could likely have penned, it bound Howard to leave the salt lakes open to all until the courts could rule, to refrain from prosecuting his abductors, to leave the county within twenty-four hours, and never to return. To guarantee the promises, he had to post a $12,000 bond, backed by local merchants. Once the paper had been signed, Howard hurried across the New Mexico line to Mesilla, where he added his outrage to the other voices angrily bombarding Austin and Washington, D.C.[7]

Warning signals had preceded the explosion. Both Sheriff Kerber and district judge Allen Blacker had alerted Governor Richard B. Hubbard that troops should be sent at once. They meant federal troops, but none were nearby. Fort Bliss had been abandoned nine months earlier. Thirty cavalrymen guarded a detail erecting a military telegraph between Mesilla and El Paso, and Lieutenant Louis H. Rucker, an officer on the staff of Colonel Edward Hatch, commanding the District of New Mexico in Santa Fe, had been in El Paso since July.[8]

Rucker's presence represented an international backdrop to the unfolding salt war. Porfirio Díaz had seized power in Mexico City; adherents of the ousted president, Sebastian Lerdo de Tejada, had gathered at points in Texas to mount a counterrevolution; and U.S. cavalry had brazenly chased Apaches on Mexican soil. As the Díaz and Hayes administrations sparred on the diplomatic front, border tensions brought Mexico and the United States to the brink of war. Because a Lerdist force gathered in the El Paso Valley with the avowed aim of retaking Paso del Norte, Colonel Hatch had dispatched Lieutenant Rucker to keep close watch on this prospective violation of the neutrality laws. By October, the Lerdist threat had subsided, but the danger of war had not. These conditions could only have further excited Howard's captors and reinforced their Mexican patriotism.[9]

On October 3 rumors of a riot in San Elizario prompted Rucker to ride down the valley, arriving just in time for Howard's release. Returning to El Paso, Rucker wired Colonel Hatch that a mob, composed of citizens of both the United States and Mexico, had supplanted lawful authority and placed at risk every American in the valley, that troops were urgently needed to protect life and property. Sheriff Kerber dispatched similarly alarming telegrams.[10]

Colonel Hatch ordered twenty of the cavalrymen assigned to the telegraph project to report to Rucker. He himself received instructions to return to San Elizario to investigate what was happening. He was to use his twenty soldiers only to prevent "encroachments upon American soil of armed bodies of Mexicans. He has nothing to do with local disturbances of the peace by citizens of Texas, whether they be Mexicans or Americans." This theme was to be repeated time and again in dispatches to Rucker and his successor. But no one ever told them what constituted an armed body of Mexicans, or how to identify them among the men at San Elizario.[11]

At the head of his platoon of black cavalrymen, Rucker rode into San Elizario on October 8. Three times in the following two days, he succeeded in meeting with the leaders. From them he learned the origins of the trouble and concluded that the Mexicans had been incited by "parties" who, when it became serious, failed to make good their promises. "The fact of the matter is," he stated, "the Mexicans had been lied to to such an extent they did not know who or what to believe." Although unnamed, the "parties" were doubtless Louis Cardis and Father Borajo. The junta assured Rucker that they had heeded his advice, reinstated the deposed judge and justice of the peace, and resolved to let the law take its course. Rucker thought they would, if left alone.[12]

They probably would have, had not a defiant but foolhardy Charles Howard ridden into El Paso on October 7 with the twenty troopers sent to Rucker. Three days later, he walked into Solomon Schutz's store, double-barreled shotgun resting on his shoulder. Inside, Don Luis

Cardis sprang from a rocking chair to face his enemy. Howard fired one load of buckshot into Cardis's stomach, the other into his chest. Howard rushed back to Mesilla, but by breaking his bonded pledge to leave forever and murdering a leader revered by all Mexicans, he had reignited the flames doused by Lieutenant Rucker.[13]

To Governor Hubbard, a lawless mob had seized power in El Paso County. The laws and legal processes of Texas had been trampled. On October 24, 1877, Major Jones received orders to proceed at once to El Paso.[14]

Jones arrived in El Paso on November 6 after a circuitous route by rail and stage through Kansas and New Mexico. He found everyone excited and fearful, for he had stepped into the next phase of the unfolding crisis. Furious over the murder of Cardis, again the multitude had assembled in San Elizario. Howard had broken his pledge never to return, and they intended to collect the $12,000 bond or execute the bondsmen. These frightened merchants and some friends, about ten altogether, fortified themselves in a dwelling and sent appeals for help to El Paso. Jones had no force to call on, Sheriff Kerber could find only two possemen, and Lieutenant Rucker had orders not to intervene. For Jones, the only option was to throw his talent for mediation into the mix.

Reaching San Elizario on November 7, Jones found the bondsmen and their allies terrified. At once he sent for Gregorio García. Leader of a small band of moderate Mexicans who opposed the rashness of the mass, García was an experienced Indian fighter who in 1871 had captained one of Governor Davis's Ranger companies. At Jones's behest, García assembled a company of armed men to keep the peace so long as the major remained in town.

Twice Jones met with a committee of ten men appointed by the junta. Quietly but unequivocally, he declared that he had not come to settle the salt question, only to keep the peace. They must look to the courts to decide that matter. Likewise, the courts would deal with Howard; he had killed Cardis, and Jones would arrest him.

The committee replied that they had the right to arrest Howard and force him to sign papers and post bond. Now that Howard had violated the terms of the bond, they had the right to collect the money for themselves. They had these rights "because they were the people and the people were the law."

Another knotty issue popped up. Jones said that he intended to raise a Ranger company to maintain order. The Mexicans said they wanted their own company, commanded by their own officers. Jones demurred, whereupon the leaders declared that no Mexican should be enrolled in Jones's company. In unintended tribute to Jones's quietly firm stance, however, the junta reiterated their vow to stir no more alarm.[15]

In El Paso, Jones turned to raising a body of twenty Rangers, not an easy task. Joseph Magoffin, the deputy customs collector, urged Jones to turn to his recent supporter, Captain García. But Jones wanted no one tainted by local factionalism. As lieutenant of what he designated as a detachment of Company C, he named John B. Tays. Brother of the town's Episcopal cleric, Tays worked at odd jobs and had no qualifications save willingness and honesty. Even Howard thought Tays "very slow" and urged Jones to turn to Captain García to recruit some Mexicans for the company. Instead, Tays signed up twenty Americans, mediocrities or worse but on the whole better than he had thought possible.[16]

Next Jones took a step that demonstrated his misreading of Charles Howard, with whom he had been conducting a friendly correspondence since his arrival. In San Elizario Jones had promised to arrest Howard for murder. In El Paso he arranged for Howard to come back from Mesilla and submit to arrest. On November 16 Jones took Howard before the local justice of the peace. That functionary, with marginal command of English and law, allowed Howard to waive examination, then set bail at $4,000 and commanded him to appear when district court next convened in El Paso in March 1878.[17]

After the court action, as Magoffin recalled, "I told Howard for Lord's sake to stay away until the court met; and he replied that he would, saying that he thought of making a trip to Chihuahua." This is what Jones assumed too, as he inspected Tays's detachment at San Elizario on November 22 and began the long stage journey to Austin.[18]

On December 11, 1877, Father Bourgade, the current parish priest, penned for Jones an ominous description of conditions in San Elizario. A train of carts had set out for the salt lakes, some said to court arrest and finish what had been left only half done, others said to sell salt in Mexico to ward off starvation wrought by drought-ridden crops. Also troubling was the character of Tays's Ranger company, quartered in a large adobe with adjoining corral. The priest thought that the men had signed up to make an easy dollar and could not be depended on to endanger themselves for the sake of the law. Worse, the Mexicans doubted that the Rangers bore any official commission but rather were mere paid hirelings of Judge Howard.[19]

Forty Mexicans had indeed gone for salt, and Howard determined to intercept them and serve legal papers sequestering the salt. These he applied for at Ysleta, the county seat, on the evening of December 12 and, leaving Sheriff Kerber to follow with them the next day, set forth for San Elizario. At Howard's request, Tays had sent ten Rangers as escort.[20]

Both Howard and Tays should have known better. Howard had barely escaped with his life from these same people at this same place, and since then he had given them immeasurably more reason to want him dead. But he was arrogant, stubborn, and contemptuous of the Mexicans. "It is like talking to a lot of jacks," he informed Major Jones, "all braying at once."[21] For his part, Tays had been in San Elizario for nearly a month, knew the temper of the people, and feared trouble. A more decisive man would have done all in his power to keep Howard away and to avoid appearing before the Mexicans as his protector.

Tays had alerted the new federal officer in El Paso that he might need help. He was Captain Thomas Blair, who had arrived on November 18 to replace Lieutenant Rucker. The twenty cavalrymen were still the only federal troops in the area. Dismayed by the armed Mexicans gathering along the road and in town, Tays had already sent word to Blair to come at once.

With a lieutenant and nineteen cavalrymen, Blair came at once. He reached the outskirts of town, only three hundred yards from the Ranger quarters, shortly before midnight on December 12. About fifty armed Mexicans blocked the road. By what authority, the captain demanded, did they presume to halt an officer of the U.S. Army? They had been ordered to bar everyone, they answered. Barela told Blair this was none of his business, that they intended to take Howard and would brook no interference. Mindful of his orders not to intervene in civil affairs, Blair wrung from the Mexican leader an assurance that every man in town was a citizen of El Paso County. "Under the circumstances," Blair explained, "I did not consider it my duty to try to force an entrance." Or as Barela laughingly put it, the captain departed "mucho pronto."[22]

In fact, sensing not only a chance for revenge on the hated gringo but for plunder as well, Mexicans had converged on San Elizario from both sides of the border, swelling the throng to more than five hundred. Chico Barela and Sisto Salcido could maintain a shaky control over their own followers, but the knots of men who crossed from Mexico could be controlled by no one. Except for the passions generated by the war furor, they came mainly for loot. By 10:00 P.M. all had begun to assemble at the home of Leon Granillo, another of the leaders.

Captain Gregorio García and others, including Howard, had gathered in Charles Ellis's store. As the crowd at Granillo's grew boisterous and unruly, Ellis, an affable, longtime resident married to a Mexican woman, slipped a pistol into his boot and walked to Granillo's home to try to reason with them. He had no sooner begun his appeal than someone shouted, "Ahora es tiempo!" A mounted man galloped up, threw a lasso over Ellis, and dragged him down the street. The rider then dismounted and slashed Ellis's throat.[23]

The rising commotion prompted Howard to seek refuge in the Ranger quarters. He gained cover none too soon, for a crowd advanced on the adobe as if to launch an assault. Tays distributed his men on the roof and in the corral for defense. No shots were fired, and the would-be attackers fell back.

The Rangers awoke on December 13 to find themselves confronted with a force organized with almost military precision—three ranks of pickets backed by compact platoons of twenty mounted men regularly spaced. Merchant John Atkinson came in with a trunk containing the negotiable assets of his store: $700 in specie together with currency and other paper amounting in all to $11,000. He brought word that Tays had three hours to surrender Howard or he would be taken by force. Unwisely, at this juncture Sergeant Charles E. Mortimer walked down the street to the Ellis store. A bullet slammed into his back. Tays helped him return, but he died that night.

The shot that felled Mortimer signaled the opening of the battle. All day of December 13 and 14 the two sides exchanged a hot fire, which dropped three or four attackers but no defenders. Three times attack forces tried to take the Ellis store, but García and his men drove them back. But on the second night, ammunition exhausted, his son killed, and he himself hit twice, García and his five-man contingent surrendered. Mexicans poured in to plunder the store and fortify the windows with sacks of flour as firing positions.[24]

On December 15, with battle raging in the streets, Captain Blair again showed up in San Elizario, this time unaccompanied by soldiers. In a long talk with the junta, he learned how determined the Mexicans were to have Howard. Barela assured him that no one had been killed and that everyone from Mexico had been sent back across the river, which gave the captain all the reason he needed to stay out of the fight. He returned to El Paso by a road on the Mexican side, a fortunate choice because a party of assassins had been posted at Socorro to shoot him down.[25]

A deputy sheriff of Pecos County, Andrew Loomis, had been caught in the Ranger quarters and not surprisingly found urgent cause to go home. At noon on the sixteenth, bearing a white flag, he walked to the nearest Mexicans. They conducted him out of sight. Encouraged that Loomis had gone free, Tays hoisted his own truce flag and went out for a parley. The two negotiators agreed to extend the truce until the next morning, when Tays would meet with the junta. In fact, Loomis had not been freed but robbed and locked in the room of one of the adobes.

The next morning, December 17, Tays met with the Chico Barela and his lieutenants. They told him that if Howard would surrender and relinquish all claim to the salt lakes, they would not harm him. Otherwise, they would blow up the Ranger quarters with gunpowder they claimed to have tunneled beneath the building during the night. Whether Tays believed either the promise or the threat, he returned to his fortress and relayed the message to Howard.

His time had run out, Howard now understood; if he failed to give up, everyone in the building would be killed. "I will go," he said, "as it is the only chance to save your lives, but they will kill me." Tays bravely vowed to defend him, but Howard had a better sense of reality. He gave his valuables to his agent, John McBride, bid farewell to all, and accompanied Tays back to the junta's headquarters.

Tays sent back for John Atkinson, who had been serving as interpreter. He had been a San Elizario merchant long enough to become involved in local feuds, to incur the wrath of Father Borajo, to get mixed up in the salt intrigues, and to reveal himself as irascible and mean-spirited. On his arrival, he was diverted to another room. There he offered his trunk crammed with $11,000 in exchange for the freedom of Howard, McBride, and the Rangers. Barela agreed and, without allowing Atkinson to confer with Tays, sent him back to tell the Rangers that all had been amicably settled and that the lieutenant ordered them all to come with their arms and join him. They did, only to be herded into a corral, disarmed, and locked in a dirty room. Barela told Tays he could rejoin his men, who, he thought, were still in their defenses. He protested that he would stay with Howard until Barela made good his promises. Barela then had him led into the same room with Deputy Loomis, where he first learned that his men had been tricked into giving up.[26]

Chico Barela was said to have intended to honor his agreement, but shouts erupted among his followers calling for death to all the gringos. The victims on whom all agreed were Howard, McBride, and Atkinson, whose trunk holding $11,000 had already been seized. The only explanation for including Atkinson, whose betrayal of Tays had brought the battle to an end, seems to have been his despicable personality and the enmity of Father Borajo.[27]

Howard went first, as the horde gathered to watch. A firing squad of eight men, half from the other side of the border, formed in line. Howard bared his chest and shouted, "Fire!" As the volley ripped into him, he fell to the ground kicking and writhing. Jesús Telles dashed up and, gripping a machete in both hands, slashed downward. But Howard rolled over and Telles cut off two of his own toes. Other men converged to hack what remained of life out of the salt king.[28]

Atkinson came next. In fluent Spanish, he taunted the crowd for breaking their agreement. Cries of "finish them!" roared from the crowd. Atkinson too bared his breast and said that he would give the command to fire, instructing the squad to aim for his heart. The volley smashed into his stomach and staggered him. "Mas arriba, cabrones," he shouted–higher. Two more shots dropped him but left him struggling. Rising on his elbows, he pointed to his head. The squad leader stepped up with a pistol and blew his brains out.

McBride followed, quietly, sadly, and baffled. He probably never understood that merely acting as Howard's agent in the salt business condemned him to die.

Unsated by the executions, the crowd cried for death to all the gringos, which meant the Rangers. Chico Barela had had enough, however, in fact more than enough. But for the passions of the crowd (and Borajo?), he probably would have stood by his bargain with Atkinson. Now he stepped forward and opened his own shirt front. "No," he shouted, "no other man shall be killed, and if you propose to kill anybody else I will take out my people and fight you." No more blood flowed, but the throng spread out to loot the stores and houses of the Americans and those Mexicans who had stood by them.[29]

Herded into their original quarters under heavy guard, Tays and his Rangers passed an anxious night. The next morning, December 18, they turned out to watch the Mexicans parade their military strength and organization. A succession of self-appointed leaders made speeches.

Two from across the border called for the death of the Rangers and then of all Americans in El Paso County. Much of the crowd clamored in agreement. But again Barela intervened, vowing to fight any who attempted more killings. He allowed the Rangers to keep their horses but not their arms and bade them leave. They did so at once, reaching El Paso to find the town in an uproar and Captain Blair, as Tays wryly reported, "making preparations to start to my assistance with his command of 18 men some time next Spring."[30]

As soon as fighting had broken out on December 13, Sheriff Kerber and others besieged Governor Hubbard with pleas for help. The governor in turn besieged President Rutherford B. Hayes, stressing the participation of Mexican citizens and imploring a rapid deployment of U.S. troops. Also, responding to a proposition advanced by Kerber, Hubbard authorized him to raise one hundred men in New Mexico to come to the aid of El Paso, a measure both would have cause to regret. And at last the army acted, pushing troops by forced marches from posts in New Mexico and West Texas. The army had reached the conclusion that Governor Hubbard's appeal to the president invoked the army's constitutional duty to put down insurrection or invasion.[31]

They arrived too late to do more than calm the citizens. The culprits had disappeared into Mexico together with all the loot gathered at San Elizario. The first troops arrived on December 20 and more the next day. Colonel Edward Hatch assumed command and on December 22, with sixty cavalrymen and a howitzer, advanced down the valley toward San Elizario.[32]

Kerber's call for volunteers from New Mexico had also been heeded, and thirty came from Silver City on the twenty-second. Most were freebooters, some even avowed outlaws, seeking whatever the state might pay or whatever they might gain in loot. They were never sworn into state service. That afternoon, several hours behind Colonel Hatch, Kerber took the road down the valley with forty-four men, about half New Mexicans and the rest Tays's Rangers. Kerber considered himself in command of all the men by authority of the governor, a conviction shared by Tays.

In Ysleta, where Kerber's force spent the night, he arrested two men said to have been members of the mob. The next morning, December 23, he resumed the advance. Two wagons bore two coffins each, in which to inter the bodies left by the executioners in San Elizario. The two prisoners, their hands bound behind them, sat on the coffins in the first wagon. They were to dig the graves.

In Socorro, four miles from Ysleta, Kerber scattered his men to search the town for firearms. A spent bullet from a house struck a Ranger sergeant, and a squad of New Mexicans blasted the doors and windows with a fusillade. Tays ordered them to search the house. They found one man dead and his wife wounded. Kerber wanted to arrest Jesús Telles, the machete-wielding executioner who cut off his own toes, who lived in Socorro. The sheriff sent a deputy with a squad of Tays's Rangers. They returned to explain that Telles had fired at them, and they had shot him down.

The gunfire left Socorro's residents either cowering in their homes or fleeing from the town. The sound also reached Colonel Hatch, returning in his buggy from San Elizario. He whipped the horses into the center of town to confront Sheriff Kerber, who described all the firing as self-defense. He also said that, before reaching Socorro, the two prisoners seated on the coffins in the first wagon had jumped out and run seventy-five yards into the chaparral. The two guards, Tays's men, had pursued and killed them, then dragged their bodies back to the road.

Hatch listened with rising skepticism. Joined by the local justice of the peace, the colonel continued to where the bodies of the two prisoners lay in the road. They found blood stains in the back of the wagon, no evidence that the bodies had been dragged, and signs suggesting they had been shot at close range. "I then denounced this inhumanity in no measured terms," Hatch recalled, "and informed the sheriff it was his duty to arrest the murderers immediately."[33]

"Rangers" perpetrated all the excesses of which Hatch complained. But the word applied both to Tays's men and to the Silver City volunteers. Witnesses later blamed all the outrages on the New Mexicans and praised the conduct of the Tays Rangers. The guards who killed the two prisoners, however, belonged to Tays's company, some of Tays's men participated in the shooting of Telles (which may or may not have been justified), and Tays himself sent a squad of New Mexicans into the house where the man and his wife had been shot. Kerber, of course, arrested no one. The next day, December 24, Colonel Hatch issued orders assuming command and declaring that "outrages in the name and under color of the law, and by those who ought to be its representatives and guardians, will not be tolerated."

Despite the presence of troops, scattered outrages continued for the next week or two. Intimidation, robbery masquerading as house searches, rape, and attempted rape plagued Ysleta. All could be attributed to the Silver City volunteers. "I wish they would clear out of here," Tays declared. They finally did, when Adjutant General Steele on January 10, 1878, ordered them discharged.[34]

An investigation followed. On December 19 Governor Hubbard asked the Texas congressional delegation to press for an inquiry into the part taken by Mexican citizens in the affair. On December 31 President Hayes turned to the army. Colonel John H. King and Lieutenant Colonel William H. Lewis showed up in El Paso in mid-January 1878 and immediately began taking testimony. Not until then did Hubbard learn that the federal officers had begun work. On February 9 he directed Major Jones to hasten to El Paso and take his place as the state's representative on the commission.

Arriving on February 18, Jones learned that his fellow commissioners were recording testimony about the conduct of state and county officials and even the Rangers. The governor had asked only for a finding on the extent of participation by Mexican citizens. At last, however, after an exchange of telegrams, Jones received authority to take his place as a commissioner. Seating himself on February 27, he laid before the two army officers a protest against any inquiry into what may have happened after December 17, the day of the executions. The actions of the sheriff, his posse, and the Rangers were purely state and local matters, of no concern to the army, which had no tribunal before which they could be brought. King and Lewis, however, blithely finished writing their report, handed it to Jones, and left El Paso.[35]

Although they proceeded without Jones and slighted him after his arrival, Colonels King and Lewis gathered a truly massive volume of evidence baring the origins, progress, and conclusion of the salt war. Jones's minority report, predictably, took refuge in legal technicalities— doubtless valid but unhelpful to a full understanding of what had happened. In all its monumental disorder, the report remains the indispensable foundation of any study of the salt war. On the commission's single substantive recommendation all could unite: federal troops should be permanently stationed at El Paso.

In retrospect, both Americans and Mexicans agreed that the enforcers of the people's law would never have fired on U.S. soldiers. The experiences of Lieutenant Rucker and Captain Blair somewhat weakened that notion, but the reactivation of Fort Bliss ensured that no upheaval of the magnitude of the salt war would ever again occur.

With district court convening in March 1878, Major Jones strengthened and extended the enlistment of Tays's Rangers. The grand jury handed down indictments of about one hundred men who could be named as part of the throng that had executed Howard and the others. Rangers would be needed to find and arrest them, although nearly all had taken refuge in Mexico, and extradition efforts had stirred no more than empty promises from Mexican officials. John Tays resigned as lieutenant in April 1878, to be succeeded by his brother James A. Tays. The Rangers did succeed in running the "American mob" out of the valley, and they actually apprehended one of the men indicted for the San Elizario affair. But Ysleta had no jail, and in November all the prisoners held by the Rangers slipped away under cover of night. James Tays resigned shortly afterward, and interim command fell to First Sergeant Marcus Ludwick.[36]

Gradually, the indicted Mexicans crept quietly back to their homes in the valley towns and resumed their traditional lives. The Austin owners of the salt lakes designated another agent, a former first sergeant of

Tays's company, who proved more a diplomat than Howard. The Mexicans dealt with him politely and paid the fees asked for the salt. The laws of Texas had been vindicated.[37]

THE SALT WAR formed one the darkest pages in the history of the Texas Rangers. No Ranger unit had ever surrendered so completely or ever would again. No Ranger unit had ever lost men under its protection to such bloody execution. On the other hand, only once had a sorrier Ranger unit ever served the state (Tobin's, in the Cortina troubles of 1859–1860). But Jones had to have Rangers in El Paso, and Tays and his twenty men seemed to him the best he could get.

The salt war was not a proud moment in the career of Major Jones. He brought reason and persuasion to his meeting with Chico Barela and his cohorts in San Elizario, and had he been able or willing to remain in El Paso for another month or two he could probably have averted the blowup. But pressing duties called at home, and he heeded the call. While in El Paso, his cultural bias and determination to play no favorites led him into misplaced friendship and trust with Charles Howard. Jones arranged for Howard's arrest and freedom under bail, then hurried back home without taking steps to ensure that Howard left Texas and did not return until he could be tried by district court in March. That was a fatal error. Had Howard carried out his promises to the San Elizario junta and his implicit commitment to Jones, the insurgents would have had no immediate cause for violence.

Jones must also bear some responsibility for the character of Tays's detachment. Had he combined Captain Gregorio García's followers with American recruits and placed the whole unit under García, a capable leader, the outcome could not have been worse than Tays made it by appearing as Howard's hireling.

The severest judgment, however, falls on the federal government. The army's generals persisted in regarding the affair as a purely local matter and convinced themselves, despite reports from their own officers on the scene, that Mexican citizens were not involved. If army intervention required no more pretext than the participation of Mexican citizens, peacekeeping troops could have been placed in San Elizario as early as the middle of October, after Lieutenant Rucker had declared soldiers to be urgently needed. Meekly, and probably with a sigh of relief, Captain Blair accepted Chico Barela's assurance that no Mexican citizens were in San Elizario, but he knew better. Had even a shadow of the force Colonel Hatch concentrated in the valley on December 22 and 23 been sent to San Elizario at any time before the battle that ended with the death of the five Americans, the crisis would have blown over.

Revisionist historians see the salt war as a "people's movement" asserting deeply held traditional rights that had been trampled by the American minority and their alien laws. Americans, of course, including the governor, adjutant general, and Major Jones, regarded it as the uprising of a lawless mob manipulated by scoundrels for their own benefit.

It seems to have been both, set against the backdrop of a brewing war with Mexico. The people surely united in feeling that they had been unjustly deprived of a livelihood they regarded as open to all. But their action was scarcely spontaneous. Their grievances had been stoked by Father Borajo and Luis Cardis for their private gain, and the tenuous organization and leadership had been prompted by their influence. Under Charles Howard's provocation, the movement cascaded into a revolt that Cardis could not contain and that Borajo did not wish to contain. Without their veiled leadership, the "people's movement" is not likely to have taken form.[38]

None of which erased the blot on the record of the Texas Rangers.

[12]

"That Far, Wild Country":
The Trans-Pecos and the Panhandle

"L IEUTENANT BAYLOR, I want you to remember out in that far, wild country that you represent the honor and dignity of the great state of Texas."

So enjoined the new governor of Texas, after administering a Ranger oath in July 1879. Like his two predecessors of Southern Redeemer persuasion, Oran M. Roberts, sixty-four, looked to the past rather than the future. Tall, with thick white hair and beard, the "Old Alcalde" had chaired the Secession Convention of 1861, had commanded a Confederate regiment in the war, and had come to the governor's office from the presiding bench of the state supreme court. He resembled Richard Coke and Richard Hubbard in his devotion to low taxes, small government, and rigid economy. Yet as the salt war had dramatized, that far, wild country beyond the Pecos demanded a stronger state presence. Commissioning George Wythe Baylor as a Ranger officer was a significant step toward asserting it.[1]

Baylor had been selected for the El Paso post by the new adjutant general. William Steele had resigned in January 1879, and Governor Roberts had elevated John B. Jones to the post. Jones chose to continue in direct command of the Rangers. To relieve himself of supply, personnel, and other administrative chores, in May he appointed Captain Neal Coldwell quartermaster of the Frontier Battalion. In addition to office duties, the able Coldwell, regularly riding the frontier as Jones had done, increasingly served as the eyes and ears of his chief.[2]

George W. Baylor was a singular choice for lieutenant of the detachment of Company C in El Paso, more a throwback to the old citizen soldier than a prototype of the new professional lawman. At forty-seven, he had lived an adventurous life—failed California argonaut, Indian fighter teamed with his famous older brother John Roberts Baylor, and combat-tested Confederate colonel. But in that role his fiery temper combined with an offended sense of justice brought him into conflict with a superior officer, Major General John A. Wharton. On April 6, 1865, quarreling in a Houston hotel room, an unarmed Wharton slapped Baylor in the face, whereupon Baylor drew his Colt and killed the general. In the collapse of the Confederacy, Baylor escaped punishment, but not the stain of dishonor. By 1879, reduced to "raising cabbages and onions" in Nueces Canyon, he asked Governor Roberts for a Ranger commission. His war record and a stack of political endorsements gained him appointment to the only vacancy in the Frontier Battalion.[3]

A small caravan of wagons and carts bore Baylor and his wife and two daughters, together with a sister-in-law, across the six hundred miles of the San Antonio–El Paso road. One wagon hauled furniture, including a piano and his treasured violin, another food, forage, and a coop of game chickens. The lieutenant had campaigned in West Texas and New Mexico early in the Civil War, and now he returned to make a new life there.

Six Rangers rode escort, including Sergeant James B. Gillett. The sergeant recalled his new commander as an erect and bearded six feet, two inches, "a perfect specimen of a hardy frontiersman." He was well educated, an engaging companion and conversationalist, a "high-minded Christian gentleman" who never swore, told dirty stories, drank, or smoked. He had demonstrated his bravery on many battlefields, and in bringing down game for the journey he revealed his superior marksmanship. Ominously, however, Gillett observed that "Baylor cared nothing for discipline in the company."[4]

Baylor's appointment coincided with mounting evidence that Austin dared ignore the Trans-Pecos no longer. The salt war drew official attention to El Paso, but voices elsewhere cried for recognition. With the close of the Red River War, the Great Comanche War Trail, slicing across the Trans-Pecos to Mexico, fell into disuse. Sheepmen and cowmen began to edge beyond the Pecos in search of new grass, the richest of which lay in the well-watered Davis Mountains. Communities sprang up around the federal garrisons of Forts Stockton and Davis, the former claiming the seat of Pecos County, the latter the seat of Presidio County. Local officials alerted Austin to the perils of the Trans-Pecos.

In the late 1870s two dangers rolled down from the north to buffet Texans gravitating westward across the Pecos. Indians were one. Although Kiowas and Comanches no longer tormented the Trans-Pecos, Mescalero Apaches did. Based at the Fort Stanton Reservation, in the Sacramento Mountains of southern New Mexico, they preyed on the stock of newly arrived ranchmen and on travelers, freighters, and mail coaches on the San Antonio-El Paso Road. Fort Stanton provided a city of refuge comparable to Fort Sill a decade earlier.

The second danger was a flood of desperadoes. New Mexico's Lincoln County War had erupted in such violence that in October 1878 President Hayes proclaimed Lincoln County in a state of insurrection, which turned the army loose as a *posse comitatus*. Many on both sides were brigands drawn by the prospect of pillage. With cavalry on their trail, they headed south, into Texas.

Two of New Mexico's most notorious outlaws forced General Jones's hand. They were Jesse Evans and John Selman. Evans led an arrogant and utterly unscrupulous band called "The Boys," who operated as hired gunmen for the Murphy-Dolan faction in the Lincoln County War. Selman, a fugitive from Texas, headed a bunch called "The Wrestlers," who terrorized Lincoln County with robbery, murder, and rape. After the army took a hand in the Lincoln County War, both Evans and Selman, with about twenty of their New Mexico followers, relocated to

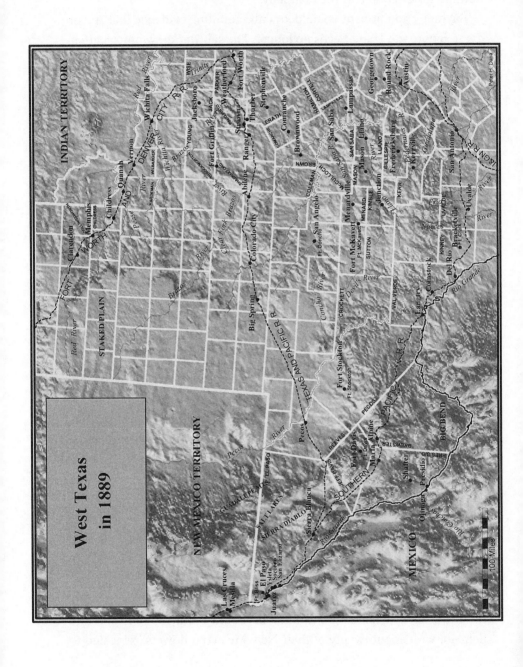

**West Texas
in 1889**

the Davis Mountains. Selman, calling himself Captain John Tyson, set up a butcher shop in the town of Fort Davis, while Evans and his henchmen kept him supplied with stolen beef.[5]

The Evans gang terrorized citizens and cowed county authorities. On May 19, 1880, Evans and four of his New Mexico fugitives engineered a brazen robbery. While two entered Keesey's saloon and called everyone to the bar for free drinks, Evans and two more strode into the Sender and Siebenborn store, held up proprietor and customers, and made off with $930 in cash and an arsenal of firearms. They then rode down to Fort Stockton, where they lazed for several days until the county judge prodded the sheriff into assembling a posse to arrest them. The posse botched the attempt but did get one, Albert Graham. Townspeople now fretted over a predictable attempt by Graham's cohorts to break him out of the rickety jail. Authorities at both Fort Davis and Fort Stockton appealed to Governor Roberts for help.[6]

Adjutant General Jones ordered Captain Dan Roberts to send a detachment of Company D by forced marches from Fort McKavett to Fort Stockton. Also, he sent Sergeant L. B. Caruthers to Fort Davis to investigate whether Rangers should be permanently stationed in Presidio or Pecos County.[7]

On June 6, after a two-week ride, Sergeant Edward A. Sieker and nine exhausted Rangers reached Fort Stockton. They arrived in time to prevent Graham's comrades from breaking him out of jail, but they could not scout the country for the rest of the gang because the jail had to be guarded. Finally they moved on to Fort Davis, taking Graham with them. Alerted to an ambush in Wild Rose Pass, they followed an alternate route and on June 18 lodged him in the more secure Fort Davis jail.[8]

On June 29 someone tipped Caruthers and Sieker that some of the Evans bunch had been spotted on the road to Presidio del Norte, the old town on the Rio Grande where travelers passed into Mexico. The two sergeants, with four privates and a Mexican guide, hurried south. Shortly after noon on July 3, after an eighty-five-mile ride, they sighted four riders, chased them into the foothills of a mountain, and fought a dismounted gun battle. It ended in the death of one of the outlaws and the surrender of Evans and two cohorts. Not until the prisoners had been disarmed did Sieker learn that one of his Rangers, George Bingham, had caught a bullet in the heart just after dismounting. Had he known that in time, Sieker vowed, he would have killed them all.[9]

In October the gangsters had their day in court. Evans drew a ten-year sentence for the murder of Ranger Bingham. Selman was packed off to stand trial for a variety of offenses in Shackelford County. But the sheriff there refused to receive him, contending that the evidence to convict had long since vanished and that if Selman showed up any-where around Fort Griffin he would be lynched. Incongruously, he turned up fifteen years later as the El Paso constable who killed John Wesley Hardin. Even Evans ended as a winner. Confined in the Huntsville Penitentiary, on May 23, 1882, he walked off a work detail and vanished from history.[10]

On one conclusion the Ranger sergeants united: Baylor could not handle Forts Stockton and Davis from El Paso. Pecos and Presidio Counties needed their own Ranger unit. On July 12, 1880, Adjutant General Jones ordered Lieutenant Charles L. Nevill to establish Company E in Fort Davis.[11]

IN SEPTEMBER 1879, at Ysleta, Lieutenant George W. Baylor took command of the detachment of Company C, which had been led for nearly a year by Sergeant Marcus Ludwick. At once Baylor plunged into the midst of a bloody Indian uprising.

Victorio, dynamic chief of the Mimbres Apaches, ranked among the ablest leaders in all the history of the Apaches. For two years, alternating war and diplomacy, he had resisted the government's attempt to make him and his people live on Arizona's sickly San Carlos Reservation. Finally, in June 1879, an accommodation had been patched together settling the Mimbres band on the Mescalero Reservation near Fort Stanton. That lasted hardly two months, until he learned that civil authorities at Silver City intended to arrest and try him for murder. With forty warriors, he broke loose, twisted and turned in the Black Range of southwestern New Mexico, fought off cavalry units trying to corner him, and in October slipped across the boundary into Mexico.[12]

Even as Victorio eluded the cavalry, Baylor had his first taste of Indian fighting in twenty years. A band of eighteen Mescaleros riding to join Victorio raided across Baylor's sector. Alerted on October 4, 1879, by a message from Captain Gregorio García at San Elizario, Baylor and nine men, including Sergeant Gillett, headed down the overland road the next morning. Baylor had formed a fast friendship with García fighting Yankees in 1861, and at San Elizario the Rangers "found that grand, brave old Mexican . . . waiting for us, his horse saddled and blankets and grub ready."[13]

The trail crossed into Mexico. No Ranger had entered Mexico since the salt war, so Baylor sent García to ask permission of the alcalde of Guadalupe. He not only gave his assent but promised reinforcements. Townsmen and the *vaqueros* of a ranch that the Apaches had raided expanded Baylor's force to about twenty-five. The trail led to a rocky canyon where Baylor was certain the Indians had laid a trap. Probing the ridges above the canyon, the pursuers uncovered the ambush.

Mexicans and Americans stumbled on foot up a rocky slope toward the base of a cliff. Hidden among the crevices, the Apaches opened fire. Baylor shouted to charge. Just short of a crest, the Rangers confronted a mass of boulders. From behind one a big Apache, his face painted red and blue, stepped out and fired at Gillett. The bullet hit a soapweed and plastered his face with sticky leaves. As he wiped them off, another bullet carried away the front brim of his hat. The warrior levered a third round into his rifle. Gillett brought his own Winchester up and took aim. The Indian turned sideways to present a smaller target. "We both fired at the same instant," recounted Gillett. "My bullet hit the redskin just above his hip and, passing straight through his body, broke the small of his back and killed him almost instantly."[14]

For the rest of the day, the two sides exchanged fire without hitting anyone. Only puffs of gun smoke presented targets, for no Indian again showed himself. Under cover of night, the Apaches withdrew.

That Baylor and his Rangers had won the confidence of their Mexican neighbors became clear a month later. On November 7, 1879, Victorio and his warriors ambushed and wiped out a party of fifteen citizens of Carrizal scouting the Candelaria Mountains for sign of Indians. When they failed to return home, another group of thirty-five set forth, only to ride into the same trap and die to a man. From Paso del Norte and the other river towns, volunteers gathered to ride south and bury the victims. An invitation reached Baylor to join the expedition. With nine men, he accepted.

Ultimately, the force numbered 179. In recognition of Baylor's experience as an Indian fighter, the leaders offered him command. This he declined because the expedition would operate on Mexican soil, but he accepted the proffered second rank.

The journey to the deadly mountain pass on the road to Chihuahua City involved no combat. The main objective was to bury the dead, a gruesome, heart-rending task. The fifty bodies represented almost the entire male population of Carrizal. For the little band of Rangers, however, it opened channels of friendship and cooperation exceptional in the wake of the salt war. Back at the border, the Mexicans expressed their gratitude and offered to join Baylor anytime Indians appeared, "so we can make a good standoff fight."[15]

Twenty-five Rangers, even under the veteran Baylor, could hardly hope to contend with several times their number of Apache fighters following such an exceptionally skilled war leader. Indeed, this mission belonged primarily to the U.S. Army. Through most of 1880 cavalry units sparred with the wily Apache in New Mexico and Texas. In July elements of Colonel Benjamin H. Grierson's Tenth Cavalry barred Victorio from crossing Texas to New Mexico. Denied critical water holes by the troops, he fell back to Mexico. Baylor and thirteen Rangers shared this operation, riding with a troop of cavalry following Indian trails across deserts and amid rocky canyons.

In Mexico Victorio had to confront another veteran Indian fighter, Colonel Joaquin Terrazas. In a newfound spirit of amity between the Díaz and Hayes administrations, the Mexican colonel invited U.S. troops to help him run down Victorio. Baylor and his thirteen men ranged widely over Chihuahua, sometimes with Mexican volunteers, sometimes with U.S. regulars. But Terrazas, citing as objectionable the Apache scouts attached to the American cavalry, asked all units from north of the border to withdraw.[16]

Back at Ysleta, Baylor welcomed two developments. First, on October 14–15, 1880, Terrazas caught Victorio amid three peaks called Tres Castillos and launched an attack. Sixty-two warriors and eighteen women and children died in the slaughter. This time Victorio's legendary cunning failed him. A bullet ended his extraordinary career.[17]

Second, Baylor found on his desk a message from Adjutant General Jones. On September 1, 1880, the detachment of Company C had been mustered out of the Ranger service and mustered back in as Company A, Frontier Battalion, *Captain* George W. Baylor commanding.[18]

Captain Baylor and his El Paso Rangers had missed out on the final battle with Victorio, but his death did not end Apache warfare in Texas. Early in January 1881 a few survivors of Victorio's decimated band– twelve warriors, four women, and four children–returned to Texas. In deadly Quitman Canyon they waylaid a stagecoach and killed the occupants. On January 16, with fourteen men, Baylor took the trail. It traced a jagged path through mountain and desert on both sides of the border, but he hung on. On January 24 Lieutenant Nevill and nine men from the company at Fort Davis joined, bringing the force to twenty-five. At dawn on January 29, as the Indians gathered for a breakfast of mescal around a campfire high in the Sierra Diablo, the Rangers rose from hiding and raked them with volley after volley from Winchester repeaters. Four men, two women, and two children fell in the burst of fire. The rest, most of them wounded, scattered. Baylor lamented their escape but quipped, "At any rate dont think they will sit down to eat breakfast without looking around to see if the Rangers are in sight."[19]

Apache warfare, like all Indian warfare, often claimed the lives of women and children. If noncombatants traveled with a raiding party, or were in a camp surprised by Rangers or U.S. cavalry, their lives were at risk. Their presence with warriors discouraged neither type of troop from attacking. Noncombatants were rarely singled out as targets but simply fell in the smoke and turmoil of battle. Baylor's Rangers regretted killing the women and children in the Sierra Diablo, but the elation at thrashing a destructive band of raiders muted the regret.

Although the old Indian fighter could not know it, with the action in the Sierra Diablo the Indian wars of Texas drew to a close. In George Wythe Baylor, El Paso had an atypical Ranger chief—older, better educated, more experienced, far more prominent in the annals of Texas, and still imbued with the aggressiveness that had marked his entire career. In only one important way could he be faulted, and it was serious. Captain Neal Coldwell, the efficient quartermaster of the battalion, had inspected Baylor's men just before the chase after Victorio. The men were a better lot than had been supposed, Coldwell informed Jones, but had poor horses and virtually no discipline. In the field they marched as they pleased, scattering the command at random over the landscape and observing hardly any security precautions to avoid surprise by Indians.[20]

Sergeant Gillett, who married Baylor's daughter and worshiped his chief, conceded that the captain would believe any story, excuse almost any offense, and enlist anyone who applied. In fact, he had to discharge more than one Ranger who turned out to be a fugitive from the law elsewhere.[21]

Still, as Coldwell granted, Baylor rigidly enforced sobriety and discharged any man who got drunk. He was well liked by his men and by the citizens of El Paso. His role in the Victorio war and in running down the last Apaches in Texas earned him praise at home and in Austin. Despite his failings, he reigned as the respected captain of Company A for six years.[22]

ON JULY 13, 1878, Major John B. Jones, not yet adjutant general, posted Company C of the Frontier Battalion to Fort Griffin, the town on the flats below the military post overlooking the Clear Fork of the Brazos. The town had already begun its decline from the boom years of the hide trade, 1876–1878, when it served as a raucous outfitting depot for the annihilation of the southern herd of bison. Farmers had edged out from the Cross Timbers, and on the plains rolling westward stockmen had begun to replace bison with longhorns. The newcomers had organized

Shackelford County in 1874, but, averse to the sordid reputation of Griffin, they had established a new county seat, Albany, fifteen miles to the south.

Lieutenant George Washington Arrington commanded Company C. In three years he had risen rapidly in the Ranger ranks. Wherever he served, admirers applauded his diligence, fairness, and effectiveness. Yet his volatile temper could explode in the face of anyone who crossed him, and he imposed an iron discipline on his men. Slightly built, with high forehead, riveting eyes, and impressively pointed mustache and beard, Arrington had acquired his combative temperament and skills as one of General John S. Mosby's Confederate guerrillas during the war. He was John C. Orrick then, but when he came to Texas in 1870 he changed his name in a move to erase a tainted postwar past.[23]

The Griffin posting led to George Washington Arrington's most significant service—leading the Rangers into the Texas Panhandle. By 1879, the Panhandle's bounteous grass beckoned stockmen. The treeless flat table of the Staked Plain remained largely uncharted, but the breaks of the Canadian River, flowing eastward from New Mexico on the north, and the headwaters of the Red and Brazos Rivers, scouring canyons in the caprock on the east, had already begun to attract settlers. In 1876 Charles Goodnight laid the foundation of his cattle empire in Palo Duro Canyon, and Thomas S. Bugbee followed with a ranch on the Canadian.

In 1876 also, the legislature drew boundaries for fifty-four Panhandle counties, attaching them all to Clay and Jack counties for judicial purposes. On Sweetwater Creek in the east, the army established Fort Elliott in 1875 and thus brought Hidetown, a buffalo hunters' camp, to life as Mobeetie, the "mother city" of the Panhandle. Tascosa followed in 1876, a "plaza" established by New Mexican sheepmen on the Canadian River to the west. It quickly transformed itself into a center for cows rather than sheep. Clarendon took root in 1878 on the Salt Fork of Red River, a colony of Methodists dubbed "Saint's Roost" by the more worldly. Fort Griffin played a minor role in the rise of the Panhandle communities; they looked instead to the railroad at Dodge City, Kansas, for commercial and transportation links to the outside world.[24]

The Texas Panhandle in the 1890s

Indians drew Arrington's attention to the Panhandle. Although now confined to the Fort Sill Reservation, the Kiowas and Comanches often embarked on hunting trips to Texas, sometimes with the agent's authority, sometimes not. Sometimes they confined their hunt to game animals but sometimes extended it to cattle as well. In the spring of 1879 the citizens of Wheeler County, which they had just organized with the seat at Mobeetie, petitioned for a visit by Rangers. In June, Arrington, newly promoted to captain, led twenty Rangers in a hot, dry march to Mobeetie.

At once the Ranger captain collided with the post commander at Fort Elliott, Lieutenant Colonel John W. Davidson, a veteran of nearly forty years widely regarded in the army as mentally unstable. His troopers had done little to turn the Indians back to the reservation, and somehow word had reached him that the Rangers came to kill Indians. Approaching Arrington in "a terrible passion," he demanded to know if he would kill Indians. He most assuredly would, the captain responded, if he found them armed, but that his orders were to protect life and property and preserve the peace, whether threatened by white or Indian.

A scout for Indians only revealed trails bearing east, back to the reservation. Warned by the colonel's couriers, Arrington concluded, "every bunch of Indians he hears of is making for the line, saying 'Texas soldiers no buenos.'"

Talking with stockmen and farmers, Arrington learned that they had lost patience with the reservation Indians. If the state or federal government would do nothing for the citizens, they would take matters into their own hands. Charles Goodnight said the same thing when Arrington dropped by his JA Ranch in Palo Duro Canyon.

The clash between Arrington and Davidson reverberated in Austin. The Wheeler County commissioners, Davidson lackeys, warned Governor Roberts that Rangers in the Panhandle would rekindle an Indian war. Davidson himself brought the quarrel to the governor's notice.

Arrington easily defended himself. The colonel and Fort Elliott's civilian sutlers had selfish motives that had nothing to do with Indians.

The sutlers had labored hard but in vain to head off the organization of Wheeler County. The new county seat would attract merchants who would compete with the monopoly of the army sutlers. Employing military intimidation, Davidson had tried to thwart the will of the citizens. No one at the fort wanted Texas Rangers anywhere nearby.

Moreover, Arrington had most of the Panhandle population on his side, and he could make a good case for posting Rangers there. Back at Griffin by early July, he had found stock ranches "thick as could be" along the base of the caprock and immigrants arriving daily to settle on all the streams heading above the caprock. He had also learned that, besides Indian hunting parties, bands of white horse thieves ranged the plains all the way to Griffin, hurried their stolen herds up Blanco or Yellow House Canyon and across to the Pecos River in New Mexico, then returned with horses stolen there. In Arrington's view, the Panhandle needed its own company of Rangers.

Captain Neal Coldwell, inspecting Company C at Griffin shortly after its return, agreed and recommended its transfer to Blanco Canyon. "Capt. Arrington," Coldwell further observed, "has won golden opinions of the people where ever he goes." He was strict and efficient, but Company C harbored a "discordant element" that kept men dissatisfied. The unit's "moral tone" suffered from "the women and wine of Fort Griffin." Arrington expected to get rid of the worst men when he reorganized on September 1. But even in the Panhandle, distant from the temptations of Griffin, Arrington's rigid discipline would never truly unite the company behind him.[25]

By early September 1879, Arrington had established his new base near the mouth of Blanco Canyon, one of two gashes in the southern caprock. Visiting in October, Captain Coldwell pronounced the unit the best mounted and best disciplined company on the entire line. The tough captain had cleansed the outfit of the Griffin carousers and rebuilt it with new but yet untried men.[26]

Arrington devoted most of his efforts to trying to turn back straying parties of Comanches from the Fort Sill Reservation. He discovered ample evidence of their routes and watering places, as well as evidence of the regular passage of horse thieves between New Mexico and Texas. His most significant achievement, however, was geographical. In wide-ranging, exhausting expeditions seeking Indians, he fleshed out blank spaces on the map of the Staked Plain.[27]

As the cavalry at Fort Sill grew more effective at keeping the Indians at home, Arrington turned to exigencies that would increasingly relegate Indians to a minor annoyance as the Panhandle filled with immigrants during the 1880s. One was cowboy rowdyism that overpowered towns with weak or no local authority. More ominous, the vast carpet of Panhandle grass attracted more and more newcomers, mostly small operators, to demand their share of the open range. Big operators like Charles Goodnight, commanding small armies of cowboy-gunmen, did not take the challenge lightly.[28]

Attracted by the free grass himself, Arrington resigned the Ranger service in the summer of 1882. Popular neither with his own men nor with his fellow captains, whom he sometimes disparaged, he nevertheless had laid the basis for a stern brand of Texas law in the Panhandle, and for seven years he had won repeated plaudits for exemplary service in every Ranger grade from private to captain. As sheriff of Wheeler County for another seven years, he indulged in unseemly quarrels with his successor captains, but until his death in 1923 Panhandle residents proudly claimed "Cap" Arrington as one of their most venerated citizens.

THROUGHOUT THE EARLY MONTHS OF 1881, captains occasionally expressed concern for their chief's health. At the same time, Jones's grip on the Ranger force weakened. Surgery for an abscess on the liver promised relief, but the little man could not stand the shock. He died on July 18, 1881, aged forty-seven. His record fully confirmed the encomiums of newspaper obituaries.[29]

John B. Jones left a widow who had broken through his stodgy bachelorhood only two years earlier. He also left a wide circle of friends and admirers, not least among his captains. And in his quiet but firm way he left a legacy more vital to the Texas Rangers than any leader who had gone before or who would come after. He gave a lasting institutional continuity to the Texas Rangers, transformed them from Indian fighters into lawmen, and imparted to them a professionalism that would endure, with some dark and conspicuous lapses, into the twenty-first century.

[13]

The King Era, 1881–1891

THE DEATH OF the revered John B. Jones stunned and saddened the Rangers of the Frontier Battalion and the Special State Troops. It also created a vacancy in the office of the adjutant general. Governor Oran M. Roberts selected Wilburn Hill King, two-term legislator from Sulphur Springs, northeast of Dallas.

King imitated Jones in retaining direct command of the Rangers. He applied Jones's high standards and ruled with the same unforgiving discipline. He expected his orders to be obeyed promptly and unquestioningly, and he adroitly rid himself of officers who failed to conform. Rigidly opinionated, King expressed himself forthrightly in language that rarely relied on one word when ten would do.

A former Confederate general with wounds to attest his combat record, King represented the old order, the Southern Redeemers who celebrated their Confederate heritage and execrated the Edmund Davis regime. King served three governors cast in the same mold as Richard Coke and Richard Hubbard—Oran Roberts, John Ireland, and Lawrence Sullivan Ross. Roberts had presided over the Secession Convention of 1861. Ireland, the slender, stern "Sage of Seguin," holding office from 1883 to 1887, had been a delegate to the Secession Convention and a Confederate colonel. Sul Ross, 1887–1891, had distinguished himself as a prewar Ranger captain and wartime Confederate general. King fit comfortably with all three and did not relinquish office until 1891, after Texans had elected a governor who looked to the future rather than the past.

While governors clung to principles of Spartan economy and minimal government, momentous changes swept Texas in the 1880s. They found an apt metaphor on the Austin hilltop crowned by the Texas statehouse. The structure was an artifact of the past, erected in 1853 and likened by one wit to "a large sized corn crib with a pumpkin for a dome." On November 9, 1881, midway through the Roberts administration, fire reduced the "grand old pile" to charred rubble. The blaze helped clear the site for the new capitol already planned. In exchange for three million acres of Panhandle grassland, Chicago capitalists backed by British investors undertook to erect a new capitol building. At the same time, they formed the famed XIT Ranch and began to convert the rich grass of ten counties into beef. For a full week in May 1888, Governor Sul Ross and Austin citizens celebrated the completion of their new capitol, a magnificent edifice of pink granite towering over twelve blocks of Congress Avenue and the Colorado River beyond.[1]

The granite walls lifting the capitol above the city symbolized the demographic, economic, political, and social transformation of Texas during the 1880s. Immigration from other states swelled population to more than two million in 1890. An expanding rail network enabled farmers to move produce, so they abandoned the self-sufficient farm for the cash crop of cotton. Railroads and cotton helped to fuel commercialism, industrialism, and urbanism. Westward fingers of the railroad system, checked for a time by the Panic of 1873, now reached for El Paso from San Antonio and Fort Worth, for Laredo from San Antonio and Corpus Christi, and for Denver across the Panhandle from Fort Worth. The railroads and associated coal mines attracted labor unions to Texas and raised the specter of labor strife. Cattlemen and sheepmen spread into the Panhandle and across the Pecos all the way to El Paso. Seeking to replace the durable longhorn with blooded stock, they enclosed pastures with barbed wire and thus doomed the open range. Democrats monopolized state offices and most local offices, but economic upheaval further roiled a historically rancorous politics.[2]

These developments held portentous implications for the executive and legislative branches of the state. They also held portentous implications for General King and his Texas Rangers. They would have to confront such new challenges as disorder in boom towns, train robbers, homicidal feudists, rampant fence cutting, labor strikes, clashes between political factions, and vigilantes turned mobs.

Wilburn King's advent alarmed the Rangers. As a legislator from an eastern county, he had stoutly opposed their appropriations, and they feared that his appointment signaled the governor's hostility. They were wrong. King promptly toured West Texas and admitted that he had changed his mind, that Rangers were essential to law and order. He never regarded them as more than a temporary force, to be sacrificed to the dictates of economy as soon they tamed the frontier. For a decade, however, even as the expansion of the Texas Volunteer Guard increasingly distracted him, King championed the cause of the Rangers and kept his captains under intense scrutiny. Indulging his weakness for verbosity, he extolled Ranger deeds in such florid hyperbole as to pump new life into a legend dormant since the time of Jack Hays and Rip Ford.[3]

Ironically, while stoking the Ranger legend King presided over a drastic shrinkage of the Ranger force. He resisted the repeated moves to abolish it altogether and made token appeals for adequate appropriations. But he shared the legislators' passion for thrift and seemed content to accept whatever level of funding they decreed. With the populous eastern counties ruling the statehouse, the Rangers counted themselves fortunate to survive the biennial sessions of the legislature with no more damage than a slashed budget.

It had been slashed in the final months of the Jones regime, from $100,000 to $80,000 for the Frontier Battalion and nothing for the Special State Troops—the old company of McNelly and Hall, now under the able Thomas L. Oglesby. To save that veteran outfit, Jones incorporated it into the Frontier Battalion as Company F.

Inheriting six companies of only twenty men each, King failed to head off further blows. By 1885, the appropriation had fallen to $60,000 a year. King disbanded two companies, including George Baylor's Company A in the far west. Later in the same year, a government-wide shortfall forced King to cut each of the remaining four companies to a mere ten Rangers. By the close of his tenure, an annual budget of $30,000 funded forty-four Rangers in three companies, widely separated and moved often to places where most needed.[4]

The cutbacks allowed captains to be choosy in selecting recruits. To fill a vacancy, applicants had only to satisfy a captain. No other qualifications were specified. Captains sought young men of strength and endurance who could handle a horse and firearms. Those traits were easily judged. Less evident were courage, the capacity for teamwork, and the potential for trouble making, within the company or in town. Rangers thus learned through experience and under the tutelage of the captain and his noncommissioned officers. Captains likewise held the power to promote worthy men and discharge the unworthy. Reporting directly to the adjutant general, captains were appointed and dismissed by the adjutant general, usually with the concurrence of the governor. Despite dwindling numbers, expanding mission, and a rugged outdoor life, Wilburn King's Rangers of the 1880s served Texas well.

AS THE KING ERA opened, railroad barons Jay Gould and Collis P. Huntington vied to build and control the nation's second transcontinental railroad. Thrusting across the Trans-Pecos from Fort Worth, Gould's Texas and Pacific not only lost its Pacific outlet to Huntington's Southern Pacific, but even lost the race for El Paso. The first SP train steamed into that dusty village from the west on May 19, 1881, instantly transforming it into a boomtown. As Gould approached from the east, the two moguls compromised. On December 16, 1881, a silver spike tied the T&P to the SP at Sierra Blanca, in the barren mountains eighty-five miles east of El Paso. The agreement permitted Gould's trains to use SP tracks into El Paso.

Huntington had already begun to piece together the chain of acquisitions that would give the SP a direct line all the way from San Francisco to New Orleans. During 1882 one link in the chain hurried from San Antonio across the Trans-Pecos to the junction at Sierra Blanca.

As Texas had spurred railroad construction with massive land grants, so Texas stood ready to aid the railroad companies with Texas Rangers. The railroads both facilitated and expanded the Rangers' mission. Now they could cover their sectors much more quickly by riding passenger coaches, hauling their horses in freight cars, and communicating by telegraph. But now too the railroad companies called on them to subdue end-of-track boomtowns and to combat the profusion of train robberies that flared as soon as express cars began to transport coin and currency.

On two of General King's best captains fell responsibility for shepherding the two railroads across the Trans-Pecos. Captain Samuel A. McMurry helped the Texas and Pacific, Captain Lamartine P. Sieker the SP subsidiary.

Sam McMurry was known as "Soft Voice" or "Say Nothing." Terse, softly spoken phrases marked his speech. A blocky frame surmounted by a full, kindly, mustachioed face and receding hairline gave him a benign aspect that matched his sobriquets. Unlike some other captains, he did not play to the press, but in ten years as commander of Company B he showed himself a man of courage, a leader with a flair for the gently effective, and a peace officer determined to enforce the law with no more gunplay than essential.[5]

"Lam" Sieker, one of four brothers who signed on with the Texas Rangers, had been a Ranger since 1874. A slim, gaunt-faced, long-necked fellow of thirty-three, Sieker proved a thoughtful, able, reliable, well-liked captain. One of his men recalled that Sieker loved to dance, and whenever the company came to town citizens gathered in the schoolhouse for a frolic. The town girls knew they had grown up when they fell in love with Captain Sieker, "and all of us loved him at one time or another."[6]

After four years as head of Company D, Sieker had so impressed General King as to win the coveted post of battalion quartermaster, held by Neal Coldwell from 1879 to 1883 and John Johnson until 1885. Lam Sieker would accumulate a record twenty-six years of Ranger service, from 1874 to 1895 and again from 1900 to 1905.[7]

The lines across the Trans-Pecos did not confront a serious Indian threat. Rather, they contended with the throngs of toughs, gamblers, whiskey peddlers, prostitutes, pimps, and crooks drawn to end-of-track. The riffraff kept the tent cities in turmoil and remained to cause constant trouble in those that survived as the rails moved on. Also, advancing across stock ranges, the railroad fleshpots attracted cowboys who periodically got drunk, shot up the towns, and disrupted railroad operations.

With courts often one or two hundred miles distant from a railroad construction camp, peace officers could do no more than attempt to keep the roughs under control. Rangers learned how to keep roughs under control: commanding presence and vocabulary, manhandling when that failed, and as last resort "bending" the barrel of a six-shooter over a man's head. (The barrel, not the butt; as a later Ranger remarked, "No one but the rankest tenderfoot would change ends with a pistol or relinquish his hold on the stock.") Almost never did one rowdy or many force a Ranger to pull the trigger to enforce a command.[8]

Rangers also dealt with train robbers. On April 20, 1882, the holdup of a T&P express car at Ranger brought three of McMurry's men from a passenger coach to the station platform to exchange gunfire with the bandits. One robber was hit and later captured, but the rest got away. After Ranger, train robbery exacted a constant drain on General King's declining manpower.[9]

After the legislature cut the Rangers' appropriations in half in 1887, leaving only three companies with scarcely a dozen men each, a rash of train robberies broke out. King, Governor Sul Ross, and railway executives met and agreed to organize a "special ranger service" for passenger trains. Selected trainmen, engineers, conductors, brakemen, and other employees were sworn in as Special Rangers, which allowed them to carry arms and protect the trains without expense to the state.[10]

"Specials" had been a King innovation since early in his administration. He reasoned that the act of 1874 authorizing the Frontier Battalion provided for 450 Rangers, a number never approached because of meager appropriations. He could therefore, he believed, swear in as many Specials as he wanted so long as they cost the state nothing and never ran the Ranger total above 450. Not only railroad personnel but stockmen, detectives, hide inspectors, former Rangers or sheriffs who had incurred enemies, and others with real need or political influence gained commissions as Special Rangers. Although of dubious legality, the device provided practical benefits if also opportunities, because of lax accountability, for misuse.[11]

The railway special service could guard trains but not chase culprits who had pulled off a successful robbery. Another of King's top captains made the most dramatic pursuit of train robbers, albeit a few months after King had stepped down as adjutant general.

Frank Jones had served two hitches in the Rangers before signing on for a third in September 1882. Under Lam Sieker, whom he adored, Jones proved an apt pupil and rose swiftly in Company D. When Sieker went to Austin in 1885 as battalion quartermaster, Lieutenant Jones, at age twenty-nine, took command of the company. His captaincy came a year later. In the next few years, with service on the lower Rio Grande, the upper Nueces, and in the Trans-Pecos, he evolved into perhaps the most widely admired lawman in Texas. General King labeled him "a most efficient, energetic, and fearless officer and Ranger."[12]

In 1891 Jones headquartered his tiny company at Alpine, a cowtown on the Southern Pacific surrounded by grasslands rolling north to the Davis Mountains and south to the rocky peaks and canyons cradled by the Big Bend of the Rio Grande. On September 1 the telegraph brought word that an SP train had been robbed in Val Verde County near Langtry, where the colorful Judge Roy Bean held court. The next morning, loading five Rangers and their horses on a special car, Jones steamed 145 miles southeast to the scene of the crime.

For more than a week the determined little squad clung to the bandit trail, made by five men on horseback who time and again scattered and reunited and crossed and recrossed the Rio Grande. Exhausted, mounts giving out, living off grub abandoned by the fugitives, the lawmen beat and burned one cane brake after another on both sides of the river before at last admitting failure and returning home.

A month later Jones got word that the wanted men had returned to Val Verde County and were thought to be some fifty miles north of Comstock, in the Devils River wilds. On October 10 he loaded seven men and their horses on a freight train and from Comstock pointed north. In tangled terrain of Sutton and Crockett Counties, the Rangers cut the fresh trail of four men and soon overtook them. A running gunfight netted two captives within a mile when their horses failed. A third had to surrender when a bullet brought down his horse. For eight exhausting miles, the fourth spurred his horse in flight. A Ranger bullet knocked him to the ground, wounded. Rather than give up, he turned his six-shooter on himself and, as Jones laconically put it, "blew his brains out."

Back at the railroad with his prisoners, Jones encountered the Val Verde County sheriff, who presented arrest warrants for the train robbers. Aware of the laxity of local courts, Jones declined to turn them over, explaining that they had robbed the U.S. mail, a federal offense, and that he held commission as a deputy U.S. marshal as well as Texas Ranger. He would take them to the federal court in El Paso.

Subordinating state to federal law later got Jones into trouble, but the federal court in El Paso sent the three train robbers off to a federal penitentiary. Captain Jones, moreover, earned the plaudits of the SP management and thereafter instant response to almost any transportation favor he might ask.[13]

"A GIGANTIC ORGANIZATION has been created with many thousands of men bound by secret oaths and obligations," General King declared darkly in 1886. "Under the mad and murderous teachings of Communists and Socialists," huge aggregations of wage workers had forced state after state to confront the dangers of labor unrest. The "gigantic organization" was the Knights of Labor, Terence Powderly's vehicle for uniting the "toilers" of every economic sector in the quest for higher wages and better working conditions. The appearance of the Knights in Texas in the early 1880s troubled the adjutant general.

In Jay Gould's Texas railroad system the Knights confronted an organization perhaps less gigantic than their own but far more ruthless. Minor strikes in 1884 and 1885 gained auspicious concessions. In the spring of 1886, however, the Great Southwest Strike shattered on corporate obduracy, public sympathy alienated by obstruction that led to violence, and most critically, railroad goon squads, Pinkertons, and militia. Responding to the company management's call for help, Governor Ireland and Adjutant General King concentrated the state troops at the flash point of Fort Worth, and the strike quickly collapsed.

The Texas Rangers played a minor role in the strike. King ordered three companies to the scene. They were too few, however, to do much more than walk the railroad yards as Texas Rangers. In fact, that was how General King, with his usual grandiloquence, applauded their influence. Their "sturdy and determined manner and appearance," he wrote, "made a powerful impression on the minds of the strikers, and had due weight in bringing about a condition of peace."[14]

The failure of the Great Southwest Strike in April 1886, followed by public outrage over the Haymarket bomb in Chicago a month later, dealt a mortal blow to the Knights of Labor, and the "giant organization" of King's dread swiftly declined. The railroad strike, however, introduced the Texas Rangers to an unpleasant mission that would cling to them well into the twentieth century.

Although crippled, the Knights tried to organize the miners of the coal beds near the Texas and Pacific tracks on both sides of the Erath-Palo Pinto County line, seventy-five miles southwest of Fort Worth. In September 1888, these mines fell under the control of Robert D. Hunter, a tough capitalist of the Jay Gould stripe. To supply the railroad with the prime bituminous fuel, he organized the Texas and Pacific Coal

Company. In December Hunter's obstinate refusal to negotiate with the Knights' organizers set off a strike and shut down the mines. The first call for Rangers came from the sheriff of Erath County, but thereafter Hunter himself made known his wants.

Sam McMurry drew the assignment. His gentle ways made him the ideal captain for such service. He took ten men to the mines, based on the newly founded company towns of Thurber in Erath County and Strawn in Palo Pinto County.

McMurry confronted a delicate mission: to protect corporate property from damage and to preserve order among angry workers inflamed by militant organizers. In the eyes of the workers, this task allied him with Hunter, especially when Hunter imported 135 scabs from Indiana. When "agitators" threatened to stop the train as it made its way through Fort Worth, McMurry's Rangers got it through without incident.

However much King abhorred the Knights of Labor, he knew the Rangers must steer a cautious path between management and labor. To management he made clear that their complaints lay largely within the jurisdiction of the civil courts and that Rangers could be relied on only to keep the peace. To McMurry King made clear that Rangers could not be used by management for any illegal or repressive purpose, and he pointedly admonished that any misstep could hand the legislature a pretext for abolishing the Rangers.

By June 1889 Hunter had won. The strike had collapsed. The scabs worked the pits. The Knights had failed to organize the mines. The remaining strikers had dwindled to thirty or forty and promised to disappear altogether.[15]

Yet the Knights had not given up. The organizers turned up again in July 1890. Again Hunter called on McMurry. Again McMurry hastened to Thurber. By October he had steered the issue into the courts and thought the trouble would subside. At Hunter's request, however, he left two Rangers to keep watch.[16]

Sam McMurry had tried to uphold the Ranger tradition of impartiality. As he discovered, however, in a conflict between labor and management, keeping the peace impartially verged on the impossible.

Popular notions of corporate rights, combined with the assertive temperament of "Colonel" Hunter, cast the Rangers, however unwillingly, as the allies of management. In keeping the peace, they had helped to break the strike and thwart the unionizers.

BARBED WIRE APPEARED suddenly in Texas in the late 1870s, fragile-looking strands that could turn back even the brawny longhorn. Barbed wire could keep cattle in or out. Farmers could fence cattle out of their crops. Stockmen could fence their herds in and other herds out, discouraging rustling and mavericking, avoiding the confusion of sorting out brands after a season of sharing the open range with others, and permitting the development of blooded stock to replace the tough longhorn.

Barbed wire could also enclose public lands still open to purchase or lease. It could block public thoroughfares. It could appropriate to one man's use water and grass that had always been considered open to all.

From South Texas to North Texas, in scarcely five years barbed wire fences transformed the landscape. They concentrated most intensely in a belt four or five counties wide extending north and south through the center of the state. In this zone cowmen grazed cattle on ranges increasingly hatched by fences while farmers, politically energized by the Granger movement, pushed in from the east to take up homesteads.

When the drought of 1883 parched grass and dried up watering holes, stockmen suddenly awoke to what they had wrought: no less than the closure of the open range, the transformation of the way of life it had supported, and negation of the common notion that water and grass, like air, lay free to all comers. The open range still survived on the western plains and in the Panhandle, but in the counties where cowmen and farmers mingled amid their fences, the drought of 1883 kindled a guerrilla war the more deadly because it was waged at night by clandestine groups.

The drought drove real or imagined victims of fences into secret, night-riding societies. The "Knights of the Knippers" threatened bodily harm to selected fence builders and cut offending fences. Their targets might be legitimate cowmen who fenced nothing but land they owned or leased from the state. As often the nippers turned on men who enlarged their range by enclosing not only their own land but land that still belonged to the state. The nippers might be disgruntled farmers or stockmen large or small. Often they were corrupted by alliance with cattle thieves and hide burners with their own sinister aims. Perhaps worst of all, nippers turned communities into cauldrons of mutual fear and suspicion. Few men identified or even spoke against the miscreants, either through sympathy or fear. Few sheriffs, dependent on votes, would arrest. Few prosecutors would prosecute because few juries would convict, either through sympathy or fear or as nippers themselves.[17]

With the local machinery of justice paralyzed, victims beseeched the state for help. Send in the Rangers, they cried. Adjutant General King had little patience with such entreaties. Rangers could keep the peace or contend with outlaws operating openly, but to bring to justice secret groups that enjoyed wide public support and intimidated opponents seemed a doomed venture. Under such conditions, King believed, citizens had to clean up their own communities and not expect the Rangers to do it for them. In verbose, hectoring letters, he lectured Texans on their civic responsibilities.[18]

Governor Ireland mounted a determined offensive against the fence-cutters. In October 1883 he called a special session of the legislature, and when the lawmakers gathered in Austin in January 1884 he presented them with a long list of remedies. The most important enactment made fence-cutting a felony. Others required gates every three miles and outlawed the fencing of lands not owned or leased. Also, in a rare burst of generosity, the legislators appropriated $50,000 for the governor's use in the war against fence-cutters.[19]

Ireland shared a common belief that only undercover operatives could ferret out fence-cutters, most of whom were ordinary, hard-working citizens except when they gathered for a nighttime mission. Rangers made poor detectives because they quickly aroused suspicion of their true identity. Besides, even skilled detectives could not reform a community that refused to convict regardless of the evidence.

But Ireland now had a fund of $50,000, and he turned to professionals–Pinkerton's National Detective Agency in Chicago and Farrell's Commercial Detective Agency in New Orleans. He also hired private detectives in Texas. In March 1884 operatives converged on the cluster of counties southwest of Fort Worth, where fence-cutters had excited the most complaint. For three months the secret agents nosed around Brownwood and surrounding communities. Pinkerton himself provided Governor Ireland with detailed summaries of his agent's daily activities. The operatives identified many culprits but never caught any in the act of cutting and never gathered enough evidence to convict even had a jury been willing to convict.[20]

While the detectives worked, the governor made combating fence-cutting the primary mission of the Rangers. On March 6, 1884, Adjutant General King summoned Captain George W. Baylor from Ysleta and placed him in temporary command of the entire Frontier Battalion, with the rank of major. His mission was to deploy the companies in such manner as to aid the secret agents and to urge local authorities to take a more aggressive role in rooting out the offenders.[21]

In another case, the combination of Rangers and detectives worked more successfully than in Brownwood. In February 1884 T. L. Odum, a member of the legislature, began fencing his ninety-thousand-acre spread near old Fort Chadbourne, about forty miles southwest of the railroad town of Abilene. A community of "nesters" (the "Fish Creek crowd") had been running cattle and sheep on Odum's range. He ordered them off and, when they refused, brought suit. At once his fences began to fall.

Farrell's detective, William Carlton, turned up a local resident, Ben Warren, willing to penetrate the Fish Creek gang and serve as a witness. Carlton inserted Warren into the gang, whose leader administered an oath of allegiance. Speeding to Abilene by rail, Baylor and twenty-five of McMurry's and Gillespie's Rangers rode into Fort Chadbourne on May 4. Armed with the roster compiled by Warren, by now enlisted as a private in Gillespie's company, the Rangers arrested eight men. A week later, in Runnels City, a grand jury indicted fifteen men named by Warren.[22]

The Odum case seemed the one bright spot in an otherwise dismal record of undercover operation. Detectives cost money, and the governor's fund could not support them indefinitely. The Odum arrests offered a pretext for declaring victory and walking away. On May 12 King congratulated Baylor and his Rangers for their success and two months later terminated Baylor's assignment as commander of the Frontier Battalion. In June Governor Ireland dismissed all undercover operatives.[23]

Yet fence-cutting had not ended. It would plague Texas for at least another decade. Even the Odum case lost its luster of triumph as it dragged its way through one session of court after another. On February 9, 1885, as Odum and Ranger Ben Warren sat with others next to a stove in a Sweetwater hotel, someone fired from outside a window. The bullet clipped Odum, then struck Warren in the face, killing him instantly.

The state had lost its star witness. Two leaders of the Fish Creek gang were indicted for Warren's murder. Their trials, like the trials of the fence-cutters Warren had identified, bumped from one continuance to another through 1885 and 1886 and finally fell from the docket. Meanwhile, Odum erected more fence, had it cut, and saw his repairmen jeered by the cutters themselves galloping up and down the fence line.[24]

Next to tackle Brownwood was a Ranger who had demonstrated a flair for undercover work. Ira Aten was a young man of twenty-four when General King sent him to Brownwood in August 1886. A protégé of Lam Sieker, he was full of ambition, ability, and self-confidence. At the same time, King ordered Captain William Scott and Company F to take station at Brownwood.

In scarcely three weeks, with a local accomplice, Aten ingratiated himself with the leading cutters. Although wrestling with a troubled conscience, he quietly arranged to betray his new friends. On November 9, 1886, he sprang the trap. As he later wrote, "One crisp, moonlit November night four men came along where the Rangers were hidden. They were leading their horses and clipping the wires between each post.

"Suddenly a challenge from Captain Scott rang out on the midnight air, and like a flash, this was answered by shots from the fence cutters.

The Rangers returned the fire, and when the smoke of battle had cleared away, the horses being led by the fence cutters had been killed and two men lay dying on the fence line. One of them proved to be the constable of that precinct.

"That stopped the fence cutting in Brown County."

In places such as Brown County, where no court would convict, this brand of summary justice came to be known as "Ranger conviction."[25]

Ira Aten detested secret service but basked in the laurels it brought him. His success at Brownwood ensured that he would not escape it easily. For more than two years, while promoted to first sergeant of Company D, he seems to have borne a roving commission from General King to operate against fence-cutters. In long letters to his friend and mentor, Lam Sieker, now battalion quartermaster, he detailed his adventures, frustrations, and complaints.

Shortly after Brownwood, a substitute for long nighttime hours guarding a fence line began to take shape in Aten's mind. At first it appears to have been in jest, but gradually it grew serious. His idea was to rig a booby trap—a "dynamite boom," he called it—that would explode in a nipper's face. The device involved a long wooden box, an old shotgun charged with powder, dynamite caps, and dynamite sticks.

Working in Navarro County near Corsicana in the autumn of 1888, Aten went so far to purchase the components and assemble a test model. At this point Sieker stepped in with instructions from General King to abandon this foolhardy plan before someone got hurt. That suited Aten, for he had shown the pasture owners how to build a bomb and made sure the word spread throughout the community.[26]

No dynamite bomb ever blew up a nipper, but the fear of one produced a marked decline in fence cutting in Navarro County. The dynamite bomb also marked the end of Aten's career as a secret agent, probably to the relief of King and Sieker as much as Aten, who happily returned to his company near Uvalde.

In the 1880s a wave of fence-cutting also rolled across New Mexico and Arizona and the entire Great Plains, but nowhere with the intensity of Texas. Elsewhere the issues were the same: farmers and small

South Texas
in 1887

50 Miles

stockmen contending against large stockmen and illegal fencing of the public domain. Outside Texas, however, the public domain was federal, not state. This brought into play laws enacted by the Congress and enforced by federal marshals and federal courts. In Texas, state lands, state laws, state courts, and state Rangers afforded weaker remedies. In the public mind and in history, therefore, fence-cutting is most prominently identified with Texas.[27]

TEXANS TOOK THEIR politics seriously, so seriously that hardly any part of the state could get through an election without rancorous feuding that sometimes erupted in violence and homicide. The issues that fed such acrimony were almost always local and personal. Factional wrangling often drew extra venom from longstanding family feuds. In border towns ethnic rivalries added still more combustibles, as did the political status of blacks in the eastern counties. In frontier counties, incendiary politics flamed against a backdrop of rampant outlawry.

The feud that ran longest and bloodiest centered in LaSalle County, bisected by the Nueces River southwest of San Antonio, and spilled over into Frio County on the north and Dimmit County on the west. This was a land dense with thorny chaparral, cattle and horse thieves, and stolen stock pausing on the way to market in the pastures of a few powerful ranchers.

Although created in 1858, LaSalle County was not organized until 1880, which marked the beginning of county politics. Extension of the International and Great Northern Railroad from San Antonio to Laredo drew the county seat to the crossing of the Nueces, and the town of Cotulla sprang to life. The county election of November 1882 pitted the Ranger faction against the Sheriff faction and set off years of contention and bloodshed. The Ranger faction consisted of those who backed former Ranger Charles B. McKinney. The Sheriff faction rallied behind the incumbent sheriff, William O. Tompkins.[28]

McKinney had risen to lieutenant of Company F after Tom Oglesby resigned to run successfully for sheriff of Maverick County. "Girlie," Rangers called McKinney, because of his curly blond hair, slight frame, and light complexion. The sobriquet belied the tough little man's exemplary four-year record in every Ranger grade from private to lieutenant. Perhaps with some prodding from Lee Hall, now an influential stockman suffering from LaSalle County fence-cutters, McKinney ran for sheriff.[29]

Sheriff Tompkins held office by appointment after the elected incumbent resigned in June 1881. Tompkins too had served four years as a Ranger, with a creditable record until marred by discharge for drunkenness. He had recently married the fourteen-year-old daughter of county commissioner George Hill, and he had close enough ties to shady characters to antagonize Lee Hall.[30]

Tompkins won the election in November 1882, but McKinney contested. A new election in February 1883 brought Tompkins to town with an armed host bent on ensuring his victory. Lee Hall showed up with his own squad of cowboy-gunmen. No one started shooting, and the election passed off without interference. McKinney narrowly won.

For four years the Tompkins faction contended with the McKinney faction as the new sheriff warred on stock thieves and murderers. The Ranger faction supported McKinney and helped fix his aggressive brand of law on LaSalle County.

In the spring of 1883, Josephus Shely replaced McKinney as commander of Company F. One of five brothers to serve at one time or another in the Rangers, Joe Shely had been a San Antonio policeman and, briefly, a Ranger under Oglesby. Shely and McKinney respected each other and worked well together.

Shely not only suffered a feeble sense of ethics but also openly dabbled in politics, by which he had gained his commission. As the election of 1884 approached, Laredo-based state senator E. F. Hall protested Shely's active policing and also accused him of swindling the state. Hall was a Republican in an overwhelmingly Democratic state. Only along the border, with the Mexican vote, did Republicans stand much chance of winning an election. Although McKinney's term ran until 1886, on election day 1884 Shely's Rangers allegedly intimidated Mexicans, who could be expected to vote Republican, and bulldozed other voters by thrusting prepared ballots into their hands.

McKinney and allied county officers stood firmly with the Ranger faction, defending Shely and absolving him and his men of any impropriety on election day. In June 1885, however, General King requested and received Shely's resignation. McKinney had lost his staunchest supporter.[31]

The old animosities continued to boil, with the Tompkins crowd plotting to rid themselves of McKinney. The sheriff had hardly launched his second term when, the day after Christmas 1886, he and his deputy, former Ranger Samuel V. "Pete" Edwards, boarded a southbound train to investigate the rape of an eleven-year-old girl near Twohig. At the station they passed a few words with George "Bud" Crenshaw and James E. McCoy. Both were Tompkins followers who had tangled repeatedly with the sheriff. Crenshaw was the brother-in-law of George Hill, father of Tompkins's wife. McCoy hobbled about on a wooden leg, the result of a factional shootout in Cotulla in 1884. Obtaining horses, the lawmen set out for their destination. En route they again encountered Crenshaw and McCoy. Crenshaw raised his Winchester and sent two fatal bullets into McKinney. McCoy blazed away with his six-shooter at Edwards, who took a painful hit but galloped to safety.[32]

Rangers quickly appeared on the scene. They were Company C, their captain George Heinrich Schmitt. Former sheriff of Comal County, he had won a Ranger commission at the same time as Joe Shely, and by the same use of political influence. "Old Schmitt" was a big man, in physique and in self-esteem, and he wrote long letters to King and Sieker extolling his virtues and achievements and disparaging his fellow captains.[33]

Schmitt appeared in Cotulla on December 28, 1886, with a resolve to get McKinney's killers. His task was complicated on January 2 when two men shot George Hill on the streets of Cotulla. County commissioner, father-in-law of Tompkins, and brother-in-law of Bud Crenshaw, Hill lived long enough to name the assassins for two Rangers: Silas Hay and Frank Hall. Since Hay was McKinney's father-in-law, the feud had grown even more intensely personal.

Schmitt learned that young Tompkins had been part of the conspiracy to murder McKinney, and he induced him, in exchange for part of the reward the governor had offered, to betray the murderers by leading them into a Ranger ambush. With five Rangers and a guide, Schmitt went to Twohig. Lying in the brush by day and scouting the country by night, he waited for the plot to unfold. Just after dark on January 17, 1887, as he and two Rangers covered a trail leading to a well, Crenshaw and Tompkins approached on horseback. The Rangers rose and commanded the horsemen to surrender. Tompkins threw up his hands, but Crenshaw leveled his pistol on Sergeant Albert Grimes. The three Rangers opened fire, hitting Crenshaw several times and knocking him to the ground. Tompkins spurred his horse into the night. The prostrate Crenshaw fired twice at his assailants. Schmitt ordered him to lay down his gun. As Grimes approached, however, Crenshaw suddenly raised and cocked his pistol. Grimes kicked it from his hand. Crenshaw died several hours later.

The other culprits took heed. Chased from one hideout to another, the stump of his leg throbbing from exertion and damp nighttime camps, McCoy finally came in and surrendered. So on January 25 did Silas Hay and Frank Hall. Tompkins also gave up, protesting his innocence of any involvement in McKinney's assassination. With Schmitt hot on their trail, and perhaps lynch mobs as well, all considered Ranger protection and the courts the safest course. For all but McCoy, this judgment proved sound. After two years of court action, he mounted the scaffold to pay the ultimate penalty for the murder Crenshaw had committed. No one thought justice had miscarried, for in the factional climate of LaSalle County Jim McCoy had done his share of killing.[34]

"Old Schmitt" had demonstrated some first-rate rangering. Newspapers heaped praise on him, and he sang his own praise in high voice. But as in his other posts, he quickly made himself unpopular. He had no sooner wrapped up the McKinney and Hill cases than King, on February 21, 1887, ordered him to move Company C to Brownwood. In the

SHOOTOUT IN ROUND ROCK. Even though his fame rested on a single exploit, a train robbery, Sam Bass flourished briefly as one of the West's most wanted outlaws. On July 19, 1878, Major Jones and a squad of Rangers cornered Bass and two cohorts in Round Rock. The gun battle killed one and mortally wounded Bass, who escaped but was found next day, dying at the foot of an oak tree. *Texian Press, Waco.*

CAMP LIFE. Two scenes typical of hundreds during the last decades of the nineteenth century. Captain Dan Roberts's Rangers dine in the open at their camp on the San Saba River, near Fort McKavett, in 1878. Near Uvalde in the 1880s, Captain Frank Jones's company pitched camp in a cottonwood grove. Roberts, *Western History Collections, University of Oklahoma Libraries.* Jones, *Texas Ranger Hall of Fame and Museum.*

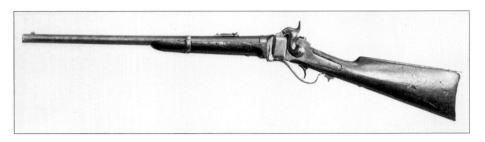

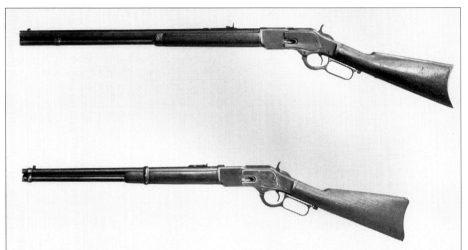

RANGER WEAPONS. At state insistence, Rangers of the Frontier Battalion purchased the single-shot Sharps, although they preferred the 1873 Winchester repeater, either rifle or carbine. By the 1880s this was the standard shoulder weapon. As the standard six-shooter, the 1873 Colt Peacemaker, with long or short barrel, endured for decades. All, *Ron Dillow and Ken Pate*.

GEORGE WYTHE BAYLOR. From 1879 to 1885 Baylor headed Company A of the Frontier Battalion in El Paso. An old soldier and prominent Texan—he had fought Indians before the Civil War and served as a Confederate colonel—he had fallen on hard times and needed a job. His men loved him, possibly because he imposed no discipline, but El Pasoans liked him too. Baylor and his Rangers successfully contended with Apaches, but the captain could never quite make the transition to lawman. *Western History Collections, University of Oklahoma Libraries.*

WILBURN H. KING. Adjutant General of Texas from 1881 to 1891, King retained direct command of the Rangers and carried on the traditions laid down by John B. Jones. His lavish praise of the Rangers helped revive a legend receding since the years of Jack Hays and Rip Ford. *Texas State Library and Archives.*

COMPANY F, FRONTIER BATTALION. Josephus Shely (standing, third from left) captained this company from 1883 to 1885. He obtained his commission through political influence and lost it for politicking against a state senator. His brother Washington ("Wash") Shely (seated, second from left) served for years as sheriff of Starr County. W. T. ("Brack") Morris (standing, second from right) was Karnes County sheriff in 1901 when killed while trying to arrest Gregorio Cortez. The Morris slaying set off the most celebrated manhunt in Texas history. *Western History Collections, University of Oklahoma Libraries.*

SAMUEL A. MCMURRY and WILLIAM J. MCDONALD. Sam ("Soft Voice") McMurry commanded Company B of the Frontier Battalion for ten years, 1881–91, to be followed by "Captain Bill" McDonald, 1891–1907. Both were effective leaders but sharply contrasted in personality and style. McMurry was quiet and unpretentious, McDonald a contentious, publicity-hungry showman. *Texas Ranger Hall of Fame and Museum.*

COMPANY B, FRONTIER BATTALION. Sam McMurry's men posed during strike duty at the Thurber coal mines in 1889. Sam Platt (fifth from left, with pipe) was McMurry's steadfast sergeant; the woman is Platt's wife. On Mrs. Platt's left is W. John L. Sullivan, who later became first sergeant and had to be discharged for drunkenness. He wrote a book full of self-praise and falsehood. *Western History Collections, University of Oklahoma Libraries.*

IRA ATEN. Adjutant General King used Sergeant Aten for undercover work against fence-cutters until he conceived the idea of rigging a "dynamite boom" to blow up the nippers. This scheme got him returned to his company. At his death in 1953, Aten was heralded as "the last of the old-time Rangers." *Western History Collections, University of Oklahoma Libraries.*

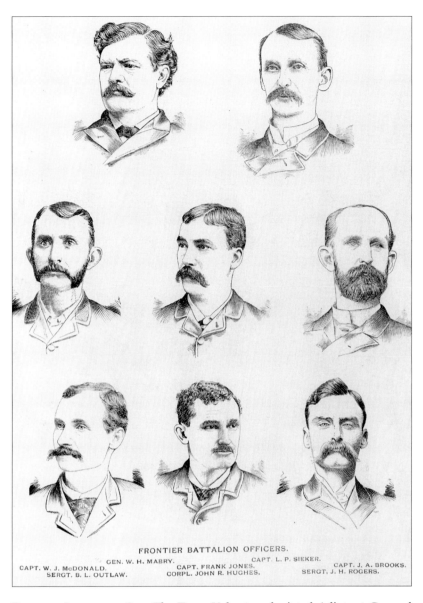

FRONTIER BATTALION OFFICERS.

GEN. W. H. MABRY. CAPT. L. P. SIEKER.
CAPT. W. J. McDONALD. CAPT. FRANK JONES. CAPT. J. A. BROOKS.
SERGT. B. L. OUTLAW. CORPL. JOHN R. HUGHES. SERGT. J. H. ROGERS.

RANGER LEADERS, 1892. *The Texas Volunteer* depicted Adjutant General Woodford H. Mabry and his principal officers in 1892. Within a few years McDonald, Brooks, Hughes, and Rogers would constitute what later writers labeled "the four great captains." Lam Sieker had been an outstanding company commander before moving to Austin as battalion quartermaster. Frank Jones, the most widely admired lawman in Texas, died in a shootout with Mexicans on the wrong side of the international boundary. Bass Outlaw was probably the best of all Ranger sergeants when sober, which was not often enough to save him from discharge. He died in a shootout at an El Paso bordello. *Texas State Library and Archives.*

SERGEANT HUGHES AND DETAIL. The silver mining town of Shafter, twenty miles north of the Rio Grande in the Big Bend, simmered with ethnic tensions and attracted both Mexican and Anglo outlaws. In 1890 Sergeant John R. Hughes (right) and three Rangers strove to keep order. *Texas State Library and Archives.*

CAPTAIN HUGHES AND COMPANY D. Headquartered at Ysleta, near El Paso, Hughes (seated on chair) performed so well that he became known as one of the "four great captains." This picture was made in 1894, shortly after the slaying of Captain Frank Jones elevated Hughes to the command. His able sergeant, Karl Kirchner, sits to his right. On the extreme left is a Mexican prisoner, his ankles in shackles. Hughes is said to have discharged Private George Tucker, next to the Mexican, for carelessly exposing his holstered six-shooter to a prisoner. *Western History Collections, University of Oklahoma Libraries.*

KEEPING THE TRAINS MOVING. In the nationwide railroad strike of 1894, Adjutant General Mabry assembled most of the Rangers to keep order. These men, drawn from three of the companies, are in front of boxcars in Temple. Captains Brooks and Hughes, standing at left, commanded this contingent. The little fellow sixth from the left, Corporal Tom Ross, later became a captain wanting enough in leadership to be dismissed. *Western History Collections, University of Oklahoma Libraries.*

COUNTERING THE SAN SABA MOB. By 1896, the San Saba mob, vigilantes turned terrorists, had murdered so many men in San Saba County that Adjutant General Mabry sent four Rangers to keep them in check. Left to right, they are Edgar T. Neal, Allen R. Maddox, Tom Johnson (cook), Dudley S. Barker, and Sergeant W. John L. Sullivan. After the mob had been broken, Barker became county sheriff. Sullivan got crosswise with his captain, Bill McDonald, and was discharged for drunkenness. *Western History Collections, University of Oklahoma Libraries.*

THE FRONTIER BATTALION, 1896. The good people of Texas and their governor grew so incensed at the impending Fitzsimmons-Maher prize fight in El Paso that almost all the Rangers were sent to prevent it. Here they pose in the only known photograph of the entire force. In the front rank, left to right, are Adjutant General Mabry and the "four great captains"—Hughes, Brooks, McDonald, and Rogers. *Texas State Library and Archives.*

autumn he came back to South Texas, where he aroused complaints from officials in Karnes and Bee Counties. Exasperated, King resorted to his favorite tactic and in November 1887, citing budgetary stresses, disbanded the company. Schmitt stirred up a ruckus in the newspapers, proclaimed himself the only honest and effective Ranger captain, and sought a legislative investigation.[35]

Captain Schmitt's swift roundup of the principals in the McKinney and related murders did not calm LaSalle County. In April 1890 Captain Frank Jones found more lawlessness there than when McKinney was elected sheriff eight years earlier. The sheriff was "a perfect nonentity." No conviction could be obtained anyway, for the good men were in the minority and afraid to talk. "Affairs are in a worse condition in this section than I have ever known in nine years service in different counties of the state," Jones concluded. For years to come, LaSalle County would confound the Texas Rangers.[36]

THE MEXICAN BORDER placed exceptional demands on the Rangers. Although cattle and horse theft flourished nearly everywhere in central and western Texas, on the border it imposed two stubborn dilemmas. First was the international boundary. Simply by crossing the Rio Grande, thieves and their stolen animals were usually safe. American lawmen violated Mexican sovereignty at their peril, and even when Mexican lawmen apprehended fugitives, the tortuous extradition proceedings rarely stood them before a Texas judge.

The second dilemma contained more ambiguity. How could Anglo lawmen tell the difference between good Mexicans and bad? Because of cultural biases, an Anglo lawman distrusted any Mexicans he did not know personally, especially if their behavior appeared suspicious.

Mexicans abhorred this stereotyping ("racial profiling" in modern terminology), and in their lexicon *rinches*–rangers–became a pejorative applied to all Anglo lawmen, not just Texas Rangers. The legislative cuts in the Frontier Battalion, however, ensured that after 1881 Rangers would appear on the border only sporadically and in diminishing numbers. Thus Mexicans suffered the consequences of stereotyping by Rangers far less than by Anglo sheriffs and their deputies and possemen and by federal border and customs officers. Even so, the legacy of earlier *rinches*, from Jack Hays and Ben McCulloch to Warren Wallace and Leander McNelly, lay heavily on the border and gave their successors a reputation not fully deserved.[37]

Still, the dilemma was real, and no encounter between Rangers and Mexicans illustrates the ambiguities and the stereotyping more vividly than the San Ambrosia affair of 1885. Rangers throughout South Texas had been alerted to search for escaped convicts thought to be hurrying for refuge in Mexico. On May 31, Sergeant Ben Lindsey and six men of Captain Lam Sieker's Company D scouted down San Ambrosia Creek, which emptied into the Rio Grande about eighty miles upstream from Laredo. A mile and a half in the distance they spotted two men on horseback trailing a led horse. The Rangers approached to within two hundred yards when the pair spurred their horses and set off a two-mile chase. Boggy ground slowed Lindsey and three Rangers, but Privates Ira Aten, then a one-year rookie, and B. C. Riley overtook the quarry on a hillside and demanded their surrender. They were Mexicans and did not fit the description of the wanted convicts. But they had run, so could well be horse thieves. As Riley reached to take their weapons, both fired, hitting him in the hip and shoulder. Aten began working his Winchester just as Frank Sieker, the captain's younger brother, joined the fray with his six-shooter. Both Mexicans took hits, one in the shoulder, the other in a hand, but one of them put a bullet in Frank Sieker's heart, killing him instantly. They disappeared over a hilltop as Lindsey and the rest of the Rangers reached the scene.

With three men, Lindsey followed the trail to a nearby ranch, where they confronted fifteen armed Mexicans and a man who identified himself as Prudencia Herrera, a deputy sheriff of Webb County. The two wounded men, he said, were named Gonzales and were father and son. They had come up from Laredo to retrieve a horse from a nearby sheep camp.

To Lindsey, the two had resisted arrest, shot two Rangers, and might be horse thieves. He intended to arrest them. After a heated argument, the sergeant had to settle for Herrera's solution. The deputy would drive the men to Laredo in a buggy. Aten and two other Rangers would follow on horseback. After tending to Sieker, Riley, and a third man whose horse had fallen on him, Lindsey and a companion would overtake the advance party in time to turn the two Gonzaleses over to the sheriff of Webb County.

That functionary was Dario Gonzales, long a political power in Webb County and, coincidentally, a relative of the two men Lindsey had insisted on arresting. On June 1, within thirty minutes of their arrival, the sheriff's kin had been released from custody and all the Rangers thrown into jail, charged with assault with intent to murder. Not for twenty-seven days did they finally get out on bail. Their cases were ultimately thrown out of court. Father and son Gonzales disappeared into Mexico.[38]

The San Ambrosia affair invites two perspectives. To Anglos, the Rangers came on two suspicious Mexicans, if not convicts, probably horse thieves as shown by their flight. They resisted arrest and shot two Rangers, one fatally, then fled with their own wounds to nearby friends. A man who may or may not have been a law officer intervened to prevent the Rangers from taking custody of the culprits. Lacking the force to contend with so many armed Mexicans, Lindsey had to agree to Herrera's course. In Laredo, a vindictive sheriff and relative of the murderers turned them loose and, to humiliate the Rangers, jailed them for nearly a month. Safe in Mexico, the father and son could not be investigated for horse theft nor stand trial for resisting arrest and murder.

To Mexicans, two countrymen innocent of any wrongdoing were going about their business when suddenly they discovered the *rinches* after them. Commanded to surrender, they moved to give up their arms but had second thoughts. Would the *rinches* shoot them down, a "Ranger conviction" as Ira Aten would label it? Mexicans believed, not without justification, that Anglo lawmen sometimes did just that. The two men decided to fight it out, then take their chances with sympathizers at the nearby ranch. In Laredo their friend and kinsman let them slip away to Mexico and made sure the Rangers got what was coming to them.

Either perspective, or a combination, could be valid. The full truth cannot be recaptured. But elements of this drama occurred time and again along the border, from Brownsville all the way to El Paso. Usually the *rinches* were Anglo sheriffs or their deputies. But the Texas Rangers fell into the cultural trap often enough to etch a troubling theme through their history.

IN MOST PARTS of Texas, the Southern Redeemers who gained power with Richard Coke's ascendancy in 1874 quickly crushed the heresies of Radical Republicanism. They purged blacks from the voting rolls and relegated them to inferior status. By 1890, Jim Crow's dark wings spread over all Texas.

Fort Bend County, in southeast Texas near Houston, was the last bastion of Black Republicanism. Washed by the Brazos River not far above its mouth, this land of coastal plain rich in salt grass supported herds of Brahma cattle and fields of cotton and sugar cane. Before the Civil War, the plantation world of the Old South had flourished here. After the war, with 90 percent of the population black, a few carpetbaggers joined with local scalawags to mobilize the freedmen and assemble a powerful political machine. Ostensibly Democratic, since Republican invited statewide contempt, it subjected an outraged white minority to county governments heavy with black office holders.

By the 1880s, the minority had begun to organize to reassert white supremacy and overturn governments that were Radical Republican in all but name. Somehow the minority faction came to be known as Jaybirds and their opponents as Woodpeckers. The two factions hurled threats, brandished arms, and slid toward violence.[39]

With tensions rising toward the election of 1888, the slaying of a Jaybird leader and the wounding of another sparked a successful Jaybird drive to run the most prominent blacks out of Richmond, the county seat. With the blacks threatening mob retaliation, the Woodpecker sheriff, James Garvey, called for help. Alerting units of the Texas Volunteer Guard, on September 6 General King himself entrained for Richmond. A white mob, however, had already dispersed the black mob, and the "best citizens" assured him that all was quiet and would remain so.[40]

The November election passed quietly, with an all-white Woodpecker slate trouncing Jaybird challengers. The election intensified some personal antagonisms, however, and on June 21, 1889, county assessor Kyle Terry reignited the feud by unloading a double-barrelled shotgun into Jaybird Ned Gibson. The Gibson brothers vowed vengeance, and both sides armed for battle.

Sheriff Garvey and the county judge (Woodpeckers) appealed to Governor Ross for help. Captain Frank Jones and his eight-man company arrived in Richmond on July 1. He cultivated both factions, and the Ranger presence, he believed, had a soothing effect. By early August, he judged Richmond calm enough to leave Sergeant Ira Aten and three men to keep watch until after district court met in September and October.[41]

Jones, anxious to attend a dying wife, took appearances at face value. Aten sensed the rising tensions but could do no more than patrol the streets and keep on friendly terms with both factions. Hardly a week after Jones's departure, on August 16, Richmond exploded. An exchange of fire between two Gibson brothers and two Woodpecker leaders set off a full-scale battle. An armed Jaybird crowd advanced on the courthouse, where Woodpecker officials took shelter behind an iron fence. Aten and his men tried to reason with both sides but failed. Volney Gibson told him to get out of the street or get killed. Aten complied, but not before gunfire erupted and severely wounded Ranger Frank Schmidt. Shotguns, Winchesters, and six-shooters filled Main Street with flying lead. Some hit flesh, but only three inflicted fatal wounds: on Woodpecker sheriff Garvey, a former Woodpecker sheriff, and Jaybird leader H. H. Frost.[42]

Aten and the county judge telegraphed Governor Ross, and by the next morning Guard companies had converged by rail to place Richmond under martial law. The governor himself arrived on the eighteenth. He sought to persuade the two factions to agree on a sheriff to replace the slain Garvey. When this failed, he obtained consent to his own candidate: Sergeant Ira Aten of the Texas Rangers. Reluctantly, Aten bowed to the governor's wishes.[43]

Besides Aten's stern justice, backed by a small Ranger detachment, two events during his tenure brought closure to the Jaybird–Woodpecker war. In January 1890, after a change of venue, Kyle Terry came to trial in Galveston for the murder of Ned Gibson. As he ascended a staircase to the courtroom, Volney Gibson stepped from the shadows and sent a bullet into Terry's heart. Neither Gibson nor any of the other participants in the feud suffered any court-imposed penalty.[44]

In the wake of the street battle, the demoralized Woodpeckers began to yield their offices and move to safer places. "Will have a Jaybird government here after a little," Aten correctly informed Captain Sieker on September 3, 1889. On October 22, 450 white citizens subscribed their names to the charter of the Jaybird Democratic Association, pledging to purify politics and ostracize any white person who did not subscribe to the group's principles. For the next sixty years, the Jaybird Association dominated the politics and government of Fort Bend County. And as Ira Aten recalled, "The negroes thereafter stayed on the plantations, worked and kept out of politics."[45]

Sheriff Aten held his post only until the election of 1890. He then headed for a new life in the Panhandle. After a term as sheriff of Castro County, he accepted the post of superintendent of the Escabarda division of the XIT Ranch, the huge spread of the syndicate that had built the state capitol. In 1904 Aten took his family to California's blossoming Imperial Valley and devoted himself to canal building and the cause of public power. Pneumonia felled "the last of the old Texas Rangers" at age ninety-four, in 1953. Coincidentally, in this same year the Jaybird Democratic Association of Fort Bend County also expired, the victim of court rulings that ran all the way to the U.S. Supreme Court.

AS DRAMATIZED BY the blowup in Fort Bend County, East Texans increasingly called on the Rangers even as their legislators opposed them in Austin. Factional disputes brought Rangers to Wharton, Waller, Chambers, Jefferson, Hamilton, and other eastern counties. A call even came from the Piney Woods of Sabine and San Augustine Counties, abutting the Louisiana border. This call led to one of the most dramatic setbacks suffered by Rangers during the King era.

The densely forested land cut by the Sabine River supported its own version of the open range. Stockmen ran hogs on unfenced commons, identifying their animals by distinctively clipped ears. As on the cattle ranges far to the west, hogmen often quarreled over ownership. Near Hemphill, a feud developed between the sprawling Conner clan—"Uncle Willis" and his six sons and their progeny—and neighbors accused of "bothering my hogs." In December 1883 the bodies of two neighbors turned up on Conner range riddled with lead from shotguns, Winchesters, and pistols. In the next two years, the courts lodged one Conner brother in the penitentiary and entangled all the others in legal proceedings. They escaped from jail, however, and took to the woods and swamps in a growing gang so cunning, ruthless, and attuned to the environment that they spread terror through the Piney Woods.[46]

In February 1886, the local district judge and a former state senator appealed to Governor Ireland for help. For several weeks Ranger Lieutenant William Scott nosed around the Conner ranges. He turned up nothing but learned much about a habitat vastly different from any the Rangers had worked before. Back in the summer of 1886, now captain of Company F, Scott bemoaned the ordeal of scouting in such hostile surroundings. "I have just gone through fifteen days of the 'toughest Rangering' that you ever saw," he complained to Lam Sieker. Ticks kept his men "scratching and kussing all night," and his stock weakened on a diet of rotten corn. "I have made quite a great failure on this scout but can stand it if I can only get back to the prairie alive."[47]

The failure was not complete. Scott and his men had apprehended two of the Conner brothers. That left Uncle Willis and three sons still at large and wanted for murder. In March 1887 King sent Scott and five men back to complete the task.[48]

Arriving on March 30, Scott recruited a few citizens volunteers and began probing south through timber and brush toward Hemphill.

Shortly after midnight they ascertained the location of the Conner camp and at daybreak deployed for a surprise attack. Four citizens and two Rangers formed the left squad, Scott and five Rangers the right. Cautiously they closed on the objective.

But the surprise was theirs. Uncle Willis and his three sons had set up their own ambush. Scott's squad walked right into it. At a range of twenty to thirty feet, from behind brush-choked trees, the Conners opened fire. The first volley fatally cut down Private J. H. Moore. The other Rangers got off several shots before the second volley felled three. Scott took a Winchester ball in his left lung. Bullets mangled both hands of Sergeant John A. Brooks. Private John H. Rogers suffered wounds in the side and arm. The remaining two Rangers kept firing, but the other squad shrank from entering the fight. The leader, none other than the state senator who had first called for Rangers, ordered his men to take cover hardly eighty yards from the battleground and even restrained his two Rangers from joining the fight. "They were more accustomed to hunting deer than desperados," observed Scott.

Ranger fire killed one of the Conner brothers and a pack horse. Uncle Willis and two sons, however, got away, although one bore wounds from which he later died. Scott almost died too. Brooks had three fingers amputated. Lawmen later caught up with Uncle Willis and his remaining son and killed them in volleys of gunfire, but by then the Rangers had withdrawn. They had been beaten by an alien, hostile environment and men who knew how to exploit its every feature.[49]

SUL ROSS WAS the last of the Southern Redeemers to occupy the governor's chair in Austin. Agrarian unrest and sentiment for curbing the power of corporations, especially the railroads, bore reformer James Stephen Hogg to the governorship in the election of 1890. Too young to have fought in the war, he dwelt less on the Confederate heritage than on shaping a state government responsive to the economic changes sweeping Texas. As Hogg took the oath of office in January 1891, Wilburn Hill King resigned after a full decade as adjutant general of Texas.

The King decade completed the transformation of the Texas Rangers from a mounted battalion of Indian fighters into a compact force of lawmen. John B. Jones had laid the groundwork for this transformation and enunciated the guiding principles. King built on the Jones tradition, although by 1891 his forty-four Rangers, striving to cover the entire state, could scarcely match the performance of the 225 Rangers of Jones and McNelly operating solely on the frontier.

The King years not only added new territory to the Ranger mission but new crimes as well. Cattle and horse theft still headed the list of offenses, as it had in earlier years. But in the 1880s the Rangers also took on fence-cutters, train robbers, vigilante mobs, labor "agitators," feuding political factions, and border troublemakers.

Like Jones, King commanded enough inferior officers and men to belie the shining image he painted in his annual reports. Discharge for drunkenness, incompetence, insubordination, and even crime weeded out men who should not have been enlisted. They were more than balanced by the able, dedicated young men of his vision. The measure of their effectiveness lay in the repeated calls for their presence. It also lay in the efforts of men whose iniquitous schemes they had disturbed to have them abolished. King fought that off, but could not fight off the drastic appropriation cuts that checked his ability to respond to the appeals for their services.

King's captains were a mixed lot. Exceptionally competent were Sam McMurry, Frank Jones, and Lam Sieker. After 1885, Sieker served King not only as quartermaster but as impromptu executive officer, the man at headquarters the captains could relate to personally. Able captains included Tom Oglesby, Charles Neville, and Tom Gillespie, all of whom later applied their Ranger skills as county sheriffs. Least effective were the political appointees, especially Joe Shely and George Schmitt. Both could boast important achievements, but both suffered personal flaws inadmissible in a Ranger captain. George Baylor, also politically appointed, was miscast as a Ranger. Although greatly beloved by his men and neighboring citizens, he could not make the transition from

Indian fighter to lawman, nor bring himself to impose even perfunctory discipline on his company.

As Wilburn King cleaned out his office in January 1891, he could look back with pride on his decade as head of the Rangers. From opponent of the Rangers as a legislator, he had made himself a worthy successor of John B. Jones.

[14]

The Four Captains

I N THE YEARS spanning the turn of the century, four captains
dominated the Texas Rangers. Ranger lore labels them the "four
great captains." They were John R. Hughes, John A. Brooks, William J.
McDonald, and John H. Rogers. Hughes joined the Rangers in 1887 and
captained a company from 1893 to 1915. Brooks signed on in 1883 and
led a company from 1889 to 1906. McDonald gained his captaincy in
1891 and held it until 1907. Rogers enlisted in 1882, rose to captain in
1893, and resigned in 1911.

As adjutant general, Governor James S. Hogg named Woodford
H. Mabry, thirty-five. Unlike Wilburn King, Mabry brought nominal
military background to the post, but he learned soldiering as quickly
and successfully as he had mastered the wholesale mercantile business in Jefferson. Like King, he concentrated on the Texas Volunteer
Guard but also kept tight control of the Rangers. Reappointed by
Governor Charles A. Culberson in 1895, Mabry served until the
outbreak of the Spanish–American War in 1898, when he led the
First Texas Infantry to Cuba. Fever killed him in Havana in January
1899.[1]

Under Mabry, the Rangers experienced the same anomaly as under King: declining strength and near extinction combined with a gleaming public image. In every session of the legislature, economizers backed by interests the Rangers had offended tried to abolish them altogether. Mabry avoided this finality. In 1891 he also persuaded lawmakers to raise the Ranger appropriation from $30,000 to $40,000, a generosity that collapsed in retrenchment in 1895. For the balance of Mabry's term, a paltry $25,000 a year gave each of the four captains one sergeant and six privates.[2]

At the same time, Mabry extolled the Rangers as lavishly as had King. "A Texas Ranger is the synonym for courage and vigilance," he wrote in his first annual report. "A bold rider, a quick eye, and a steady hand, he is the terror of the criminal, and merely his presence has its moral effect and acts as a wholesome restraint." During the widely publicized Mexican border troubles of 1891–1892, both state and national press echoed Mabry's acclaim.[3]

Jack Hays and Ben McCulloch had given birth to the legend of the Texas Rangers, but it had dimmed with the passing of the citizen soldier. As Texas Rangers reincarnated themselves as lawmen, Wilburn King revived and gave new luster to the legend. The four great captains propelled it into the twentieth century.

A KENTUCKIAN WHO came to Texas in 1876, John A. Brooks punched cows before joining Company F of the Texas Rangers in 1883, at the age of twenty-seven. Tall, lean, and tough, he was also modest, quiet-spoken, and courteous, and possessed of a high sense of duty fortified by determination, courage, and a mind that grasped both the larger mission and the immediate task. A masterful marksman, horseman, and outdoorsman, he seasoned himself in the cockpit of Cotulla, the clash with Brown County fence cutters, and the Piney Woods battle with the Conners, where he lost three fingers. Under Joe Shely and William Scott, Brooks rose to sergeant and lieutenant, and in 1889 Governor Sul Ross made him captain of Company F.[4]

In 1891 Brooks and his company worked out of Cotulla, contending with the bad men of stubbornly bad LaSalle County, when all of South Texas came alive with still another Mexican revolutionary movement. Reflecting rising discontent with the dictatorial regime of President Porfirio Díaz, Catarino E. Garza formed a small army in South Texas for an invasion of Mexico. A Texas resident, he had achieved notoriety as an eloquent newspaper editor and charismatic orator, but as a rebel general he proved altogether incompetent. Although he boasted an army of more than a thousand men, in three incursions he got less than a hundred across the border, and they accomplished no more than to prod Díaz into demanding that the United States enforce the neutrality laws.[5]

Scattered in bands across the South Texas brush country, *Garzistas* took on a dual character: revolutionary patriots and border bravos. As patriots, they enjoyed the nearly unanimous support or sympathy of the Mexican population and of many Anglos as well. As bravos, they preyed on rancheros and behaved like stereotypical Mexican bandits. In the first role, they challenged the U.S. cavalry and federal marshals to enforce federal neutrality laws. In the second role, they challenged county peace officers and Texas Rangers to enforce state laws.

The Garza movement captured the nation's imagination. Reporters converged on South Texas, and wild stories appeared in newspapers from New York to San Francisco. Public expectation combined with the diplomatic demands of Díaz spurred both U.S. regulars and Texas Rangers to produce Garza. With the people, the land, and the climate arrayed against them, they could not.[6]

In February 1892, Garza slipped out of Texas and made his way to exile in Central America. The roving bands of *Garzistas* lost their character as revolutionists and increasingly behaved like brigands. Because they had killed a soldier and two Rangers, however, they had broken Texas law. The companies of Brooks and J. S. McNeel kept the field, but they could not catch the murderers.

The Garza war spotlighted the performance of three Ranger officers. J. S. McNeel, a former San Antonio lawman with political connections, captained Company E. His boastful ways and operational lethargy weighed against him, and in August 1892 General Mabry resolved to remove him. By contrast, despite the obstacles, Brooks proved smart, energetic, and persistent, and he displayed his usual qualities of leadership.

So did Brooks's sergeant, John H. Rogers. In recognition of his work, much of it independent of Brooks, on January 1, 1893, he replaced McNeel as captain of Company E. A ten-year veteran at thirty, Rogers had risen under Sam McMurry and John Brooks. With Brooks, Rogers had been badly wounded in the fight with the Conner gang in 1887. With blocky frame and grandly mustachioed face, he had shown himself to be a committed, indefatigable, and courageous Ranger with a flair for leadership. Like Brooks and McMurry, he was soft-spoken and modest. Unlike any other captain, however, he was so deeply religious that he was said to carry a Bible in one hand and a six-shooter in the other, and he understood the uses of both. Rogers proved to be another of the four great captains.[7]

Except for hardship and perseverance, the Garza campaign earned neither the U.S. Army nor the Texas Rangers any laurels. A few exchanges of gunfire and a few captures scarcely offset the toil, torture, and frustration of constantly scouting an unforgiving land peopled by unsympathetic rancheros. The population, the environment, and the quarry made the mission of both Rangers and regulars virtually impossible to carry out.

ANOTHER OF THE great captains was William J. McDonald, thirty-eight when commissioned in 1891. He did not come from within the Ranger ranks but got the nod because he and Governor Hogg had known each other years earlier, when Hogg was a justice of the peace in East Texas. McDonald had tried many ways to make a living while also serving as a deputy sheriff in two counties and as a deputy United States marshal. Only as a lawman had he succeeded, and respectable credentials validated his political appointment.[8]

"Captain Bill" possessed courage, bravery, dedication, persistence, mastery of horse and gun, and criminal investigative skill. Six feet tall, wiry, lithe of movement, he projected authority with riveting blue eyes deeply set in a face framed by big ears and adorned with a mustache merging into muttonchop whiskers. More than any other captain, he was a showman, a colorful character, a self-promoter who reveled in notoriety. He cultivated politicians and newsmen and made certain that his exploits received public acclaim, often at the expense of his men.

McDonald gained a merited reputation for talking down mobs. "I used to tell him," recalled one of his men, "Cap, you're going to get all of us killed, the way you cuss out strikers and mobs." "Don't worry, Ryan," was the response. "Just remember my motto." He repeated his motto often enough to bequeath it to all successive generations of Rangers: "No man in the wrong can stand up against a fellow that's in the right and keeps on acomin.'"[9]

McDonald also was the inspiration for the enduring legend of "one riot, one ranger." The story survives in many versions, but in all an impending riot leads to a call for Rangers. One arrives, and when asked where the others are, he answers that there is only one riot.

Aside from the theatrics, McDonald's biggest fault was an inability to embrace any point of view but his own. All who disagreed were not only wrong but classed as the enemy. He never doubted that he was the fellow in the right, and he always just "kept on acomin." In the factional squabbles that roiled the Panhandle counties as fiercely as elsewhere in Texas, McDonald failed the test of impartiality and indeed often became a factional issue himself. As an Amarillo critic charged, "He is so constituted that he thinks that a man who does not like the ranger force is a scoundrel and can't be too badly treated by them."[10]

Headquartered in Amarillo, McDonald's little company of a dozen or more, cut in half in 1895, policed a huge territory. The Panhandle encompassed fifty-four counties, established in 1876 but organized in the 1890s in the wake of the Fort Worth and Denver City Railroad, completed in 1888. On the west, a tier of counties stacked against the New Mexico boundary formed "no-man's land," a stamping grounds for cattle and horse thieves from both sides of the line. On the east lay Oklahoma Territory, base for notorious outlaw gangs that forayed both into the Panhandle and across Red River to North Texas. Finally, Company B covered the counties south of the Panhandle as far as the Texas and Pacific Railroad, accessing them by rail via Fort Worth.

Like other captains, McDonald contended with horse and cattle thieves, train robbers, and the factional disputes that arose in newly organizing counties. Some county political conflicts centered on the location of the county seat, but most swirled around the sheriff, who was also the tax collector. Some sheriffs were flagrantly partisan, some incompetent, some outright crooks. Some welcomed Rangers, some wanted no part of them.

Compounding the county problems were the lords of the big open-range outfits backed by foreign capital, such as the XIT, the JA, the Espuela, and the Matador. Men like Charles Goodnight and Murdo Mackenzie did not welcome little cowmen, nesters, or any other of the newcomers who organized counties and disturbed the old ways. Many were Grangers, adherents of the agrarian movement to aid and organize small farmers. "Range versus Grange" oversimplified the division, but McDonald often stood between the cowboy pistoleers of the range and the town and county builders of the Grange.

One such disturbance drew McDonald to Motley County in the summer of 1893. It was a complicated conflict between range and Grange, and it spilled over into Childress County to bring McDonald into conflict with Sheriff John Matthews and a "dirty little paper" that reviled the Rangers.[11]

On December 9, 1893, Matthews and two companions came down to Quanah for a meeting with the Hardeman County sheriff. That evening at the train depot the Matthews party came face-to-face with McDonald. After a brief exchange of words, both men drew their pistols and started firing. Both went down, severely wounded. Two of McDonald's bullets hit Matthews above the heart but were stopped by a tobacco plug and a notebook. McDonald took bullets in the neck and shoulder and had his lung punctured and ribs shattered. In a puzzle never solved, the rounds that felled Matthews came in three different calibers from somewhere in his rear and hit him in the back. Matthews died of blood poisoning three weeks later. McDonald almost died, but after months of convalescence he returned to duty.[12]

IN JUNE 1894 labor issues again hit the Rangers. Again trouble boiled up in Thurber, where the stern Robert D. Hunter still managed the Texas and Pacific coal mines. In March he had reduced wages, and a strike seemed in the offing. He called on Adjutant General Mabry for help.

Arriving on June 8, Captain Bill quickly got to the root of the alarm. Union activists from striking Oklahoma mines were trying to get up a strike at Thurber. They used as their headquarters a saloon on the edge of the company town but across the line in Palo Pinto County, beyond the reach of Erath County authorities. On Saturday and Sunday afternoons they lured miners with free beer. By evening, most patrons had lost any reluctance to pay. The proprietors and the firebrands from outside subjected the miners to harangues against the company and got them so drunk they were unfit for work. On the grounds of safety, Hunter fired every drunk or hungover workman. Hunter and his pit bosses received death threats. Handbills circulated in town at night. Word spread that dynamite would be dropped into the pits if the entire force did not walk off the job. Everyone in Thurber was excited and scared.

McDonald quieted passions. He talked with all groups and made clear that he meant to keep the peace. Most of the miners wanted simply to continue to dig coal if only the storms brewed by outsiders could be calmed. After meeting with McDonald, the minority trying to get up a strike backed off.[13]

Even as McDonald soothed Thurber back to normal, a labor crisis erupting in Chicago threatened to spread into Texas. A strike against the Pullman Palace Car Company had drawn Eugene V. Debs's fledgling American Railway Union into the fray, and President Grover Cleveland's use of federal troops against the strikers so infuriated workers that railroads everywhere braced for disruption and violence. By the middle of July 1894, Mabry had the Rangers of McDonald, Brooks, and recently commissioned John R. Hughes working the lines all the way from Galveston through Fort Worth to the Red River. They handled a few minor disturbances, but federal troops and court injunctions broke the strike and the American Railway Union as well.[14]

THE TERM "MOB" recurs constantly in the postwar history of Texas. It signified a vigilante mob, a lynch mob, an outlaw mob, a feud mob, or a political mob. A mob did not require spontaneity of formation or action. Indeed, the most insidious mobs methodically preyed on their communities for years.

Typically, such mobs began as vigilante groups forged early in an area's settlement, when horse and cow thieves easily evaded a weak system of criminal justice. Vigilantes, usually leading citizens, accorded swift justice on the nearest tree limb.

Over time some vigilante associations lost their original purpose and evolved into sinister leagues featuring signs, passwords, and rituals; numbering in their ranks prominent and successful men; and enforcing their designs by assassination and terror. Their victims were men with coveted property, men who had not heeded an ultimatum to leave, and simply men who had spoken out against mob rule.

The deadliest and longest-lasting mob reached its zenith in 1896 in the cow country grassland gashed by the Colorado and San Saba rivers. It had surfaced in San Saba and the adjoining counties of Mills, Brown, and McCulloch as early as 1884. But it displayed all the hallmarks of a mob that since the late 1870s had cowed the counties on the east—Erath, Comanche, Hamilton, and Lampasas. These may have been two different mobs, one mob that unfolded out of the other, or the same mob shifting westward.

Besides the usual victims, the earlier mob dedicated itself to running out all blacks and all sheepmen. On occasion Rangers sought to counter mob depredations, which shook Erath and Hamilton counties especially hard, but without success. As one citizen complained of these "midnight legislators" in 1884, "No animal that grows wool will be endured . . . and Gov. Ireland himself would not be allowed a negro coachman or a cook." Indeed, in 1886 the mob drove every black resident out of Comanche County, and as late as the middle of the twentieth century the county still boasted of its all-white population.[15]

Between 1884 and 1896, the San Saba mob murdered between twenty and fifty men. Despite the secret oaths and rituals, everyone knew the mobsters, who included clergymen and prominent stockmen as well as men of lesser stature. No one could speak out against them without risk of life. Some had been killed for the offense, one on the basis of a child's schoolyard report of her father's antimob comments at the dinner table. The sheriff and other county officers either held membership or understood the power relationships well enough to do what they were told.[16]

In June 1896, following two murders within five days, District Judge W. M. Allison asked Adjutant General Mabry to station a detachment of Rangers on the Colorado River north of the county seat, the area most afflicted by mob violence. Mabry could spare only four men, two from McDonald's company and two from Rogers's company. Under W. John L. Sullivan, McDonald's sergeant, the four took station at Regency, on the north side of the Colorado in Mills County, twenty miles from San Saba.

Sergeant Sullivan combined some of the same traits as his captain. His big muscular frame and big wavy beard matched his big ego. Commanding his own outfit and reporting directly to the adjutant general inflated his customary self-importance. Yet Sullivan was fearless, energetic, smart, and adept at acquiring vital information. Within a month he had identified three of the murderers, although he doubted that he could get enough evidence to convict.[17]

The Rangers threw the mob off balance. As threats to the mob, they made themselves prime targets. "I will tell you Gen," Sullivan wrote Mabry, "we boys dont sleep too sound on this River as these men are ambush, & do ambush." The danger subsided when the detachment moved to San Saba for district court in November.[18]

Based on Sullivan's evidence, the newly elected district attorney, W. C. Linden, got the grand jury to indict two men for murder. Judge Allison changed their venue to Austin. A sensational trial there in February 1897 produced a hung jury, and another trial was set for June. That trial also ended in a hung jury.

Meantime, Sullivan experienced a change of fortune. The mob had manipulated the malleable new sheriff, A. J. Hawkins, to pick a fight with Sullivan and get the Rangers withdrawn. With his usual bellicosity, Sullivan fell for it. In a courthouse encounter in March 1897, Hawkins provoked Sullivan into drawing his pistol. One of his men intervened, and Judge Allison ordered the Rangers into the street, where they made such a turbulent scene that the judge asked Mabry to withdraw Sullivan from San Saba.[19]

Sullivan also got into trouble with his own captain. In Austin McDonald sternly counseled him about his imperious conduct and his growing addiction to strong drink. Even so, he stood up for Sullivan and persuaded Mabry to return him to San Saba. Mabry did, but also insisted that McDonald take command there.

His vanity wounded, Sullivan resented the criticism and resented being superseded. Through June 1897, he grew sullen and uncommunicative, went off fishing for days, and spread word everywhere that he had done all the work in the Panhandle while McDonald got the credit. Next he began consorting with the enemy, passing hours drinking with the sheriff and other known mob leaders. On July 2 he staggered into camp so drunk he had lost his way, and the very next day he returned to the saloon for another drinking bout with the same crowd. McDonald demanded his resignation.[20]

Captain Bill proved no more temperamentally suited than Sullivan to handle the delicate relationships in San Saba County. Over the next six months, McDonald's aggressive pursuit of witnesses unsettled the malefactors and elicited threats to "do us up and kill us out." He had nothing but contempt for Sheriff Hawkins and, despite Mabry's urging, made no effort to get along with him. District Attorney Linden thought McDonald overzealous yet conceded that he was doing what he was sent to do.

McDonald began to harbor doubts about Judge Allison. First he tried to get the Rangers moved back to the Colorado, later to Richland Springs, sixteen miles up the San Saba. In either place, McDonald pointed out, no resident would dare be seen talking to Rangers. The constructive work was to be done in the county seat, mob headquarters, where he would be gathering evidence against leading citizens who were friends of the judge. They must have their thumb on him in some way, McDonald thought, or else "he has certainly lost a few joints of his back bone."

Because McDonald did his work thoroughly and provided a sense of protection for witnesses and jurors, in November 1897 Linden persuaded the grand jury to indict some of these civic leaders for murder. They posted bail at once, but McDonald had clearly shaken the organization. They hurled anonymous threats at him. One missive ordered him to leave at once or "we will fill you so full of led that it wil take a frait trane to holl you to the grave yard . . . and after you are gon we wil not leve a single anty mob man in the county we will kill the hole damd shootin match."

Clearly, the mob had not been banished. McDonald regarded the bail posted by the indicted men as worthless, but he could not persuade Judge Allison to investigate. All went free. None, McDonald thought, would ever come to trial. With one exception, he was right. Only one man went to prison. The rest had their cases continued from one court session to the next and finally dropped.

The Texas Rangers did not quell the San Saba mob, but they made an important contribution. They provided protection to witnesses and juries and gathered the evidence for District Attorney Linden to bring mobsters into court and expose them before the community. He could not obtain convictions, but in the end it was Linden, not McDonald, who drove them from the county. In May 1899, when some tried to intimidate Linden on the streets of San Saba, he faced them down with a pistol. He then commanded them all to sell out and leave the county on pain of a legal hounding so relentless that he would bankrupt them all—the same tactic Lee Hall had used to make an honest man out of King Fisher. They left.[21]

LEGISLATIVE PARSIMONY SWEPT the Trans-Pecos entirely clear of Rangers just as increased immigration, spurred by two railroads, raised fresh challenges to law enforcement. George W. Baylor's Company A, at Ysleta, was the first casualty, in 1885. Captain J. T. Gillespie's Company E, at Alpine, followed in 1887. In this same year, Presidio County spawned two new counties: Brewster, with the seat at Alpine, and Jeff Davis, with the seat at Fort Davis. Marfa inherited from Fort Davis the seat of Presidio County. Between Marfa and the Rio Grande at Presidio, silver mines gave rise to the boomtown of Shafter. Cattle grazed wherever grass grew, their market reached by the Southern Pacific and the Texas and Pacific railroads.

Constant appeals from the West finally prompted a response from Adjutant General King. In the spring of 1889 he sent four men from Captain Frank Jones's company at Uvalde to take station at Alpine, where former Ranger captain Gillespie was sheriff of Brewster County. When three decamped for better paying jobs in Mexico, responsibility fell to rookie Charles H. Fusselman. Furnished three more men, within a year Corporal, then Sergeant Fusselman made a name for himself, notably in keeping the peace in Shafter. In April 1890, however, while in El Paso on court business, he joined local lawmen in chasing horse thieves. They turned and fought, killing the sergeant. Yielding to the need, General King ordered Captain Jones to move his headquarters and entire company (all of ten men) to Alpine and take responsibility for the Trans-Pecos.[22]

While based in Alpine, Jones performed impressively, cementing his reputation as the first among Ranger captains. At Shafter Mexicans stole silver ore by night and hurried it across the Rio Grande to a smelter in Mexico, and tensions between Mexicans and Anglos called for constant monitoring. But El Paso, even though accessible by rail, lay distant from Alpine. With Baylor's company no longer on duty, stock theft escalated. Mexican gangs, working with accomplices in Texas, rounded up cattle and horses and drove them across the river before posses could be formed. In June 1893, Mabry ordered Jones to move his headquarters to Baylor's old station of Ysleta.[23]

Jones had been settled at Ysleta only ten days when he led a detail of five Rangers to San Elizario to arrest two men for horse and cattle theft and assault with intent to murder. They were Jesús María Olguin and his son Severio. At daybreak on June 30 the Rangers "rounded up" the ranch of old Clato Olguin, patriarch of the Olguin clan, but the son and grandson had been tipped off and had taken refuge a few miles distant with Antonio Olguin, Jesús's brother. After escaping from the Texas Penitentiary, where he had been sent for rape, he had settled on the Mexican side of the boundary.

The Ranger squad turned back toward Ysleta. The road crossed and recrossed into Mexico, for here the boundary lay not in the flowing Rio Grande but in an abandoned channel overgrown with chaparral. The wedge of brush-choked bottoms between the old riverbed and the flowing river to the south, an area of several square miles, was known as Pirate Island and served a purpose consistent with its name.[24]

After a three-mile ride, the Rangers spotted two Mexicans approaching them. Seeing the Rangers, they wheeled and galloped back up the road. The Rangers spurred in pursuit. At a cluster of adobes on each side of the road, the two men flung themselves from their mounts and ran inside one of the buildings. As the Rangers came abreast, gunfire blazed from the house and adjoining adobe wall. Jones and his men dismounted and advanced to within thirty feet of the little fortress, exchanging Winchester fire with at least half a dozen men.

A bullet struck Jones in the thigh. He crumpled to the ground but after straightening his leg resumed firing. Private F. F. Tucker bent over and asked, "Captain, are you hurt?" "Yes," answered Jones, "shot all to pieces." At this moment another round, fired from over the wall, hit him just above the heart and ranged downward. "Boys, I am killed," uttered Jones as he fell back dead.

The shootout erupted at the home of Antonio Olguin, two hundred yards south of the boundary. Almost certainly, Jones never knew he had left Texas. Private E. D. Bryant knew, however, and he told his comrades they had better get back to Texas before Mexican soldiers came. Ranger fire had wounded both Jesús and Severio Olguin, and the firing subsided enough for the Rangers to withdraw.

The Pirate Island affair prompted an outpouring of sympathy for the popular captain. Authorities at Juárez cooperated by returning his body and, later, his personal effects. They also clamped three of the Olguins in jail. They were American citizens, one an escaped convict, and the district attorney in El Paso promptly filed extradition papers. But the Díaz government took offense at this invasion of Mexican soil and lodged a diplomatic protest in Washington. The State Department called on Governor Hogg for an explanation, and federal authorities sent an army officer from Fort Bliss to investigate. In a few months the clamor subsided, but the Olguins were never extradited.[25]

Frank Jones's death dramatized the weakness to which a stingy legislature had reduced the Texas Rangers. Ironically, only five months earlier Jones had written words that could have served as his epitaph: "Of late years the Rangers have been compelled to do killing simply because they were so few in numbers it emboldened fugitives. During the first years of my Ranger service we never went out except there were 8 or 10 men and we never had to kill anyone."[26]

The death of Frank Jones had one beneficial result. It elevated to the head of Company D the ablest of the four great captains: John R. Hughes.

THIRTY-EIGHT IN 1893, John R. Hughes brought experience, maturity, and talent to the captaincy of Company D. As Jones's sergeant, he had won the confidence of sheriffs, judges, county officials, federal lawmen, and all others with whom he worked. Support for his promotion was instant and widespread. At once he revealed himself as the equal of Frank Jones in every measure of a Ranger captain, and in time he emerged as the best of them all.[27]

"A braver or cooler officer has never been commissioned," observed the editor of a Pecos newspaper. To those expected qualities Hughes brought others. He had a sharp mind, rugged physique, vigor and endurance, and unquenchable zest for rangering. He was a skilled outdoorsman, especially adept at tracking. Service at Shafter and Presidio had given him an understanding of the unique demands of the border. Of prime importance, Hughes selected his recruits with great care and exacted high standards of performance. Like successful captains since

Jack Hays, he led by example rather than edict. His men accorded him respect, affection, and loyalty, which he returned in full measure. "Folks trust John," observed one of his men. In short, John Hughes loved his job and did it incomparably.[28]

Hughes confronted the same handicap as Jones—not enough men to cover the huge Trans-Pecos, especially after the cutback of 1895 pared his company to a sergeant and six privates. Explosive county feuds in Pecos and Fort Stockton demanded constant attention. Train robbers had to be tracked for miles in the forbidding Devils River headlands or along the desolate Rio Grande. The boundary crackled with border disturbances, while ethnic troubles rumbled at Shafter, Presidio, Terlingua, and even Marfa and Fort Davis. These alarms, combined with the usual cow and horse theft, prompted one appeal after another from the sheriffs of Reeves, Brewster, Jeff Davis, and Presidio Counties. Often Hughes had to answer that he simply had no men to send.[29]

Stock theft also bedeviled the El Paso Valley, left largely uncovered even though company headquarters was at Ysleta. Pirate Island, scene of Jones's demise, was a favored holding grounds. But thieves operated more safely around the abandoned army post of Fort Hancock, ninety miles below El Paso. Fully fifty were said to be involved, including some of the same men who followed Chico Barela in the salt war of 1877. In November 1893 Hughes captured two of the prime leaders, Bernal and Tranquilino Barela, and believed he had broken up the gang.[30]

Another took its place in the spring of 1899. Four men operated at Fort Hancock and four at Crow Flat, ninety miles to the north at the base of Guadalupe Peak, on the New Mexico line. The four at Fort Hancock drove stock stolen on the Rio Grande to Crow Flat to exchange for stock stolen in New Mexico. With three Rangers and a federal customs officer, Hughes tracked these men for the entire month of April 1899 and returned with six of the eight outlaws and most of the purloined animals.[31]

Captain Hughes set himself two missions, almost obsessions, that he worked on whenever he found the time. One was to catch the Olguins who had killed Frank Jones. The other was to catch the killers of

Sergeant Fusselman, Hughes's friend and superior at Shafter in 1890. While still based in Alpine, Captain Jones had worked around El Paso long enough to identify the men who shot Fusselman: Desidario Pasos and Geronimo Parra. While scouting upriver from El Paso in late July 1893, Hughes learned from a New Mexico deputy that the Olguins were in Mesilla and that Parra had been jailed in Las Cruces for horse theft and attempted murder.[32] The Olguins disappear from the official record, presumably never captured.[33]

With one of Fusselman's killers, Hughes gained satisfaction. Geronimo Parra had been lodged in the New Mexico penitentiary at Santa Fe. Hughes wanted him to stand trial in Texas for the murder of Fusselman. At Ysleta in October 1898 Hughes and a New Mexico lawman sealed a bargain. The latter was the sheriff of Doña Ana County, Pat Garrett, who had killed Billy the Kid. If Hughes would find a man Garrett wanted, he would get Parra out of the penitentiary and turn him over to Hughes. Garrett got his fugitive, and Hughes, after complicated extradition proceedings, got Parra. On March 13, 1899, the sheriff and the Ranger escorted the prisoner by train from Santa Fe to El Paso. Convicted of murder, Parra went to the gallows on January 5, 1900. He did not go quietly. He and another murderer, wielding knives fashioned from smuggled wire, bloodied several guards before they were subdued and hanged. Captain Hughes watched the execution, doubtless with a feeling of relief that the promising young Ranger, after ten years, had at last been avenged.[34]

NO RANGER OPERATION of the 1890s attracted more state and national attention than one that seems like official overreaction. Governor Charles A. Culberson, reflecting the sentiments of a vocal minority, intended that no prizefight take place in Texas. The legislature made explicit an ambiguous law to that effect. The controversy over staging a world heavyweight bout in Texas raged throughout 1895 and finally centered on El Paso. Encouraged by local merchants, promoter Dan Stuart set February 14, 1896, as the date for "Ruby Bob" Fitzsimmons and Pete Maher to climb in the ring together. Newspapers everywhere gave major attention to the event, and special trains brought hundreds of fans to the border town.

The event also brought the Texas Rangers to town. The governor sent Adjutant General Mabry to take charge, and Captains Hughes, Brooks, McDonald, and Rogers assembled nearly their entire companies for him to command. Rangers kept Stuart and everyone else involved under constant surveillance. Clearly, the fight would not take place in Texas. The governor of Chihuahua ruled Mexico out of bounds. President Grover Cleveland sent federal marshals to ensure that, as decreed by the Congress in response to church groups, the public lands of New Mexico also remained off-limits.

"Judge" Roy Bean, the fabled "law west of the Pecos," came up with the answer. Everyone crowded aboard Southern Pacific trains and steamed nearly four hundred miles down to Langtry. The Rangers went too. On a tiny island in the middle of the Rio Grande, Fitzsimmons knocked out Maher in less than two minutes.

The episode afforded the entire nation, and a fair share of the world, constant amusement for more than a year. It also spotlighted the Texas Rangers and yielded the only opportunity in the history of the Frontier Battalion for all the companies and their captains to assemble with their commander. A camera recorded the occasion for posterity.[35]

IN THE SPRING OF 1899 smallpox struck Laredo. The state health officer came from Austin to isolate the infected and inoculate the uninfected. In a classic case of failure to communicate across cultural barriers, he encountered resistance from the Mexican community. In particular, families refused to surrender their diseased loved ones for transfer to the "pesthouse."

On March 18, with Ranger Augie Old, Captain John H. Rogers came from Cotulla to help enforce the state regulations. The next day, when they and local officers broke down a door and forcibly removed a person, a throng of protesters grew so threatening as to cause the enforcers to back off until Rogers could get the rest of his men down from Cotulla. When they arrived on March 20, he posted them at a hotel to await orders.

Meantime, Rogers and Old backed the sheriff and his deputies in presenting search warrants at homes suspected of stockpiling ammunition for armed resistance. Agipito Herrera barred the door to his home. Friends began to converge, and someone fired a pistol. The street filled with angry men and women. The sheriff and his deputies vanished. Herrera appeared with a Winchester and aimed at Rogers, who leveled his own. Both fired at the same time. Rogers went down with a bullet in the right arm, Herrera with a bullet in the chest. Augie Old walked over to the prostrate Herrera and put two rounds into his head.

Sergeant H. G. Dubose and the other four Rangers rushed to the scene. Rounding a corner, they confronted several score Mexicans gathered around Herrera's body. The Mexicans opened fire on the Rangers, who returned the fire and, believing the fallen man to be Old, charged. After a street battle lasting thirty minutes, the crowd dispersed. A detachment of federal soldiers from Fort McIntosh moved in and restored order. Health officers enforced the regulations, and the epidemic subsided.

The clash between Rangers and townspeople cost one citizen his life and ten, including two women, severe wounds. A less confrontational, more reasoning approach might have avoided violence. In light of the long-standing bitterness of the Mexican population toward Anglo authority, however, their cooperation probably could not have been gained quickly enough to enable health officers to halt the spread of the contagion. The "smallpox war" was but one of many border eruptions that dramatized the cultural gulf separating the Mexican majority from the Anglo minority.[36]

The "war" also inflicted a heavy cost on Captain Rogers. Herrera's bullet forced the removal of a piece of bone from his right arm. With the arm thus shortened, he could no longer align the sights of his Winchester. He had another specially constructed to compensate.

As for Ranger Old, who had ensured that Herrera received a "Ranger conviction," he was as deeply committed to Methodism as Rogers was to

Presbyterianism. After leaving the Rangers, Old became a respected Methodist clergyman.[37]

WHEN THE SPANISH–AMERICAN WAR broke out in the spring of 1898, rumors reached Austin that Mexicans would try to show their sympathy for Spain by raiding in Texas. Overreacting, Adjutant General Mabry (who would command a Texas regiment in Cuba) dispatched the entire Ranger force to stations on the Southern Pacific Railroad. Even had the rumors not turned out to be groundless, the handful of Rangers could have done no more to head off such incursions than they had in the Garza uprising seven years earlier. They had hardly reached their assigned posts when they turned back to their original locations.[38]

BY THE TURN of the century, many Texans looked on the Frontier Battalion as an anachronism. It had been created to protect the Texas frontier from Indian raids. Texas no longer suffered from Indian raids and no longer had a frontier. Battalion, moreover, implied a much larger force than fifty Rangers. However deceptive the label, the Frontier Battalion had always functioned as a state police force, and Texas needed a state police force.

From the beginning, a legal technicality had waited as if in ambush. Adjutant General King recognized it as early as 1882, when three Rangers were indicted for killing a man in the line of duty. The law that authorized the Special State Troops, he pointed out, endowed all the members of the unit with the powers of a peace officer. In the Frontier Battalion, however, formed to fight Indians, the legislature had named only officers as lawmen, whether carelessly or deliberately was never explained. King recommended that the terminology be clarified, but the legislature took no action. In practice, all Rangers continued to function as peace officers.[39]

The ambush snapped shut in 1900.

The waning years of the nineteenth century entangled the Texas Rangers in a host of ugly county feuds. Usually they accomplished no more than keep the peace while the factions worked out a compromise or the courts disposed of the issues. Especially virulent were Hall County in the Panhandle and Orange County in the far southeast, next to Louisiana. Both fell to Captain Bill McDonald.

In Hall County nesters faced off against stockmen. The rise of the People's or Populist Party gave the little fellows a shot at county offices. From the Populist perspective, McDonald's Rangers worked in behalf of the big cowmen, and early in 1900 petitions to the governor got them entirely removed.

Orange County was much more deadly. Here too Populists, fusing with Republicans and drawing on the black vote, gained county offices. The Orange County feud of 1899–1900 featured a lethal array of ingredients: lynchings, assassinations, efforts to purge the county of blacks, arson, anonymous death threats, a corrupt county judge, and, not least, the mercurial Captain Bill himself. In the line of duty, a Ranger shot and killed the son of the county judge, only to be shot down himself, from behind.

In both Hall and Orange Counties, Ranger Lou Saxon was one of McDonald's most efficient men. In Orange, attempting to arrest two drunken men, he had to "bend" his pistol barrel over their heads. In Hall County, he arrested some fence-cutters. In both counties he found himself indicted for false arrest and swiftly convicted. The judges ruled that only a commissioned Ranger, not a private, possessed the authority to make arrests.[40]

"It is the most outrageous thing that has happened since I have been in the service," exploded McDonald; but he now had new superiors to convince. Joseph D. Sayers had succeeded Charles Culberson as governor in 1899 and appointed Thomas Scurry as adjutant general. "Have governor act at once," McDonald wired Scurry on May 21, 1900.

But Sayers was not ready to act at once. He had Scurry request a legal opinion from the state attorney general. After a labored analysis of law, that official concluded, as had the judges, that only commissioned officers could execute criminal process or make arrests. For twenty-five years the Texas Rangers had been making illegal arrests.[41]

The attorney general's opinion spelled the end of the Frontier Battalion. Until the legislature could meet, Scurry performed a prodigious feat of paperwork that in effect left everyone in place but commissioned them lieutenants.

Finally, on March 29, 1901, the legislature acted. Responding to Scurry's recommendations, it created a Ranger Force of four companies of mounted men, each composed of a captain, a sergeant, and twenty privates. All Rangers, regardless of rank, were clothed with the powers of a peace officer. Pay was set at $100 a month for captains, $50 for sergeants, and $40 for privates (up from thirty). Rangers still had to furnish their own horse and rifle. Rations were specified and a quartermaster authorized.[42]

The law of 1901 did nothing other than make all Rangers peace officers, a legal technicality that simply legitimized what had been standard practice for twenty-five years. The institutional continuity of the Texas Rangers remained unbroken. They were now the Ranger Force. In law they had never been the Frontier Battalion, which was an administrative term to describe what the legislature had created but not named. Captains still reported to the adjutant general. For the first decade of the new century, moreover, the legislature never appropriated enough to support the authorized strength of eighty-eight; $30,000 a year, dropped to $25,000 in 1906, allowed each company no more than eight privates rather than the authorized twenty.

Under the law of 1901, nothing had been lost and nothing gained except correction of a legal error. The four captains—Hughes, Brooks, McDonald, and Rogers—still commanded the four diminutive companies. Texas still had a state police force.

[15]

End of an Era

FOR THE TEXAS RANGERS, the first decade of the twentieth century brought a decline in their role as lawmen of the Old West. The Old West itself faded while the Rangers stretched thinly to accommodate the entire state. As the force shrank, so did its quality. Low pay led to high turnover and, in those who stayed, mediocrity or worse. Drunkenness and other misbehavior grew more common. Like King and Mabry, Adjutant General Scurry occasionally burnished the Ranger image, but the burden of upholding the Ranger reputation fell chiefly to the four captains.[1]

Along the border, Rangers remained the men Mexicans loved to hate. Often cited as fuel for this abhorrence is the saga of Gregorio Cortez. Twenty-six in 1901, he had been reared in a family of horse thieves and became one of the most accomplished, wanted in several Texas counties. On June 12, 1901, Karnes County sheriff W. T. "Brack" Morris, a former Ranger, attempted to arrest Cortez. Three bullets downed Morris with fatal wounds. Gonzales County sheriff Richard Glover, a boyhood friend of Morris's, organized a six-man posse and traced Cortez to the farm of Henry Schnabel, near Ottine south of Austin. On the night of

June 14, with Schnabel as guide, the posse, tired and well lubricated with whiskey, launched what a later Ranger called a "wild sashay" on the tenant house where Cortez supposedly hid. Everyone fired in every direction. A posseman's bullet killed Schnabel. Cortez emerged to fire at any mounted form and brought down Glover, dead.

The killing of two sheriffs set off the biggest manhunt in South Texas history. In nearly every county sheriffs raised posses and took the field. On foot and on stolen horses, Cortez eluded all his pursuers. June 22 brought him, exhausted, to a sheep camp northwest of Laredo, only eight miles from the Rio Grande. A vaquero attracted by the reward tipped off Captain John Rogers, headquartered in Laredo. Accompanied by a federal customs officer, Rogers quietly arrested Cortez.

Dodging scores of pursuers in a ten-day chase across three hundred miles of South Texas chaparral instantly secured Gregorio Cortez a lasting niche in the folklore of border Mexicans. Verse after verse of *corridos*—folk ballads—celebrated the incredible adventure by which this lone Mexican outwitted, outran, and humiliated the host of posses tracking him on horseback and by rail. Not only the fortitude and skill of the pursued but the evil designs and ineptitude of the pursuers resonated in cadences that would live forever on the border and endure as a stinging reproach to the *rinches*.

Although the reproach fell chiefly on the Texas Rangers, in the hunt for Gregorio Cortez *rinches* were sheriffs and posses, not Rangers. One of Rogers's men accompanied a posse, and Rogers himself made a routine arrest. In the succession of trials that finally put Cortez in the penitentiary, Rangers escorted the prisoner and discouraged lynch mobs. But the identity of *rinches* and Rangers in popular thought, combined with the subsequent transformation of Cortez from a horse thief into a simple tenant farmer, cast the Rangers as the villains of the balladry. Rogers enjoyed wide acclaim for the arrest, but hardly any Rangers could number themselves among the *rinches* who struggled to snare Gregorio Cortez.[2]

The Cerda brothers gained no such glory as Gregorio Cortez, but they got the Rangers into serious trouble. In January 1902, Captain Brooks and his company, always responsive to the King Ranch interests, pitched camp outside Brownsville to contend with the depredations that periodically swept the southern part of the King Ranch, now the domain of Richard King's widow. Brooks entrusted most of the scouting to his sergeant, A. Y. Baker, a tough, truculent veteran of proven competence.

Political conflict wracked the lower valley as "Reds" and "Blues" mobilized for the election of 1902. Federal customs officers, Republican appointees, roused Mexican voters against the "good people" of the blue Democratic establishment. The collector of customs published a Spanish-language newspaper that excoriated the Rangers and roused hostility that spilled into the streets. Incensed, Baker and his comrades responded by bullying their tormentors.

Against this unstable backdrop, Baker and his men scouted the King range. A nighttime sweep on May 16, 1902, turned up several King calves tied to chaparral limbs, and in a sudden encounter Baker rode on Ramón Cerda, bent over a tied calf searing his own brand into its hide. Both men fired. Cerda's round hit Baker's horse in the head and killed it. Baker's round caught Cerda above the right eye and killed him. The next morning Justice of the Peace Estévan García and seven witnesses examined the scene. Noting the partly branded calf, Baker's dead horse, and Cerda's weapon with one round fired, they filed a record of inquest supporting Baker's plea of self-defense.

At Baker's examining trial, however, the purported results of another inquest were introduced. Six days after Cerda's death, another justice, Encarnacion Garza, and another seven witnesses had dug up Cerda's body and concluded that he had been tied and dragged before he was shot. This inquest had never been entered in the official record, and the Rangers and their "blue" supporters could hardly be faulted for regarding it as manufactured to tar Baker as an assassin. Ranger critics readily embraced this version of Cerda's death, and feeling against Brooks and his men ran higher than ever.

On September 9, as Baker, Ranger Emmet Roebuck, and a King herder, Jesse Miller, rode from Brownsville toward camp, a storm of shotgun fire from ambush swept the trail. It severely wounded Baker in the back, killed Roebuck, and dropped Miller's horse. Brooks had already been alerted to a plot to kill the Rangers and had learned enough to sweep through Brownsville and arrest Alfredo Cerda, Ramón's brother, and five accomplices, including Encarnacion Garza, the justice who had conducted the second inquest on Ramón Cerda.

Released on bond, Alfredo Cerda publicly vowed to kill Baker. When the two chanced to meet in a Brownsville store on October 3, Baker's Winchester ended the impasse. Alfredo's hand had flashed to his right hip, Baker contended, and a jury later concluded that he had acted in self-defense. Whether the hip bore a pistol is not apparent. Another jury acquitted Baker of murdering Ramón Cerda.

The explosive political setting in Brownsville ensured that shock waves from the Cerda affair hit Austin. Governor Joseph D. Sayers dispatched Adjutant General Scurry to investigate. Scurry found Brooks's Rangers blameless of any offense but overreacting to provocative insults. Both Scurry and the governor, however, understood that Brownsville could know no peace so long as Brooks and his company remained. Captain Hughes received orders to take over the Brownsville sector.

The Cerda affair achieved prominence because political strife lifted it above ordinary relations between Rangers and border Mexicans. Whether in the lower valley, at Presidio and Shafter, or around El Paso, such encounters featured similar uncertainties. Mexicans had been conditioned to believe the worst of Rangers, and killings like those of the Cerdas easily translated into official executions. As in the Cerda case, Rangers could usually justify their actions, but never to Mexicans who had been reared on stories of Leander McNelly and Jack Hays and had seen their countrymen, "bandits" or not, gunned down by Rangers.[3]

TWO EPISODES FORESHADOWED missions that would increasingly occupy Rangers in the twentieth century. One was dealing with labor troubles. The other was imposing order on oil boomtowns.

In September 1903, for the third time, the Texas and Pacific Coal Company at Thurber called for Rangers. The company had successfully fended off all attempts to unionize the workforce. Organizers found managers adamant and stirred so much dissatisfaction among the miners that Adjutant General John A. Hulen (commissioned in 1902 by Governor Samuel W. T. Lanham) sent Captain Rogers and his company to keep the peace. Under the watchful eyes of the Rangers, all but twenty-five of the eight hundred diggers quietly walked off the job and entrained, at union expense, for unionized mines. Mine managers paid high tribute to Rogers and his men. In June 1904 Captain Brooks and his company earned similar praise for preventing disorder among strikers at the Minera coal mines near Laredo. As unions grew stronger and more aggressive in coming decades, Rangers would not always find strikers so easily calmed.[4]

On January 10, 1901, the Spindletop gusher blew from a Gulf salt dome near Beaumont and launched Texas, and much of the world, into a new industrial age. Beaumont's population exploded, and Texas had its first oil boomtown, complete with throngs of men on the take, muddy streets, drunken rowdies, turbulence, violence, homicide, crime, and brutality toward blacks. An oil company executive warned the adjutant general that Beaumont needed "a good bunch of Rangers."

Nearby Batson, however, drew the Rangers into what would become a recurring ordeal during the twentieth century. The Batson field blew in 1903, and in January 1904 Governor Lanham sent Captain Brooks to investigate. He found "every thing wide open here," local officers grudgingly cooperative, and the task of keeping order his alone. "It is very unpleasant for one ranger to be compelled to police a tough place like this," he complained. Through 1904, however, Brooks and three of his men set the pattern for the future: brush aside corrupt lawmen, round up fugitives and other criminals, and keep order with the techniques developed two decades earlier in the railroad camps, where firm authority backed by physical violence tamed many a rowdy. In Batson Brooks confronted a new challenge, met it decisively and creatively, pointed the way for Rangers to come, and confirmed his stature as one of the four great captains.[5]

. . .

IN 1904 BROWNSVILLE at last gained its long-sought rail connection with Corpus Christi and the rest of Texas. Northern immigrants immediately boosted the population and began to transform the lower valley into an agricultural bonanza of irrigated truck and citrus farming.

Racial and ethnic tensions continued to unsettle Brownsville. The northerners either brought with them or quickly adopted the prejudices of Anglo Texans. The battalion of the black Twenty-fifth Infantry posted to Fort Brown in July 1906 found welcome from neither Anglos nor Mexicans. Nor did these soldiers, boasting a distinguished combat record in Cuba and the Philippines, readily tolerate the racial attitudes or the random acts of thuggery that occasionally befell them. As one example, federal customs inspector A. Y. Baker, who had killed the Cerda brothers four years earlier as a Ranger sergeant, threw a drunken black soldier into the Rio Grande. Even so, neither townspeople nor soldiers considered relations strained enough to portend trouble.

Near midnight on August 13, 1906, rifle fire erupted outside the brick wall separating Fort Brown from the city. Certain that the fort was under attack, the gate sentinel twice fired his rifle into the air as a signal. As the garrison turned out under arms, ten to twenty shadowy figures made their way up an alley leading from the fort to the town and began firing into lighted buildings. Before vanishing ten minutes later, they had killed a man, shattered the arm of a police lieutenant, left homes and commercial buildings riddled with bullets, and spread terror through the population. In the dark of night, no one identified any of the raiders, but at daybreak the mayor gathered spent shell casings and clips from the army Springfield and spread them before the post commander, Major Charles W. Penrose. A volley of telegrams sped to Austin and Washington, D.C., demanding the removal of the black troops, measures to prevent a recurrence, and an inquiry to identify and bring to justice the guilty.

Recognizing the "Brownsville affray" as essentially a federal matter, the governor and adjutant general procrastinated several days while they and the state's congressional delegation worked with army officials. The commanding general in Texas dispatched his inspector general, Major Augustus P. Blocksom, to conduct an official investigation.

The army promised to replace the garrison of Fort Brown with white troops.

Many townspeople wanted Texas National Guard units sent to patrol the city. Instead Governor Lanham sent Texas Rangers: Captain Bill McDonald and the four men who made up his company.

McDonald stepped off the train on August 21, to find that a citizens' committee had been working with Majors Penrose and Blocksom for almost a week without making progress. No soldier admitted to participating in the raid. No soldier conceded knowledge of a raid. An unshakable conspiracy of silence seemed designed to thwart all probes. Penrose vowed "to ferret it out if it took him ten years." McDonald grumped that Penrose could do it in ten minutes if he tried. The committeemen thereupon added the captain to their ranks and vested him with full power to press forward in their name.

A committed lawman as well as an arrant racist, McDonald launched the inquiry in his usual style. Some of the "lovable coons" had shot up Brownsville. Despite the dawdling of the army officers, by questioning a few soldiers he could quickly find out which "black devils" to charge. He marched up to the fort's gate, commanded a squad of guards to lower their Springfields and get out the way (or so his biographer would have us believe), and confronted Majors Penrose and Blocksom. He interrogated enough soldiers and gathered enough other evidence to convince him that he had the names of thirteen guilty men, and he persuaded Judge Stanley Welch to issue warrants for their arrest for "conspiracy to commit murder." Actually, he believed everyone at the fort culpable and that no mistake would be made "if Penrose and the three companies of soldiers were all placed under arrest for those that were not actually engaged in the murder knew all about it and this of course made them accessories."

For Captain Bill, serving the arrest warrants proved more difficult than naming the culprits. Major Penrose had been unable to identify anyone, nor had Major Blocksom, although the latter's investigation led him to lay the deed to members of the garrison. Twice on the evening of August 24 McDonald sent the warrants to Penrose and demanded custody of the thirteen soldiers. Twice Penrose refused, citing concern for the safety of the men and adding that he had been unable to find anyone connected in any way with the crime.

More significant, McDonald learned that Penrose had received orders to move his battalion to Fort Reno, Oklahoma, dropping the thirteen men at Fort Sam Houston in San Antonio to be held until called for by the state of Texas. The white soldiers to take their place had reached Brownsville on the same train that brought McDonald.

But McDonald intended to prevent the departure of the battalion until he had his men. At midnight a train stood ready, but he ordered it held. "It is possible," Major Blocksom later wrote, that "McDonald might have fought the entire battalion with his four or five rangers were their obedience as blind as his obstinacy." The obstinacy also alarmed local officials, who saw the removal of the troops as the best way to end an ugly situation. During the night Judge Welch rescinded the warrants. McDonald refused to accept this action, even though threatened with a citation for contempt. The obstinacy collapsed only when the governor, much to the captain's surprise and hurt, sided with the judge. "Consult district judge and sheriff and act under and through them," read the telegram from Lanham. McDonald saw the futility of further dispute. Early on August 25 a train bearing the battalion of the Twenty-fifth Infantry steamed out of Brownsville.

From beginning to end, the incident was essentially a matter for the army to investigate and resolve. McDonald could see nothing beyond the laws of Texas, the color of the offenders' skin, and his duty to bring the lawbreakers to justice. His imperious and belligerent investigation played no constructive part in the process. Until the governor finally intervened, Captain Bill played the fellow in the right who "just keeps acomin.'"

Aside from antagonizing army officers and Brownsville officials, McDonald's sole contribution was to name thirteen blacks who had violated the laws of Texas. The army confined them at Fort Sam Houston, subject to a call from Texas, until a Brownsville grand jury failed to find enough evidence to sustain indictments. McDonald's case collapsed.

Who shot up Brownsville bedevils historians to this day. The army could never decide, and Major Blocksom's recommendations finally prevailed, all the way up to President Theodore Roosevelt. The major believed that the battalion had closed ranks to protect the guilty and should be handed an ultimatum to name the culprits or face dishonorable discharge. Still, every soldier denied knowledge of the affair. In November 1906 President Roosevelt ordered every one of them, 167 men, discharged "without honor." This action immediately sparked a partisan controversy, and senate hearings brought forth new but not conclusive evidence. Springfield shell casings may have been planted to shift blame from smugglers, irate Mexicans, grudge-bearing Brownsville men, or still others. Or in fact black raiders may have struck out at racist townspeople.[6]

Whatever the explanation, the dishonorable discharge of all three companies could not withstand the scrutiny of a later generation struggling against racism. In 1972 the Congress converted the discharges to honorable and authorized back pay and allowances to the victims. Only one old man survived to claim the reparation. "None of us said anything because we didn't have anything to say," he explained. "It was a frameup through and through."[7]

Brownsville did not provide the blaze of glory through which Captain Bill left the Ranger Force. That came in November 1906, when he and his four men, called to Rio Grande City by the political assassination of Judge Stanley Welch, rode into a nighttime ambush. When the smoke cleared, none of the Rangers had been hit, while four Mexicans lay dead and two stood with their hands up. "I don't guess I missed any of them," explained McDonald, whose new Winchester had jammed after the first shot.[8]

Early in 1907 a new governor, Thomas Campbell, elevated McDonald to the post of state revenue agent. Although reluctant to leave the Ranger Force, the aging lawman accepted. Not everyone was unhappy to see him leave. Especially in Brownsville, his role in the "affray" of August 1906 portrayed him for many as a troublemaking blowhard. Yet Captain Bill never lacked for champions. As a Falfurrias realtor wrote the adjutant general in September 1906, "WE WANT RANGERS AND MORE OF THEM, LIKE CAPT MCDONALD."[9]

OF ALL THE TASKS that bedeviled the Texas Rangers in the twentieth century, none would prove messier than prohibition. In 1907–1909 Amarillo gave them a taste of what the 1920s held in store.

Amarillo's Bowery, next to the railroad depot, featured streets lined with saloons and brothels and reverberated nightly with drunken rowdyism, fights, muggings, robberies, and occasional homicides. City officials, reacting to church and temperance groups, exercised local option to impose prohibition of liquor. The police force and Sheriff's Department, however, frequently at odds with the city administration, ignored the laws. Bowery entrepreneurs and their customers, and many townspeople, disliked attempts to regulate business and morality. The district judge and other community leaders asked Governor Campbell to send in Rangers. His adjutant general, James O. Newton, who took office in January 1907, assigned the task to Captain Frank Johnson, headquartered at Colorado City.

Johnson already had two men in Amarillo. One of them, Ranger N. P. "Doc" Thomas, made himself odious to Bowery operators as well as the sheriff and police chief. Rarely did he meet local lawmen without losing his temper and pouring forth verbal abuse. The sheriff's two sons, who spent all their time carousing in local "hoar houses," clashed with Thomas repeatedly. Hostility toward the Rangers spread throughout the city, but the "good people" urged them to keep at the task.[10]

Finally, in August 1908, Captain Johnson and three Rangers pitched camp at Amarillo and, with the two already on the scene, went aggressively after bootleggers and saloon keepers. Working night and day, they filled the county jail with one hundred offenders. "We cleaned up the town and closed all the joints and turned it over to the local officers in fine shape," Johnson proudly proclaimed early in December 1908.[11]

As soon as the "joint men" discovered the Rangers no longer enforcing prohibition, they reopened for business. Neither police nor sheriff intervened. Moreover, they remained furious with the indiscretions of Ranger Thomas and sought ways to get rid of him. On January 5, 1909, as Thomas sat in the county attorney's office, jailor James Keeton crept up behind him and with a six-shooter blew open his head. All circumstances pointed to premeditated assassination, but with everyone near the scene prepared to swear that Keeton had fired in self-defense, conviction seemed unlikely.[12]

Such was the conclusion of Captain Tom Ross, who had been assigned Amarillo in a routine shifting of headquarters. While Ross worked with a grand jury unsympathetic to Rangers, he also continued the onslaught against the whiskey traffickers. Although he brought several before the courts, he operated with the same insensitivity to public opinion as had the slain Thomas. The impasse with the local lawmen continued. On October 16, 1909, a Ranger picked a fight with the chief of police, who in turn assaulted a second Ranger.[13]

Adjutant General Newton had never approved of the Amarillo mission. Local authorities, he believed, ought to handle local laws, especially one fraught with such controversy and emotion as prohibition. He thought the Rangers ought to withdraw from the prohibition mess and concentrate on more serious crime. The drive behind the Amarillo policing seems to have come from Governor Campbell, a champion of local option.

After the clash between the police chief and Ranger, Newton decided how to get out of what had become a public relations disaster for the Rangers: turn Amarillo over to Captain John R. Hughes and let him make peace with all factions. Arriving on November 10, Hughes gathered the local officers and quietly lectured them. If they would do their duty, he said, he would sit in Amarillo all winter and send in blank monthly reports. He would be watching, however, and would not allow violations of law to go unnoticed.[14]

Captain Ross resented Newton's solution. But Ross's methods had worked no better than Johnson's. Hughes's tact and firmness eased the Rangers out of the morass. The two-year ordeal had demonstrated how unfitted they were to deal with laws many citizens opposed, especially when high-handed behavior offended public sentiment. Hardly three months after exchanging stations with Hughes, Ross received notice from Newton that, having failed to exercise proper control of his men, the "discipline of the Ranger Force" required his resignation.[15]

Ross's OUSTER SIGNALED how much the Ranger Force had declined during the opening years of the twentieth century. Captain Johnson, who had bungled Amarillo as badly as Ross, lost his commission in 1910 when his company was abolished. That left but three companies: three captains, three sergeants, and fifteen privates.[16]

Of the four captains of the 1890s, only Hughes and Rogers remained. The departure of Brooks in 1906 and McDonald in 1907 had hurt. They were men of stature and effectiveness who upheld the reputation of the Rangers. Brooks settled in Falfurrias and went on to a distinguished career as state legislator and county judge. When the legislature carved a new county out of Starr County in 1911, it took the name of Brooks. He died in 1944.

As for Captain Bill, President Woodrow Wilson named him United States Marshal for the Northern District of Texas. Pneumonia killed him in 1918. Even in death he proclaimed his motto. His tombstone in a Quanah cemetery bears the inscription: "No man in the wrong can stand up against a fellow that's in the right and keeps on a-comin.'"

Hughes and Rogers continued to serve with distinction, but they could not prevent the breakdown in Ranger discipline. Reports of drunkenness, internal quarrels, abuse of authority, and other misdeeds found their way into newspapers and armed those who wanted to see the force abolished.

Symptomatic of the decline was a letter written to Adjutant General Hulen in 1906 by state senator W. W. Turney of El Paso. He credited himself with having saved the Rangers from legislative extinction for a full decade, but now he doubted the wisdom of his efforts. El Paso County had just lost Hughes's company. Captain Rogers and his men and by inference all others did not measure up to Hughes, the ideal Texas Ranger.

Sober, fearless, industrious, Hughes required his men to be the same, wrote Turney. He was not afraid of his horse, and he was usually found riding through the hiding places of outlaws. He cared nothing for a railroad pass or a Pullman berth and hardly ever used either. Nor did his men. When a dollar was paid out, Texas got the worth of her money.

Not so with other Rangers. Too often they were mere figureheads, thinking only of their own business and advancement and never the interest of the state. Duty seemed not to carry them beyond a fireside in some county seat. Perhaps after all the Ranger Force had no future.[17]

It did, but not so bright and publicly applauded as in the years of Jones and McNelly, or the more recent time of the four captains. In the first decade of the twentieth century, the first for the newly styled "Ranger Force," decline set in, increasingly evident even though obscured by the achievements of the four captains.

The last two lived out long lives as honored veterans. John Rogers resigned his commission in 1911, served as a U.S. marshal for eight years, and returned in 1927–1930 to round out his career as a Ranger captain. He died in 1930, aged sixty-seven. From an office in Austin, John Hughes presided over the force as senior captain and retired in 1915 after twenty-eight years as a Ranger and twenty-two as a captain, a record unrivaled then or since. He prospered in banking and other enterprises, received awards and honors and repeatedly saw his story in print, adorned many a Ranger reunion with his massive white beard and cherubic countenance, and reigned for thirty-two years as the most venerated icon of the old Rangers. In 1947, ninety-two years old and dying of cancer, he took his own life.

After 1910, even as Rogers and Hughes served out their remaining years, the Texas Rangers sank in a political mire, committed atrocities that would bring them again to the brink of extinction, and relegated to their past the traditions of lawmen of the Old West.

[16]

A Summing Up

FOR THE YEARS 1823 to 1910, Texas Ranger is a label that describes two distinctively different bodies of men. From 1823 to 1874, Rangers were citizen soldiers, periodically mobilized to fight Indians or Mexicans. After 1874, they were Old West lawmen who belonged to an institution administratively named the Frontier Battalion and, after 1901, legislatively named the Ranger Force.

Similarities linked the citizen soldiers and the state lawmen who were designated Texas Rangers. They wore no uniform, as lawmen not even a badge. Men dressed however they wished for the task at hand, be it trailing Indians or horse thieves, fighting Mexicans with the armies of Taylor and Scott, or imposing order on a fractious courtroom during an incendiary trial. Officers and men related to one another informally, without the exacting discipline of the regular army or a metropolitan police force. In both roles men retained the sense of individual freedom and independence characteristic of the Anglo Texan. Either as soldiers or lawmen, their effectiveness depended on their leadership. Officers who understood the Texan makeup and led by example rather than fiat usually had good men and good units. Officers lacking this quality fell short, either as soldiers or lawmen, and their units failed to measure up to the Texas Ranger ideal.

Beyond these similarities, beyond the starkly different missions, the citizen soldiers and the lawmen drew from and molded a different order of man. Citizen soldiers enlisted for three months, sometimes six, but if they served longer it was in response to another callup. They were young men between jobs and frontier farmers who left their fireside to fight off Indians or take on the Mexicans and then come back home. Some, like those who signed on time and again under Jack Hays and Rip Ford, so loved the life and their captains that they made rangering a career limited only by the frequency of callups. They, and those who fought in the Mexican War, served together long enough to perfect their horsemanship and marksmanship and to develop a cohesion and teamwork that made them superior combat outfits. Nearly all, however, were sturdy outdoorsmen who knew how to ride and shoot. An occasional Indian or Mexican turned up on the muster rolls, even on rare occasion entire units of Indians or Mexicans, but nearly all citizen soldiers were Anglo Texans who despised Indians and Mexicans.

The Ranger lawmen responded to no callup. They enlisted on their own initiative and joined the ranks only after undergoing close scrutiny by their captain. They came from all walks of life and all parts of the state, although cowboys from the western counties predominated. Military structure, discipline, and accountability, while informal, were nevertheless strict, curbing individual freedom more rigidly than the citizen soldier would have tolerated. Rangers rarely served more than one or two years. For some, the life proved too strenuous and the pay too paltry. For some, the lure of a cattle spread or other more lucrative enterprise beckoned. For some, drunkenness, insubordination, misuse of authority, or troublemaking in the company earned discharge, often dishonorable. For most, however, the periodic budget cuts so drastically reduced the companies that men had to be let go. Captains retained only the best, and many who stayed developed into career lawmen. Some of these, deficient in judgment, intellect, imagination, commitment, diligence, honesty, or other marks of the good policeman, darkened the reputation of the Rangers. Others evolved into true professionals, a credit to the Rangers and the pride of Texans. They were a mixed lot, these Ranger lawmen of the Old West Texas.[1]

OVER THE PAST CENTURY, two competing images of the Texas Rangers have emerged, both in scholarly studies and in popular thought. At the beginning of the twenty-first century, they still war with each other, the one sustaining the bright legend of the state's criminal investigative arm, the other inspiring periodic attempts to abolish it altogether. The first and older image is best captured by two of Texas's most distinguished historians, Walter Prescott Webb and T. R. Fehrenbach. Webb:

> To speak of courage among Texas Rangers is almost a superfluity. They all have it to a high degree, and the man who lacks it cannot long remain a private. A captain not only had courage, which may be a purely emotional thing, but he had what is better, a complete absence of fear. For him fear and courage are unknown; he is not conscious of either. This means that he is free, with every faculty about him, to act in complete accord with his intelligence.
>
> The real Ranger has been a very quiet, deliberate, gentle person who could gaze calmly into the eye of a murderer, divine his thoughts, and anticipate his action, a man who could ride straight up to death. In fatal encounter—the last resort of a good officer—the Ranger has had the unhurried courage to take the extra fraction of a second essential to accuracy which was at a premium in the art and the science of the Western pistology.[2]

Fehrenbach:

> From 1836 onward, the history of the Texas Rangers was . . . only a little less than the history of Texas, while the history of all west Texas was only a little more than the story of the Ranger force.
>
> Very soon, the Rangers had certain marked characteristics, which they did not soon lose. They were not typical Texas farmers—the man

with a farm and family could not spend his time riding the wild frontier. They were for the most part extremely young. Most great Ranger leaders earned their fame long before the age of thirty. That they were adventurous and uniformly courageous needs no explanation; they were all volunteers. More significant was the repeated assertion by observers that the Ranger captains were unusual men—not merely brave, but officers who showed an utter absence of fear. This breed of captain was called forth both by the rough nature of the men he led, and the incredibly perilous situation of the tiny Ranger bands on the war frontier.[3]

That *the* real Ranger or even *the* Ranger captain was quiet, deliberate, gentle, courageous, fearless, and endowed with other sterling traits defies plausibility. Rangering neither attracted nor produced such a man. Many possessed one or more of these attributes, but few displayed them all. Certainly there were outstanding Rangers. Jack Hays, Matt Caldwell, Ben McCulloch, Sam McMurry, Lam Sieker, Frank Jones, Ira Aten, and the four captains come to mind. On the other hand, William Tobin, Warren Wallace, George Schmitt, Joe Shely, J. S. McNeel, and Tom Ross hardly measured up to the stereotype.

And then there was the improbably named Bass Outlaw, an incomparable sergeant when sober but such a terror when drunk that he had to be discharged. His end came in an El Paso bordello in 1894, when he shot and killed a Ranger and was gunned down himself by none other than Constable John Selman, the outlaw-turned-lawman who killed John Wesley Hardin. Bass Outlaw possessed qualities of the ideal Ranger, but he had one failing that disqualified him.[4]

The records of the Rangers identify many, both commissioned and enlisted, both frontier fighters and lawmen, who resembled the stereotype alongside many lacking even scanty qualifications. One searches the documents in vain for Webb's "real Ranger."

During their fighting years the Rangers did not dominate the history of frontier Texas, as Fehrenbach contends. The "Rangers" existed only as an intermittently invoked tradition, not as a continuously operating institution. Some, mainly in Jack Hays's outfit, saw enough service to qualify as professional Indian fighters and, on occasion, Mexican fighters. Most Rangers of that time were not professional Rangers but footloose young volunteers or, to take issue with Fehrenbach, farmers, stockmen, businessmen, or laborers who left their families for weeks at a time to campaign against Indians or Mexicans. The history of frontier Texas is replete with episodes of wives and children fighting off or falling victim to Comanche raiders while their menfolk were absent.

Best but by no means alone in representing the competing Ranger image are folklorist Américo Paredes and three collaborating Chicano scholars, Julian Samora, Joe Bërnal, and Albert Peña. Paredes:

> There is evidence . . . that not all Rangers lived up to their reputation as a fearless breed of men. Their basic techniques of ambush, surprise, and shooting first—with the resultant "mistake" killings of innocent bystanders—made them operate at times in ways that the average city policeman would be ashamed to imitate. The "shoot first and ask questions later" method of the Rangers has been romanticized into something dashing and daring, in technicolor, on a wide screen, and with Gary Cooper in the title role.[5]

Samora, Bërnal, and Peña:

> It is a matter of historical record that the Rangers have operated without restraint and with seemingly unchecked power. This power has been abused under the guise of maintaining law and order; unchecked power invariably will be abused. The agency has never been responsible to a local electorate as have sheriffs and policemen. It is a matter of historical record that the Rangers have been brutal (Webb would say "vigorous") in their methods of upholding *their* interpretation of law and in their violations of the civil rights of citizens.[6]

Américo Paredes and the trio of Julian Samora, Joe Bërnal, and Albert Peña etch a dark portrait of the Texas Ranger. Like Webb and

Fehrenbach, they deal with him as lawman, but their larger work makes clear that they also are describing the earlier Rangers. This portrait features a brutal, lawless Ranger, one who as a soldier indiscriminately slaughtered Indians and Mexicans and as lawman systematically practiced the *ley de fuga*–the law of the fugitive, in which prisoners were routinely shot while supposedly trying to escape. A later generation would call this Ranger a "rogue cop." Unlike the county sheriff, the Ranger was unaccountable to the citizenry and thus unrestrained in his violent tendencies.

No more than Webb's "real Ranger" is this Ranger grounded in credible evidence. Primary sources fail to disclose the systematic misconduct of which the Rangers are accused. Surely some were brutal, lawless, practitioners of the *ley de fuga*, or "rogue cops." They key word, however, is systematic: were they routinely guilty of such misdeeds and thus deserving of the generality? As for accountability, the Ranger's ran to his captain, who was accountable to the adjutant general, who was accountable to the governor, who was accountable to the citizenry and, more immediately, the legislature. Ample evidence demonstrates that this chain of command ensured accountability. The sheriff's direct accountability to the local citizenry, on the other hand, involved election to the office and frequently undermined law and order, and sometimes even abetted crime.

The revisionist case seems built on four supports. The first is the well-documented atrocities of the Mexican War and McNelly's border operations. The second is an interpretation of such incidents as the San Ambrosia affair of 1885 (chap. 13) and the Cerda killings of 1902 (chap. 15) that brushes aside all uncertainty and ambiguity, uncritically embraces the popular Mexican belief of what happened, and assumes that they occurred regularly. The third is the popular belief itself, unquestionably a deeply held belief passed from one generation to the next, but rooted in folklore and a scattering of anecdotes. The fourth, which undergirds the popular belief as well as the conclusions of the revisionists, is a tendency to tar the Rangers of two centuries with the actions of some in the twentieth century. The border excesses of 1915–1919 and the strike-breaking operation of the 1960s against Mexican agricultural workers are but two of several twentieth-century grievances resented by Mexicans.

The revisionists target the Webb portrayal of Texas Rangers in general but are primarily concerned with their conduct in relations with border Mexicans. What border Mexicans believed, however unwarranted or distorted, is part of the history of the Texas Rangers. As recorded by Américo Paredes, here is what they believed, as revealed in border sayings and anecdotes:

1. The Texas Ranger always carries a rusty old gun in his saddlebags. This is for use when he kills an unarmed Mexican. He drops the gun beside the body and then claims he killed the Mexican in self-defense and after a furious battle.
2. When he has to kill an armed Mexican, the Ranger tries to catch him asleep, or he shoots the Mexican in the back.
3. If it weren't for the American soldiers, the Rangers wouldn't dare come to the Border. The Ranger always runs and hides behind the soldiers when the real trouble starts.
4. Once an army detachment was chasing a rider, and they were led by a couple of Rangers. The Mexican went into the brush. The Rangers galloped up to the place, pointed it out, and then stepped back to let the soldiers go in first.
5. Two Rangers are out looking for a Mexican horse thief. They strike his trail, follow it for a while, and then turn at right angles and ride until they meet a half-dozen Mexican laborers walking home from the fields. These they shoot with their deadly Colts. Then they go to the nearest town and send back a report to Austin: "In pursuit of horse thieves we encountered a band of Mexicans, and though outnumbered we succeeded in killing a dozen of them after a hard fight, without loss to ourselves. It is believed that others of the band escaped and are making for the Rio Grande."[7]

However much such beliefs are drawn from events of the twentieth century, they do not reflect a pattern apparent in the nineteenth century. To be sure, McNelly and his men unjustifiably abused Mexicans, as did the Rangers during the Mexican War. But in the aftermath of the Civil War, as Texans bemoaned the consequences of defeat, outrage over the Alamo, Goliad, and other Mexican offenses of the revolution and the republic subsided. Anglo-Texan hostility toward Mexicans fueled by these old grievances lessened, although prejudice, discrimination, and oppression did not. Rangers of course not only shared these attitudes but were an arm of the Anglo Texan establishment. Even so, evidence of consistent Ranger persecution of Mexicans, as distinct from the occasional, appears to rest on dubious foundations. If Mexican sources other than popular belief exist with sufficient substance to establish a pattern, they have not been set forth. No persuasive documentation now sustains the revisionist characterization of the nineteenth-century Rangers.

As with Mexicans, so with Indians. Rangers embodied the attitudes of Anglo Texans and also of Mexicans. Even though Indians antedated white immigrants by centuries, Texans regarded them as interlopers, uncivilized wretches who did not know how to make proper use of the land. When the tribes that lived in Texas behaved, they were to be tolerated. When they did not, they were to be expelled or eliminated. Texans reserved special enmity for Kiowas and Comanches on the northwestern frontier and for Apaches in the Trans-Pecos. These Indians were not being displaced by Texans. They came from outside Texas, intent on murder and plunder. They were almost impossible to catch, but when they were brought to battle Rangers paid no more heed to humanitarian principles than their foe.

The present study, like Walter Webb's, draws heavily on the official records of the Rangers, the state adjutant generals, and the governors of Texas. That these records point to interpretations different from Webb's may be explained by the different ways two historians read the same evidence—not uncommon in the historical profession—and also by a social and cultural environment separated by more than seventy years.

The official records are voluminous and indispensable to a true understanding of the Texas Rangers. Critics argue that official records are biased, as indeed they are. Although official records rarely contain self-incrimination, they are not free of negative material. People offended by Ranger conduct poured out their complaints to the governor and the adjutant general. Moreover, as most historians understand, *all* written documents are in some degree biased. The historian's challenge is to identify the bias and extract the genuine. The revisionist works cited above do not disclose any use of official records.

Beyond the official records, newspapers, observations of travelers, biographies, autobiographies, reminiscences, and scholarly monographs fill out the Ranger portrait. When a newspaper had a correspondent on the scene of a major event, such as the killing of Sam Bass or the El Paso salt war, the dispatches can constitute a major firsthand source. Newspapers also frequently contained letters from knowledgeable participants or observers that add to the historical record. At the same time, newspapers routinely ground out wild rumors and fabrications that have to be recognized and discarded. Like the official records, biographies, autobiographies, and reminiscences contain biases—often blatant biases—that call for skeptical scrutiny. Ranger biographies are all cast more or less in the heroic mold. Reminiscences suffer from time-clouded memories as well as the impulse to embroider.

In short, most sources contain material of value, and most sources must be employed with caution. For the Texas Rangers, that is no less true than with any other subject. The test lies in how well the historian uses them.

THAT THE TEXAS RANGER remains the hero of an enduring legend can be confirmed by anyone with a television. In Texas, Jack Hays gave birth to the legend in the early 1840s, as he squared off against Comanche raiders from his base in San Antonio. His pioneering employment of the Colt five-shooter gave impetus to the accolades showered on him in Texas newspapers. With the passing years, reminiscences of Rangers who rode with him, embellished by popular writers, inflated Hays's deeds and created some that likely did not happen. A life-size diorama in the Texas Ranger Hall of Fame at Waco, for example, depicts Hays alone atop Enchanted Rock fighting off hordes of converging Comanches. This exploit commands no contemporary documentation, and all reminiscent accounts are chronologically vague.[8]

With the Mexican War, the legend spread from Texas throughout a nation caught up in war. Samuel Walker's exploits in General Zachary Taylor's service introduced the Rangers to the American people. The well-publicized deeds of Hays and his regiment of mounted volunteers, even though not officially labeled Rangers, inflated and burnished the legend on the national stage. Their combat success and unconventional appearance and behavior made good newspaper copy. In the postwar years, with Texas Rangers secure in the American vocabulary and Rip Ford's Indian fighters maintaining their vibrancy, dime novels further popularized these vigorous frontiersmen.

By 1860 the legend of the Texas Rangers was well established. The war dimmed the public focus, however, and the legend subsided. The Rangers of Jones, McNelly, and King brought it back to life, and by the early 1880s it burned even more brightly. The official reports of Adjutant Generals King and Mabry routinely vested the Rangers with superhuman qualities. As early as 1882, a newspaper captured the rekindled spirit: "The Texas Ranger can ride harder, fight longer, lives rougher, and makes less talk about it than anybody else that walks on two feet."[9]

Popular fiction revived and verse and balladry celebrated the strong, silent, fast-shooting lawman of legend. In 1892 a frontier housewife composed her own six-stanza homage, concluding:

> *He may not win the laurels,*
> *Nor trumpet tongue of fame,*
> *But beauty smiles upon him,*
> *And ranchmen bless his name.*
> *Then here's to the Texas Ranger,*
> *Past, present, and to come,*

Our safety from the savage,
The guardian of our home.[10]

Even as the twentieth-century Ranger came under severe criticism and verged on extinction, the Old West lawman flourished in print and film. Comic books and pulp westerns continued to star the Rangers. Zane Grey's *The Lone Star Ranger* (1915), dedicated to the Rangers, reached theaters twice as a silent and once as a talkie (1930). Films featuring Texas Rangers appeared as early as 1910 and never stopped. Mike Cox's "Texas Ranger Filmology" lists 118 Ranger movies between 1910 and 1995, nearly all about nineteenth-century Rangers.[11]

The Lone Ranger galloped into radio in 1933. With William Tell as overture, the masked rider of the Plains and his faithful Indian companion, Tonto, warred against frontier evil and with a silver bullet disarmed bad men without ever drawing blood. As radio gave way to television after World War II, Clayton Moore and Jay Silverheels appeared in 1949 in a long-running series that gave visual form to the heroes of the radio generation. The Lone Ranger still lives. Internet Web sites provide every arcane detail any aficionado may want about this icon of popular culture.[12]

The Lone Ranger did not dominate television portrayals of the Rangers. Series came and went, and feature-length films exploited and fueled the legend. In 1989 the miniseries drawn from Larry McMurtry's *Lonesome Dove* gained a huge audience, giving graphic expression to four books about Rangers that enjoyed triumphant sales. As this book goes to press, filmdom presents Leander McNelly with a company of punks resembling the Young Guns of Billy the Kid. "An epic adventure of love and courage in a rugged land," we are promised, *"Texas Rangers* revives the great tradition of the pure American Western."

Despite the continuing efforts of scholars to recast the image of the Texas Ranger, in the legendary embodiment inspired by Jack Hays and fleshed out by the Old West lawmen he still rides in the popular imagination.

. . .

THE LEGEND WEIGHS heavily in assessing the historical significance of the Texas Rangers. Historical significance is measured in historical consequence. That the legend has so profoundly and for so long flourished in the public mind is a consequence of major proportions. That people the world over know of the Texas Rangers, no matter how false or distorted the image, endows the Rangers with a significance eclipsing their influence on the course of history.

As for impact on the course of history, this evaluation centers on how well the Rangers achieved the purposes for which they were created. Three major purposes furnish the framework, two of citizen soldiers and one of lawmen. The first is protecting the Texas frontier from Indians. The second is contending with Mexicans—during the decade of the republic, in the American war with Mexico, and on a constantly troubled international frontier. The third is enforcing the laws of Texas.

From homegrown ranging companies to units of volunteer state troops, Rangers found their primary mission in protecting the frontier of settlement. Beginning in the 1820s, the frontier invaded the lands of agricultural tribes on the upper Trinity and Brazos Rivers, threatened the range of the Southern Comanches on the Edwards Plateau, and drew near enough to the raiding trails of Northern Comanches and Kiowas from north of Red River to entice marauders into the settlements. During the Texas Republic, except for the brief time of the moribund Texas army, frontier defense fell entirely to ranging companies. After Texas entered the American union in 1845, the responsibility belonged to the U.S. Army. A chain of frontier forts failed to shield the settlements, and military operations failed to stop the raiding. Texans ridiculed the army and demanded that the federal government pay for Rangers, who knew better than the regulars how to fight Indians. From the beginning of statehood, Rangers took the field against Indians almost continuously, but the state, not the nation, footed the bill.

When well led, Rangers did in fact know better than the soldiers how to fight Indians, as Jack Hays and Rip Ford demonstrated. Rangers tracked Indians, skirmished with Indians, and on several occasions surprised and destroyed Indian villages and inflicted severe casualties. So did the more numerous regulars. Although the agricultural tribes had virtually collapsed by the advent of statehood, the Kiowas and Comanches ravaged the frontier for another thirty years. During that period, both Rangers and regulars occasionally punished raiders and made their forays dangerous and sometimes fatal. But no more than temporarily did either curtail the pace of raiding. Sometimes, as when Rip Ford thrashed Iron Jacket at Antelope Hills in 1858, the result was escalated raiding in retaliation. Despite occasional triumphs, therefore, the citizen soldiers in the long term did not accomplish their purpose. Raiding ended only after the Red River War of 1874–1875 confined the Kiowas and Comanches to reservations in the Indian Territory and the Victorio War of 1880–1881 eliminated the Apache menace to the Trans-Pecos. Those were U.S. military operations in which Texas Rangers participated only marginally.

Rangers scored better against Mexicans. During the republic, Santa Anna discovered that denying Texas independence worked better in rhetoric than in action. General Adrián Woll's occupation of San Antonio in 1842 roused a response that fixed an unacceptable cost on Mexican military incursions. The victory of Matt Caldwell and his Rangers at the battle of Salado is not diminished by the military debacle that followed when Texans tried to invade Mexico and ended by drawing seventeen black beans. That was not a Ranger operation.

The record of the Rangers in the war with Mexico was a triumph, qualified only by their undisciplined troublemaking and penchant for indiscriminate revenge for the Alamo, Goliad, and the black beans. In the battle of Monterey, the regiments of Hays and Wood proved first-rate combat soldiers, unsurpassed by any of the regular army formations. Throughout Zachary Taylor's operations in northern Mexico, the reconnaissance missions of Ben McCulloch and other Ranger captains gathered intelligence about enemy and terrain crucial to the general's planning. And in central Mexico, Hays demonstrated that Rangers not only fought superbly in formal battle but excelled in the partisan warfare that Mexican guerrillas imposed on General Winfield Scott's supply lines. *Los Diablos Tejanos* were a terror to the Mexicans and a vexation to the generals, but they contributed significantly to the progress and outcome of the war.

Rangers again faced Mexicans in the revolt of Juan Nepomuceno Cortina on the lower Rio Grande in 1859–1860. Here they operated in tandem with U.S. regulars against Mexicans who, like their leader, were a combination of patriot and brigand. The first Rangers on the scene, those of William Tobin, performed abominably and pillaged more diligently than their adversaries. After Tobin's withdrawal, however, Rip Ford and his Rangers worked closely with the U.S. cavalry to scatter the rebels and end the rebellion.

In the twilight year of the citizen soldier, Leander McNelly's company moved to the Rio Grande in 1875 to operate against Mexican cattle thieves. McNelly scored one success near Brownsville, but his most celebrated feat was crossing the Rio Grande to confront Mexicans at Las Cuevas. The sheer bravado of this act, followed by his stubborn refusal to withdraw in the face of more than ten times his number, made him a hero to Texans but obscured the paucity of the result. Thereafter, McNelly's company performed more effectively against outlaws than Mexicans.

As lawmen, the Rangers' significance—how well they achieved their purpose—has to be judged in two ways: performance and the result of performance. These Rangers were good at tracking and apprehending fugitives. They were good at mediating between contending factions, such as family against family, political bloc against political bloc, labor against management, and mob against antimob. They were good at easing public excitement and heading off prospective riots. They were good at maintaining orderly courtrooms. And they were good at taming places where rowdies gathered, such as new towns overrun by fun-loving cowboys, railroad end-of-tracks, and oil boom-towns.

Assessing results dilutes the high marks earned by performance. Texans insisted on the supremacy of local authority, which established the political culture in which governors and adjutant generals functioned. Rangers rarely found it possible to override the wishes of a sheriff. When Rangers offended segments of a county's electorate, the sheriff usually sided with the voters, and the governor or adjutant general usually curbed the Rangers or removed them altogether.

Also limiting performance was a criminal justice system in which convictions were very difficult to obtain. Legal technicalities and forgiving juries set free many an offender the Rangers had worked hard to bring to the bar. Rare was the defense lawyer who could not find a legal loophole to win a continuance for his client. As witnesses scattered and evidence dissipated, cases dragged from one continuance to another and finally dropped from the docket. The fault lay not entirely with the system. Frequently the citizens were too intimidated or too tolerant to perform their civil duty as witnesses and jurors.

In quelling riots, controlling rowdies, calming feuds, and keeping the peace in excited communities, the Rangers did exceptionally well. In sending bad men to the penitentiary, they went down to defeat in a defective criminal justice system.

While asked to do more and more with fewer and fewer men, the lawmen Rangers served Texas well.

They also served the nation well, for they provided a model for a mounted constabulary with broad jurisdiction. Often compared with Canada's Northwest Mounted Police, the Texas Rangers formed a law enforcement agency with statewide powers. By century's end, of all the states and territories only Massachusetts and North Carolina had experimented with a state constabulary. E. J. Davis's Texas State Police had been a powerful arm of the governor for purposes both worthy and unworthy, but it had been transitory. All the states and territories had U.S. marshals, but they and their deputies served federal law, not state law. To be sure, governors commanded the state militia, but these citizen soldiers enforced the law only in times of crisis. For two decades after the death of John B. Jones, except for the shadowy organizations in Massachusetts and North Carolina, the Frontier Battalion was the only police force in the nation with statewide jurisdiction. Although theoretically if not always in practice subordinate to county authority, it could operate anywhere in Texas.

By early in the twentieth century the Texas Rangers had provided the inspiration and the model for the Arizona Rangers, the Nevada Rangers, and the New Mexico Mounted Police. They had also planted the roots for a system of state police that quickly spread over the entire nation.[13]

As citizen soldiers and Old West lawmen, the Texas Rangers left an indelible mark on history. As legendary heroes and legendary knaves, they left an indelible mark on human minds the world over. They fully merit their niche in the annals of Texas and the nation.

ABBREVIATIONS

To abbreviate the citations for documents in the Texas State Archives, I have adopted a system that combines record group, box, and folder as here exemplified: 401-406-6. This translates to record group 401, box 406, folder 6.

AAAG	Acting assistant adjutant general
AAG	Assistant adjutant general
AG	Adjutant general
AGO	Adjutant General's Office
CAH, UTA	Center for American History, University of Texas at Austin
CO	Commanding officer
GO	General order
LR	Letters received
NARA	National Archives and Records Administration
OAG	Office of the Adjutant General
RG	Record group
SO	Special order
SWHQ	*Southwestern Historical Quarterly*
TSA	Texas State Archives

NOTES

Chapter 1

1. Harry Cage to Sam Houston, Wilkinson County, Mississippi, November 29, 1837, Andrew Jackson Houston Papers, Box 2-22/165, Folder 1436, Archives Division, Texas State Library (hereafter TSA). The standard biography of Hays is James K. Greer, *Colonel Jack Hays: Texas Frontier Leader and California Builder* (New York: E.P. Dutton, 1952). An edition covering only the Texas years was published as *Texas Ranger: Jack Hays and the Frontier Southwest* (College Station: Texas A&M Press, 1987). Thinly researched, Greer's biography invites replacement. Greer has Hays arriving in Texas immediately after San Jacinto in the spring of 1836, but no contemporary evidence documents his presence before 1838, and the Cage letter, while not necessarily barring an earlier arrival, suggests that the boys brought it with them from Mississippi after its date of November 29, 1837. Greer and others rely heavily on a manuscript entitled "Sketch of Colonel John C. Hays, Texas Ranger," a typescript of which is in the Center for American History, University of Texas at Austin (hereafter CAH UTA). Although the typescript is not so identified, this seventy-seven-page document was prepared by John C. Caperton in California in 1879 "from material furnished by Col. Hays and Major John Caperton." After the Mexican War Hays went to California, where he became a distinguished surveyor and community leader. Caperton, whose friendship with Hays did not begin until after the Mexican War, is quoted in the manuscript, but Hays is not. Caperton turned over the manuscript to historian Hubert Howe Bancroft, who used it in his *History of the North Mexican States and Texas*. The original is now in the Bancroft Library at the University of California at Berkeley. How much of what Caperton recorded may be directly attributed to Hays is unknown. Much of it prompts skepticism in a careful historian. It rarely provides dates or even years for many of the adventures and is rife with hyperbole. I shall use it only occasionally. Greer bases his account of Hays's arrival in Texas in 1836 on this source and no other. The Caperton manuscript intersects several others. James T. DeShields obtained a copy from Bancroft himself and used it and other sources to prepare a series of articles, "Sketches concerning the Life of John C. Hays," which ran serially in a Belton, Texas, newspaper in

the 1880s. The manuscript is in the DeShields Papers, CAH, UTA. John S. Ford, Hays's adjutant in the Mexican War, also wrote a manuscript entitled "John C. Hays in Texas," in the John Salmon Ford Papers, CAH, UTA. The DeShields manuscript, the Caperton manuscript, and the Ford manuscript were used with other sources by J. D. Affleck to prepare "History of John C. Hays," a typescript in two volumes in the Affleck Papers, CAH, UTA. Like the Caperton manuscript, all these biographical undertakings contain useful material but on the whole are unreliable. They are testimony to the legendary status Hays attained after the Mexican War and are responsible for some of the more enduring mythology of his life.

2. This description is drawn primarily from the impressions of a New Orleans diarist who met Hays two years later, during the Mexican War. Samuel C. Reid, Jr., *The Scouting Expeditions of McCulloch's Texas Rangers* (Philadelphia: G. B. Zeiber, 1847; Austin: Steck, 1935), 108–9. Such was Hays's fame, however, that descriptions abound. An excellent character sketch is in Caperton, "Sketch of Col. John C. Hays," 38–40. Caperton knew Hays well, although after his Ranger service. See note 1 for this source.

3. J. W. Wilbarger, *Indian Depredations in Texas* (Austin: Hutchings Printing House, 1889; Austin: State House, 1985), 72–73.

4. First quote: Mary A. Maverick, *Memoirs of Mary A. Maverick*, ed. Rena Maverick Green (San Antonio: Alamo Printing, 1921), 28–29. Second quote: Wilbarger, *Indian Depredations*, 73.

5. Maverick, *Memoirs*, 29.

6. Nelson Lee, *Three Years among the Comanches: The Narrative of Nelson Lee, the Texas Ranger* (1859; Norman: University of Oklahoma Press, 1957), 14. Caperton, "Sketch of Col. John C. Hays," 10.

7. Caperton, "Sketch of Col. John C. Hays," 10.

8. James W. Nichols, *Now You Hear My Horn: The Journal of James Wilson Nichols, 1820–1887*, ed. Catherine W. McDowell (Austin: University of Texas Press, 1967), 123; J. C. Duval, *Early Times in Texas* (Austin: H. P. N. Gammel, 1892), 70–74; Wilbarger, *Indian Depredations in Texas*, 290–95. Caperton, "Sketch of Col. John C. Hays," 36.

9. Nichols, *Now You Hear*, 123.

10. Frederick Wilkins, *The Legend Begins: The Texas Rangers, 1823–1845* (Austin: State House Press, 1996), chap. 3; Louis A. Garavaglia and Charles G. Worman, *Firearms of the American West, 1803–1865* (Albuquerque: University of New Mexico Press, 1984). For the emergence of the "plains rifle," see chapter 4.

11. Charles T. Haven and Frank A. Belden, *A History of the Colt Revolver and Other Arms Made by Colt's Patent Fire Arms Manufacturing Company from 1836 to 1940* (New York: Bonanza, 1978), chaps. 2–3. Garavaglia and Worman, *Firearms of the American West, 1803–1865*, 144–45. Wilkins, *The Legend Begins*, 64–68, 177–78. The navy ordered 180 Paterson Colts, but Wilkins can find records of only 130 delivered.

12. This account draws on several contemporary or near contemporary sources. Hays's report, typically brief and lacking details, was dated June 16, 1844, and printed in the *Annual Report of the Secretary of War and Marine, Republic of Texas, 1844*, 7–8. Immediately after returning to San Antonio, he recounted the action in more detail to Mary Maverick, who at once set it to paper and included it in *Memoirs of Mary A. Maverick*, 81–83. Hays journeyed at once to Washington-on-the-Brazos, where he told his story to an anonymous correspondent who immediately recorded it in a letter of June 23 to the editor of the Houston *Morning Star*, where it appeared in the issue of June 29, 1844. The *Telegraph and Texas Register* reprinted the letter on July 3, 1844. Lee, *Three Years among the Comanches*, 23–26, is the reminiscent account of a participant. Samuel Reid got the story in 1847 from Hays and others who had been in the fight and wrote of it in *The Scouting Expeditions of McCulloch's Texas Rangers*, 109–11. On June

9, Ben McCulloch sent a partial report, based on a courier from Hays, in a letter to a friend, who passed it on to Superintendent of Indian Affairs Thomas Western, who in turn reported it to President Sam Houston by letter of June 16. Western's letter is in Dorman H. Winfrey and James H. Day, eds., *The Indian Papers of Texas and the Southwest, 1825-1916* (Austin: Texas State Historical Association, 1995), 2:72-74. Wilkins, *The Legend Begins*, 178-85, gives an authoritative account and reprints Hays's official report. Caperton, "Sketch of Col. John C. Hays," 20-23, tells of this battle in exaggerated though generally accurate form. The battle site lies on the east bank of Walker Creek just above its confluence with the west fork of Sister Creek, about a mile northwest of present Sisterdale. For map and identification, see Kenneth F. Neighbours, "The Battle of Walker's Creek," *West Texas Historical Association Year Book* 41 (October 1965): 121-30.

Chapter 2

1. Donald W. Meinig, *Imperial Texas: An Interpretive Essay in Cultural Geography* (Austin: University of Texas Press, 1969), 35. See also David J. Weber, *The Mexican Frontier, 1821-1846: The American Southwest under Mexico* (Albuquerque: University of New Mexico Press, 1982), chap. 9.

2. Proclamation of Baron de Bastrop, August 4, 1823, in Eugene C. Barker, ed., *The Austin Papers*, American Historical Association *Annual Report 1919* (Washington: Government Printing Office, 1924), 2: 677-78. Austin's words, undated, were written on the reverse of a proclamation by the baron dated August 5, 1823, printed in ibid., 678-79. That these words constituted a call for volunteers and thus mark the beginning of the Texas Rangers is disproved by Allen G. Hatley, *The Indian Wars of Stephen F. Austin's Texas Colony, 1822-1835* (Austin: Eakin, 2001). Documentation for the formation of Morrison's ten-man unit is in the Bexar Archives, CAH, UTA. Based on these Mexican documents, which include Morrison's "Returns of Inspection," the story has been pieced together by Dan E. Kilgore, *A Ranger Legacy: 150 Years of Service in Texas* (Austin: Madrona, 1973), 7-19. Neither Eugene C. Barker, *The Life of Stephen F. Austin* (Nashville: Cokesbury, 1925), nor the standard history, Walter Prescott Webb, *The Texas Rangers: A Century of Frontier Defense* (Boston: Houghton Mifflin, 1935; Austin: University of Texas Press, 1965), drew on these records.

3. Significantly, the most recent and thoroughly researched and interpreted biography of Austin says nothing of Rangers or the Ranger tradition. Barker's outdated biography, and the sources on which it rests, provide a weak basis for fixing Ranger origins at 1823. Gregg Cantrell, *Stephen F. Austin: Empresario of Texas* (New Haven: Yale University Press, 1999).

4. Barker, *Life of Stephen F. Austin*, 165-66.

5. These strands of Texan history are well developed by T. R. Fehrenbach, *Lone Star: A History of Texas and Texans* (New York: Macmillan, 1968), 304-5, 313-14, 447-48. See also Mark E. Nackman, "The Making of the Texan Citizen Soldier, 1835-1860," *SWHQ* 78 (January 1975): 233-53; and Nackman, *A Nation within a Nation: The Rise of Texas Nationalism* (Port Washington, N.Y.: Kennikat, 1975).

6. Arnoldo de Leon, *They Called Them Greasers: Anglo Attitudes toward Mexicans in Texas, 1821-1900* (Austin: University of Texas Press, 1983), chap. 1.

7. H. M. P. Gammel, comp., *The Laws of Texas, 1822-1897* (Austin: Gammel., 1898), 1:1134.

8. Malcolm D. McLean, comp., *Papers concerning Robertson's Colony in Texas*, 19 vols. (Fort Worth: Texas Christian University Press, 1974-1976; Arlington: University of Texas at Arlington Press, 1977-1987), 10:43-49, 465-67, 503-10, 546-47. McLean deserves

credit for documenting Coleman's precedence as the first Ranger captain, a connection unrecognized by other historians of the Rangers, including Webb, *Texas Rangers*. See also John Henry Brown, *Indian Wars and Pioneers of Texas* (Austin: L. E. Daniell, 189?; Austin: State House Press, 1988), 26, 61; James T. DeShields, *Border Wars of Texas* (1912; Austin: State House Press, 1993), 116-18; Lucy B. Erath, ed., *The Memoirs of Major George B. Erath, 1813-1891* (Austin: Texas State Historical Association, 1923; Waco: Heritage Society of Waco, 1956), 23-24; and George B. Erath, "Sketches of Milam and Robertson Counties, 1843," in Charles A. Gulick et. al., eds., *The Papers of Mirabeau Buonaparte Lamar* (Austin: various publishers, 1921-1927; New York: AMS, 1973), 4:31.

9. The ordinance and decree is printed in John H. Jenkins, ed., *Papers of the Texas Revolution* (Austin: Presidial, 1973), 9:390. For previous measures culminating in this one, see ibid., 9:251, 259, 264, 382; and 2:303, 440, 490-91. The October actions of the Permanent Council are in Eugene C. Barker, ed., "Journal of the Permanent Council (October 11-27, 1835)," *Texas State Historical Association Quarterly* 7 (April 1904): 249-77. The council appointments to the new Ranger Corps appear in a long list of appointments to various posts during November and December 1835 printed in *Telegraph and Texas Register* (San Felipe), January 16, 1836. See also Frederick Wilkins, *The Legend Begins: The Texas Rangers, 1823-1845* (Austin: State House Press, 1996), 12-14. Deliberations leading to authority to raise a Corps of Rangers occurred within the much larger context of the unfolding Texas Revolution, which is skillfully set forth in two works: Stephen L. Hardin, *Texian Iliad: A Military History of the Texas Revolution* (Austin: University of Texas Press, 1994); and Paul D. Lack, *The Texas Revolutionary Experience: A Political and Social History, 1835-1836* (College Station: Texas A&M Press, 1992).

10. Noah Smithwick, *The Evolution of a State, or Recollections of Old Texas Days* (Austin: H. P. M. Gammel, 1900; Austin: University of Texas Press, 1983), 82-96. Smithwick was one of the Rangers. Williamson's order to Tumlinson, date not given, is repeated in Williamson to Governor and Council, Gonzales, February 25, 1836, in Jenkins, *Papers of the Texas Revolution*, 4:434-35. Wilkins, *The Legend Begins*, 18-23. For the company enlisted under the October authority of the Permanent Council, see Silas M. Parker to General Council, Sterling, November 2 and December 17, 1835; and D. B. Friar to Permanent Council, Viesca, November 23, 1835, in Jenkins, *Papers of the Texas Revolution*, 2:203, 490-91, 3:230.

11. Amelia W. Williams and Eugene C. Barker, eds., *The Writings of Sam Houston, 1813-1863* (Austin: University of Texas Press, 1938-1943; reprint, Austin and New York: Pemberton, 1970), 1:476-82. Gammel, *Laws of Texas*, 1:1113-14. The law of December 10 is identified earlier in this chapter as setting the legislative beginning of the ranging service as July 1835. Indian relations during the decade of the republic are well documented in Dorman H. Winfrey and James H. Day, eds., *The Indian Papers of Texas and the Southwest, 1825-1916* (Austin: Texas State Historical Association, 1995), vols. 1-2. For Indian policy during the republic, see Anna Muckleroy, "The Indian Policy of the Republic of Texas," *SWHQ* 25 (April 1922): 229-60; 26 (July 1922): 1-29; (October 1922): 128-48; (January 1923): 184-206.

12. The treaties are in Winfrey and Day, *Indian Papers*, 1:28-32, 46-48, 50-55.

13. Ernest Wallace and E. Adamson Hoebel, *The Comanches: Lords of the South Plains* (Norman: University of Oklahoma Press, 1952). T. R. Fehrenbach, *The Comanches: The Destruction of a People* (New York: Alfred A Knopf, 1974; New York: Da Capo Press, 1994). Thomas W. Kavanagh, *Comanche Political History: An Ethnohistorical Perspective, 1708-1875* (Lincoln: University of Nebraska Press, 1996). Rupert N. Richardson, *The Comanche Barrier to South Plains Settlement*, ed. Kenneth R. Jacobs, rev. ed. (Austin: Eakin, 1996).

14. Meinig, *Imperial Texas*, 42.

15. For Lamar's grand design, see his message to Congress of December 21, 1838, in Gulick, *Lamar Papers*, 2:351–55. The laws of December 1838 and January 1839 are in Gammel, *Laws of Texas*, 2:15–20, 2:29–30, 2:31, 2:44, 2:78, 2:84–85, 2:93, 2:126.

16. Thomas W. Cutrer, "Army of the Republic of Texas," *New Handbook of Texas*. (Austin: Texas State Historical Association, 1996), 1:247–50. For the difficulties in building the new military force, see Secretary of War Albert Sidney Johnston to President Lamar, November 1839, *Annual Report of the Secretary of War, Republic of Texas, 1839*, 3–5; and Johnston to Lamar, December 12, 1839, 401-1306-9, Archives Division, Texas State Library (hereafter TSA). Military developments, along with virtually everything else that occurred in the Republic of Texas from 1836 to 1842, are exhaustively detailed in two works by Joseph Milton Nance: *After San Jacinto: The Texas–Mexican Frontier, 1836–1841* (Austin: University of Texas Press, 1963); and *Attack and Counter-attack: The Texas-Mexican Frontier, 1842* (Austin: University of Texas Press, 1964).

17. Col. John H. Moore to Secretary of War A. S. Johnston, La Grange, March 10, 1839, in Winfrey and Day, *Indian Papers*, 1:57–59. This is Moore's official report, in which he portrays the fight as a victory and fails even to mention the loss of his horses. See also Smithwick, *Evolution of a State*, 154–57. Smithwick commanded the Bastrop company. Brown, *Indian Wars and Pioneers of Texas*, 74–76; and John Henry Brown, *History of Texas, from 1685 to 1892* (St. Louis: L. E. Daniell, 1892–93; Austin: Jenkins, 1970), 2:182. J. W. Wilbarger, *Indian Depredations in Texas* (Austin: Hutchings, 1889; Austin: State House, 1985), 144–46. *Telegraph and Texas Register* (Houston), February 27, 1839.

18. The Cherokee expulsion is marginal to the Ranger story and beyond the scope of this book except as an expression of Lamar's Indian policy. For the full story, see Dianna Everett, *The Texas Cherokees: A People between Two Fires, 1819–1840* (Norman: University of Oklahoma Press, 1990). See also *Telegraph and Texas Register* (Houston), May 29, 1839; and William L. Mann, "James O. Rice: Hero of the Battle on the San Gabriels," *SWHQ* 55 (January 1951): 30–42.

19. Mary A. Maverick, *Memoirs of Mary A. Maverick*, ed. Rena Maverick Green (San Antonio: Alamo, 1921), 44.

20. Hugh McLeod to Albert Sidney Johnston, San Antonio, March 20, 1840, in *Journals of the House of Representatives of the Republic of Texas*, 5th Congress, 1st session (1840–1841), appendix to the *Annual Report of the Secretary of War, 1840*, 136–39. Additional details are in *Telegraph and Texas Register* (Houston), April 8 and 29, 1840; and *Austin City Gazette*, March 25, 1840. Maverick, *Memoirs of Mary A. Maverick*, 31–37. Kavanaugh, *Comanche Political History*, 262–63, contends that Matilda Lockhart had been ransomed during the winter and gave her story in ample time for Texas authorities to plot the Council House affair. Kavanaugh bases this on Brown, *Indian Wars and Pioneers of Texas*, 51. However, the official reports and contemporary accounts are all explicit that the Indians delivered the Lockhart girl when they came in on March 19, and Brown himself, in his account of the Council House fight later in the book (76–78), contradicts his earlier statement and agrees with all other reporters.

21. Donaly E. Brice, *The Great Comanche Raid: Boldest Indian Attack of the Texas Republic* (Austin: Eakin, 1987), 29–31. This is a carefully researched study based on newspaper and archival sources and is the best treatment of the subject. John J. Linn, *Reminiscences of Fifty Years in Texas* (New York: D. & J. Sadlier, 1883; Austin: State House Press, 1986), 338–41. Linn, founder of Linnville, was in Victoria when the Comanches attacked.

22. Brice, *Comanche Raid* 31–33. Linn, *Reminiscences*, 341–44, although in Victoria, describes in detail the events that occurred in his home town.

23. There is no full-scale biography of Caldwell. See George R. Nielsen, "Mathew Caldwell," *SWHQ* 64 (April 1961): 478–502.

24. Thomas W. Cutrer, *Ben McCulloch and the Frontier Military Tradition* (Chapel Hill: University of North Carolina Press, 1993). Less interpretive but in many ways more detailed is Victor M. Rose, *The Life and Services of Gen. Ben McCulloch* (Philadelphia: Pictorial Bureau of the Press, 1888; Austin: Steck, 1958). Nelson Lee, *Three Years among the Comanches: The Narrative of Nelson Lee, the Texas Ranger* (1859; Norman: University of Oklahoma Press, 1957), 16.

25. The best source for the movements of the McCulloch-Zumwalt-Tumlinson force is W. D. Miller, a participant, who wrote a day-by-day account at Gonzales on August 17, had it attested by Ben McCulloch and David Murphree of Victoria, and sent it to the *Austin City Gazette*, where it appeared on September 2. It was reprinted in the *Telegraph and Texas Register* (Houston), September 9, 1840. See also Brown, *Indian Wars and Pioneers of Texas*, 80; Rose, *Life and Services of General Ben McCulloch*, 55–56; Cutrer, *Ben McCulloch and the Frontier Military Tradition*, 41–42; and Brice, *Great Comanche Raid*, 34. Brown was a nineteen-year-old volunteer in the subsequent battle of Plum Creek, and his account of the entire operation is a reliable source.

26. Brown, *Indian Wars and Pioneers of Texas*, 81.

27. James W. Nichols, *Now You Hear My Horn: The Journal of James Wilson Nichols, 1820–1887*, ed. Catherine W. McDowell (Austin: University of Texas Press, 1967), 61.

28. Ibid., 62.

29. Zachariah N. Morrell, *Flowers and Fruits from the Wilderness; or, Thirty-six Years in Texas with Two Winters in Honduras* (New York: Sheldon, 1872), 129.

30. Huston to Secretary of War Branch T. Archer, August 12 and September 28, 1840, in *Journals of the House of Representatives of the Republic of Texas*, 5th Congress, 1st session (1840–1841), appendix to the *Annual Report of the Secretary of War*, September 30, 1840, 141–45. Brown, *Indian Wars and Pioneers of Texas*, 82. Accounts by other participants are John Holland Jenkins, *Recollections of Early Texas: The Memoirs of John Holland Jenkins*, ed. John Holmes Jenkins (Austin: University of Texas Press, 1958), 62–68; and "Brazos," *Life of Robert Hall: Indian Fighter and Veteran of Three Great Wars* (Austin: Ben C. Jones, 1898; Austin: State House, 1992), chap. 15.

31. Huston's official report, written on the evening of the battle, counted one man killed and seven wounded, one mortally. So it was thought at the time, but this man recovered. See Brice, *Great Comanche Raid*, 100, n. 38.

32. Linn, *Reminiscences of Fifty Years in Texas*, 343. Nichols, *Now You Hear My Horn*, 171–72, describes the division of the spoils.

33. Principal source is Moore to Secretary of War Branch T. Archer, Austin, November 7, 1840, in *Telegraph and Texas Register* (Houston), November 18, 1840. See also Jenkins, *Recollections of Early Texas*, 171–74; Brown, *Indian Wars and Pioneers of Texas*, 83–85; and Brown, *History of Texas*, 2:182–83. Brice, *Great Comanche Raid*, chap. 6, presents an authoritative account.

34. Brice, *Great Comanche Raid*, chap. 7, has a good analysis of these results. Texans had ample evidence of Mexican tampering with the Comanches, and there were probably some Mexicans in the Comanche raiding party at Victoria and Linnville.

35. Gulick, *Lamar Papers*, 3:352–53. *Austin City Gazette*, May 13, 1840. *Telegraph and Texas Register* (Houston), July 8 and August 3, 1840, and January 6, 1841. *Austin City Gazette*, February 17 and May 5, 1841. Secretary of War Branch T. Archer to Colonel William G. Cooke, Austin, March 2, 1841, 401-1307-11, TSA. See also *Annual Report of Secretary of War Branch T. Archer, September 30, 1841*, in Texas Congress, *Journals of the Sixth Congress, 1841–42*, ed. Harriet Smither (Austin: Texas Library and Historical Commission, 1945), 3:357, 360.

36. Gammel, *Laws of Texas*, 2:646–48.

37. Address to Congress, December 21, 1841, RG 307, Executive Record Book: Sam Houston, 1841–44, pp. 5–6, TSA.

38. Houston to House of Representatives, January 6, 1842, in Williams and Barker, *Writings of Sam Houston*, 2:423. Houston to Senate, January 25, 1842, RG 307, Executive Record Book: Sam Houston, 1841–44, p. 25, TSA. The *Telegraph and Texas Register* (Houston), December 15, 1841, charged that in some counties land surveyors and speculators and even cattle thieves had applied to the chief justices for certificates that they had been in the field on Indian expeditions.

39. Houston's peace offensive is a significant and dramatic aspect of Texas history but marginal to the Ranger story. It is well documented in Winfrey and Day, *Texas Indian Papers*, vols. 1–2. For the council minutes and treaty of October 7–9, 1844, see 2:103–21.

Chapter 3

1. I shall use South Texas to define the area south and west of the San Antonio River to the Rio Grande from its mouth upstream to the mouth of the Pecos River.

2. Enlightening perspectives on this civilization, usually ignored in conventional Texas histories, are Arnoldo De Leon, *The Tejano Community, 1836–1900* (Albuquerque: University of New Mexico Press, 1982; Dallas: Southern Methodist University Press, 1997); Armando C. Alonzo, *Tejano Legacy: Rancheros and Settlers in South Texas, 1734–1900* (Albuquerque: University of New Mexico Press, 1998), chaps. 1–3; and Andres Tijerina, *Tejano Empire: Life on the South Texas Ranchos* (College Station: Texas A&M Press, 1998).

3. John Brown to Secretary of War A. S. Johnston, San Antonio, September 13, 1839; Henry F. Foote to President M. B. Lamar, New Bahia, September 15, 1839; both in Charles A. Gulick et al., eds., *The Papers of Mirabeau Bounaparte Lamar* (Austin: various publishers, 1921–1927; New York: AMS 1973), 3:106–10. *Telegraph and Texas Register* (Houston), January 5, 1839.

4. The classic account by a New Orleans newsman who accompanied the expedition is George Wilkins Kendall, *Narrative of the Texan Santa Fe Expedition*, 2 vols. (New York: Harper, 1844). There have been many subsequent reprint editions. See also Noel M. Loomis, *The Texan-Santa Fe Pioneers* (Norman: University of Oklahoma Press, 1958).

5. Victor M. Rose, *The Life and Services of Gen. Ben McCulloch* (Philadelphia: Pictorial Bureau of the Press, 1888; Austin: Steck, 1958), 66–67. Thomas W. Cutrer, *Ben McCulloch and the Frontier Military Tradition* (Chapel Hill: University of North Carolina Press, 1993), 50–51.

6. The Vasquez raid is recounted in ample and documented detail in Joseph Milton Nance, *The Texas-Mexican Frontier, 1842* (Austin: University of Texas Press, 1964), chaps. 1–5. See also *Telegraph and Texas Register* (Houston), March 16, 1842; and Mary A. Maverick, *Memoirs of Mary A. Maverick*, ed. Rena Maverick Green (San Antonio: Alamo, 1921), 60–61, 71. Mrs. Maverick was part of the second Runaway Scrape.

7. Nance, *Texas-Mexican Frontier*, 280–81. *Report of the Secretary of War and Marine*, November 12, 1842, appendix to *Journals of the House of Representatives, Seventh Congress*, 30–31. *Telegraph and Texas Register* (Houston), September 7, 1842.

8. A. Hutchinson et al. to Citizens of Gonzales County, San Antonio, September 12, 1842, 10:00 P.M., in appendix to *Journals of the House of Representatives, Seventh Congress*, 18–19; Hays to citizens of Texas, San Antonio, September 12, 1842, and Hays to Secretary of War, Seguin, same date, ibid., 16 and 21. Anderson Hutchinson's diary in E. W. Winkler, ed., "The Bexar and Dawson Prisoners," *Texas State Historical Association Quarterly* 13 (1909–10): 294–95. *Telegraph and Texas Register*, September 21, 1842.

9. Joseph M. Nance, *Attack and Counter-Attack: The Texas-Mexican Frontier, 1842* (Austin: University of Texas Press, 1964), chap. 14. See also Nance, trans. and ed., "Brigadier General Adrián Woll's Report of His Expedition into Texas in 1842," *SWHQ* 58 (April 1955): 523-52.

10. Nance, *Attack and Counter-Attack*, 342-44. Caldwell to Ezekiel Williams, Cibolo, September 14, 1842, in *Telegraph and Texas Register*, September 21, 1842. George R. Nielsen, "Mathew Caldwell," *SWHQ* 64 (April 1961): 495-96.

11. One of the most informative sources, detailing events day by day, is J.H.B. to Editor, Lavaca River, October 2, 1842, *Telegraph and Texas Register* (Houston), November 2, 1842. A. J. Sowell, *Early Settlers and Indian Fighters of Southwest Texas* (Austin: B. C. Jones, 1900; Austin: State House, 1986), 24-25. My reconstruction of the battle rests on "J.H.B." as cited above; an account by Memucan Hunt in *Telegraph and Texas Register*, October 26, 1842; Caldwell's report to the Secretary of War, September 18, 1842, in appendix to *Journals of the House of Representatives, Seventh Congress*, 15-18; James W. Nichols, *Now You Hear My Horn: The Journal of James Wilson Nichols, 1820-1887*, ed. Catherine W. McDowell (Austin: University of Texas Press, 1967), 95-103; Zachariah N. Morrell, *Flowers and Fruits from the Wilderness; or, Thirty-six Years in Texas with Two Winters in Honduras* (New York: Sheldon., 1872), chap. 15; and John Henry Brown, *History of Texas, from 1685 to 1892* (St. Louis: L. E. Daniell, 1892-93; Austin New York: Jenkins, 1970), 2: chap. 22; Nelson Lee, *Three Years among the Comanches: The Narrative of Nelson Lee, Texas Ranger* (1859; Norman: University of Oklahoma Press, 1957), chap. 7; Nance, *Attack and Counter-Attack*, chap. 15; Wilkins, *The Legend Begins*, 125-38.

12. Nichols, *Now You Hear My Horn* 96, describes the position but gives directions in terms of a north-south rather than east-west stream. I believe Wilkins, 221, has correctly clarified the confusion of the Nichols account, except that Wilkins has the Salado here flowing from east to west while I believe it was the reverse. Only a west-east configuration could account for Hays's decoy party and the pursuing Mexican cavalry crossing the Salado and turning right to Caldwell's position. The battlesite is within the bounds of the Fort Sam Houston military reservation in San Antonio.

13. Morrell, *Flowers and Fruits*, 169. Morrell was part of Hays's decoy expedition.

14. Ibid.

15. Nichols, *Now You Hear My Horn*, 98-99.

16. Brown, *History of Texas*, 2:225. There are other versions of Córdova's death by participants, but Brown witnessed the fight.

17. J.H.B., October 2, 1842, in *Telegraph and Texas Register*, November 2, 1842.

18. The best source for the Dawson massacre is A. A. Gardenier to Editor, LaGrange, October 21, 1842, in *Telegraph and Texas Register*, November 16, 1842, based on an interview with one of the two survivors. Joseph C. Robinson, "Dawson's Defeat–The Massacre," *Texas Democrat*, May 27, 1846, as taken from *LaGrange Intelligencer*. All the sources cited in note 12 above deal with the Dawson massacre. Especially valuable, however, are the J.H.B. and Memucan Hunt accounts because also based on interviews with survivors. Nance, *Attack and Counter-Attack*, chap. 16, tells the story in detail. Like the Salado Battlefield, the Dawson massacre site is within the Fort Sam Houston reservation in San Antonio.

19. As related by Henry Woods to A. A. Gardenier.

20. Miller as told to J.H.B.

21. *Memoirs of Mary A. Maverick*, 74.

22. Woods at told to Gardenier.

23. Caldwell to (?), 7:00 P.M. September 18, 1842, *Telegraph and Texas Register*, September 28, 1842. This newspaper received the appeal in Houston on September 22. To whom and where it was dispatched is unknown. Caldwell also dated his official report to

the secretary of war September 18, but did not finish and dispatch it until he had recounted the events of the next few days.

24. Mayfield to E. Burleson, Camp Salado, "Tuesday morning September 20, 1842," ibid., September 28, 1842. Mayfield thus introduces a problem of chronology that I can reconcile only by dating his arrival early on Monday the nineteenth rather than Tuesday the twentieth. His letter recounts Caldwell's battle of "yesterday" and Dawson's catastrophe of "last night." (A detachment from Caldwell's command had discovered the Dawson dead that morning.) Billingsley to (?), 9:00 P.M. Sunday, September 18, 1842, in ibid., October 5, 1842, reports that he has been joined by Wallace and that they had observed cannon smoke on the Salado and knew Caldwell to be engaged. If they did not join Caldwell that night, where were they all day and part of the night of the nineteenth? Moreover, J.H.B.'s day-by-day chronicle, under date of September 18, states "On the night after the battle were joined by 100 Coloradoans under Capt. Jesse Billingsley and William I. Wallace, with J. S. Mayfield as major." Finally, Mayfield's letter dated the morning of the twentieth states that spies reported Woll still holding San Antonio, whereas at this time Caldwell learned that Woll had evacuated San Antonio and was withdrawing. The problem is compounded by Caldwell himself, whose official report, dated September 18 but obviously not completed until September 23 or even later, has the Mayfield contingent arriving on the Salado during the night of the eighteenth, but then has the entire command, learning of Woll's withdrawal, move out in pursuit on the nineteenth. This, however, did not happen until the twentieth. Perhaps Mayfield had his days confused, or perhaps a typesetter made an error. Nance and other historians accept Mayfield's dating.

25. Memucan Hunt and J.H.B. A famous story, repeated by Texas historians, has Hays and McCulloch wrapping themselves in blankets and boldly strolling around the Mexican camp during the night of the twentieth. It is a beguiling drama, but alas, its roots are in Caperton, "Sketch of Colonel John C. Hays," and in the absence of any contemporary hint of such an adventure, I suspect that, like many other adventures set forth in that document, it did not happen.

26. *Fruits and Flowers*, 176–77. See also Sowell, *Early Settlers and Indian Fighters of Southwest Texas*, 25–27.

27. The quotation is J.H.B. See also Morrell, 176–80. Memucan Hunt. Nance, *Attack and Counter-Attack*, chap. 17, is a detailed reconstruction. His analysis of the command breakdown is especially pertinent. *Memoirs of Mary Maverick*, 75–76, also deals with the command issue. John Holland Jenkins, *Recollections of Early Texas* (Austin: University of Texas Press, 1958), 99–101, gives eyewitness observations of the fight and the dissensions in the ranks.

28. Quoted in Nance, *Attack and Counter-Attack*, 396.

29. *Telegraph and Texas Register*, October 12, 1842. Caldwell took responsibility in his report dated September 18 but not completed until after the retreat from the Hondo. Caldwell to Secretary of War, September 18, 1842, in Appendix to *Journals of the House of Representatives, Seventh Congress*, 15–18. Nielsen, "Mathew Caldwell," 501.

30. Nance, *Attack and Counter-Attack*, 406.

31. Ibid., 420–21.

32. An excellent history of the Somervell expedition and its aftermath is Sam W. Haynes, *Soldiers of Misfortune: The Somervell and Mier Expeditions* (Austin: University of Texas Press, 1990), whose interpretations I follow. Nance, *Attack and Counter-Attack*, chaps. 18–24. Appendix to *Journals of the House of Representatives, Seventh Congress*, 3–13. Somervell's final report, undated, is in *Telegraph and Texas Register*, February 22, 1843. Authoritative reports by participants are Memucan Hunt, January 8, 1842, in ibid., January 18, 1843; Sterling Brown Hendricks, "The Somervell Expedition to the Rio Grande, 1842," ed. E. W. Winkler, *SWHQ* 23 (October 1919): 112–40; and Thomas Jefferson

Green, *Journal of the Texian Expedition against Mier* (New York: Harper, 1845; New York: Arno, 1973). See also Ralph A. Wooster, "Texas Military Operations against Mexico, 1842–1843," *SWHQ* 67 (April 1964): 465–84.

33. A participant described this incident in Joseph D. McCutchan, *Mier Expedition Diary*, ed. Joseph Milton Nance (Austin: University of Texas Press, 1978), 39–40.

34. A detailed history of the Mier expedition was to have been the third of Joseph Milton Nance's volumes on Texas–Mexican military relations 1836–1842. Nance died before it could be completed. It has now been published as Nance and Archie McDonald, *Dare-Devils All: The Texan Mier Expedition, 1842–44* (Austin: Eakin, 1998). An account of the battle of Mier from Ampudia's perspective, based on reports from Matamoros, appeared in the *Telegraph and Texas Register*, January 25, 1843. Participant accounts are in ibid., same date and February 15, 1843.

Chapter 4

1. K. Jack Bauer, *The Mexican War, 1846–1848* (New York: Macmillan, 1974; Lincoln: University of Nebraska Press, 1992). John S. D. Eisenhower, *So Far from God: The U.S. War with Mexico, 1846–1848* (New York: Random House, 1989). Justin H. Smith, *The War with Mexico*, 2 vols. (New York: Macmillan, 1919). Although modern scholars regard Smith as hopelessly antiquated, his work is exhaustively researched, stylistically engaging, comprehensive in coverage, and replete with forthright judgments that remain persuasive even in a time when students favor a far more sympathetic view of the Mexican side.

2. Whether Walker suggested the idea to Taylor or responded to an idea already formed by Taylor is uncertain. For the clearest reconstruction of the chronology, based on Ranger service records, see Henry W. Barton, *Texas Volunteers in the Mexican War* (Wichita Falls: privately published, 1970), 9–13. Two good overall histories of the Rangers in the Mexican War are Charles D. Spurlin, *Texas Volunteers in the Mexican War* (Austin: Eakin, 1998) and Frederick Wilkins, *The Highly Irregular Irregulars: Texas Rangers in the Mexican War* (Austin: Eakin, 1990).

3. The best characterization of Walker is by his lieutenant in the 1847 offensive against Mexico City: Thomas Claiborne, "Memoirs of the Past," *Vidette*, April 1, 1886. A copy of this obscure military newspaper is in the Walker Papers, Box 1982/47, Folder 77, TSA. See also Charles D. Spurlin, "Walker, Samuel H.," in *New Handbook of Texas* (Austin: Texas State Historical Association, 1996), 6: 797–98; and Spurlin, "Ranger Walker in the Mexican War," *Military History of Texas and the Southwest* 9 (1971): 259–79. The quotation is in Sam W. Haynes, *Soldiers of Misfortune: The Somervell and Mier Expeditions* (Austin: University of Texas Press, 1990), 20. Walker's escape is described in ibid., 160–61.

4. Barton, *Texas Volunteers in the Mexican War*, 10–12. Wilkins, *Highly Irregular Irregulars*, 25–26. Charles T. Haven and Frank A. Belden, *A History of the Colt Revolver and Other Arms Made by Colt's Patent Fire Arms Company from 1836 to 1940* (New York: Bonanza, 1978), 272. After years of trying to sell his arms to the War Department, Colt had given up and gone out of business. With the outbreak of war, the Ordnance Department entered the open market and bought up all the Colt repeaters that could be found–150 carbines and pistols. Some of these pistols found their way to Point Isabel. Walker kept many of the issue and turn-in slips, which are in the Walker Papers, TSA.

5. Taylor to AG, Camp near Matamoros, April 26, 1846, *Mexican War Correspondence*, House Executive Document 60, 30th Congress, 1st Session (serial 520), 288. Taylor to Governor J. Pinckney Henderson, April 26, 1846, in *Texas Democrat* (Austin), May 6, 1846. In this letter, Taylor states that Walker's company "is already rendering important service here" and asks that he be commissioned as one of the captains of the Texas volunteers.

6. Taylor to AG, Point Isabel, May 3, 1846, *Mexican War Correspondence*, 288–90. One of the escapees described his experience to a researcher for historian H. H. Bancroft: "George Washington Trahern: Texan Cowboy Soldier from Mier to Buena Vista," ed. A. Russell Buchanan, *SWHQ* 58 (July 1954): 70–72. Barton, *Texas Volunteers*, 12, quotes an account in *The American Flag*, January 20, 1847, a soldiers' paper published in Matamoros. Creed Taylor left a greatly embellished recollection in "John W. Hunter Literary Efforts," 2-23/933, TSA. The recollection of another escapee, Maurice Simmons, is quoted from an unpublished manuscript by editor Joseph E. Chance in Abner Doubleday, *My Life in the Old Army: Reminiscences of Abner Doubleday from the Collections of the New-York Historical Society* (Fort Worth: Texas Christian University Press, 1998), 310 n. 31. The *Texas Democrat* (Austin), May 20, 1846, ran a reasonably accurate account. The most detailed and authoritative narrative appeared in John S. Jenkins, *History of the War between the United States and Mexico* (Philadelphia: John E. Potter, 1851), 98–99. Walker tells of the picket fort in Walker to Taylor, April 24, 1846, RG 94, Mexican War Army of Occupation LR, Entry 133, Box 4, NARA.

7. Jenkins, *History of the War between the United States and Mexico*, 98–99. Jenkins has this exploit occurring during the day of the twenty-ninth. However, an officer at Taylor's headquarters recorded on April 30 that "Capt. Walker came up this morning bringing a communication from Major Munroe." A nighttime ride through this enemy-held country makes more sense. Rhoda van Bibber Tanner Doubleday, ed., *Journal of the Late Brevet Major Philip Narabourne Barbour* (New York: G. P. Putnam's, 1936), 49–50.

8. Capt. William S. Henry, *Campaign Sketches of the War with Mexico* (New York: Harper, 1847), 88–89. Taylor to AG, Point Isabel, May 5, 1846, *Mexican War Correspondence*, 292–93. Lt. George G. Meade to wife, Point Isabel, May 5, 1846, in *Life and Letters of George Gordon Meade, Major-General, United States Army* (New York: Charles Scribner, 1913), 1: 75–76. Meade added that during the fourth several other scouts were sent toward Brown's fort, but all were turned back by Mexican horsemen.

9. *LaGrange Intelligencer*, May 30, 1846, quoting New Orleans papers.

10. Henderson to Taylor, Austin, May 3, 1846, 301-17-3, TSA.

11. Henderson transferred his powers to Lt. Gov. A. C. Horton on May 19, 301-17-3, TSA. Taylor to AG, Matamoros, July 31, 1846, *Mexican War Correspondence*, 321–22, acquiesced in Henderson's muster as a major general and added: "All the Texan troops are anxious to go forward; they are hardy, and can subsist on little." For the organization and names of all Texans mustered during the Mexican War, see appendixes of Spurlin, *Texas Volunteers in the Mexican War*. See also Barton, *Texas Volunteers in the Mexican War*, 16–22.

12. Rankin Dilworth, *The March to Monterrey: The Diary of Rankin Dilworth, U.S. Army: A Narrative of Troop Movements and Observations on Daily Life with General Taylor's Army during the Invasion of Mexico*, ed. Lawrence R. Clayton and Joseph E. Chance (El Paso: Texas Western Press, 1996), 24. Taylor to Dr. R. C. Wood, Matamoros, July 7, 1846, in *Letters of Zachary Taylor from the Battle-Fields of the Mexican War, Reprinted from the Originals in the Collection of Mr. William K. Bixby of St. Louis, Mo.*, ed. William H. Samson (Rochester, N.Y.: Genesee, 1908), 24. Wilkins, *Highly Irregular Irregulars*, 61, points to the other meanings of licentious, which I find confirmed in the Random House dictionary.

13. McCulloch's outfit found able chroniclers in two men from New Orleans. George Wilkins Kendall, *Dispatches from the Mexican War*, ed. Lawrence Delbert Cress (Norman: University of Oklahoma Press, 1999), 57. Correspondent for the *Picayune*, Kendall rode with McCulloch wherever possible. His dispatches are a prime source for Taylor's Monterey campaign. Kendall had shared the trials of the Texan Santa Fe prisoners and so had a special affinity for the Texans. McCulloch's operations are covered in more

detail in Samuel C. Reid Jr., *The Scouting Expeditions of McCulloch's Texas Rangers* (Philadelphia: G. B. Zieber, 1847; Austin: Steck, 1935).

14. McCulloch's movements are detailed in Reid, *Scouting Expeditions*.

15. The question of terms of service and the governing laws is almost impossible to make sense of, especially since Taylor ignored the law when expedient. See, however, Barton, *Texas Volunteers*, for a discussion of this question and for the administrative history of every company sworn into the service. Spurlin, *Texas Volunteers*, also deals with each company, setting forth data drawn from official muster rolls. Not all the foot regiment went home, some electing to enlist in one of the mounted regiments. Likewise, not all the mounted men reenlisted; many took their discharge, but their places were filled by others. For Johnston's remorse and his subsequent part in the battle of Monterey, see Charles P. Roland, *Albert Sidney Johnston: Soldier of Three Republics* (Austin: University of Texas Press, 1964), chap. 8.

16. Taylor to AG, Camargo, September 3, 1846, *Mexican War Correspondence*, 417–19.

17. Order No. 115, by command of Major General Taylor, Cerralvo, September 11, 1846; Taylor to AG, Cerralvo, September 12, 1846, *Mexican War Correspondence*, 421, 504–5. Wood's movements are followed by the only diarist to leave a record: James K. Holland, "Diary of a Texan Volunteer in the Mexican War," *SWHQ* 30 (July 1926): 22–23.

18. Reid, *Scouting Expeditions*, 140–41. Doubleday, *Journal of Barbour*, 105–6. George Wilkins Kendall, *The War between the United States and Mexico, Illustrated* (New York: D. Appleton, 1851; Austin: Texas State Historical Association, 1994), 5–6. Order No. 119, Camp near Marin, September 17, 1846; Order No. 120, San Francisco, September 18, 1846, by command of Major General Taylor, *Mexican War Correspondence*, 506. Holland diary, 23–25.

19. Luther Giddings, *Sketches of the Campaigns in Northern Mexico by an Officer of the First Ohio Volunteers* (New York: Putnam, 1853), 143–44. See also John R. Kenly, *Memoirs of a Maryland Volunteer: War with Mexico, in the Years 1846-7-8* (Philadelphia: J. B. Lippincott, 1873), 99. Kenly watched the Texan antics from a tree.

20. Worth's official report, Monterey, September 28, 1846, *Report of the Secretary of War, 1847*, House Executive Document 4, 29th Congress, 2nd Session (serial 497), 102–8. Hays's official report, Monterey, c. September 24, 1846, in Charles A. Gulick et al., eds., *The Papers of Mirabeau Bounaparte Lamar* (Austin: various publishers, 1921–1927; New York: AMS Press, 1973), 6: 138–40. Reid, *Scouting Expeditions*, 156–58. Wilkins, *Highly Irregular Irregulars*, 88–90. Spurlin, *Texas Volunteers*, 72–105.

21. *Texas Democrat* (Austin), November 4, 1846.

22. Reports of Worth and Hays cited in note 21. Reid, 162–65. Wilkins, 90–92. Hays reported two Rangers killed and nine wounded. Service records show one killed and eleven wounded, none fatally. Barton, *Texas Volunteers in the Mexican War*, 58–59.

23. Joseph E. Chance, ed., *The Mexican War Journal of Captain Franklin Smith* (Jackson: University Press of Mississippi, 1991), 150–51. The surgeon related this story to Smith in Monterey after the battle. He associated it with an action that occurred later in the day, but all sources agree that Gillespie fell in the first fire. Another witness related that Gillespie was hit in the abdomen, leaned on his elbow for a time against a rock, asked passing men for water, then urged them forward when they had none. *Texas Democrat* (Austin), October 21, 1846. For a lengthy biographical sketch of Gillespie, including his part in the battle of Monterey, see ibid., October 28, 1846.

24. Smith, *War with Mexico*, 1: 246–48, has a good account of this action. See also Kendall, *War between the United States and Mexico*, 8; and *Dispatches from the Mexican War*, chap. 2. Hays reported two Rangers killed and six wounded, but service records show two officers (Gillespie and Lt. Daniel McCarty) and a private killed and an officer and a private wounded. Barton, 60–61. Hays had seven companies in the assault, those of Richard Gillespie, Ben McCulloch, Tom Green, Kit Acklin, James Gillespie, Claibourne

Herbert, and Samuel Ballowe. Captain Childs is usually identified by his brevet rank of lieutenant colonel.

25. Only after the withdrawal, Taylor states, did he learn by courier that Worth was fighting on the other side of the plaza. Taylor to AG, Monterey, October 9, 1846, *Report of the Secretary of War, 1847,* 87. This is Taylor's final and most detailed report on the action.

26. Reid, *Scouting Expeditions,* 204. Giddings, *Campaign Sketches,* 212. Taylor's explanation, together with the documents tracing the negotiations, are in *Report of the Secretary of War, 1847,* 78–82. More extensive documentation is in Reid, 200–210, who includes a justification of Taylor's course by Col. Jefferson Davis of the Mississippi Rifles, who was one of the negotiators.

27. Taylor to AG, Monterey, October 6, 1846, *Mexican War Correspondence,* 430. Giddings, *Campaign Sketches,* 221–22.

28. Walker to Colt, New York, November 30, 1846, in John E. Parsons, ed., *Samuel Colt's Own Record* (Hartford: Connecticut Historical Society, 1949), 9–10.

29. Charles T. Haven and Frank A. Belden, *A History of the Colt Revolver and the Other Arms Made by Colt's Patent Fire Arms Manufacturing Company from 1836 to 1940* (New York: Bonanza, 1978), 272–96. Robert D. Whittington III, *The Colt Whitneyville-Walker Pistol: A Study of the Pistol and Associated Characters, 1846–1851* (Hooks, Texas: Brownlee, 1984). Louis A. Garvaglia and Charles G. Worman, *Firearms of the American West, 1803–1865* (Albuquerque: University of New Mexico Press, 1984), 141–46. Wilkins, *Highly Irregular Irregulars,* chap. 8.

30. Barton, *Texas Volunteers in the Mexican War,* 81–108. I have examined some of the official documents in the Governors' Papers and the Executive Record Books in TSA.

31. Colt to Hays, New York, June 8, 1847, in Parsons, 81–82.

32. Reid, *Scouting Expeditions,* 233. Barton, *Texas Volunteers,* 81–82.

33. McCulloch to William R. Scurry, Dyersburg, Tennessee, April 30, 1849, printed in Pat B. Clark, *The History of Clarksville and Old Red River County* (Dallas: Mathis, Van Nort, 1937), 118–26. This is a graphic and detailed account of this and subsequent scouts for Taylor. In addition to McCulloch's letter, Phillips left a detailed account printed in the *Telegraph and Texas Register* (Houston), August 2, 1847. See also Thomas W. Cutrer, *Ben McCulloch and the Frontier Military Tradition* (Chapel Hill: University of North Carolina Press, 1993), 91–100.

34. Bauer, *Mexican War,* 218. Wilkins, *Highly Irregular Irregulars,* 136.

35. Joseph E. Chance, ed., *Mexico under Fire: Being the Diary of Samuel Ryan Curtis, 3rd Ohio Volunteer Regiment, during the American Occupation of Northern Mexico, 1846–1847* (Fort Worth: Texas Christian University Press, 1994), 137, 261–62. Chance includes an extended discussion of Gray and his exploits in an endnote. See also Frank Wagner, "Gray, Mabry B.," in *New Handbook of Texas* 3: 293–94. Giddings, *Campaign Sketches,* 324–27.

36. Wilkins, chap. 10. *Mexican War Correspondence,* 1131–32. Walter P. Lane, *The Adventures and Recollections of General Walter P. Lane* (Austin: Jenkins, 1970), 49–74.

37. S. Compton Smith, *Chili con Carne: or, The Camp and the Field* (New York: Miller and Curtiss, 1857), 294.

38. Taylor to AG, Monterey, June 16, 1847, *Mexican War Correspondence,* 1178. Wilkins, *Irregulars,* 141–45, vigorously defends Chevallie's companies from such charges.

39. Barton, *Texas Volunteers in the Mexican War,* 109–12. Wilkins, *Irregulars,* 159–62. Much of what is known of the operations of Hays's command is contained in John S. Ford's papers at the CAH, UTA. I have used the selection published as *Rip Ford's Texas,* ed. Stephen B. Oates (Austin: University of Texas Press, 1963), book 2. The regiment's lieutenant colonel, P. Hansbrough Bell, remained in Texas commanding the other half of the regiment.

40. Whittington, *Colt Whitneyville-Walker Pistol*, 51–54. *Rip Ford's Texas*, 70. Walker to Dear Brother, Perote, June 6 and October 5, 1847, Walker Papers, Box 1982/47, Folder 76 and Folder 8, TSA. The second letter is printed in Haven and Belden, *History of the Colt Revolver*, 292–93.

41. Albert G. Brackett, *General Lane's Brigade in Central Mexico* (Cincinnati: H. W. Derby, 1854), 173–74.

42. Lane to AG, Puebla, December 1, 1847, *Report of the Secretary of War, 1848*, House Executive Document No. 1, 30th Congress, 2nd Session (serial 537), 86–89. *Rip Ford's Texas*, 78–81.

43. Ethan Allen Hitchcock, *Fifty Years in Camp and Field: The Diary of Major-General Ethan Allen Hitchock, U.S.A.*, ed. W. A. Croffut (New York: G. P. Putnam, 1909), 310. An Indiana colonel, Ebenezer Dumont, described the Ranger entry into Mexico City in colorful detail in a letter home, reprinted from the *Indiana Register by the New Orleans Weekly Delta*, February 14, 1848.

44. *Rip Ford's Texas*, 83–85.

45. Ibid., 86–91. E. M. Daggett, "Adventures with Guerrillas," in Isaac George, *Heroes and Incidents of the Mexican War* (Greensburg, Pa.: Review Publishing, 1898), 200–13. Scott to AG, January 13, 1848, *Mexican War Correspondence*, 1067. Spurlin, *Texas Volunteers*, 201.

46. Allan Peskin, ed., *Volunteers: The Mexican War Journals of Private Richard Coulter and Sergeant Thomas Barclay, Company E, Second Pennsylvania Infantry* (Kent: Kent State University Press, 1991), 269.

47. Official reports are in *Report of the Secretary of War, 1848*, 95–103. An extended account is in *Rip Ford's Texas*, 91–98. Josiah Pancoast, *Sketches of Life on the Western Frontier and in the Army in Mexico during the '40s* (Woodstown, N.J.: First National Bank, 1911), 37. Ronnie Tyler, "The Rangers at Zacualtipan," *Texana* 4 (Winter 1966): 343–45.

48. Donald S. Frazier, ed., *The United States and Mexico at War: Nineteenth-Century Expansionism and Conflict* (New York: Macmillan Reference, 1998), 210–11.

49. Henry W. Barton, "The United States Cavalry and the Texas Rangers," *SWHQ* 63 (April 1960): 507.

50. Kenly, *Memoirs of a Maryland Volunteer*, 394–97.

51. *Rip Ford's Texas*, 103–4. Ford does not mention the conspicuous display of U.S. troops and the U.S. flag, which may have added a moderating influence to the speech he had already delivered.

Chapter 5

1. Speech to Senate on February 1, 1858, in Amelia W. Williams and Eugene C. Barker, eds., *The Writings of Sam Houston, 1813–1863* (Austin: University of Texas Press, 1938–1943), 6:468. For the complete debate, see *Congressional Globe*, 35th Congress, 1st session (1857–58), 1: 492–97, 633–34, 643–46, 667–79. The quotation, "Give us rangers in Texas," is on p. 672.

2. Dorman H. Winfrey and James M. Day, eds., *The Indian Papers of Texas and the Southwest, 1825–1916* (Austin: Texas State Historical Association, 1995), 3:43–61, 130–37.

3. *Report of the Commissioner of Indian Affairs, 1855*, 179. For these events, see Rupert N. Richardson, *The Comanche Barrier to South Plains Settlement* (Glendale: Arthur H. Clark, 1933; Austin: Eakin, 1996), chaps. 5–6. The latter edition restores much material deleted by the publisher in the first edition. See also Kenneth F. Neighbours, *Robert Simpson Neighbors and the Texas Frontier, 1836–1859* (Waco: Texian, 1975).

4. Robert M. Utley, *Frontiersmen in Blue: The United States Army and the Indians, 1846–1865* (New York: Macmillan, 1967; Lincoln: University of Nebraska Press, 1981), 70–76. Both Brooke and Smith were colonels of the line but serving in the brevet grades they had earned for gallantry in the Mexican War.

5. For Hays's subsequent career, see James K. Greer, *Colonel Jack Hays: Texas Frontier Leader and California Builder* (New York: E.P. Dutton, 1952). For McCulloch, see Thomas W. Cutrer, *Ben McCulloch and the Frontier Military Tradition* (Chapel Hill: University of North Carolina Press, 1993).

6. Ford's grandson told Walter Prescott Webb that the sobriquet originated in the Mexican War, when as adjutant of Hays's regiment Ford wrote death certificates for men killed in battle and scrawled on them "R.I.P." as an abbreviation for rest in peace. See Webb, *The Texas Rangers: A Century of Frontier Defense* (New York: Houghton Mifflin, 1935; Austin, University of Texas Press, 1965, 1980), 124 n. 65. Most Texas historians have repeated this explanation. Ford's biographer, however, does not: W. J. Hughes, *Rebellious Ranger: Rip Ford and the Old Southwest* (Norman: University of Oklahoma Press, 1964), 79. Hughes does not find the appellation in use until the early 1850s, when it was a common term to describe people involved in one scrape after another. I share Hughes's skepticism. For one thing, very few Rangers died in battle; such deaths as occurred were from disease. For another, I doubt that the Rangers paid any more attention to death certificates (or whatever document the army required) than to muster rolls and all the other paperwork for which the paper keepers repeatedly and in vain called on the Rangers.

7. In addition to Hughes, *Rebellious Ranger*, see the biographical sketch by Stephen B. Oates, ed., in *Rip Ford's Texas* (Austin: University of Texas Press, 1963). Ford lived a long life and left a voluminous body of papers, both contemporary and retrospective. Some of his convoluted prose is difficult to make sense of, but his papers are an indispensable source for four decades of Texas history. Oates has edited the best in this volume. The papers themselves are in CAH, UTA.

8. *Rip Ford's Texas*, chaps. 12–15. The quotation is on p. 142.

9. Brooke to AG, San Antonio, August 31 and September 20, 1849, in *Report of the Secretary of War, 1849*, 143, 147–48.

10. Richardson, *Comanche Barrier*, 98–102, deals with this background. It is also laid out in compelling detail by a Mexican investigative commission that compiled exhaustive documentation in the North Mexican States in 1873. See *Reports of the Committee of Investigation Sent in 1873 by the Mexican Government to the Frontier of Texas*, trans. B. V. Pfeuffer (New York: Baker & Godwin, 1875). This is a translation of the official Mexican report.

11. Brooke to Governor P. H. Bell, San Antonio, January 30, 1850, 301-19-Bell5, TSA. For the AG's complaint, see Jones to Brooke, September 20, 1850, *Report of the Secretary of War, 1850*, 55–56. For the call and muster of the companies, see Brooke to Wood, August 11, 1849; Orders No. 57, Headquarters 8th Military Department, San Antonio, August 19, 1848; and Orders No. 53, September 11, 1849; all in 301-18-Wood20, TSA. For a listing of companies in state service, see resolution of legislature calling for federal reimbursement, in H. P. M. Gammel, comp., *The Laws of Texas, 1822–1897* (Austin: Gammel, 1898), 3:465–68.

12. Richardson, *Comanche Barrier*, 102.

13. Beginning in the 1960s, revisionist scholars challenged the conventional interpretation of South Texas affairs by Anglo historians. Their case is persuasive even though sometimes overstated. For succinct accounts of conditions on the lower Rio Grande in the 1850s, see David Montejano, *Anglos and Mexicans in the Making of Texas, 1836–1986* (Austin: University of Texas Press, 1987), 30–34; and Robert J. Rosenbaum, *Mexican*

Resistance in the Southwest (Austin: University of Texas Press, 1981; Dallas: Southern Methodist University Press, 1998), chap. 3.

14. Pease to Callahan, July 5, 1855, in Winfrey and Day, *Indian Papers*, 3:220–21. Subsequent pages reproduce further correspondence between Pease and citizen groups, General Smith, and Captain Callahan. Documents relating to Callahan's Indian operations are in 401-1153-3; and 301-24-Pease21, 22, and 23, TSA. Ernest C. Shearer, "The Callahan Expedition, 1855," *SWHQ* 54 (April 1951): 430–51. Ronnie C. Tyler, "The Callahan Expedition of 1855: Indians or Negroes?" *SWHQ* 70 (April 1967): 574–85. J. Fred Rippy, "Border Troubles along the Rio Grande, 1848–1860," *SWHQ* 23 (October 1919): 99–103.

15. Smith to AG, October 17, 1855, 401-1153-3, TSA.

16. Traditional Texas historians have portrayed the Callahan expedition just as Governor Pease did–a legitimate "hot pursuit" of Indian raiders across the border. Some concede that slave hunting might have been a secondary objective. But the evidence presented by Tyler in the article cited above leaves no question of the true intent of Callahan and Henry.

17. Smith to AG, October 17, 1855, 401-1153-3, TSA. For the details of Callahan's occupation of Piedras Negras and crossing of the boundary, see two detailed reports by Captain Burbank to Smith's adjutant general, Fort Duncan, October 4 and 8, 1855, in *Rip Ford's Texas*, 217–18.

18. Gammel, *Laws of Texas*, 4:186–87. See also Pease to Callahan, Austin, October 10, 1855; Smith to Pease, October 11, 1855; and Pease to Smith, October 13, 1855, in Winfrey and Day, *Indian Papers*, 3:253–56. See also Smith to Don Emilio Langberg, commanding Mexican forces in Coahuila, San Antonio, December 6, 1855, 401-1153-3, TSA.

19. *United States and Mexican Claims*, Senate Executive Document 31, 44th Congress, 2nd session (Serial 1720), February 2, 1877, 76, 78, 88, 90, 92. This is a report of the secretary of state on claims submitted by citizens of the United States and Mexico under the Convention of July 4, 1868.

20. Shearer, "Callahan Expedition," 451.

21. Neighbours, *Robert Simpson Neighbors and the Texas Frontier*.

22. Gammel, *Laws of Texas*, 3:1495–99. Richardson, *Comanche Barrier*, chap. 9. Kenneth F. Neighbours, *Indian Exodus: Texas Indian Affairs, 1835–1859* (Wichita Falls, Texas: Nortex, 1973), chaps. 7–8. Neighbours, *Robert Simpson Neighbors*, chaps. 8–14.

23. Neighbors to Acting Commissioner of Indian Affairs, Brazos Agency, September 10, 1855, *Report of the Commissioner of Indian Affairs, 1855*, 177–82. Neighbors to Commissioner of Indian Affairs, Brazos Agency, September 18, 1856, ibid., 1856, 173–76. Richardson, *Comanche Barrier*, 110.

24. Neighbors to Commissioner of Indian Affairs, Brazos Agency, September 16, 1857, *Report of the Commissioner of Indian Affairs, 1857*, 552. Twiggs to AG, San Antonio, January 20, 1858, *Report of the Secretary of War, 1858*, 249–50. Twiggs was a brigadier general of the line commanding in his brevet grade of major general.

25. Neighbors to Twiggs, San Antonio, July 17, 1857, *Report of the Commissioner of Indian Affairs, 1857*, 553–55. Twiggs to AG, San Antonio, June 16, 1857, 301-26-Pease43, TSA.

26. Pease to Twiggs, Austin, August 13, 1857; Twiggs to Pease, San Antonio, August 20 and 29, 1857, 301-26-Pease45, TSA. Pease to Congressmen Guy M. Bryan and John H. Reagan, Austin, November 3, 1857, in Winfrey and Day, *Indian Papers*, 3:266. Gammel, *Laws of Texas*, 4:1137.

27. Runnels to President of Senate, January 22, 1858, in Winfrey and Day, *Indian Papers*, 3:270–71. Gammel, *Laws of Texas*, 4:949–50. Undated clipping from Austin *Intelligencer*, encl. to Twiggs to AG, January 30, 1858, *Report of the Secretary of War, 1858*, 253–54.

28. Runnels to Ford, Austin, January 28, 1858, in Winfrey and Day, *Indian Papers*, 3:272–73.

29. Ford to Runnels, Camp Adams, Brown County, February 27, 1858, 301-27-Runnels3, TSA. Same to same, Brazos Agency, April 7, 1858, ibid., Runnels5. Same to same, Camp Brown, March 11, and Camp Runnels, March 31, 1858, in Winfrey and Day, *Indian Papers*, 3:275–77, 279–81.

30. Ford to Runnels, Camp Runnels, May 22, 1858; Lt. A. Nelson to Ford, May 21, 1858, 301-27-Runnels6, TSA. Significantly, although technically mounted volunteers, Ford dated his report at "Headquarters Texas Rangers" and signed it as "Captain Commanding Texas Rangers." See also Ford's reminiscent account in *Rip Ford's Texas*, chap. 19. An extended account is also in J. W. Wilbarger, *Indian Depredations in Texas* (Austin: Hutchings, 1889; Austin: Eakin, 1985), 320–26. Hughes, *Rebellious Ranger*, chap. 6. Hughes has the village Tenawa Comanches and the village from which reinforcements came as Nokonis. Richardson identifies Iron Jacket and his people as Kotsotekas. Some interesting and somewhat bizarre Comanche perspectives, based on oral tradition, are in Thomas W. Kavanagh, *Comanche Political History: An Ethnohistorical Perspective, 1708–1875* (Lincoln: University of Nebraska Press, 1996), 365–67.

31. Richardson, *Comanche Barrier*, 120. Ford to Runnels, June 2, 1858, 301-27-Runnels7, TSA.

32. Ford to Runnels, June 2, 1858, 301-27-Runnels7, TSA.

33. Twiggs's correspondence with army headquarters and Governor Runnels, together with operational reports, are in *Report of the Secretary of War, 1858*, 268–76. See also Utley, *Frontiersmen in Blue*, 127–35; and William Y. Chalfant, *Without Quarter: The Wichita Expedition and the Fight on Crooked Creek* (Norman: University of Oklahoma Press, 1991).

34. Hugh Allen to Runnels, San Saba River, November 21, 1858, Winfrey and Day, *Indian Papers*, 3:309–10. This volume is full of similar protests showing hardly a break in Indian raiding. For Buffalo Hump at the federal distribution on the Arkansas, see Agent Robert C. Miller to Superintendent of Indian Affairs at St. Louis, Bent's Fort, Kansas Territory, August 17, 1858, in *Report of the Commissioner of Indian Affairs, 1858*, 98.

35. Neighbours, *Indian Exodus*, 131–32.

36. Ibid. Runnels to Ford, Austin, February 11, 1859, in Winfrey and Day, *Indian Papers*, 3:314. The issue led to a rancorous newspaper controversy between Ford and the prosecuting attorney. See Hughes, *Rebellious Ranger*, 159, and Ford's own rendering in *Rip Ford's Texas*, chap. 21. To have attempted the arrests, Ford contended (p. 247), "would have caused a civil war on the frontier."

37. Acting Commissioner of Indian Affairs Charles Mix to Neighbors, March 30, 1859; Neighbors to Mix, May 12, 1859, *Report of the Commissioner of Indian Affairs, 1859*, 263–64, 269–71.

38. Plummer to AAG Department of Texas, Brazos Agency, May 23, 1859; Agent S. P. Ross to Neighbors, Brazos Agency, May 26, 1859, *Report of the Commissioner of Indian Affairs, 1859*, 276–78.

39. Neighbours, *Exodus*, 137. George Klos, "'Our People Could Not Distinguish One Tribe from Another': The 1859 Expulsion of the Reserve Indians from Texas," *SWHQ* 97 (April 1994): 599–619. *Report of the Commissioner of Indian Affairs, 1859*, 165–66, 215–334. *Report of the Secretary of War, 1859*, 365–74. Winfrey and Day, *Indian Papers*, 3:312 passim.

Chapter 6

1. Llrenna B. Friend, *Sam Houston: The Great Designer* (Austin: University of Texas Press, 1954), 162–270.

2. J. Fred Rippy, *The United States and Mexico* (New York: Alfred A. Knopf, 1926), chap. 12.

3. Friend, *Sam Houston*, 270–320.

4. Brownsville *American Flag*, August 20, 1856, quoted in *Reports of the Committee of Investigation Sent in 1873 by the Mexican Government to the Frontier of Texas*, 132. Cortina's political activities run through much of the documentation but are best stated in the report of the commission Houston sent to investigate the origins and progress of the Cortina troubles: Angel Navarro and Robert Taylor to Houston, Brownsville, February 4, 1860, 301-34-Houston40, TSA.

5. Cortina lacks a balanced biography. Lyman I. Woodman, *Cortina: The Rogue of the Rio Grande* (San Antonio: Naylor, 1950), presents the standard bandit portrayal long prevalent in Texas histories. Charles W. Goldfinch, *Juan N. Cortina, 1824-1892: A Reappraisal* (Brownsville: Bishop's Print Shop, 1950), is a scholarly study that emphasizes Cortina's patriotic side while minimizing the criminal. It became a base for much of the revisionism that began in the 1960s, in which Cortina emerges as a classic "social bandit," battling a selfish and brutal establishment in behalf of the poor and powerless. See the introduction to Jerry D. Thompson, ed., *Juan Cortina and the Texas-Mexico Frontier, 1859-1877* (El Paso: Texas Western Press, 1994). This is an edited edition of Cortina's string of *pronunciamentos*. See also Thompson's introduction to his editing of the Heintzelman journals: *Fifty Miles and a Fight: Major Samuel Peter Heintzelman's Journal of Texas and the Cortina War* (Austin: Texas State Historical Association, 1998). None of these sources should be blamed for my rendition of Cortina, which is drawn not only from them but from a reading of the massive official documentation that Cortina inspired on both sides of the boundary. On the American side, most of the official reports and correspondence appear in RG 301, Runnels and Houston Papers, TSA; *Difficulties on the Southwestern Frontier*, House Executive Document 52, 36th Congress, 1st session (Serial 1050), April 2, 1860; *Troubles on the Texas Frontier*, House Executive Document 81, 36th Congress, 1st session (Serial 1056), May 5, 1860; *Report on the Texas Frontier Troubles*, House Report 343, 44th Congress, 1st session (Serial 1709), March 2, 1876; Amelia W. Williams and Eugene C. Barker, *The Writings of Sam Houston, 1813-1863* (Austin: University of Texas Press 1938-43), vol. 7; and Stephen B. Oates, ed., *Rip Ford's Texas* (Austin: University of Texas Press, 1963), chaps. 22-24. For the Mexican perspective, see *Reports of the Committee of Investigation Sent in 1873 by the Mexican Government to the Frontier of Texas*.

6. Angel Navarro and Robert Taylor to Houston, Brownsville, February 4, 1860, 301-34-Houston40, TSA. Affidavit of City Marshal Robert Shears, January 14, 1860, 301-30-Houston37. Affidavit of Francisco Yturria, January 19, 1860, 301-30-Houston38. Statement of William Neal to Commissioners Robert Taylor and Angel Navarro, January 16, 1860, ibid. Report of Cameron County Grand Jury, c. late November 1859, *Difficulties on the Southwestern Frontier*, 92-93. U.S. Customs Collector Francis W. Latham to Gen. David E. Twiggs, Brownsville, September 28, 1859, ibid., 31-32. Eleven (Anglo) citizens of Brownsville to Gov. H. R. Runnels, October 2, 1859, ibid., 20-22. Appraiser General W. P. Reyburn to Collector of Customs F. A. Hatch, New Orleans, November 21, 1859, ibid., 64-68. Maj. Samuel P. Heintzelman to Capt. John Withers (adjutant to the department commander), Brownsville, March 1, 1860, *Troubles on the Texas Frontier*, 3-4. This is Heintzelman's comprehensive final report recording the beginning and progress of the Cortina affair. An especially good summary of events as of the end of 1859 is Cameron County Chief Justice Edmund J. Davis, Mayor Stephen Powers et al. to Governor of Texas, Brownsville, December 30, 1859, 301-29-Runnels24, TSA.

7. Thompson, *Juan Cortina*, chap. 1. *Difficulties on the Southwestern Frontier*, 70-71.

8. Heintzelman to Withers, March 1, 1860, *Troubles on the Texas Frontier*, 4-5. Mayor Stephen Powers to Gov. H. R. Runnels, Brownsville, October 25, 1859, 301-29-Runnels23, TSA. Thompson, *Juan Cortina*, 21.

9. Brownsville *American Flag*, October 25, 1859, in *Difficulties on the Southwestern Frontier*, 44–47. See other newspaper accounts, pp. 47–51. Capt. W. B. Thompson to Mayor Powers, October 25, 1859, ibid., 68–69. Powers to Runnels, October 25, 1859, 301-29-Runnels23, TSA. Heintzelman to Withers, March 1, 1860, *Troubles on the Texas Frontier*, 5. Thompson, *Juan Cortina*, 21.

10. Tobin to Runnels, San Antonio, October 11, 1859, 301-29-Runnels23. Runnels to Tobin, Austin, October 13, 1859, 401-1153-10, TSA. Tobin to Runnels, November 16, 1859, in *State Gazette* (Austin), November 26, 1859.

11. Heintzelman to Withers, March 1, 1860, *Troubles on the Texas Frontier*, 5. Appraiser General W. P. Reyburn to Collector of Customs F. A. Hatch, New Orleans, November 21, 1859, *Difficulties on the Southwestern Frontier*, 67. John S. Ford, soon to appear in this narrative, knew the truth: "On the 13th November he was hung by members of Capt Tobin's company." Ford to W. C. Thomas, February 22, 1860, Heintzelman Papers, Library of Congress, copy kindly furnished by Jerry Thompson. See also Thompson, *Fifty Miles and a Fight*, 32. Governor Houston, reacting to Ford's report to Heintzelman, called on Tobin for a complete report of his operations. "Make particular reference to the hanging of Cabrera at Brownsville and who participated in it," he directed. Houston to Tobin, March 5, 1860, in Williams and Barker, eds., *Writings of Sam Houston*, 7:499–500. If Tobin complied, I have not found the answer.

12. Tobin to Runnels, Brownsville, November 27, 1859, 301-29-Runnels24, TSA. Heintzelman to Withers, March 1, 1860, *Troubles on the Texas Frontier*, 6. Newspaper clippings quoting letters from Brownsville in *Difficulties on the Southwestern Frontier*, 82–85.

13. Thompson, *Juan Cortina*, 23–28. *Difficulties on the Southwestern Frontier*, 79–82.

14. Heintzelman's movements are most clearly traced in Thompson, *Fifty Miles and a Fight*, in which the major's journal affords pithy insights that do not find their way into official reports. See also Heintzelman's summary report, March 1, 1860, *Troubles on the Texas Frontier*, 7. Throughout October and November General Twiggs, clearly traumatized, alternated between exaggerating and minimizing the Cortina threat, and his troop dispositions and reports to Washington reflected his fluctuating state of mind. Heintzelman's force numbered far fewer than had originally been alerted for the Brownsville operations. Stability returned to department headquarters early in December, when Twiggs finally left on sick leave, and Lt. Col. Washington Seawell took over as acting commander. See Twiggs's orders and reports in *Difficulties on the Southwestern Frontier*, 54–59, 72–74, 86.

Governor Runnels was almost as ambivalent as Twiggs. His first orders to Ford were to gather all the volunteers he could en route to Brownsville. These were subsequently modified to direct Ford to recruit one hundred men, unite them with Tobin's authorized one hundred, and call an election to determine who would command as major. Runnels to Ford, November 17, 1859, 401-1153-10. Same to same, November 22 and 23, 1859, 301-20-Runnels24, TSA. Ford to Runnels, Goliad, November 22, 1859, ibid.

15. Heintzelman to Lt. T. A. Washington (AAAG in department headquarters), Fort Brown, December 16, 1859, *Difficulties on the Southwestern Frontier*, 87–88. Same to AG, December 18, 1859, ibid., 89–90. Same to Withers, March 1, 1860, *Troubles on the Texas Frontier*, 7–9. Thompson, *Fifty Miles and a Fight*, 138–41. Tobin to Runnels, December 16, 1859; Ford to Runnels, same date, 301-29-Runnels25, TSA.

16. Heintzelman to AG, Ringgold Barracks, December 27, 1859, *Difficulties on the Southwestern Frontier*, 97–98. Same to Withers, March 1, 1860, *Troubles on the Texas Frontier*, 8–10. Thompson, *Fifty Miles and a Fight*, 154–56. Oates, *Rip Ford's Texas*, 269–75. Tobin to Gov. Sam Houston, Rio Grande City, December 28, 1859, 401-1153-10, TSA. This is a very brief report in which Tobin declares that *he* overtook Cortina, completely routed him, and took two cannons.

17. Tobin to Houston, Ringgold Barracks, January 2, 1860, 301-30-Houston36. Same to Heintzelman, same date, 401-1153-12, TSA. Thompson, *Fifty Miles and a Fight*, 142, 164. Oates, *Rip Ford's Texas*, 276–77.

18. Taylor to Houston, Brownsville, January 16, 1860, 301-30-Houston38. Navarro to Houston, January 26, 1860, 301-30-Houston39. Navarro and Taylor to Houston, February 4, 1860, 301-30-Houston40. Navarro and Taylor to Tobin, January 12, 1860; and Navarro to Houston, Austin, February 15, 1860, *Difficulties on the Southwestern Frontier*, 116, 120–22. Navarro to Heintzelman, Heintzelman to Navarro and Taylor, Navarro and Taylor to Ford, all February 2, 1860, ibid., 118–19. Oates, *Rip Ford's Texas*, 277–80. Contemporary documents use Cortina and Cortinas interchangeably. Williams and Barker, *Writings of Sam Houston*, 7:395–96.

19. Heintzelman to Withers, January 29, 1860, *Difficulties on the Southwestern Frontier*, 106–7.

20. Heintzelman to AG, Fort Brown, March 7, 1860, ibid., 137. Thompson, *Fifty Miles and a Fight*, 218. On March 17, he wrote in his diary (ibid., 114), "I wish I could get instructions, so as to dispense with the Rangers. Everything is going on well & I fear that they will spoil it."

21. Ford to Heintzelman, La Bolsa, February 4, 1860; Tobin to Houston, Brownsville, February 6, 1860; Heintzelman to Joaquin Angeles, February 9, 1860; Heintzelman to Withers, same date, *Troubles on the Texas Frontier*, 95–98, 68–70. Oates, *Rip Ford's Texas*, 282–87. Heintzelman gives the enemy force as 150 infantry and 50 cavalry. A printer's error badly scrambled the Tobin report of February 6 with one of March 24 from Ford. The latter (p. 99), which is erroneously ascribed to Tobin, contains Tobin's account of the battle and belongs with the former, while the final few sentences of the former (p. 97) belongs with the latter.

22. Oates, *Rip Ford's Texas*, 286. The casualty figures are from Heintzelman to Withers as cited in the previous note.

23. Houston to Floyd, Austin, February 13 (two letters) and 17, 1860, Williams and Barker, *Writings of Sam Houston*, 7:379–85, 474–75, 478–79. Telegram, Houston to Floyd, New Orleans, February 20, 1860, *Difficulties on the Southwestern Frontier*, 131.

24. Gammel, *Laws of Texas*, 4:1375–77, 1400. Williams and Barker, *Writings of Sam Houston*, 7:407–13, 423–29, 473.

25. AG to Lee, February 24, March 2 and 3, 1860, *Difficulties on the Southwestern Frontier*, 133–35.

26. Ford's beliefs and intentions are manifest, both explicitly and implicitly, throughout his narrative of the Cortina affair, in Oates, *Rip Ford's Texas*, chaps. 22–23.

27. Stoneman and Ford to Heintzelman, Camp on Rio Grande [in Mexico], March 18, 1860, *Troubles on the Texas Frontier*, 80–81. Oates, *Rip Ford's Texas*, 290–95.

28. Heintzelman to Stoneman, Fort Brown, March 19, 1860, *Troubles on the Texas Frontier*, 81.

29. Ford to Heintzelman, March 24, 1860 (see explanation in note 22 of printer's scrambling of report; this is Ford's report even though shown as Tobin's, and contains Tobin material), *Troubles on the Texas Frontier*, 99. Heintzelman to AG, March 25, 1860; Heintzelman to Withers, same date, all in ibid., 81–83. Oates, *Rip Ford's Texas*, 295–98. Hughes, *Rebellious Ranger*, 173–8.

30. See for one of many examples Orders to Ranger Captains, March 22, 1860, in Williams and Barker, 7:535–36. For specifics, see for example Houston to Dalrymple, Burleson, and Conner, January 1, 1860, ibid., 7:423–29.

31. The theory that Houston mobilized Johnson's regiment and other Ranger units to have ready for a sudden descent on Mexico is propounded by Walter Prescott Webb, *The Texas Rangers: A Century of Frontier Defense* (New York: Houghton Mifflin, 1935; Austin:

University of Texas Press, 1965, 1980), chap. 10. Webb reprints the pertinent correspondence, which I have examined in the Governors Papers at TSA. I find Webb's argument unpersuasive. He ends the Cortina affair three months prematurely, minimizes the Indian threat to the northwestern frontier, portrays Johnson as wholly ignored by the governor, and seems to postulate (unrealistically, I believe) a dash on Mexico by a force in the service of the state of Texas. In the absence of further evidence, Houston's avowal that were he to pursue Mexican ambitions he would do so as a filibuster rather than governor of Texas seems more convincing to me.

32. Houston to Johnson, March 17 and May 7, 1860, Williams and Barker, 7:525-67, 8:48-49.

33. Johnson to Houston, Fort Belknap, May 16 and 30, 1860, 301-32-Houston52 and 53, TSA.

34. The Johnson expedition is amply documented in RG 301, Boxes 32-33 (Houston governor's papers), TSA; and in Williams and Barker, 7:525-27 and 8:48-49,113-14, 142, 176-77.

35. Houston to Ross (at Waco), Austin, September 11, 1860, Williams and Barker, 8:139-40. Judith Ann Benner, *Sul Ross: Soldier, Statesman, Educator* (College Station: Texas A&M Press, 1983). Roger N. Conger, "Lawrence Sullivan Ross," in *Rangers of Texas* (Waco: Texian, 1969), 115-30.

36. The battle of Pease River occurred in the midst of the Texas secession crisis, and if Ross ever wrote an official report, it has yet to come to light. After the Civil War, however, he compiled an authoritative account printed in J. W. Wilbarger, *Indian Depredations in Texas* (Austin: Hutchins, 1889; Austin: Eakin, 1985), 333-47; and *History of Texas* (Chicago: Lewis, 1896), 234-36. Benner, *Sul Ross*, chap. 5, is a thorough account drawing on Ross family papers as well as other sources. J. Evetts Haley, *Charles Goodnight: Cowman and Plainsman* (1936; Norman: University of Oklahoma Press, 1949), chap. 4. Goodnight was guide for a citizen group following Ross. During his reservation years, Quanah Parker denied that his father had been killed at Pease River, and some authors have taken his claim at face value. A convincing discussion of the issue, which supports Ross's account, is Robert H. Williams, "The Case for Peta Nocona," *Texana* 10 (1972): 55-72.

Chapter 7

1. David P. Smith, *Frontier Defense in the Civil War: Texas Rangers and Rebels* (College Station: Texas A&M University Press, 1992), 21-32. This is a thoroughly researched work, drawing heavily on both state and Confederate records. Although I have examined many of the relevant documents in the Texas State Archives, I concluded it unnecessary to duplicate Smith's exhaustive research. My treatment of the Civil War years, therefore, rests heavily on his book. See also W. C. Holden, "Frontier Defense in Texas during the Civil War," *West Texas Historical Association Year Book* 4 (June 1928): 16-31. The pertinent acts of the legislature and ordinances of the Convention are in H. P. M. Gammel, comp., *The Laws of Texas, 1822-1897* (Austin: Gammel, 1898), 4:1530-32, 5:346-47, 353, 360, 368, 421.

2. Smith, *Frontier Defense*, 41-44. Gammel, *Laws of Texas*, 5:452-54.

3. James K. Greer, ed., *A Texas Ranger and Frontiersman: The Days of Buck Barry in Texas, 1845-1906* (Dallas: Southwest, 1932; Lincoln: University of Nebraska Press, 1978), 154. The description is Greer's in ibid., 222-23. Barry also contributed an account of his services in J. W. Wilbarger, *Indian Depredations in Texas* (Austin: Hutchins, 1889; Austin: Eakin, 1985), 439-56.

4. Smith, *Frontier Defense*, 53-54, 69-70. For the distinction between the farmers of the Cross Timbers and the cattlemen newcomers of the open plains, see Ty Cashion, *A Texas*

Frontier: The Clear Fork Country and Fort Griffin, 1849-1887 (Norman: University of Oklahoma Press, 1996), chap. 3. For the military market for the Texas beef, see T. H. Fehrenbach, *Comanches: The Destruction of a People* (New York: Da Capo, 1974), 452.

5. Smith, *Frontier Defense*, chap. 4.

6. Ibid., 81-86. John Henry Brown, *Indian Wars and Pioneers of Texas* (Austin: L. E. Daniell, c. 189?; Austin: State House Press, 1988), 115-18.

7. Gammel, *Laws of Texas*, 5:677-79, 688-89.

8. Smith, *Frontier Defense*, chap. 6. Greer, *A Texas Ranger and Frontiersman*, 169-72.

9. Smith, *Frontier Defense*, 131-35. James B. Barry in Wilbarger, *Indian Depredations in Texas*, 449-52. Kenneth Neighbours, "Elm Creek Raid in Young County, 1864," *West Texas Historical Association Year Book* 40 (October 1864): 83-89. Rupert N. Richardson, *The Frontier of Northwest Texas, 1846 to 1876* (Glendale: Arthur H. Clark, 1963), 246-47. Fehrenbach, *Comanches*, 452-57. Cashion, *A Texas Frontier*, 66-68.

10. I. D. Ferguson in J. Marvin Hunter, ed., "The Battle of Dove Creek," *West Texas Historical Association Year Book* 10 (October 1934): 78-79.

11. McAdoo to Adjutant and Inspector General John Burk, Fredericksburg, February 7, 1865; same to same, Burnet, February 28, 1865; Totten to Erath, no place, no date; Barry to Burk, Camp Colorado, January 20, 1865; Erath to Burk, South Bosque, February 2, 1865, 401-387-8, -9, and -11, TSA. Smith, *Frontier Defense*, 151-55. Greer, *Texas Ranger and Frontiersman*, chap. 16. A. M. Gibson, *The Kickapoos: Lords of the Middle Border* (Norman: University of Oklahoma Press, 1963), chap. 15. William C. Pool, "The Battle of Dove Creek," *SWHQ* 53 (April 1950): 367-85. Hunter, ed., "Battle of Dove Creek," 74-85. Lucy A. Erath, *The Memoirs of Major George B. Erath* (Austin: Texas State Historical Association, 1923), 98-99.

12. The standard histories of Reconstruction in Texas were written by earlier generations of historians who viewed Texans as hapless victims of a tyrannical rule of carpetbaggers and scalawags. More balanced is the treatment of Carl H. Moneyhon, *Republicanism in Reconstruction Texas* (Austin: University of Texas Press, 1980). See also Moneyhon's shorter essay in *The New Handbook of Texas* (Austin: Texas State Historical Association, 1996), 5:474-81. Another solid work is William L. Richter, *The Army in Texas during Reconstruction, 1865-1870* (College Station: Texas A&M Press, 1987). Dale Baum, *The Shattering of Texas Unionism: Politics in the Lone Star State during the Civil War Era* (Baton Rouge: Louisiana State University Press, 1998). For a good summary of revisionist trends, see Edgar P. Sneed, "A Historiography of Reconstruction in Texas: Some Myths and Problems," *SWHQ* 72 (April 1969): 435-48.

13. Gammel, *Laws of Texas*, 5:928-30. Letters from the frontier are in Dorman H. Winfrey and James M. Day, eds., *The Indian Papers of Texas and the Southwest, 1825-1916* (Austin: Texas State Historical Association, 1995), 4:95ff.

14. *Report of the Secretary of War, 1866*, 48. Sheridan to Chief of Staff John A. Rawlins, November 11, 1866, in *Claims of the State of Texas*, Senate Executive Document 19, 45th Congress, 2nd Session, 1878 (Serial 1780), 8-9. This source also contains related correspondence through September and October 1866, 2-9. Additional telegrams and letters are in 301-53-Throckmorton1-5, TSA. Richter, *Army in Texas during Reconstruction*, chap. 4.

15. *Report of the Secretary of War, 1867*, 470-73.

16. The literature of the Fort Sill reservation is voluminous. I have dealt with and documented the subject in *Frontier Regulars: The United States Army and the Indian, 1866-1890* (New York: Macmillan, 1973; Lincoln: University of Nebraska Press, 1984), 207-14; and *The Indian Frontier of the American West, 1846-1890* (Albuquerque: University of New Mexico Press, 1984), 140-48.

17. *U.S. Relations with Mexico*, House Report 701, 45th Congress, 2nd Session, 1878 (Serial 1824), 209-11.

18. Gammel, *Laws of Texas*, 6:179–82. For the militia act of June 14, 1870, and the state police act of July 1, 1870, see ibid., 185–90, 193–94.

19. Ibid., 6:45–46.

20. GO No. 3, Hq. State of Texas, AGO, Austin, August 3, 1870, 401-1156-15, TSA. *Report of the Adjutant General of the State of Texas from June 24, 1870, to December 31, 1870* (Austin: Tracy, Siemering, 1870), 6–7, 61–63.

21. *Claims of the State of Texas*, Senate Executive Document 19, 45th Congress, 2nd Session, 1878 (Serial 1780), 10–12. *Report of the Adjutant General of the State of Texas from June 24, 1870, to December 31, 1870*, 6–7.

22. Message of Governor E. J. Davis, January 10, 1871, 301-89-Davis350, TSA. and *Report of the Adjutant General of the State of Texas for the Year 1872* (Austin: James P. Newcomb, 1873), 6–8.

23. Richarz to AG, Fort Inge, December 4 and 12, 1870, 401-389-13, TSA. Periodic reports from are in ibid., Folders 9–16. For Davis's view of the Mexican refuge, see his message to the legislature of January 10, 1871, 301-89-Davis350, TSA.

24. Terry G. Jordan, *North American Cattle-Ranching Frontiers: Origins, Diffusion, and Differentiation* (Albuquerque: University of New Mexico Press, 1993), chap. 7, revises the traditional interpretation of the origins and characteristics of the Mexican and Texas systems.

25. The fight is described in graphic and convincing detail by Ranger A. J. Sowell, *Rangers and Pioneers of Texas* (San Antonio: Shepard, 1884; New York: Argosy-Antiquarian, 1964), 298–345. The official report is also detailed: Lt. A. C. Hill to Davidson, Thompsonville Station, Wise County, February 9, 1871, 401-1156-18, TSA.

26. GO No. 4, AGO, February 27, 1871, 401-984: General Orders AGO, 21-22, TSA.

27. Utley, *Frontier Regulars*, 207–12. Utley, *Indian Frontier*, 143–48. More recent studies are Charles M. Robinson III, *The Indian Trial: The Complete Story of the Warren Wagon Train Massacre and the Fall of the Kiowa Nation* (Spokane: Arthur H. Clark, 1997); and Robinson, *Satanta: The Life and Death of a War Chief* (Austin: State House Press, 1997).

28. Gammel, *Laws of Texas*, 7:36–38. *Report of the Adjutant General of the State of Texas for the Year 1872*, 8–9.

29. Moneyhon, *Republicanism in Reconstruction Texas*, chaps. 9–10. For a revisionist view of the state police, see Ann Patton Baenziger, "The Texas State Police during Reconstruction: A Reexamination," *SWHQ* 72 (April 1969): 470–91.

Chapter 8

1. *Report of the Secretary of War, 1874*, 70–71.

2. Message of Governor Richard Coke to the Fourteenth Legislature, January 26, 1874, 301-95-49, TSA. For details of cost and inadequacy of companies in the field under calls of Governor Davis, see AG William Steele to Coke, March 5, 1874, Ledger 401-621, p. 70, TSA.

3. H. P. M. Gammel, *The Laws of Texas, 1822–1897*. (Austin: Gammel, 1898), 8:86–91.

4. File for House Bill 128, Fourteenth Legislature, Regular Session, RG 100, Records of the Legislature, TSA.

5. Billy Mac Jones, "John B. Jones," in *Rangers of Texas* (Waco: Texian, 1969), 151–59. James B. Gillett, *Six Years with the Texas Rangers* (New Haven: Yale University Press, 1925), 62. Frederick Wilkins, *The Law Comes to Texas: The Texas Rangers, 1870–1901* (Austin: State House, 1999), 43.

6. A graphic view of Ranger camp life appears in the reminiscences of a captain's wife who lived for a time with her husband: Lou Conway Roberts, *A Woman's Reminiscences of Six Years in Camp with the Texas Rangers* (Austin: Von Boeckman-Jones, 1928), 11–18.

Her husband published his own memoirs, which are not as well done: Dan W. Roberts, *Rangers and Sovereignty* (San Antonio: Wood Printing & Engraving, 1914).

7. Gillett, *Six Years with the Texas Rangers*, 21.

8. Wilkins, *The Law Comes to Texas*, 38–40, 77. Louis A. Garavaglia and Charles G. Worman, *Firearms of the American West, 1866–1894* (Albuquerque: University of New Mexico Press, 1985), 81–92, 141–58, 183–92. Specimens of all Ranger arms are displayed in the Texas Ranger Hall of Fame, Waco, Texas.

9. Gillett, *Six Years with the Texas Rangers*, 22. Official reports abound in RG 401, both AG Correspondence and Ranger Records, in TSA.

10. Jones to Steele, Camp at Flat Top Mountain, Young County, July 14, 1874, 401-392-5, TSA. Jones to Steele, Camp Eureka near Big Wichita, Archer County, July 23, 1874, ibid.-6. The Kiowa accounts are in W. S. Nye, *Carbine and Lance: The Story of Old Fort Sill* (Norman: University of Oklahoma Press, 1942), 192–200.

11. Z. T. Wattles, August 22, 1874, in unidentified newspaper clipping (probably Corsicana *Observer*, in Jones's home town), 401-1158-17, TSA.

12. The standard history of the Red River war is James L. Haley, *The Buffalo War: The History of the Red River Indian Uprising of 1874* (Norman: University of Oklahoma Press, 1985). I have dealt with it in *Frontier Regulars: The United States Army and the Indian, 1866–1890* (New York: Macmillan, 1973; Lincoln: University of Nebraska Press, 1984), chap. 13. See also Charles M. Robinson III, *Satanta: The Life and Death of a War Chief* (Austin: State House Press, 1997).

13. Message of Governor Richard Coke to Second Session, Fourteenth Legislature, January 1875, 301-96-52; GO 15, March 20, 1877, 401-395-7, TSA.

14. Erik Rigler, "Frontier Justice: In the Days before NCIC [National Crime Information Center]," *FBI Law Enforcement Bulletin* 54 (July 1985): 16–22. Harold J. Weiss Jr., "The Texas Rangers Revisited: Old Themes and New Viewpoints," *SWHQ* 97 (April 1994): 636. David M. Horton and Ryan Kellus Turner, *Lone Star Justice: A Comprehensive Overview of the Texas Criminal Justice System* (Austin: Eakin, 1999), 100.

15. The classic study of this subject is Richard Maxwell Brown, *Strain of Violence: Historical Studies of American Violence and Vigilantism* (New York: Oxford University Press, 1975). Brown devotes sixty-four pages to violence and vigilantism in Texas.

16. Hand to Jones, Jim Ned, Coleman County, June 1, 1876, 401-1158-21, TSA.

17. *Supplemental Report of the Adjutant General*, December 1, 1874, 3–10. *Report of the Adjutant General, 1876*, 5–9. Wilkins, *The Law Comes to Texas*, 53–57, 62–63.

18. The phrase is borrowed from the classic study of Texas feuding: C. L. Sonnichsen, *I'll Die Before I'll Run: The Story of the Great Feuds of Texas* (New York: Devin-Adair, 1962; Lincoln: University of Nebraska Press, 1988).

19. *The Penal Code of Texas Passed by the Sixteenth Legislature, February 21, 1879, Took Effect July 24, 1879* (Austin: State Printing Office, 1887), bound with *Revised Statutes of Texas, 1879*. The relevant passage is Title 9, Chapter 4, "Unlawfully Carrying Arms," p. 42. Each article references as source Act of April 12, 1871–ironically, a measure enacted by the Davis legislature to keep better control over the unrepentant war generation. For the issue in the broader context, see Philip D. Jordan, "The Wearing of Weapons in the Western Country," in his *Frontier Law and Order: Ten Essays* (Lincoln: University of Nebraska Press, 1970), chap. 1.

20. Steele to Jones, September 23, 1875, 401-393-11, TSA. For a general history see C. L. Sonnichsen, *Ten Texas Feuds* (Albuquerque: University of New Mexico Press, 1957), chap. 5. Captain Dan Roberts told of his participation in *Rangers and Sovereignty*, 87–93. Ranger James B. Gillett, who was close to the action but not a participant, gave his version in *Six Years a Texas Ranger*, chap. 5. See also Lou Conway Roberts (Mrs. Dan W. Roberts), *A Woman's Reminiscences of Six Years in Camp with the Texas Rangers*, 7–10.

21. In addition to sources cited in the previous note, my account is drawn from *Report of the Adjutant General, 1876*, 5–7, and Jones to Steele, September 28 and 30, October 20 and 28, 1875, 401-393-11, TSA.

22. Steele to Coke, August 31, 1876, in *Report of the Adjutant General, 1876*, 3.

23. SO 2, AGO, Austin, July 14, 1874, Ledger 401-1012, 73–74; AG William Steele to [Capt. L. H. McNelly], July 14, 1874, Ledger 401-621, and 303-05, TSA.

24. George Durham, as told to Clyde Wantland, *Taming the Nueces Strip: The Story of McNelly's Rangers* (Austin: University of Texas Press, 1962), 16. Durham and Napoleon A. Jennings, *A Texas Ranger* (New York: Charles Scribner, 1899; Norman: University of Oklahoma Press, 1997), furnish the basis for most accounts of McNelly's Rangers and their successors under Lee Hall. Both are colorful reminiscent accounts that must be used with care. How much Wantland influenced Durham is speculative. Jennings, who wrote for newspapers, placed himself in events that occurred before his enlistment and embellished those in which he participated. Often contemporary sources contradict their memory. Nevertheless, both knew the main players and pronounced judgments that are worth considering. The authoritative biography is Chuck Parsons and Marianne E. Hall Little, *Captain L. H. McNelly, Texas Ranger: The Life and Times of a Fighting Man* (Austin: State House, 2001).

25. Steele's detailed report is of special value because contemporary: Steele to Coke, July 10, 1874, Ledger 401-621, 297½.

26. McNelly to Steele, August 31, 1874, 401-392-9, TSA.

27. The quotation is by the anonymous "Pidge," who wrote a series of satirical letters from Clinton published in the Austin *Democratic Statesman*, for which he had once worked. Pidge remained anonymous in Ranger histories until his identity was exposed by historian Chuck Parsons as T. C. Robinson, whom McNelly elevated from sergeant to lieutenant in October 1874. Parsons, *"Pidge," A Texas Ranger from Virginia: The Life and Letters of T. C. Robinson, Washington County Volunteer Militia Company "A"* (Wolf City, Texas: Henington, 1985).

28. McNelly to Steele, August 31, 1874, 401-392-9, TSA.

29. McNelly to Steele, Clinton, October 18 and December 10, 1874, 401-392 -13 and -17. Events in DeWitt County are recounted in the Clinton letters of "Pidge," in Parsons, *Pidge*, chap. 2.

Chapter 9

1. Steele to Coke, July 1, 1876, *Report of the Adjutant General, 1875*, 8–9. Steele investigated conditions on the scene, traveling as far south as Brownsville. His report describes the Corpus Christi raid. See also *Report on Texas Frontier Troubles*, House Report 343, 44th Congress, 1st Session (Serial 1709), March 2, 1876, xix–xxi; William M. Hager, "The Nuecestown Raid of 1875: A Border Incident," *Arizona and the West* 1 (Autumn 1959): 258–70; and Paul S. Taylor, *An American-Mexican Frontier: Nueces County, Texas* (New York: Russell & Russell, 1934), 55–57.

2. SO 15, AGO, Austin, April 2, 1875, Ledger 401-1012, 80, TSA.

3. Coldwell to Jones, Hidalgo County, May 4, 1875, 401-393-6. TSA. Earlier reports in the same vein are in ibid. Coldwell's findings were reinforced by federal military officers, especially scouting reports forwarded by Col. Edward Hatch to AAG Department of Texas, Ringgold Barracks, December 6, 1874, in RG 94, 5543 AGO 1874, NARA. For Wallace's company, see Steele to Wallace, July 31, August 10 and 31, and September 14, 1874, and Steele to Justice of the Peace John Berney at Floresville, Wilson County, August 31, 1874, Ledger 401-621, 338, 352, 389, 390, and 420, TSA.

4. Steele to Coke, March 30, 1875, 301-94-24, TSA.

5. For Cortina's career after the 1859–1860 troubles, see Jerry D. Thompson, ed., *Juan Cortina and the Texas-Mexico Frontier, 1859–1877* (El Paso: Texas Western Press, 1994).

6. McNelly to Steele, Brownsville, August 13, 1875, 401-393-10, TSA, tells of the spy system.

7. Affidavit of Jesús Sandoval, Brownsville, May 3, 1875, *Report of the Adjutant General, 1875*, 19. Sandoval's affidavit is also in *Texas Border Troubles*, House Executive Document 64, 45th Congress, 2nd Session (Serial 1820), 1878, 83–84.

8. Quoted in Walter Prescott Webb, *The Texas Rangers: A Century of Frontier Defense* (1935; Austin: University of Texas Press, 1965), 243. Callicott's phonetically rendered manuscript is in the Webb Papers, CAH, UTA. Webb cleaned up the text for inclusion in his book. Of course McNelly never officially reported his torture of Mexicans, which is explicit in the accounts of Callicott and two other Rangers: Durham, *Taming the Nueces Strip*; and Jennings, *A Texas Ranger*.

9. Testimony of Ord, *Texas Border Troubles*, 95.

10. McNelly's official report, June 1875, has apparently disappeared from TSA but is printed in Webb, *Texas Rangers*, 239–41. Durham, Callicott, and "Pidge," cited previously, all give their accounts. Chuck Parsons and Marianne E. Hall Little, *Captain L. H. McNelly: Texas Ranger: The Life and Times of a Fighting Man* (Austin: State House Press, 2001), chap. 14. In hearings before a congressional committee in Washington, D.C., January 29, 1876, McNelly told of this affair: *Texas Border Troubles*, 14–15. Correspondence and affidavits concerning it are in ibid., 81–97.

11. Steele to Coke, July 1, 1875; Dwyer to Coke, August 14, 1875, in *Report of the Adjutant General, 1875*, 6–16. An appendix contains numerous affidavits to support the conclusions.

12. Randlett penned a very detailed report at Edinburg, December 1, 1875, in *Texas Border Troubles*, 92–95. Clendenin's report, Ringgold Barracks, December 5; and Alexander's report, Fort Brown, November 29, are in ibid., 90–91. McNelly to Steele, Brownsville, November 12, 1875, 401-393-14, TSA.

13. This account is drawn from the reports of Alexander, Clendenin, and Randlett cited in the previous footnote and from extended excerpts from McNelly's official report, November 22, 1875, in Webb, *Texas Rangers*, chap. 13. The original is recorded in the TSA as received by the AG but has disappeared since Webb used it. Callicott's account is in ibid. McNelly's telegram to Steele, November 20, 1875, is in 401-393-15, TSA. Durham and "Pidge," previously cited, also give extended accounts. Parsons and Little, *Captain L. H. McNelly*, chaps. 15–17. Wilkins, *The Law Comes to Texas*, 99–109. Durham, 119, quotes a dispatch from Colonel Potter relaying orders of Secretary of War William W. Belknap for Alexander to demand McNelly's return from Mexico and McNelly's answer to "Give my compliments to the Secretary of War and tell him and his United States soldiers to go to hell." Not surprisingly, no such documents have ever been discovered, but writers nonetheless delight in recounting the story.

14. Rippy, *The United States and Mexico*, chap. 17. Utley, *Frontier Regulars*, chap. 18.

15. For a biography of King Fisher, see Ovie Clark Fisher and Jeff C. Dykes, *King Fisher: His Life and Times* (Norman: University of Oklahoma Press, 1966). Parsons and Little, *Captain L. H. McNelly*, chap. 18.

16. Telegram, McNelly to Steele, Eagle Pass, June 4, 1876, 401-394-8, TSA. See also McNelly to Steele, Laredo, May 31, 1876, ibid.-7. *Report of the Adjutant General, 1876*, 9.

17. Both Jennings, *A Texas Ranger*, chap. 14, and Durham, *Taming the Nueces Strip*, 129–37, tell the Fisher story as participants but in probably exaggerated fashion. McNelly did not report in detail, but see *Report of the Adjutant General, 1876*, 9. He did give an account to a newspaper reporter, *San Antonio Daily Express*, June 17, 1876. Parsons and Little, *Captain L. H. McNelly*, chap. 18.

18. Gammel, *Laws of Texas*, 8:891–92, 1187. McNelly's testimony was reported by most newspapers, along with his commentary on King Fisher's misdeeds. See *San Antonio Daily Express* (news item and editorial), June 25, 1876.

19. Petition of July 23, 1876, in 401-394-9, TSA. W. H. King, "The Texas Ranger Service," in Dudley C. Wooten, ed., *A Comprehensive History of Texas, 1685–1897* (Dallas: William G. Scarff, 1898), 2:352. A competent though overdrawn biography is Dora Neill Raymond, *Captain Lee Hall of Texas* (Norman: University of Oklahoma Press, 1940).

20. Durham, *Taming the Nueces Strip*, 158, 161–62.

21. GO 4, AGO, Austin, January 18, 1877, Ledger 401-984, 52, TSA. *Galveston News*, February 6, 1877.

22. Parsons and Little, *Captain L. H. McNelly*, chaps. 19–20.

23. C. L. Sonnichsen, *I'll Die before I'll Run: The Story of the Great Feuds of Texas* (New York: Devin-Adair, 1962; Lincoln: University of Nebraska Press, 1988), 90–115. Parsons, "The DeWitt County Feud." Raymond, *Captain Lee Hall*, chap. 7.

24. W. R. Friend to Steele, Cuero, May 27, 1877, 401-395-12, TSA.

25. The most authoritative biography of Hardin is Leon Metz, *John Wesley Hardin: Dark Angel of Texas* (El Paso: Mangan, 1996). While in prison, Hardin himself wrote a self-justifying autobiography, which was found among his papers after his death in 1895 and published by his family in 1896 as *The Life of John Wesley Hardin as Written by Himself* (Norman: University of Oklahoma Press, 1961). Deftly separating Hardin's fictions from probable truths, Metz makes excellent use of the book as a source. Much valuable detail of the Comanche episode is related in Mollie Moore Godbold, "Comanche and the Hardin Gang," *SWHQ* 67 (July 1963): 55–77; (October 1963): 247–66.

26. Gammel, *Laws of Texas*, 8:561.

27. Duncan's critical role in the capture of Hardin is authoritatively related in a deeply researched study by Rick Miller, *Bounty Hunter* (College Station, Texas: Creative, 1988), chap. 4. Hall gives his memory of the preliminaries in *San Antonio Daily Express*, September 12, 1895, but he could not tell of the capture itself.

28. Official records of this mission are strangely sparse. If Armstrong submitted an official report to Hall or Steele, it has gone astray. Hall tells of his intent to join in the expedition in Hall to Steele, September 1, 1877, 401-396-5. Armstrong's accident is reported in Telegram, Hall to Steele, May 29, 1877, 401-1157-17, TSA. Based on contemporary newspaper accounts and the testimony of participants, Miller, *Bounty Hunter*, chap. 4; Metz, *John Wesley Hardin*, chap. 9; and Chuck Parsons, *The Capture of John Wesley Hardin* (College Station, Texas: Creative, 1978), have authoritatively reconstructed the story.

29. "Texas, by God!" is recounted in Webb, *The Texas Rangers*, 299–301. His source is an account written by one of Armstrong's two sons, Tom, in 1934. I have examined this document in the Webb Papers, Box 2M275, CAH, UTA. In a transmittal letter to his brother Charles, manager of the Armstrong Ranch in South Texas, Tom wrote that he had heard his father tell this story twice, once in 1905 and again in 1910. So colorful a detail would likely have remained in John Armstrong's memory and taken its place in his telling of Hardin's arrest. Not without misgivings, I have included it.

30. The only surviving official records of the Armstrong mission are six telegrams to Steele, August 23, 24 (three), and 25 (two), 1877, in 401-396-4, TSA.

31. Metz, *John Wesley Hardin*, chaps. 21–28.

32. Hall to Steele, Cuero, January 1, 1878, 401-396-14, TSA.

33. Hall's many reports detailing the activities of his Rangers from 1877 to 1880 are in 401-395, -396, -397, and -398, TSA. Raymond, *Captain Lee Hall of Texas*, chaps. 11–14.

34. Hall to Steele, Eagle Pass, May 16, 1877, 401-395-12. Telegram, Hall to Steele, May 16, 1877, 401-1157-17, TSA. Judge, Clerk, and Commissioners of Maverick County to Governor R. B. Hubbard, Eagle Pass, May 17, 1877, 401-395-13, TSA. Hall to Steele, Castroville, July

28, 1877, ibid.-17. Lt. Pat Dolan to Maj. John B. Jones, Uvalde, November 22, 1877, 401-396-10. Capt. Neal Coldwell to AG John B. Jones, Dimmit County, June 28, 1879, 401-398-9. Hall to Jones, Carrizo Springs, Dimmit County, August 8, 1879, ibid.-11. Hall to Jones, Cuero, September 20, 1879, ibid.-12. Hall to Jones, San Diego, November 20, 1879, ibid.-15. Dykes and Fisher, *King Fisher*, chaps. 11–12. Their book relies heavily on Durham, Jennings, and other reminiscent sources of dubious value, but it sets forth the legal sequence as revealed in court records.

35. Fisher and Dykes, *King Fisher*, chaps. 13–15.

Chapter 10

1. Kerr County Justice of the Peace A. McFarland to Jones, Kerrville, March 26, 1877; Blackburn to Jones, Lampasas, March 30, 1877; Jones to Blackburn, Austin, April 1, 1877; and Blackburn to Jones, Burnet, April 6, 1877, 401-395-7 and -8, TSA.

2. Jones to Steele, Camp Wood, Edwards County, April 16, 1877; Jones to Blackburn, Junction City, April 23, 1877; Telegrams, Jones to Steele, Junction, wired from Fort McKavett, April 24 and 27, 1877; Jones to Steele, Fredericksburg, April 28, 1877; Jones to Steele, Fort McKavett, May 6, 1877, 401-395-9, -10, and -11, TSA.

3. Jones to Steele, Fort McKavett, May 6, 1877, 401-395-11, TSA.

4. Ibid.

5. C. L. Sonnichsen, *I'll Die before I'll Run: The Story of the Great Feuds of Texas* (New York: Devin-Adair, 1962; Lincoln: University of Nebraska Press, 1988), 125–49. James B. Gillett, *Six Years with the Texas Rangers* (New Haven: Yale University Press, 1925), chap. 7. Gillett was a Ranger sergeant in the Reynolds detail. Jerry Sinise, *Pink Higgins, the Reluctant Gunfighter, and Other Tales of the Panhandle* (Quanah, Texas: Nortex, 1973). Bill O'Neal, *The Bloody Legacy of Pink Higgins* (Austin: Eakin, 1999). Wilkins, *The Law Comes to Texas*, 130–33. I have also profited from two unpublished manuscript articles by Lampasas historian Jeff Jackson, who kindly made them available to me: "Gunfight in the Lampasas Saloon" and "The Horrell-Higgins Feud" (both April 1997).

6. Sparks to Jones, Lampasas, March 30, 1877, 401-395-7, TSA.

7. O'Neal, *Pink Higgins*, 44–48, reconstructs the battle, complete with map. Jones to Steele, Lampasas, June 11 and 15; and Jones to Sparks, June 15, 1877, 401-395-14, TSA.

8. My account is based on sources previously cited plus Jones to Steele, July 6, 11, 12, 18, 22, 25, 28, and 31, 401-395-16 and -17, TSA. See also Reynolds's record of operations for July 1877, in ibid.-17. The letters exchanged by the feudists, undoubtedly written by Jones, are in 17. Reynolds gave his account of the arrest of the Horrells to the *Lampasas Dispatch*, August 9, 1877, reprinted in Sinise, *Pink Higgins*, 36–37.

9. Sinise, *Pink Higgins*. Sonnichsen, *I'll Die before I'll Run*, 145–49. O'Neal, *Pink Higgins*, chap. 5. Sam's death is from obituary in *The Humboldt Standard*, August 4, 1936, copy furnished by Jeff Jackson.

10. The Bass literature is voluminous, but I have relied chiefly on the exhaustively researched and definitive biography by Rick Miller, *Sam Bass and Gang* (Austin: State House, 1999). See also Wilkins, *The Law Comes to Texas*, chap. 6. Lengthy accounts of the chase appeared in the *Galveston News*, July 21 and 24, 1878.

11. Steele to Jones, Austin, April 11 and 12, 1878, 401-1159-7, TSA.

12. Telegram, Jones to Steele, Dallas, April 16, 1878, 401-1159-8, TSA. Jones to Denton County Sheriff W. T. Eagan, Dallas, April 28, 1878, 401-397-2, TSA.

13. The "bargain" is recorded in Memorandum of U.S. District Attorney Andrew J. Evans in regard to James Murphy, Tyler, May 21, 1878, 401-1159-7, TSA. Murphy tells how the bargain was arranged in a statement dated Austin, July 26, 1878, in ibid. The sequence is thoroughly detailed by Miller, *Sam Bass and Gang*, 201–3.

14. The convergence of Rangers and outlaws on Round Rock is set forth in Miller, *Sam Bass and Gang*, chap. 15. The flurry of telegrams sent by and to Jones are in 401-397-8, TSA. Almost twenty years later, Lee Hall gave a detailed account that fits nicely with other evidence: *San Antonio Daily Express*, September 12, 1895.

15. Gillett, *Six Years with the Texas Rangers*, chap. 9. Gillett was a Ranger sergeant in the Reynolds detail.

16. Steele to Jones, July 21, 1878, 401-397-8, TSA.

17. Miller, 263, discusses the evidence and reaches the conclusions I have built into the narrative: Herold killed Bass, Ware killed Barnes.

Chapter 11

1. The standard history is C. L. Sonnichsen, *The El Paso Salt War* (El Paso: Texas Western Press, 1961). See also Sonnichsen's *Pass of the North: Four Centuries on the Rio Grande* (El Paso: Texas Western Press, 1968), chaps. 15-16. A mass of firsthand evidence is *El Paso Troubles in Texas*, House Executive Document 93, 45th Congress, 2nd Session (Serial 1809), 1878. This is the report of a commission composed of two army officers and Major Jones charged with investigating the salt war. It contains the testimony and affidavits of most of the principals and copies of dozens of official documents. Official documents are also in *Relations of the United States with Mexico*, House Executive Document 701, 45th Congress, 2nd Session (Serial 1824), 1878. Col. Edward Hatch, commanding the District of New Mexico, and Lt. Col. William H. Lewis, one of the commission members, submitted separate reports in *Report of the Secretary of War, 1878*, 50-57. The towns and populations are given by longtime residents J. P. Hague and J. A. Zabriski in *El Paso Troubles*, 50 and 53.

2. Nicholas P. Houser, "Tigua Pueblo," in William C. Sturtevant, ed., *Handbook of North American Indians* (Washington, D.C.: Smithsonian Institution, 1979), 9:336-42. Visiting Ysleta in 1881, anthropologist (and army officer) Capt. John G. Bourke found vestiges of the Tigua heritage and pride that the people had served the U.S. Army as "Pueblo scouts" in the campaigns of 1879-1880 against the Apache Victorio. Lansing B. Bloom, ed., "Bourke on the Southwest," *New Mexico Historical Review* 13 (April 1938): 204-9.

3. W. H. Timmons, "La Isla," *The New Handbook of Texas* (Austin: Texas State Historical Association, 1996), 4:12.

4. Hatch to AAG Department of the Missouri, El Paso, January 11, 1878, in *Report of the Secretary of War, 1878*, 52. Hague and Zabriski, *El Paso Troubles*, 50 and 53, offer the most lucid explanations.

5. Kerber to AG Steele, Ysleta, October 5, 1877, *El Paso Troubles*, 151-52. *Mesilla Independent*, October 6, 1877. The editor, Albert J. Fountain, had been a participant in earlier battles over the lakes and had represented El Paso in the Texas state senate. El Paso factionalism grew so deadly, however, that he moved to New Mexico and established the *Independent*. Because of Fountain's background, his newspaper is a good source for the developing crisis.

6. I infer this from Ranger Capt. George W. Baylor, introduced in the next chapter, who called Barela "the *pueblo cacique*." George Wythe Baylor, *Into the Far, Wild Country*, ed. Jerry D. Thompson (El Paso: Texas Western Press, 1996), 287.

7. Many participants in this affair gave their testimony, but the most detailed and reliable is that of Father Bourgade. *El Paso Troubles*, 99-100. A good account of the origins of the dispute and the Howard ordeal is collector of customs S. C. Slade to secretary of the treasury, El Paso, October 22, 1877, in *Relations of the United States with Mexico*, 279-80. Howard told his own story in detail in *Mesilla Independent*, October 6, 1877, which also printed the text of the document he had signed.

8. Testimony of Judge Blacker, *El Paso Troubles*, 123. Telegram, Blacker and Kerber to Hubbard, El Paso, September 14, 1877, 401-396-6, TSA.

9. None of this background appears in *El Paso Troubles* nor in any of the histories of the salt war. For the larger picture see Chapter 9. For Rucker's assignment and reports, see RG 393, LR District of New Mexico, 1877, NARA, available on microfilm as M1088, Reels 30–31.

10. Telegram, Rucker to AAAG District of New Mexico, El Paso, October 4, 1877, *Relations of the United States with Mexico*, 277.

11. The words are those of Brig. Gen. John Pope, Hatch's superior as department commander at Fort Leavenworth, in telegram, Platt (AAG) to CO District of New Mexico, October 13, 1877. They were repeated many times by Pope both to his superiors and subordinates, and they were embraced by Pope's superior, Lt. Gen. Philip H. Sheridan, division commander in Chicago. The telegram of October 13 is in RG 94, LR OAG, NARA, available on microfilm as M666, "Mexican Border Troubles," Reel 203, Frame 122. Many documents not included in the published volume, *El Paso Troubles*, are found in this compilation, in Reels 200–203.

12. Rucker to AAAG District of New Mexico, El Paso, October 11, 1877, *El Paso Troubles*, 277–78.

13. There were ample witnesses to the murder. For the best of the testimony, see *El Paso Troubles*, 59–64. See also detailed account in *Mesilla Independent*, October 18, 1877.

14. Virtually all the records of the Texas AG relating to the salt war are reproduced in *El Paso Troubles*. Governor Hubbard was kept abreast of developments by Sheriff Charles Kerber, District Judge Allen Blacker, and various citizens of El Paso.

15. Bourgade, *El Paso Troubles*, 99–100. Jones's report contains his account, ibid., 26. For the formation of García's company, see García, March 2, 1878, ibid., 101.

16. Magoffin, *El Paso Troubles*, 79. Howard to Jones, Mesilla, November 13, 1877, Walter Prescott Webb Papers, Box 2R288, Transcripts of AGO Correspondence, vol. 5, p. 103, CAH, UTA. This document, and many others relating to the salt war, have disappeared from the TSA since Webb researched there.

17. Jones, *El Paso Troubles*, 26. Joseph Magoffin, ibid., 81.

18. Magoffin, *El Paso Troubles*, 81. Jones wired Steele from San Elizario on November 22 that he was leaving for Austin this day. Ibid., 155.

19. Bourgade to Jones, San Elizario, December 11, 1877, Walter Prescott Webb Papers, Box 2R288, Transcripts of AGO Correspondence, vol. 5, p. 132, CAH, UTA. This document has not been found in the TSA.

20. This and what follows rest largely on Sheriff Kerber's lengthy report to the governor of December 25, 1877, and Tays's report to Jones of December 20, both in *El Paso Troubles*, 76–79 and 157–58. The accounts of other first-hand witnesses and second-hand authorities are scattered through this frustratingly unorganized volume. Additional documents appear in RG 94, LR OAG, NARA, M666, "Mexican Border Troubles," Reel 204.

21. Howard to Jones, Mesilla, November 13, 1877, Walter Prescott Webb Papers, Box 2R288, Transcripts of AGO Correspondence, vol. 5, p. 103, CAH, UTA.

22. Blair to AAG Department of the Missouri, El Paso, December 19, 1877, *El Paso Troubles*, 55–57. Account of Ranger Cpl. H. O. Matthews, *Mesilla Independent*, January 5, 1878.

23. The most detailed account of what occurred within the Mexican ranks is by Juan Nepomuceno García, *Mesilla Independent*, January 17, 1878, reprinted in *El Paso Troubles*, 96–98. In the article he claims to have witnessed all that he describes. In his testimony before the investigating commission, he admits that he did not, but obtained some details from those who did. Nevertheless, his is the best evidence we have, is not contradicted by other evidence, and meets the test of plausibility.

24. Testimony of Gregorio García, *El Paso Troubles*, 37. "Franklin," from El Paso, December 21, 1877, in *Mesilla Independent*, December 22, 1877 (but issue delayed two days for further dispatches from the scene).

25. Blair to AAG Department of the Missouri, El Paso, December 19, 1877, *El Paso Troubles*, 56–57. Kerber to Hubbard, December 25, 1877, is authority for some of the conversation, which it was to Blair's advantage to minimize in light of later events. Blair wanted very much to believe that it was a "local affair," as Kerber put it, so he could avoid taking any action. But the same could be said also of Generals Pope and Sheridan and, in Washington, General in Chief William T. Sherman and Secretary of War George W. McCrary.

26. This seems the most likely scenario, based on Tays's report and Juan García's newspaper account, previously cited, together with the testimony of Vidal García and Ranger John K. Ball, the latter two in *El Paso Troubles*, 73 and 103. Matthews in *Mesilla Independent*, January 5, 1877.

27. E. Stine's testimony, *El Paso Troubles*, 66, explains how both Ellis, as sheriff and tax collector, and Atkinson, as his heavy-handed deputy, had made themselves odious to the people and, as school trustees, had tangled with Father Borajo over the education of Catholic children.

28. The description of the three executions comes from Juan N. García, in *El Paso Troubles*, 98.

29. Mary Antonio Cooper, wife of Price Cooper, one of the Rangers, *El Paso Troubles*, 74. This is confirmed by Tays in his report of December 20, p. 158.

30. This is Tays's report of December 20, but the sentence quoted was omitted from the printed version in *El Paso Troubles*. For copy of the original, which was not found in the TSA, see Walter Prescott Webb Papers, Box 2R288, Transcripts of AGO Correspondence, 5, pp. 147–49, CAH, UTA. A valuable summary of the San Elizario episode, although wrong in some aspects, is customs collector S. C. Slade to secretary of the treasury, El Paso, December 20, 1877, *Relations of the United States with Mexico*, 281–82.

31. These telegrams, dated between December 12 and December 18, are in *El Paso Troubles*, 144–48. For the army's new reasoning, see Gen. William T. Sherman to Lt. Gen. Philip H. Sheridan, December 15, 1877, RG 94, LR OAG, NARA, M666, "Mexican Border Troubles," Reel 203, Frame 65.

32. The sequence is established in Kerber's report of December 25, 1877, *El Paso Troubles*, 149. Telegrams and orders governing the movement of troops are in RG 94, LR OAG, M666, "Mexican Border Troubles," Reel 203.

33. Hatch to Col. John H. King, Santa Fe, February 8, 1878, *El Paso Troubles*, 87. For Kerber's version, see his report of December 25, ibid., 79 and 117. For Tays, 115–16. For Justice of the Peace Demitrio Urtiago, 89. See also customs collector S. C. Slade to secretary of the treasury, El Paso, December 24, 1877, *Relations of the United States with Mexico*, 282.

34. For rape and other outrages, see *El Paso Troubles*, 95, 113–14. For discharge, see Steele to Kerber, January 10, 1878, ibid., 158.

35. Relevant correspondence is appendix A of the commission's report, *El Paso Troubles*, 47–49.

36. Jones to Kerber, Austin, May 7, 1878; Jones to Lt. J. A. Tays, Austin, July 12, 1878; Tays to Jones, Ysleta, July 15 and November 6, 1878; Bryan Callaghan to Jones, San Elizario, December 9, 1878, 401-397-3, -7, -15, and -17, TSA.

37. Sonnichsen, *Pass of the North*, 210. Sgt. M. Ludwick to Jones, Ysleta, January 6, 1879, 401-398-1, TSA.

38. For the Chicano perspective, see Rodolfo Acuña, *Occupied America: A History of Chicanos*, 3d ed. (New York: HarperCollins, 1988), 47–49. Mary Romero, "El Paso Salt War: Mob Action or Political Struggle?" *Aztlan* 16 (1985): 119–43, promotes the notion of

political struggle, which of course it was; but, except for Acuña, she cites only the traditional sources I have used, as indeed does Acuña. Note, however, that *El Paso Troubles* contains a wealth of testimony by Mexican participants, observers, and victims. The basic conclusion is my own.

Chapter 12

1. George Wythe Baylor, *Into the Far, Wild Country: True Tales of the Old Southwest,* ed. Jerry D. Thompson (El Paso: Texas Western Press, 1996), 1, 275. This is a collection of articles Baylor wrote for an El Paso newspaper at the turn of the century. Thompson's introduction is a concise biography of Baylor, and his annotations are valuable.

2. Frederick Wilkins, *The Law Comes to Texas: The Texas Rangers, 1874–1901* (Austin: State House, 1999), 175–77.

3. Thompson's introduction to *Into the Far, Wild Country.* For Baylor's application, supported by sixteen signatures, see Baylor to Gov. O. M. Roberts, San Antonio, February 3, 1879, in Dorman H. Winfrey and James M. Day, eds., *The Indian Papers of Texas and the Southwest, 1825–1916* (Austin: Texas State Historical Association, 1995), 4:412–14.

4. James B. Gillett, *Six Years a Texas Ranger, 1875–1881* (New Haven: Yale University Press, 1925) 140–49.

5. Grady E. McCright and James M. Powell, *Jessie Evans: Lincoln County Badman* (College Station, Texas: Creative, 1983). Ed Bartholomew, ed., *Jesse Evans: A Texas Hide-Burner* (Houston: Frontier Press of Texas, 1955). Leon C. Metz, *John Selman: Gunfighter* (Norman: University of Oklahoma Press, 1980).

6. Capt. Neal Coldwell to Jones, Fort Davis, July 10, 1880; Fort Davis merchants to Jones, Fort Davis, May 21, 1880; Presidio County Attorney John M. Dean to Gov. O. M. Roberts, Fort Davis, May 21, 1880 (with petition); telegrams, Pecos County Judge G. M. Frazer to Jones, Fort Stockton, May 24 and June 2, 1880, 401-399-11, -12, -14, and -17, TSA. McCright and Powell, Bartholomew, and Metz all narrate these events.

7. Telegrams, Jones to Frazer, May 25 and June 3, 1880; Jones to Caruthers, May 31, 1880 (two); Jones to Dean, May 31, 1880; Ledger 401-628, 210, 223, 224, 226, 232, TSA.

8. Telegram, Frazer to Roberts, Fort Stockton, June 15, 1880; Sieker to Jones, Fort Stockton, June 15, 1880; Coldwell to Jones, Fort Davis, July 10, 1880, 401-399-13, -15, and -17, TSA.

9. Capt. Coldwell, still at Fort Davis, wrote a long description of the fight, and Capt. Dan Roberts forwarded Sieker's report, which is even more detailed and reliable. Coldwell to Jones, Fort Davis, July 10, 1880; Roberts to Jones, Camp Hancock, Menard County, July 12, 1880, 401-399-17, TSA.

10. Lt. C. L. Nevill to Jones, Musquiz Canyon, Presidio County, October 16 and 23, 1880, 401-400-4, Shackelford County Sheriff W. R. Cruger to Jones, Albany, July 2, 1880, 401-399-16, TSA. McCright and Powell, *Jesse Evans,* chaps. 14–15. Metz, *John Selman,* chap. 12.

11. Roberts to Jones, July 12, 1880, 401-399-17, TSA. Jones to Nevill (at Austin), July 12, 1880; Jones to Sieker (at Fort Davis), July 12, 1880; Jones to Coldwell (at Fort Davis), July 12, 1880; Jones to Roberts (at Fort McKavett), July 14 and 23, 1880; Jones to Caruthers (at Fort Davis), July 15, 1880, Ledger 401-628, 299, 300, 304, 314, 321-22, 354, TSA.

12. Dan L. Thrapp, *Victorio and the Mimbres Apaches* (Norman: University of Oklahoma Press, 1974).

13. Baylor penned a detailed account in 1900, plainly based on contemporary documents: *Into the Far, Wild Country,* 276–81. Gillett prepared a similarly detailed account: *Six Years in the Texas Rangers,* chap. 12. Jerry Thompson, editor of the Baylor articles, established that Gillett plagiarized parts of Baylor's newspaper articles.

14. Gillett, 157–58. Baylor gives a slightly different version.

15. Baylor to Jones, Ysleta, December 3, 1879, 401-398-16, TSA. Baylor, *Into the Far, Wild Country*, 284–91. Gillett, *Six Years in the Texas Rangers*, chap. 13. Gillett's account is largely plagiarized from Baylor's.

16. Gillett, *Six Years in the Texas Rangers*, 183–89.

17. Thrapp, *Victorio*, chap. 22.

18. SO 71, AGO, signed John B. Jones, September 8, 1880, 401-400-1, TSA.

19. Baylor to Jones, Ysleta, February 9, 1881; Nevill to Jones, Camp Mauske [Musquiz] Canyon, February 6, 7, and 8, 1881, 401-400-11, TSA. Baylor, *Into the Far, Wild Country*, 304–19.

20. Coldwell to Jones, Fort Davis, August 1, 1880, 401-399-19, TSA.

21. Gillett, *Six Years with the Texas Rangers*, chap. 16.

22. *Report of the Adjutant General, 1880*, 25. James M. Day, "El Paso's Texas Rangers," *Password* 24 (Winter 1979): 153–72.

23. Jerry Sinise, *George Washington Arrington: Civil War Spy, Texas Ranger, Sheriff and Rancher: A Biography* (Burnet, Texas: Eakin, 1979).

24. Frederick W. Rathjen, *The Texas Panhandle Frontier* (Austin: University of Texas Press, 1973), chap. 8. L. F. Sheffy, "Old Mobeetie–The Capital of the Panhandle," *West Text Historical Association Year Book* 6 (June 1930): 3–16.

25. Arrington to Jones, Sweetwater [the name until changed to Mobeetie, Indian for Sweetwater], June 18 and 21, July 12, 1879; Coldwell to Jones, Fort Griffin, July 17, 1879; Davidson to Gov. O. M. Roberts, Fort Elliott, June 25, 1879; Wheeler County commissioners Benjamin Williams, John Donnelly [sutler's clerk], and J. W. Huselby to Roberts, Fort Elliott [n.b. not Mobeetie], July 4, 1879, 401-398-9 and -10. Arrington to Davidson, Fort Elliott, June 18, 1879, 401-1159-12. TSA.

26. Arrington to Jones, Camp Roberts, Crosby County, September 11, 1879; Coldwell to Jones, Blanco Canyon, Crosby County, October 22, 1879, 401-398-12 and -14, TSA.

27. Arrington to Jones, Camp in Sand Hills NW corner of Gaines County, January 20, 1880, 401-1159-5. Arrington to Jones, Camp Roberts, February 9, 1880, 401-399-2. TSA.

28. Arrington to Jones, Camp Roberts, February 10, 1880; Sgt. W. C. Bradley to Jones, Camp Roberts, April 29, 1880; Judge E. R. Morris to Jones, Seymour, April 7, 1880; Arrington to Jones, Seymour, April 9, 17, 23 and May 8, 1880, 401-399-1, -7, -8, -9, and -13. B. E. Tower to Postal Inspector A. P. Foster, Worsham P.O., Wilbarger County, March 16, 1881; Arrington to Jones, Camp Roberts, April 30, June 18, 1881; Coldwell to Jones, Blanco Canyon, June 27, 1881, 401-400-14, -16, and -19, TSA.

29. Cf. *Dallas Daily Herald*, July 20, 1881.

Chapter 13

1. David C. Humphrey, *Austin* (Austin: Texas State Historical Association, 1997), 9–10 (quotations). Frederick W. Rathjen, "The Texas State House: A Study of the Building of the Texas Capitol Based on the Reports of the Capitol Building Commissioners," *SWHQ* 60 (April 1957): 433–62. J. Evetts Haley, *The XIT Ranch of Texas and the Early Days of the Llano Estacado* (1929; Norman: University of Oklahoma Press, 1967), chap. 4.

2. John S. Spratt, *The Road to Spindletop: Economic Change in Texas, 1875–1901* (Dallas: Southern Methodist University Press, 1955). Alwyn Barr, *Reconstruction to Reform: Texas Politics, 1876–1906* (Austin: University of Texas Press, 1971).

3. *Report of the Adjutant General, February 1882*, 26–27, 39–52. This report, the first of two for 1882, was issued three months after King's return from his western tour. Each of his annual reports contains examples of his legend-building effusions.

4. The sequence may be traced in the AG's biennial reports.

5. Robert W. Stephens, *Texas Ranger Sketches* (Dallas: privately published, 1972), 99–102.

6. Alonzo Van Oden, *Texas Ranger's Scrapbook*, ed. Ann Jenson (Dallas: Kaleidograph, 1936), 8.

7. Stephens, *Texas Ranger Sketches*, 144–46.

8. The quotation is from William W. Sterling, *Trails and Trials of a Texas Ranger* (Norman: University of Oklahoma Press, 1959), 367. Reports of McMurry and Sieker of railroad duty are scattered throughout 401-401 and -402, TSA.

9. McMurry to King, Colorado, May 1 and 31, June 30, 1882, 401-401-17, -18, and -19, TSA. See also McMurry to King, Colorado, April 4, 1882, and telegrams, McMurry to King, April 21 and 26, May 2, 1882 (first and last from Colorado, second from Ranger), 401-1159-23, TSA.

10. *Report of the Adjutant General, 1888*, 47–48.

11. King to George A. Helm, April 11, 1889, Ledger 401-1135, 682-86, TSA.

12. Stephens, *Texas Ranger Sketches*, 65-69. Stephens, *Walter Durbin: Texas Ranger and Sheriff* (Clarendon, Texas: Clarendon, 1970), 56–57. Van Oden, *Texas Ranger's Scrapbook*, 71. W. H. King, "The Texas Ranger Service and History of the Rangers," in Dudley C. Wooten, ed., *A Comprehensive History of Texas, 1685–1897* (Dallas: William G. Scarff, 1898), 2:349.

13. Jones to AG W. H. Mabry, Camp Hogg (Alpine), September 11, 1891; Jones to Mabry, El Paso, October 24, 1891; Jones to Mabry, Camp Hogg, November 2, 1891; Jones to Mabry, El Paso, April 4, 1892; Val Verde County Sheriff August S. Kieffer to Attorney General, Del Rio, October 23 and November 3, 1891, all in 401-421-2, -11, -17, and -20, TSA.

14. *Report of the Adjutant General, 1886*, 4–12, 54–55. Ruth A. Allen, *The Great Southwest Strike* (Austin: University of Texas Press, 1942).

15. Telegram, Erath County Judge J. L. Humphries to Gov. L. S. Ross, Stephenville, December 13, 1888; telegrams, McMurry to King, Gordon, December 20 and 28, February 2, 11, and 17, 1889, 401-413-13, -17, and -18. Erath County Deputy Sheriff F. W. Freeman to King, Stephenville, March 13, 1889; J. G. Watkins, Secretary-Treasurer, Palo Pinto Coal Mining Co., to Gov. L. S. Ross, Fort Worth, March 26, 1889; Harton Walker, president of Palo Pinto Co., to King, Fort Worth, March 28, 1889; McMurry to King, Strawn, April 6 and May 8, 1889, 401-414-1, -2, and -5. King to McMurry, February 15, 1889; King to Watkins, March 28, 1889, Ledger 401-1135, 579-80, 655. McMurry to King, Thurber, June 6 and July 2, 1889, 401-414-12 and -17. TSA. Marilyn D. Rhinehart, "Hunter, Robert Dickie," *The New Handbook of Texas* (Austin: Texas State Historical Association, 1996), 3:789.

16. Hunter to King, Coal Mines Junction, July 5, 1890; McMurry to King, Thurber, July 12, 1890; McMurry to King, Amarillo, October 7, 1890, 401-417-7 and -18.

17. R. D. Holt, "The Introduction of Barbed Wire into Texas and the Fence Cutting War," *West Texas Historical Association Year Book* 6 (1930): 72–88. Henry D. McCallum, "Barbed Wire in Texas," *SWHQ* 61 (October 1957): 207–19. Henry D. McCallum and Francis T. McCallum, *The Wire That Fenced the West* (Norman: University of Oklahoma Press, 1965). Wayne Gard, "The Fence-Cutters," *SWHQ* 51 (July 1947): 1–15.

18. *Report of the Adjutant General, 1884*, 34–43.

19. *Message of Governor John Ireland to the Eighteenth Legislature, Convened in Special Session, . . . January 8, 1884* (Austin: State Printer, 1884), copy in 301- 123-7, TSA. H. P. N. Gammel, comp., *The Laws of Texas, 1822–1897* (Austin: Gammel, 1898): 9:566–69.

20. Allen Pinkerton to Ireland, Chicago, March 9, 11, 12, 16, 21, and 27, April 7, 11, 23, and 29, May 9 and 14, 1884. T. N. Vallins to King, Brownwood, April 14 and 23, May 4 and 16, June 3, 1884. A. E. Kramer to King, Brownwood, March 10, April 9 and 14, 1884. Capt. J. T. Gillespie to King, Brownwood, March 13, April 23, May 14 and 31, 1884. Capt. George W. Baylor to King, Brownwood, March 16, 1884. All in 401-404-1, -2, -3, -5, -7, -9, -11, and -16, TSA.

21. King to Baylor, n.d. (c. March 6, 1884), Ledger 401-631, 152-54.

22. Carlton to King, Fort Chadbourne, March 7 and 29, April 22, May 14, 1884; Baylor to King, Runnels City, May 4 and 7, 1884, 401-404-2, -8, -10, and -11, TSA.

23. King to Baylor, May 12 and July 15, 1884, Ledger 401-631, 64-65, 424, TSA. See King's long analysis of fence cutting in *Report of the Adjutant General, 1884*, 16-22.

24. Odum to King, Chadbourne, February 13 and 24, 1885; Henry Luckett to King, Abilene, March 6, 1885; Gillespie to QM Capt. John Johnson, Abilene, March 12, 1885; Thomas N. Boylan to King, Farrell's Commercial Detective Agency, New Orleans, March 19 (three) and 28, September 25 (two), 1885, 401-406-4, -6 and -7. Odum to Ireland, Abilene, February 5, 1886, 401-407-18, TSA.

25. The quotation is from Aten's memoir, *Six and One-Half Years in the Ranger Service: Memoirs of Sergeant Ira Aten, Company D, Texas Rangers* (Bandera, Texas: Frontier Times, 1945), 20. King to Aten, August 26, 1886; King to Scott, September 6, 1886, Ledger 401-634, 69, 93. Banker Henry Ford to King, Brownwood, September 16, 1886, 401-408B-6. Scott to Sieker, Brownwood, December 12, 1886, 401-1160-4. Aten to Sieker, Camp Ross (near Uvalde), June 11, 1887, 401-410-8. TSA. *Report of the Adjutant General, 1886*, 66. Harold Preece, *Lone Star Man: Ira Aten, Last of the Old Texas Rangers* (New York: Hastings House, 1960), 130–42.

26. Aten to Sieker, Corsicana, August 20 and 31, September 1 and 17, October 8 and 15, 1888, 401-412-18, -19; -413-1, TSA. Aten, *Six and One-Half Years in the Ranger Service*, 20–22. Preece, *Lone Star Man*, chap. 14.

27. Gard, "Fence Cutters," 12–15.

28. Chuck Parsons and Gary P. Fitterer, *Captain C. B. McKinney and the Law in South Texas* (Wolfe City, Texas: Henington, 1993). Parsons has brought together official records, newspaper coverage, and other original sources to trace a story that surfaces only sporadically in the Ranger record.

29. The characterization is from Napoleon A. Jennings, *A Texas Ranger* (1899; Norman: University of Oklahoma Press, 1997), 50.

30. Hall's role is touched on, with some expense to truth, in Dora Neill Raymond, *Captain Lee Hall of Texas* (Norman: University of Oklahoma Press, 1940), 206.

31. King to Shely, June 19, 1884; King to E. F. Hall (at Laredo), July 5, 1884, Ledger 401-631, 348. Hall to Ireland and Hall to King, Laredo, July 4, 1884, 401-405-3 and -4. John A. Kerr (merchant) to Ireland, Cotulla, November 21, 1884; Petition of three judges and forty citizens to Ireland, Cotulla, November 13, 1884; LaSalle County commissioners, treasurer, attorney, and Sheriff McKinney to Ireland, November 26, 1884, 401-405B-6. King to Shely, June 4, 1885; King to Hall, June 29, 1885; King to Sieker, June 30, 1885, Ledger 401-632, 336, 371, 377. Shely to King, Uvalde, June 10, 1885; Hall to King, Laredo, July 1 (two letters) and 16, 1885, 401-406-15. King to Gov. L. S. Ross, August 26, 1887, Ledger 401-635, 262. All in TSA. See also *Dallas Daily Herald*, January 31, February 7, 9, and 10, 1885.

32. Parsons and Fitterer, 97–99, reconstruct the murder in detail.

33. Stephens, *Texas Ranger Sketches*, 131–33. Stephens, *Walter Durbin: Texas Ranger*, 15.

34. Schmitt to Sieker, January 4 and 20, 1887, 401-1160-4 and -6. Schmitt to Sieker, December 30, 1886; Schmitt to King, Cotulla, January 4, 18, 25, and 31, February 4, 10, and 21, 1887, 401-409, -9, -11, -12, -13, and -15. Stephens, *Walter Durbin*, 37–44. Durbin was one of the two Rangers with Schmitt when Crenshaw was killed. Students dispute whether Durbin or Grimes fired the fatal shot. Parsons and Fitterer, chaps. 13–15, treat these events in detail, with frequent quotation from original sources.

35. E. R. Lane to King, Cotulla, February 22, 1887, 401-409-12. King to Schmitt, February 21 and March 9, 1887, Ledger 401-634, 345, 374, TSA.

36. Jones to King, Cotulla, April 7, 21, and 25, 1890, 401-416-15 and -16, TSA.

37. For the broad application of the term *rinches*, see Américo Paredes, *"With His Pistol in His Hand": A Border Ballad and Its Hero* (Austin: University of Texas Press, 1958), 24. William Y. Sterling, who was reared in the border setting, makes the same point in *Trails and Trials of a Texas Ranger*, 510.

38. Lindsey to Sieker, Camp San Ambrosia, July 10, 1885, in *Report of the Adjutant General, 1886*, 60–61. See also King's account in ibid., 52–53, and in Wooten, *Comprehensive History*, 2:362–64. Aten's account is in *Six and One-Half Years in the Ranger Service*, 3–4. Senator E. F. Hall and Rep. E. A. Aten to King, Laredo, June 18, 1885; Sieker to King, Eagle Pass, July 1, 1885, 401-406-16 and -17, TSA.

39. C. L. Sonnichsen, *I'll Die before I'll Run: The Story of the Great Feuds of Texas* (1951; Norman: University of Oklahoma Press, 1988), 232–81.

40. *Report of the Adjutant General, 1888*, 8–9.

41. Judge J. M. Weston to Gov. L. S. Ross and Sheriff T. J. Garvey to Ross, Richmond, June 24, 1889; Jones to Sieker, Wharton, July 1, 1889; Jones to King, Richmond, July 12 and August 8, 1889, 401-414-15 and -16; -415-2, TSA. Sonnichsen places the Gibson killing on January 21 instead of June 21, which confuses his chronology and that of all who rely on him. Aten's oft-cited memoirs and biography introduce further confusion because he narrates his adventures without any reference to Captain Jones. Aten, *Six and One-Half Years in the Ranger Service*, 26–31. Preece, *Lone Star Man*, chap. 17.

42. No official report has been found in the AG's records. Sonnichsen, 260–65, gives a detailed account. Aten, 27–28, and Preece, 189–95, also have accounts.

43. Ibid. Judith Ann Benner, *Sul Ross: Soldier, Statesman, Educator* (College Station: Texas A&M Press, 1983), 171–73.

44. Sonnichesen, *I'll Die before I'll Run*, 274–77.

45. Aten to Sieker, Richmond, September 3, 1889; Jones to King, Boerne, September 9, 1889, 401-415-7, TSA. Sonnichsen, *I'll Die before I'll Run*, 271–72. Pauline Yelderman, "Jaybird-Woodpecker War," *New Handbook of Texas*, 3:917–18.

46. Joseph F. Combs, *Gunsmoke in the Redlands* (San Antonio: Naylor, 1968), chap. 19.

47. Judge James I. Perkins to Gov. John Ireland, Hemphill, February 8, 1886, 401-407-18. King to Scott and King to Senator William W. Weatherred, June 11, 1886, Ledger 401–633, 371, 372. Scott to Sieker, Hemphill, July 31 and August 1, 1886, 401-1160-4. All TSA.

48. Judge Perkins to King, Rusk, September 28, 1886; Scott to King, Brownwood, January 28, 1887, 401-408B-6; and -409-11. King to Scott, March 7, 1887, Ledger 401–634, 371–72. All TSA. *Report of the Adjutant General, 1886*, 55.

49. Weatherred to King, Hemphill, April 1, 1887; Scott to King, Hemphill, April 6, 1887; Dr. J. J. Nash to Sieker, Hemphill, May 20, 1887, 401-409-19; and -410-6. Dr. J. W. Smith to Sieker, Hemphill, May 19, 1887, 401-1160-6. All TSA. *Report of the Adjutant General, 1888*, 44, 46, 48. King later wrote that Scott and Brooks later killed Willis Conner, some of his sons, and a grandson, a rendering roughly according with the account of Combs, *Gunsmoke in the Redlands*. Combs does not identify the lawmen. See King, "Texas Ranger Service and History," in Wooten, *Comprehensive History*, 2:362. If King is correct, no trace of it appears in official records or in his annual reports. Interesting perspectives on the Conner battle, partly derived from Brooks, are in Sterling, *Trails and Trials of a Texas Ranger*, chap. 36.

Chapter 14

1. Lewis E. Daniell, *Personnel of the Texas State Government, with Sketches of Representative Men of Texas* (San Antonio: Maverick, 1892), 113–14. Alonzo Van Oden, *Texas Ranger Scrapbook*, ed. Ann Jenson (Dallas: Kaleidograph, 1936), 9.

2. H. P. M. Gammel, comp., *The Laws of Texas, 1822–1897* (Austin: Gammel., 1898), 10:113, 516, 850, 1476.

3. *Report of the Adjutant General, 1891*, 8. The same encomium is repeated in ibid., 1892, 33. For a national perspective, see Richard Harding Davis, *The West from a Car-Window* (New York: Harper, 1892), 8–15.

4. Sterling, *Trails and Trials of a Texas Ranger*, chap. 36. Harold J. Weiss, "Brooks, John Abijah," *New Handbook of Texas* (Austin: Texas State Historical Association, 1996), 1:750. An admiring sketch appears in *The Texas Volunteer*, June 15, 1892, 6.

5. Gilbert M. Cuthbertson, "Catarino E. Garza and the Garza War," *Texana* 13 (1975): 335–48. More succinct and less florid is Cuthbertson's sketch of Garza in *New Handbook of Texas*, 3:106–7. The Díaz perspective is well presented in M. Romero (Mexican minister of finance), "The Garza Raid and Its Lessons," *North American Review* 155 (September 1892): 324–37.

6. Romero, "The Garza Raid and Its Lessons" recounts many newspaper exaggerations and falsehoods. A graphic view of the army operation is Richard Harding Davis, "Our Troops on the Border," which appeared in *Harper's Weekly* 36 (March 26, 1892), 7, and also as chapter 2 of *The West from a Car-Window*, published the same year. Especially insightful analyzes of people and conditions in South Texas were penned by state legislator John J. Dix of Benavides, a longtime resident, to Mabry, January 2 and 9, February 15, and May 12, 1892, 401-422-7 and -11; -423-15, TSA.

7. Sterling, *Trails and Trials of a Texas Ranger*, chap. 38. Harold J. Weiss, "Rogers, John Harris," *New Handbook of Texas*, 5:664. *The Texas Volunteer*, June 15, 1892, 6–7.

8. An adulatory biography, based on extensive interviews with McDonald, is Albert B. Paine, *Captain Bill McDonald, Texas Ranger: A Story of Frontier Reform* (New York: J. J. Little & Ives 1909; Austin: Eakin, 1986). The book contains much of value but also much embellishment that has left McDonald the best known of the captains. In similar vein is Madeline Mason-Manheim, *Riding for Texas: The True Adventures of Captain Bill McDonald of the Texas Rangers, as Told by Colonel Edward M. House to Tyler Mason* (New York: Rynal & Hitchcock, 1936). More balanced is Harold J. Weiss, "'Yours to Command': Captain William J. 'Bill' McDonald and the Panhandle Rangers of Texas" (Ph.D diss., Indiana University, 1980).

9. Weiss, "'Yours to Command'," 38–39.

10. E. B. Pendleton to Mabry, Amarillo, January 28, 1893, 401-427-2, TSA.

11. McDonald to Mabry, Matador, August 17, 1893; Quanah, August 21, 1893, 401-429-13 and -15. County Judge H. H. Campbell to Gov. J. S. Hogg, Matador, September 10, 1893, 301-140-230. TSA. Weiss, "'Yours to Command'," 87–93.

12. Weiss, "'Yours to Command'," 94–97, reconstructs the shooting in detail. Official papers are in 401-430-15; -431-1, -3, -6, and -11, TSA. Important affidavits of witnesses are printed in Michael G. Ehrle, comp. and ed., *The Childress County Story* (Childress: Ox Bow, 1971), chap. 40. I am indebted to Harold Weiss for providing me a copy of this obscure publication.

13. Hunter to Mabry, Thurber, June 10, 1894; McDonald to Mabry, June 13, 1894, 401-432-8 and -11, TSA. This Thurber disturbance produced voluminous documentation in the form of long letters as well as affidavits of both managers and laborers, in 401-432-8, -11, -12, -14, -15, -18, and -19, TSA.

14. Brooks to Mabry, Temple, July 13, 14, 15, and 20, 1894; Hughes to Mabry, Temple, July 14, 16, 17, 18, and 23, 1894; McDonald to Mabry, Quanah, July 15, 1894, 401-433-5, -9, -10, -11, and -12, TSA.

15. T. S. Myers to Gov. John Ireland, Carlton, Hamilton County, May 29, 1884, 401-404-16, TSA. Billy Bob Lightfoot, "The Negro Exodus from Comanche County, Texas," *SWHQ* 56 (June 1953): 407–16. For this earlier mob action and its origins, see also John F. Pinney to AG W. H. King, Menardville, February 11, 1884; T. R. Nugent to Ireland, Stephenville, February 19, 1884; County Attorney M. F. Martin to Ireland, Stephenville, February 24,

1884, and to King, February 29, 1884; George W. Jenks (editor, *Stephenville Empire*) to Ireland, Stephenville, August 29, 1884; George W. Hollister to Ireland, Thrifty, Brown County, September 1, 1884; Attorneys H. H. Neil and Lee Young to King, Stephenville, October 19, 1884, 401-403-18, -19, and -20; -405-9 and -12; -405B-3, TSA.

16. C. L. Sonnichsen, *I'll Die before I'll Run: The Story of the Great Feuds of Texas* (1951; Norman: University of Oklahoma Press, 1988), 206–32.

17. Allison to Mabry, San Saba, June 29, 1896, 401-439-17. Mabry to McDonald (at Amarillo), July 30 and August 6, 1896; Mabry to Rogers (at Alice), August 6, 1896; Mabry to Sullivan (at Regency), August 21, 1896, Ledger 401-660, 52, 85, 86, 146. Sullivan to Mabry, San Saba, August 15, 17, and 26; Regency, September 14 and 17, 1896, 401-440-6, -10, -11, and -15, TSA. Sullivan wrote his own story of San Saba, portraying himself as dispatched by Governor Culberson and otherwise badly scrambling chronology and embellishing his role: W. John L. Sullivan, *Twelve Years in the Saddle for Law and Order on the Frontiers of Texas* (Austin: Von Boeckman Jones, 1909: Lincoln: University of Nebraska Press, 2001), chaps. 13–14.

18. Sullivan to Mabry, Regency, September 14 and 17 and November 13, 1896; San Saba, November 30, 1896, 401-440-15; -441-2 and -4, TSA.

19. Mabry to McDonald (at San Saba), April 2 and May 17, 1897; Mabry to Linden (at Llano), May 17, 1897, Ledger 401-662, 36–37, 111. McDonald to Mabry, San Saba, May 5, 6, 7, 14, 15, 18, 19, and 29, 1897; Allison to Mabry, San Saba, May 8, 1897; Linden to Mabry, Llano, May 11, 1897, 401-442-12, -13, -14, -15, and -16, TSA.

20. McDonald to Mabry, San Saba, June 23, July 3 and 4, 1897, 401-443-12, -16, and -17, TSA.

21. Much documentation is in 401-444 and -446, and Ledger 401-664, 8–9, 59, 60, 62, 111, 112, 149-50, 272, 297, TSA. Sonnichsen, *I'll Die before I'll Run*, 224–31, tells of Linden's confrontation with mobsters, based on an interview with Linden; this is corroborated by Sheriff E. T. Neal to AG Thomas Scurry, San Saba, May 17, 1899, 401-451-14, TSA. Richard Maxwell Brown, *Strain of Violence: Historical Studies of American Violence and Vigilantism* (New York: Oxford University Press, 1975), 292–95, points out that Lyndon B. Johnson was named in honor of W. C. Linden and adopted as his own much of Linden's aggressive method in dealing with bad men.

22. *Report of the Adjutant General, 1890*, 24–26. Robert W. Stephens, *Walter Durbin: Texas Ranger and Sheriff* (Clarendon, Texas: Clarendon, 1970), 70–71. Cpl. J. W. Durbin to Capt. L. P. Sieker, Alpine, May 9, 1889; Jones to Sieker, Uvalde, May 21, 1889; Fusselman to King, Alpine, June 5, 1889; Presidio County officials and state legislators to Gov. L. S. Ross, Presidio, June 29, 1889; Henry E. McCulloch to Ross, Shafter, October 27, 1889; Fusselman to King, Marfa, November 16 and 26 (Shafter); Fusselman to Sieker, Marfa, November 29, 1889; Jones to King, Del Rio, November 29, 1889; U.S. Marshal Paul Fricke to King, San Antonio, December 12, 1889; Fusselman to Sieker, Marfa, February 29, 1890; Fusselman to King, Marfa, April 2, 1890; Fusselman to Sieker, Marfa, April 9, 1890; Pvt. John R. Hughes to Sieker, Marfa, April 18, 1890, 401-414-9, -10, -11, and -12; -415-13, -17, and -20; -416-7, -15, and -16. King to Fusselman (at Marfa), November 7, 1889, and March 31, 1890; King to Jones (at Cotulla), May 3, 1890; King to S. J. Hensley (at Presidio), May 3, 1890 Ledger 401-438, 60, 417. TSA.

23. Jones to Mabry, Camp Hogg (Alpine), August 3 and 12, November 27, December 5, 1891, January 15, 1892; Jones to Gov. James S. Hogg, Camp Hogg, March 18, 1892; Special Ranger Ernest St. Leon to Mabry, Shafter, June 30, 1892; Jones to Mabry, Camp Hogg, June 30, 1892; County Judge F. E. Hunter to Hogg, El Paso, December 16, 1892; Jones to Mabry, Camp Cleveland, December 22 and 25, 1892; 401-420-15; 421-18; -422-1 -7, and -17;- 424-7; -426-14 and 15. TSA.

24. Below El Paso, the notoriously unstable Rio Grande had flooded so violently in the 1830s as to cut a new course south of the towns of Ysleta, Socorro, and San Elizario, cre-

ating La Isla between the old and new river beds. La Isla figured in the El Paso salt war of 1877 (chap. 11). In 1848 the Treaty of Guadalupe Hidalgo, ending the Mexican War, placed the international boundary in the middle of the Rio Grande and thus threw La Isla and its towns into Texas. In subsequent years, the ever-changing river caused endless confusion and complex questions of ownership and jurisdiction. In 1884 the United States and Mexico by treaty applied established international practice to the Rio Grande boundary: when the river changed course suddenly (avulsion), the boundary moved with it; when the river changed course slowly (erosion and accretion), the boundary remained in the abandoned channel. In the El Paso Valley, this happened so often that some segments of the boundary lay unseen and unmarked in long abandoned and overgrown river beds. Such a segment coincided erratically with the road from San Elizario to Socorro. I have dealt with this and other boundary questions in *Changing Course: The International Boundary, United States and Mexico, 1848–1963* (Tucson: Southwest Parks and Monuments Association, 1996).

25. Documentation for the Pirate Island affair is voluminous. The most thorough and reliable account was penned by George W. Baylor, Jones's father-in-law, long a resident of Ysleta, who knew all the characters, investigated carefully, and even drew a map of the battlefield: Baylor to Mabry, Ysleta, July 9, 1893, 401-428-21. Other important documents are Sgt. John R. Hughes to Mabry, Ysleta, July 1, 1893; Cpl. Carl Kirchner to Mabry, Ysleta, July 2, 1893; Sheriff F. B. Simmons to Mabry, El Paso, July 7, 1893; Gov. J. S. Hogg to Mabry, August 22, 1893 (transmitting diplomatic correspondence from Washington); Capt. J. R. Hughes to Mabry, Ysleta, September 4 and 6, 1893, 401-428-18, -19; -429-15 and -16. Mabry to Hughes (at Ysleta), September 2, 1893; Mabry to Hogg, September 9, 1893, Ledger 401-650, 388, 431-37. Acting Secretary of War to Secretary of State, September 19, 1893, enclosing Monthly Return of Capt. Frank Jones for June 1893 and Lt. H. W. Royden to Post Adjutant Fort Bliss, September 4, 1893, 301-140-232. All TSA.

26. Jones to Mabry, Ysleta, February 17, 1893, 401-427-9, TSA. Jones, still based at Alpine, was in Ysleta visiting his sick wife.

27. An admiring biography, which must be used with care, is Jack Martin, *Border Boss: Captain John R. Hughes, Texas Ranger* (San Antonio: Naylor, 1942). See also Virgil E. Baugh, *A Pair of Texas Rangers: Bill McDonald and John Hughes* (Washington, D.C.: Potomac Westerners Corral, 1970).

28. The first quotation is from Martin, 142; the second from Van Oden, *Texas Ranger Scrapbook*, 21.

29. The demands on Hughes's company and his responses are amply documented in the AG records, 401-430 through 401-454, TSA.

30. Jones to Mabry, Marathon, April 16, 1893; Hughes to Mabry, Ysleta, November 12 and 24, 1893, 401-427-21; -430-10 and -13, TSA.

31. Hughes to AG Thomas Scurry, Ysleta, July 18, 1900, 401-459-12, TSA.

32. Mabry to Jones (at Alpine), April 23 and 29, 1891, Ledger 401-640, 308, 350. Jones to Mabry, Camp Hogg, April 26 and May 8, 1891, 401-419-3 and -4. Hughes to Mabry, Ysleta, July 26, 1893, 401-429-7. All TSA.

33. Hughes's biographer, who drew on interviews with Hughes, weaves an elaborate tale of the Olguins' undoing. A secret operative, one "Diamond Dick" St. Leon (who does appear in the records), eliminated two Olguins, scared Jesús deep into Mexico, and provided a list of the men involved in the fight with Jones. Hughes's Rangers scooped them up and eventually saw them all hang. Most of this yarn is false or improbable and all undocumented, but it may rest on something Hughes recounted. Martin, *Border Boss*, 122–30.

34. Hughes to AG Thomas Scurry, Ysleta, March 9 and 14, 1899; Hughes to Capt. E. M. Phelps, March 14, 1899, 401-450-18, TSA. Leon C. Metz, *Pat Garrett: The Story of a Western*

Lawman (Norman: University of Oklahoma Press, 1974), 216–17. Douglas V. Meed, "Daggers on the Gallows: The Revenge of Texas Ranger Captain 'Boss' Hughes," *True West* 46 (May 1999): 44–49.

35. Leo N. Miletich, *Dan Stuart's Fistic Carnival* (College Station: Texas A&M Press, 1994). *Report of the Adjutant General, 1896*, 10–13. Charles M. Robinson III, *The Men Who Wear the Star: The Story of the Texas Rangers* (New York: Random House, 2000), chap. 16. Ample official documentation is in 401-438, TSA.

36. Sgt. H. G. Dubose, "Report of Rangers Work at Laredo Texas from March 19th to March 25th 1899," 401-450-22. Rogers to AG Thomas Scurry, Cotulla, c. June 30, 1900, 401-459-12, TSA. *Report of the Adjutant General, 1900*, 22.

37. Sterling, *Trails and Trials of a Texas Ranger*, 376.

38. Mabry to Hughes, McDonald, Rogers, and Brooks, April 19, 1898, Ledger 401-666, 39-42, TSA.

39. *Report of the Adjutant General, 1882*, 27–28.

40. Orange is amply documented in 401-453, -456, and 457, TSA, and *Report of the Adjutant General, 1900*, 22-23, 25. Hall County is documented in Ledger 401-676, 763; and 401-456, TSA. Weiss, "Yours to Command," 145–52.

41. Telegram, Sayers to Scurry, Fort Worth, May 22, 1900; Attorney General T. S. Smith to Sayers, Austin, May 24, 1900, 401-457-18 and -21, TSA.

42. *General Laws of the State of Texas, 1901*, 41–43. *Report of the Adjutant General, 1900*, 27, 127–31; *1902*, 28–29.

Chapter 15

1. *Report of the Adjutant General, 1908*, 15. AG to Ranger captains, December 31, 1908, 401-516-5, TSA.

2. The standard authority is Américo Paredes, *"With a Pistol in His Hand": A Border Ballad and Its Hero* (Austin: University of Texas Press, 1958). This work taps into both border folklore and conventional documents, including the records of Cortez's trials preceding conviction and his final pardon by the governor. It is frankly revisionist, designed to cast the Rangers in the worst light and the protagonist in the best, including his identity as a tenant farmer. More objective and also well researched is Richard J. Mertz, "'No One Can Arrest Me': The Story of Gregorio Cortez," *Journal of South Texas* 1 (1974): 1–17. William W. Sterling, *Trails and Trials of a Texas Ranger* (Norman: University of Oklahoma Press, 1958), chap. 48. Reflecting the minimal Ranger role, official records contain little relating to Cortez. Rogers sent three telegrams reporting his arrest and conveyance to San Antonio: 401-464-17 and -18, TSA. *Report of the Adjutant General, 1902*, 32–33.

3. Report of Captain J. A. Brooks in *Report of the Adjutant General, 1903*, 153–54. Brooks to Scurry, Saltillo, Cameron County, May 18 and June 2, 1902, 401-469-14 and -22. Brooks to Scurry, Brownsville, September 10, 11, 12, 13, and 18; October 5, 1902, 401-472-8, -9, -13, and -17. W. E. Caldwell to Brooks, Realitos, November 12, 1902; Judge Stanley Welch to Gov. J. D. Sayers, Corpus Christi, November 8, 1902; Scurry to Sayers, Austin, November 11, 1902, 401-473-6. All TSA. Brooks to Scurry, Brownsville, October 4, 1902, Walter Prescott Webb Papers, Box 2R289, Transcripts of AGO Correspondence, vol. 15, CAH, UTA. This important document was not found in the records at TSA. Sterling, *Trails and Trials of a Texas Ranger*, 321–26. For interpretations that contradict mine, see Américo Paredes, *"With His Pistol in His Hand": A Border Ballad and Its Hero* (Austin: University of Texas Press, 1958), 29–30; and Julian Samora, Joe Bérnal, and Albert Peña, *Gunpowder Justice: A Reassessment of the Texas Rangers* (Notre Dame, Ind.: Notre Dame University Press, 1979), 56–58.

4. Reports of Rogers and Brooks, *Report of the Adjutant General, 1904*, 155, 160–161. General Manager W. K. Gordon, Texas and Pacific Coal Co., to Gov. S.W.T. Lanham, Thurber, August 30, 1903; Erath County Sheriff Mack Creswell to Lanham, Thurber, September 1, 1903; Rogers to Hulen, Thurber, September 9, 11, 14, 17, 401-478-8, -11, -13, and -14, TSA. Rogers to Hulen, Thurber, n.d., September 19 and 21, 1903, Walter Prescott Webb Papers, Box2R289, Transcripts of AGO Correspondence, vol. 16, CAH, UTA. These documents were not found in Ranger records at TSA.

5. Brooks's report in *Report of the Adjutant General, 1904*, 155. Brooks to Hulen, Batson, January 24, February and 27, 1904; Hulen to Brooks (at Batson), February 13, 1904, 401-480-8, -13, -16, and -24, TSA. Sterling, *Trails and Trials of a Texas Ranger*, 326–31.

6. I have relied heavily on Harold J. Weiss, "'Yours to Command': Captain William J. 'Bill' McDonald and the Panhandle Rangers of Texas," (Ph.D diss., Indiana University, 1980), chap. 6; and Garna L. Christian, *Black Soldiers in Jim Crow Texas, 1899–1917* (College Station: Texas A&M Press, 1995), chap. 4. For a heroic portrayal of McDonald's role, full of material that arouses skepticism, see Albert B. Paine, *Captain Bill McDonald, Texas Ranger: A Story of Frontier Reform* (New York: J. J. Little & Ives., 1909; Austin: Eakin, 1986), chaps. 38–40. McDonald wrote a long, rambling, self-pitying report to Governor Lanham, undated but c. August 26, 1906, 401-496-6, TSA. Other relevant documents, dated from August 14–25, are in 401-495 and -496; and 301-215 and -219, TSA. See also Ben Procter, *Just One Riot: Episodes of Texas Rangers in the 20th Century* (Austin: Eakin, 1991), chap. 2.

7. Christian, *Black Soldiers in Jim Crow Texas*, 85–86. Two pioneering works that brought about the reparation effort of 1972 are Anne J. Lane, *The Brownsville Affair: National Crisis and Black Reaction* (Port Washington, N.Y.: Kennikat, 1971); John D. Weaver, *The Brownsville Raid* (New York: W. W. Norton, 1970); and Weaver, *The Senator and the Sharecropper's Son: Exoneration of the Brownsville Soldiers* (College Station: Texas A&M Press, 1997). Weaver flatly exonerates the soldiers.

8. Weiss, "'Yours to Command,'" 210–18. Extract from Monthly Report of Co. B for November 1907, Walter Prescott Webb Papers, Box 2R289, Transcripts of AGO Correspondence, vol. 16, CAH, UTA. This document does not appear in the Ranger records at TSA.

9. Weiss, "'Yours to Command,'" 220–22. W. E. Caldwell to Hulen, Falfurrias, September 8, 1906, 401-496-11, TSA.

10. Johnson to Newton, Amarillo, February 15, 1907, 401-499-6. Thomas to Johnson (at Colorado City), Amarillo, February 20, 1910, 401-498-3. Thomas to Johnson, March 1 and 11, 1907; Thomas and Murchison to Newton, Amarillo, March 3, 1907, 401-499-11. Newton to Johnson (at Colorado City), March 9 and 11, 1910, 401-499-11 and -16, TSA.

11. Johnson to Newton, Weatherford, November 30, 1908, Walter Prescott Webb Papers, Box 2R290, Transcripts of AGO Correspondence, vol. 17, CAH, UTA. This document does not appear in the Ranger records at TSA. Johnson to Newton, Weatherford, December 9, 1908; Newton to Johnson (at Weatherford), December 11, 1908, 401-515-25, TSA.

12. Thomas to Gov. T. M. Campbell, Amarillo, December 28, 1908; W. A. Stewart to Campbell, Amarillo, January 6, 1909, 401-516-7 and -9, TSA.

13. Ross to Newton, Amarillo, January 9 and 15, 1909; Newton to Ross, Amarillo, January 13, 1909, 401-516-15, -16, and -20. Ross to Newton, Amarillo, February 14 and 25, 1909, 401-517-14 and 401-520-6. Ross to Newton, Amarillo, June 12 and July 3, 1909, 401-520-4 and 401-521-3. Telegrams, all October 16, 1909: Ross to Newton, Amarillo; AAG Phelps to Newton (at El Paso, with governor), Austin; Newton to Phelps, El Paso; Rogers to Phelps, El Paso; Phelps to Ross, Austin. Ross to Phelps, Amarillo, October 17, 1909; Rogers to Newton, Amarillo, October 19, 1909, 401-523-14 and -15. TSA.

14. Telegram 5, Hughes to Newton, Ysleta, October 28, 1909; Ross to Newton, Amarillo, October 29, 1909, 401-523-19 and -20. Ross to Newton, Amarillo, November 10, 1909; Hughes to Newton, Amarillo, November 13, 1909; Pastor L. C. Kirkes to Newton, Amarillo, November 15, 1909, 401-524-2, -4, and -5, TSA. Jack Martin, *Border Boss: Captain John R. Hughes, Texas Ranger* (San Antonio: Naylor, 1942), 180.

15. Newton to Ross (at Ysleta), February 12, 1910, Walter Prescott Webb Papers, Box 2R290, Transcripts of AGO Correspondence, vol. 18, CAH, UTA. This document was not found in Ranger records at TSA.

16. *Report of the Adjutant General, 1910*, 8–9.

17. W. W. Turney to AG, El Paso, August 30, 1906, 401-496-10, TSA.

Chapter 16

1. The variety of personalities and rhythm of company life emerges in the diary of one of Capt. Sam McMurry's men: John Miller Morris, *A Private in the Texas Rangers: A. T. Miller of Company B, Frontier Battalion* (College Station: Texas A&M Press, 2001).

2. Walter Prescott Webb, *The Texas Rangers: A Century of Frontier Defense* (1935; Austin: University of Texas Press, 1965), 79, xv–xvi.

3. Theodore R. Fehrenbach, *Lone Star: A History of Texas and the Texans* (New York: Macmillan, 1968), 472–473.

4. For Outlaw's death, see Hughes to Mabry, Ysleta, April 6, 1894, 401-1160-13. For Capt. Frank Jones's testimonial to Outlaw's qualities when sober, see Jones to Mabry, Alpine, June 21, 1892, 401-424-8, TSA. Another glowing tribute is Alonso Van Oden, *Texas Ranger Scrapbook*, ed. Ann Jenson (Dallas: Kaldidograph, 1936), 40–41.

5. Américo Paredes, *"With His Pistol in His Hand": A Border Ballad and Its Hero* (Austin: University of Texas Press, 1958), 28. The reference is to the 1939 film *Northwest Mounted Police*, in which Gary Cooper as a Texas Ranger trails a fugitive to Canada.

6. Julian Samora, Joe Bërnal, and Albert Peña, *Gunpowder Justice: A Reassessment of the Texas Rangers* (Notre Dame, Ind.: Notre Dame University Press, 1979), 166.

7. Paredes, *"With His Pistol in His Hand,"* 24–25.

8. For an informed discussion, see Frederick Wilkins, *The Legend Begins: The Texas Rangers, 1823–1845* (Austin: State House Press, 1996), 202–4. My own research bears out Wilkins's conclusion that Enchanted Rock is a myth.

9. Quoted in Mike Cox, *Texas Ranger Tales II* (Plano, Texas: Republic of Texas Press, 1999), 230.

10. *Texas Volunteer*, June 15, 1892.

11. Cox, *Texas Ranger Tales II*, 265–79.

12. Cox, *Texas Ranger Tales II*, 249–79, presents an excellent chapter on "Hollywood Rangers." Anyone with a search engine can type in "Lone Ranger" and access informative Web sites. "Texas Rangers," however, will usually yield abundant information about a baseball team.

13. Frank R. Prassel, *The Western Peace Officer: A Legacy of Law and Order* (Norman: University of Oklahoma Press, 1972), chap. 6. H. Kenneth Bechtel, *State Police in the United States: A Socio-Historical Analysis* (Westport, Conn.: Greenwood, 1995), 31–39. Harold J. Weiss Jr., "Organized Constabularies: The Texas Rangers and the Early State Police Movement in the American Southwest," *Journal of the West* 34 (January 1995): 27–33.

SOURCES

THIS STUDY RESTS heavily on the official records in the Archives Division of the Texas State Library. The richest record group is 401, correspondence of the adjutant general of Texas. Record group 301 contains the correspondence of the governors of Texas and has many Ranger documents that do not appear in the AG files. Finally, especially for the earlier period, record group 307 contains the executive record books of the governors. Voluminous finding aids have been compiled for these collections and may be obtained from the archives or downloaded from the Texas State Library Web site. Also used at the archives were the Andrew Jackson Houston Papers, the Samuel H. Walker Papers, and the John W. Hunter Literary Efforts.

The Center for American History at the University of Texas at Austin preserves numerous bodies of personal papers. Among those I consulted were the papers of Walter Prescott Webb, James T. DeShields, J. D. Affleck, and John C. Caperton's "Sketch of Colonel John C. Hays, Texas Ranger," a typescript from the Bancroft Library at the University of California at Berkeley.

Among the newspapers consulted, the most helpful were the *Telegraph and Texas Register* (Houston), the *Galveston News*, the *San Antonio Daily Express*, and for the salt war the *Mesilla Independent*, published in Mesilla, New Mexico. Other newspapers were the *Austin City Gazette*, the *Texas Democrat* (Austin), and the *LaGrange Intelligencer*.

In some instances I have drawn from documents in the National Archives researched for earlier works. These are identified in the citations. However, two sets of federal documents proved important to the story of the salt war: RG 393, LR District of New Mexico, 1877, on microfilm as M1088, Reels 30–32; and RG 94, LR OAG, "Mexican Border Troubles," on microfilm as M666, Reels 200–204.

Acuña, Rodolfo. *Occupied America: A History of Chicanos*. 3d ed. New York: Harper-Collins, 1988.

Allen, Ruth. *The Great Southwest Strike*. University of Texas Publications 4214. Austin: University of Texas Press, 1942.

Alonzo, Armando C. *Tejano Legacy: Rancheros and Settlers in South Texas, 1734–1900*. Albuquerque: University of New Mexico Press, 1998.

Anon. "The Mexican and Indian Raid of '78." *Texas State Historical Association Quarterly* 5 (January 1902): 212–51.

Aten, Ira. *Six and One-Half Years in the Ranger Service: The Memoirs of Sergeant Ira Aten, Company D, Texas Rangers*. Bandera, Texas: Frontier Times, 1945.

Baenziger, Ann Patton. "The Texas State Police during Reconstruction: A Reexamination." *Southwestern Historical Quarterly* 72 (April 1969): 470–91.

Barbour, Philip N. *Journals of the Late Brevet Major Philip Norbourne Barbour . . . and His Wife Martha Isabella Hopkins Barbour, Written during the War with Mexico—1846*. Edited by Rhoda van Bibber Tanner Doubleday. New York: G. P. Putnam, 1936.

Barker, Eugene C. *The Life of Stephen F. Austin, Founder of Texas, 1793–1836: A Chapter in the Westward Movement of the Anglo-American People*. Nashville: Cokesbury, 1925.

——, ed. *The Austin Papers*. American Historical Association *Annual Report 1919*. Vol. 2. Washington, D.C., Government Printing Office, 1924.

——. "Journal of the Permanent Council (October 11–27, 1835)." *Texas State Historical Association Quarterly* 7 (April 1904): 249–77.

Barr, Alwyn. *Reconstruction to Reform: Texas Politics, 1876–1906*. Austin: University of Texas Press, 1971.

Barringer, Graham A., ed. "The Mexican War Journal of Henry S. Lane." *Indiana Magazine of History* 53 (December 1957): 383–434.

Barry, James B. *A Texas Ranger and Frontiersman: The Days of Buck Barry in Texas 1845–1906*. Edited by James K. Greer. Dallas: Southwest, 1932.

Bartholomew, Ed, ed. *Jesse Evans: A Texas Hide-Burner*. Houston: Frontier Press of Texas, 1955.

Barton, Henry W. "Five Texas Frontier Companies during the Mexican War." *Southwestern Historical Quarterly* 66 (July 1962): 17–30.

——. *Texas Volunteers in the Mexican War*. Wichita Falls: Texian, 1970.

——. "The United States Cavalry and the Texas Rangers." *Southwestern Historical Quarterly* 63 (April 1960): 495–510.

Bauer, K. Jack. *The Mexican War, 1846–1848*. New York: Macmillan, 1974; Lincoln: University of Nebraska Press, 1992.

Baugh, Virgil E. *A Pair of Texas Rangers: Bill McDonald and John Hughes*. Washington, D.C.: Potomac Westerners Corral, 1970.

Baum, Dale. *The Shattering of Texas Unionism: Politics in the Lone Star State during the Civil War Era*. Baton Rouge: Louisiana State University Press, 1998.

Baylor, George W. *Into the Far Wild Country: True Tales of the Old Southwest*. Edited by Jerry D. Thompson. El Paso: Texas Western Press, 1997.

Bearley, H. C. "The Pattern of Violence." In *Culture in the South*. Edited by W. T. Couch. Westport, Conn.: Greenwood, 1970

Bechtel, H. Kenneth. *State Police in the United States: A Socio-Historical Analysis*. Westport, Conn.: Greenwood, 1995.

Benham, Henry W. *Recollections of Mexico and the Battle of Buena Vista, Feb. 22 and 23, 1847*. Boston: n.p., 1871.

Benner, Judith Ann. *Sul Ross: Soldier, Statesman, Educator*. College Station: Texas A&M Press, 1983.

Blackwood, Emma Jerome, ed. *To Mexico with Scott: Letters of Captain E. Kirby Smith to His Wife*. Cambridge: Harvard University Press, 1917.

Bloom, Lansing B., ed. "Bourke on the Southwest." *New Mexico Historical Review* 13 (April 1938): 204–9.

Bollaert, William. *William Bollaert's Texas*. Edited by W. Eugene Hollon and Ruth Latham Butler. Norman: University of Oklahoma Press, 1956.

Brackett, Albert G. *General Lane's Brigade in Central Mexico*. Cincinnati: H. W. Derby, 1854.

"Brazos." *Life of Robert Hall: Indian Fighter and Veteran of Three Great Wars*. Austin: Ben C. Jones, 1898; Austin: State House Press, 1992.

Brice, Donaly E. *The Great Comanche Raid*. Austin: Eakin, 1987.

Brown, John Henry. *History of Texas, from 1685 to 1892*. 2 vols. St. Louis: L. E. Daniell, [1892–1893]; Austin: Jenkins, 1970.

——. *Indian Wars and Pioneers of Texas*. Austin: L. E. Daniell [1896]; Easley, S.C.: Southern Historical Press, 1978.

Brown, Richard M. *Strain of Violence: Historical Studies of American Violence and Vigilantism*. New York: Oxford University Press, 1975.

Buchanan, A. Russell, ed. "George Washington Trahern: Texas Cowboy Soldier from Mier to Buena Vista." *Southwestern Historical Quarterly* 58 (July 1954): 69–90.

Bustamento, Jorge A. "The Texas Rangers: Heroes or Oppressors?" Paper presented at American Sociological Association, 1971.

Calvert, Robert A., and Arnoldo De Leon. *The History of Texas*. Wheeling, Ill.: Harlan Davidson, 1996.

Cantrell, Gregg. *Stephen F. Austin: Empresario of Texas*. New Haven: Yale University Press, 1999.

Caperton, John. *Jack Hays: The Intrepid Texas Ranger*. Bandera, Texas: Frontier Times, 1927.

Carlson, Paul H. *Texas Wollybacks: The Range Sheep and Goat Industry*. College Station: Texas A&M Press, 1982.

Cashion, Ty. *A Texas Frontier: The Clear Fork Country and Fort Griffin, 1849–1887*. Norman: University of Oklahoma Press, 1996.

Chalfant, William Y. *Without Quarter: The Wichita Expedition and the Fight on Crooked Creek.* Norman: University of Oklahoma Press, 1991.

Chamberlain, Samuel E. *My Confessions: The Recollections of a Rogue.* Edited by William H. Goetzmann. Austin: Texas State Historical Association, 1996. Originally published in 1956.

Chatfield, W. H. *The Twin Cities of the Border and the Country of the Lower Rio Grande.* New Orleans: E. P. Brandao, 1893; Brownsville: Harbert Davenport Memorial Fund, 1959.

Christian, A. K. "Mirabeau Buonaparte Lamar." *Southwestern Historical Quarterly* 23 (April 1920): 231–69; 24 (January 1921): 195–234.

Christian, Garna L. *Black Soldiers in Jim Crow Texas, 1899–1917.* College Station: Texas A&M Press, 1987.

Claiborne, Thomas. "Memories of the Past." *Vidette*, April 1, 1886.

Clark, Pat B. *The History of Clarksville and Old Red River County.* Dallas: Mathis, Van Nort, 1937.

Coker, Caleb, ed. *The News from Brownsville: Helen Chapman's Letters from the Texas Military Frontier, 1848–1852.* Austin: Texas State Historical Association, 1992.

Combs, Joseph F. *Gunsmoke in the Redlands.* San Antonio: Naylor, 1968.

Conger, Roger N., et al. *Rangers of Texas.* Waco, Texas: Texian, 1969.

Cox, Mike. *Silver Stars and Sixguns: The Texas Rangers.* Austin: Department of Public Safety, 1987.

———. *Texas Ranger Tales: Stories That Need Telling.* Plano, Texas: Republic of Texas Press, 1997.

———. *Texas Ranger Tales II.* Plano, Texas: Republic of Texas Press, 1999.

Curtis, Samuel Ryan. *Mexico under Fire: Being the Diary of Samuel Ryan Curtis, 3rd Ohio Volunteer Regiment, during the American Occupation of Northern Mexico, 1846–1847.* Edited by Joseph E. Chance. Fort Worth: Texas Christian University Press, 1994.

Cuthbertson, Gilbert M. "Catarino E. Garza and the Garza War." *Texana* 13 (1975): 335–48.

Cutrer, Thomas W. *Ben McCulloch and the Frontier Military Tradition.* Chapel Hill: University of North Carolina Press, 1993.

Dana, Napoleon J. Tecumseh. *Monterrey Is Ours: Mexican War Letters of Lieutenant Dana, 1845–1847.* Edited by Robert H. Ferrell. Lexington: University of Kentucky Press, 1990.

Daniell, Lewis E. *Personnel of the Texas State Government, with Sketches of Representative Men of Texas.* San Antonio: Maverick, 1892.

Davis, John L. *The Texas Rangers: Images and Incidents.* San Antonio: Institute of Texan Cultures, 1991.

———. *The Texas Rangers: Their First 150 Years.* San Antonio: University of Texas at San Antonio, Institute of Texan Cultures, 1975.

Davis, Richard Harding. "Our Troops on the Border." *Harper's Weekly*, March 26, 1892, 294.

———. *The West from a Car-Window.* New York: Harper, 1892.

Day, James M. "El Paso's Texas Rangers." *Password* 24 (Winter 1979): 153–72.

De Leon, Arnoldo. *The Tejano Community, 1836–1900.* Albuquerque: University of New Mexico Press, 1982.

———. *They Called Them Greasers: Anglo Attitudes toward Mexicans in Texas, 1821–1900.* Austin: University of Texas Press, 1983.

De Shields, James T. *Border Wars of Texas.* Tioga, Texas: Herald, 1912; Austin: State House Press, 1993.

Denman, Clarence P. "The Office of Adjutant General in Texas, 1835–1881." *Southwestern Historical Quarterly* 28 (April 1925): 302–22.

Dilworth, Rankin. *The March to Monterrey: The Diary of Rankin Dilworth, U.S. Army: A Narrative of Troop Movements and Observations on Daily Life with General Zachary Taylor's Army during the Invasion of Mexico.* Edited by Lawrence R. Clayton and Joseph E. Chance. El Paso: Texas Western Press, 1996.

Doubleday, Abner. *My Life in the Old Army: Reminiscences of Abner Doubleday from the Collection of the New York Historical Society.* Edited by Joseph E. Chance. Fort Worth: Texas Christian University Press, 1998.

Doubleday, Rhoda van Bibber Tanner, ed. *Journal of the Late Brevet Major Philip Norbourne Barbour Captain in the 3rd Regiment, United States Infantry and His Wife Martha Isabella Hopkins Barbour, Written during the War with Mexico 1846.* New York: G. P. Putnam, 1936.

Durham, George, as told to Clyde Wantland. *Taming the Nueces Strip: The Story of McNelly's Rangers.* Austin: University of Texas Press, 1962.

Duval, John C. *The Adventures of Big-Foot Wallace, the Texas Ranger and Hunter.* Philadelphia: Claxton, Remsen & Haffelfinger, 1871.

——. *Early Times in Texas.* Austin: H.P.N. Gammel, 1892.

Ehrle, Michael G., comp. and ed. *The Childress County Story.* Childress, Texas: Ox Bow Printing, 1971.

Eisenhower, John S. D. *So Far from God: The U.S. War with Mexico, 1846–1848.* New York: Random House, 1989.

Erath, George B. *Memoirs of Major George Bernard Erath.* Dictated to and arranged by Lucy A. Erath. Edited by E. W. Winkler. Austin: Texas State Historical Association, 1923.

Everett, Dianna. *The Texas Cherokees: A People between Two Fires, 1819–1840.* Norman: University of Oklahoma Press, 1990.

Fehrenbach, T. R. *Comanches: The Destruction of a People.* New York: Alfred A. Knopf, 1974; New York: Da Capo, 1994.

——. *Lone Star: A History of Texas and Texans.* New York: Macmillan, 1968.

Ferguson, I. D., "The Battle of Dove Creek." Edited by J. Marvin Hunter. *West Texas Historical Association Year Book* 10 (October 1934): 78–79.

Fisher, Ovie Clark, and Jeff C. Dykes. *King Fisher: His Life and Times.* Norman: University of Oklahoma Press, 1966.

Ford, John S. *Rip Ford's Texas.* Edited by Stephen H. Oates. Austin: University of Texas Press, 1963.

Frantz, Joe B. "Lone Star Mystique." *American West* 5 (May 1968): 6–9.

——. *Texas: A Bicentennial History.* New York: Norton, 1976.

Frazier, Donald S., ed. *The United States and Mexico at War: Nineteenth-Century Expansionism and Conflict.* New York: Macmillan Reference, 1998.

Friend, Llrenna B. *Sam Houston: The Great Designer.* Austin: University of Texas Press, 1954.

——. "W. P. Webb's Texas Rangers." *Southwestern Historical Quarterly* 74 (January 1971): 293–323.

Gammel, Hans Peter Nielson, comp. *The Laws of Texas, 1822–1897.* 10 vols. Austin: Gammel Book Co., 1898.

Garavaglia, Louis A., and Charles G. Worman. *Firearms of the American West.* Albuquerque: University of New Mexico Press, 1984.

Gard, Wayne. "The Fence-Cutters." *Southwestern Historical Quarterly* 51 (July 1947): 1–15.

George, Isaac. *Heroes and Incidents of the Mexican War.* Greensburg, Pa.: Review Publishing, 1898; Hollywood: Sun Dance, 1971.

Gibson, A. M. *The Kickapoos: Lords of the Middle Border*. Norman: University of Oklahoma Press, 1963.

Giddings, Luther. *Sketches of the Campaign in Northern Mexico by an Officer of the First Ohio Volunteers*. New York: Putnam, 1853.

Gillett, James B. *Six Years with the Texas Rangers, 1875 to 1881*. Austin: Von Boeckmann-Jones, 1921; New Haven: Yale University Press, 1925.

Godbold, Mollie Moore. "Comanche and the Hardin Gang." *Southwestern Historical Quarterly* 67 (July 1963): 55–77; (October 1963): 247–66.

Goldfinch, Charles W. *Juan Cortina, 1824–1892: A Reappraisal*. Brownsville: Bishop's Print Shop, 1950.

Gournay, Luke. *Texas Boundaries: Evolution of the State's Counties*. College Station: Texas A&M Press, 1995.

Green, Rena Maverick, ed. *Samuel Maverick, Texan, 1803–1870: A Collection of Letters, Journals, and Memoirs*. San Antonio: privately printed, 1952.

Green, Thomas Jefferson. *Journal of the Texian Expedition against Mier*. New York: Harper, 1845; New York: Arno, 1973.

Greer, James K. *Colonel Jack Hays: Texas Frontier Leader and California Builder*. New York: E. P. Dutton, 1952; College Station: Texas A&M Press, 1987.

Hager, William M. "The Nueces Town Raid of 1875: A Border Incident." *Arizona and the West* 1 (Spring 1959): 258–70.

Haley, J. Evetts. *Charles Goodnight: Cowman and Plainsman*. Norman: University of Oklahoma Press, 1949.

——. "The Comanchero Trade." *Southwestern Historical Quarterly* 35 (January 1935): 157–76.

——. *Jeff Milton: A Good Man with a Gun*. Norman: University of Oklahoma Press, 1948.

——. *The XIT Ranch of Texas and the Early Days of the Llano Estacado*. Norman: University of Oklahoma Press, 1967.

Haley, James L. *The Buffalo War: The History of the Red River Indian Uprising of 1874*. Norman: University of Oklahoma Press, 1985.

Hamilton, Allen Lee. *Sentinel of the Southern Plains: Fort Richardson and the Northwest Texas Frontier, 1866–1878*. Fort Worth: Texas Christian University Press, 1988.

Hardin, John Wesley. *The Life of John Wesley Hardin, from the Original Manuscript, as Written by Himself*. Seguin, Texas: Smith & Moore, 1896; Norman: University of Oklahoma Press, 1961.

Hardin, Stephen. *The Texas Rangers*. London: Osprey, 1991.

——. *Texian Iliad: A Military History of the Texas Revolution*. Austin: University of Texas Press, 1994.

Hatley, Allen G. *The Indian Wars in Stephen F. Austin's Texas Colony, 1822–1835*. Austin: Eakin, 2001.

Haven, Charles T., and Frank Belden. *A History of the Colt Revolver and Other Arms Made by Colt's Patent Fire Arms Manufacturing Company from 1836 to 1940*. New York: Bonanza, 1978.

Haynes, Sam W. *Soldiers of Misfortune: The Somervell and Mier Expeditions*. Austin: University of Texas Press, 1990.

Heintzelman, Samuel P. *Fifty Miles and a Fight: Major Samuel Peter Heintzelman's Journal of Texas and the Cortina War*. Edited by Jerry Thompson. Austin: Texas State Historical Association, 1997.

Hendricks, Sterling Brown. "The Somervell Expedition to the Rio Grande, 1842." Edited by E. W. Winkler. *Southwestern Historical Quarterly* 23 (October 1919): 112–40.

Hendrickson, Kenneth E., Jr. *The Chief Executives of Texas, from Stephen F. Austin to John B. Connally, Jr.* College Station: Texas A&M Press, 1995.

Henry, William S. *Campaign Sketches of the War with Mexico*. New York: Harper, 1847.

Hitchcock, Ethan Allen. *Fifty Years in Camp and Field: The Diary of Major-General Ethan Allen Hitchcock, U.S.A.* Edited by W. A. Croffut. New York: G. P. Putnam, 1909.

Holland, James K. "Diary of a Texan Volunteer in the Mexican War." *Southwestern Historical Quarterly* 30 (July 1926): 1–33.

Holley, Mary Austin. *Texas: Observations Historical, Geographical, and Descriptive, in a Series of Letters, Written during a Visit to Austin's Colony, with a View to a Permanent Settlement in that Country in the Autumn of 1831.* Baltimore: Armstrong & Plaskitt, 1833; Austin: Overland, 1981.

Holt, Roy D. "The Introduction of Barbed Wire into Texas and the Fence Cutting War." *West Texas Historical Association Year Book* 6 (1930): 72–88.

Horton, David M., and Ryan Kellus Turner. *Lone Star Justice: A Comprehensive Overview of the Texas Criminal Justice System.* Austin: Eakin, 1999.

Houston, Sam. *The Writings of Sam Houston, 1813–1863.* Edited by Amelia Williams and Eugene C. Barker. 8 vols. Austin: University of Texas Press, 1938–1943. Austin: Pemberton, 1970.

Hughes, John R. *The Killing of Bass Outlaw.* Austin: Brick Row Bookshop, 1963.

Hughes, William J. *Rebellious Ranger: Rip Ford and the Old Southwest.* Norman: University of Oklahoma Press, 1964.

Humphrey, David C. *Austin.* Austin: Texas State Historical Association, 1997.

Ingmire, Frances Terry. *Texas Ranger Service Records, 1830–1846.* St. Louis: privately printed, 1982.

Jeffries, C. C. "The Character of Terry's Texas Rangers." *Southwestern Historical Quarterly* 64 (April 1961): 454–62.

Jenkins, John Holland. *Recollections of Early Texas: The Memoirs of John Holland Jenkins.* Edited by John Holmes Jenkins III. Austin: University of Texas Press, 1958.

Jenkins, John Holmes III, ed. *The Papers of the Texas Revolution, 1835–36.* 10 vols. Austin: Presidial, 1973.

Jenkins, John S. *History of the War between the United States and Mexico.* Philadelphia: John E. Potter, 1851.

Jennings, Napoleon Augustus. *A Texas Ranger.* New York: Charles Scribners, 1899.

Johnston, William Preston. *The Life of Albert Sidney Johnston.* New York: D. Appleton, 1878.

Jordan, Philip D. *Frontier Law and Order: Ten Essays.* Lincoln: University of Nebraska Press, 1970.

Jordan, Terry G. *North American Cattle-Ranching Frontiers: Origins, Diffusion, and Differentiation.* Albuquerque: University of New Mexico Press, 1993.

Kavanagh, Thomas W. *Comanche History: An Ethnohistorical Perspective, 1708–1875.* Lincoln: University of Nebraska Press, 1996.

Keating, Bern. *An Illustrated History of the Texas Rangers.* Chicago: Rand McNally, 1975.

Kendall, George Wilkins. *Dispatches from the Mexican War.* Edited by Lawrence Delbert Cress. Norman: University of Oklahoma Press, 1999.

——. *The War between the United States and Mexico, Illustrated.* Edited by Ron Tyler. Austin: Texas State Historical Association, 1994. Originally published in 1851.

Kenly, John R. *Memoirs of a Maryland Volunteer: War with Mexico, in the Years 1846-7-8.* Philadelphia: J. B. Lippincott, 1873.

Kilgore, Dan E. *A Ranger Legacy: 150 Years of Service in Texas.* Austin: Madrona, 1973.

King, Edward, and J. Wells Champney. *Texas, 1874: An Eyewitness Account of Conditions in Post-Reconstruction Texas.* Edited by Robert S. Gray. Houston: Cordovan, 1974.

King, W. H. "The Texas Ranger Service and History of the Rangers, with Observations on Their Value as a Police Protection." In *A Comprehensive History of Texas, 1685 to 1897*, edited by Dudley G. Woolen, 329–67. 2 vols. Dallas: William G. Scharff, 1898.

Knowles, Thomas W. *They Rode for the Lone Star: The Saga of the Texas Rangers*. Dallas: Taylor, 1998.

Koch, Lena Clara. "The Federal Indian Policy in Texas, 1845–1860." *Southwestern Historical Quarterly* 28 (January 1925): 223–34; 28 (April 1925): 259–86; 29 (July 1925): 19–35; 29 (October 1925): 98–129.

Kuykendall, J. H. "Reminiscences of Early Texas." *Texas State Historical Association Quarterly* 6 (January 1903): 236–53; 6 (April 1903): 311–29; 7 (July 1903): 29–64.

Lack, Paul D. *The Texas Revolutionary Experience: A Political and Social History, 1835–1836*. College Station: Texas A&M Press, 1992.

Lamar, Mirabeau Buonaparte. *The Papers of Mirabeau Buonaparte Lamar*. Edited by Charles A. Gulick et al. 6 vols. New York: AMS Press, 1973.

Lane, Anne J. *The Brownsville Affair: National Crisis and Black Reaction*. Port Washington, N.Y.: Kennikat, 1971.

Lane, Walter P. *The Adventures and Recollections of General Walter P. Lane, a San Jacinto Veteran, Containing Sketches of the Texian, Mexican, and Late Wars, with Several Indian Fights Thrown In*. Marshall, Texas: Tri-Weekly Herald Job Print, 1887; Austin: Pemberton, 1970.

Lee, Nelson. *Three Years among the Camanches: The Narrative of Nelson Lee, the Texas Ranger, Containing a Detailed Account of His Captivity among the Indians, His Singular Escape through the Instrumentality of His Watch, and Fully Illustrating Indian Life as It Is on the War Path and in the Camp*. Albany: Baker Taylor, 1859; Norman: University of Oklahoma Press, 1957.

Linn, John J. *Reminiscences of Fifty Years in Texas*. New York: D. & J. Sodlier, 1883; Austin: Steck, 1935; Austin: State House Press, 1986.

Loomis, Noel M. *The Texan-Santa Fe Pioneers*. Norman: University of Oklahoma Press, 1958.

Lowrie, Samuel H. *Culture Conflict in Texas, 1821–1836*. New York: AMS Press, 1967.

Maltby, William J. *Captain Jeff; or, Frontier Life in Texas with the Texas Rangers*. Colorado, Texas: Whipkey, 1906.

Mann, William L. "James O. Rice, Hero of the Battle on the San Gabriels." *Southwestern Historical Quarterly* 55 (July 1951): 30–42.

Martin, Jack. *Border Boss: Captain John R. Hughes, Texas Ranger*. San Antonio: Naylor, 1942; Austin: State House Press, 1990.

Mason-Manheim, Madeline. *Riding for Texas: The True Adventures of Captain Bill McDonald of the Texas Rangers, as Told by Colonel Edward M. House to Tyler Mason*. New York: Reynal & Hitchcock, 1936.

Maverick, Mary Ann. *Memoirs of Mary A. Maverick, Arranged by Mary A. Maverick and Her Son, Geo. Madison Maverick*. San Antonio: Alamo, 1921.

McCallum, Henry D. "Barbed Wire in Texas." *Southwestern Historical Quarterly* 61 (October 1957): 207–19.

McCallum, Henry D., and Frances T. McCallum. *The Wire That Fenced the West*. Norman: University of Oklahoma Press, 1965.

McCarty, John L. *Maverick Town: The Story of Old Tascosa*. Norman: University of Oklahoma Press, 1946.

McComb, David G. *Texas: A Modern History*. Austin: University of Texas Press, 1989.

McConnell, H. H. *Five Years a Cavalryman; or, Sketches of Regular Army Life on the Texas Frontier Twenty Odd Years Ago*. Jacksboro, Texas: J. N. Rogers., 1889; Norman: University of Oklahoma Press, 1996.

McCright, Grady E., and James M. Powell. *Jessie Evans: Lincoln County Badman*. College Station, Texas: Creative, 1983.

McCutchan, Joseph D. *Mier Expedition Diary*. Edited by Joseph Milton Nance. Austin: University of Texas Press, 1978.

McLean, Malcolm. *Papers concerning Robertson's Colony*. 19 vols. Fort Worth: Texas Christian University Press, 1974–1976; Arlington: University of Texas at Arlington Press, 1974–1987.

McSherry, Richard. *El Puchero; or a Mixed Dish from Mexico Embracing General Scott's Campaign with Sketches of Military Life, in Field in Camp, of the Character of the Country, Manners and Ways of People, etc.* Philadelphia: Lippincott, Grambo, 1850.

Meade, George G. *The Life and Letters of George Gordon Meade, Major-General United States Army*. 2 vols. New York: Charles Scribner's Sons, 1913.

Meed, Douglas V. "Daggers on the Gallows: The Revenge of Texas Ranger Captain 'Boss' Hughes." *True West* 46 (May 1999): 44–49.

Meinig, Donald W. *Imperial Texas: An Interpretive Essay in Cultural Geography*. Austin: University of Texas Press, 1969.

Mertz, Richard J. "'No One Can Arrest Me': The Story of Gregorio Cortez." *Journal of South Texas* 1 (1974): 1–17.

Metz, Leon C. *John Selman: Gunfighter*. Norman: University of Oklahoma Press, 1980.

——. *John Wesley Hardin: Dark Angel of Texas*. El Paso: Mangan, 1996.

——. *Pat Garrett: The Story of a Western Lawman*. Norman: University of Oklahoma Press, 1974.

Mexico. *Reports of the Committee of Investigation Sent in 1873 by the Mexican Government to the Frontier of Texas*. New York: Baker & Godwin, 1875.

Miletich, Leo N. *Dan Stuart's Fistic Carnival*. College Station: Texas A&M Press, 1994.

Miller, Rick. *Bounty Hunter*. College Station, Texas: Creative, 1988.

——. *Sam Bass and Gang*. Austin: State House Press, 1999.

Mirande, Alfredo. *Gringo Justice*. Notre Dame, Ind.: University of Notre Dame Press, 1987.

Moneyhon, Carl H. *Republicanism in Reconstruction Texas*. Austin: University of Texas Press, 1980.

Montejano, David. *Anglos and Mexicans in the Making of Texas, 1836–1986*. Austin: University of Texas Press, 1987.

Morrell, Zachariah N. *Flowers and Fruits from the Wilderness; or, Thirty-Six Years in Texas and Two Winters in Honduras*. New York: Sheldon, 1872.

Morris, John Miller. *A Private in the Texas Rangers: A. T. Miller of Company B Frontier Battalion*. College Station: Texas A&M Press, 2001.

Muckleroy, Anna. "The Indian Policy of the Republic of Texas." *Southwestern Historical Quarterly* 25 (April 1922): 229–60; 26 (July 1922): 1–29; 26 (October 1922): 128–48; 26 (January 1923): 184–206.

Nackman, Mark E. "The Making of the Texan Citizen Soldier, 1835–1860." *Southwestern Historical Quarterly* 78 (January 1975): 233–53.

——. *A Nation within a Nation: The Rise of Texas Nationalism*. Port Washington, N.Y.: Kennikat, 1975.

Nance, Joseph M. *After San Jacinto: The Texas-Mexican Frontier, 1836–1841*. Austin: University of Texas Press, 1963.

——. *Attack and Counter-Attack: The Texas–Mexican Frontier, 1842*. Austin: University of Texas Press, 1964.

——, trans. and ed. "Brigadier General Adrián Woll's Report of His Expedition into Texas in 1842." *Southwestern Historical Quarterly* 58 (April 1955): 523–52.

Nance, Joseph Milton, and Archie McDonald. *Dare-Devils All: The Texan Mier Expedition, 1842–44*. Austin: Eakin, 1998.

Neighbours, Kenneth F. "The Battle of Walker's Creek." *West Texas Historical Association Year Book* 41 (October 1965): 121–30.

——. "Elm Creek Raid in Young County, 1864." *West Texas Historical Association Year Book* 40 (October 1964): 83–89.

——. *Indian Exodus: Texas Indian Affairs, 1835–1859.* Wichita Falls, Texas: Nortex, 1973.

——. *Robert Simpson Neighbors and the Texas Frontier, 1836–1859.* Waco: Texian, 1975.

Nichols, James W. *Now You Hear My Horn: The Journal of James Wilson Nichols, 1820–1887.* Edited by Catherine W. McDowell. Austin: University of Texas Press, 1967.

Nielsen, George R. "Mathew Caldwell." *Southwestern Historical Quarterly* 64 (April 1961): 478–502.

Nye, W. S. *Carbine and Lance: The Story of Old Fort Sill.* Norman: University of Oklahoma Press, 1942.

Oates, Stephen B. "Los Diablos Tejanos: The Texas Rangers." In *The Mexican War: Changing Interpretations*, edited by Odie B. Faulk and Joseph A. Stout, 120–36. Chicago: Swallow Press, 1973.

Olmsted, Frederick Law. *A Journey through Texas: Or, a Saddle-Trip on the Southwestern Frontier, with a Statistical Appendix.* New York: Dix, Edwards, 1857; Austin: University of Texas Press, 1978.

O'Neal, Bill. *The Arizona Rangers.* Austin: Eakin, 1997.

——. *The Bloody Legacy of Pink Higgins.* Austin: Eakin, 1999.

——. *Cattlemen vs. Sheepherders: Five Decades of Violence in the West, 1880–1920.* Austin: Eakin, 1989.

Paine, Albert B. *Captain Bill McDonald, Texas Ranger: A Story of Frontier Reform.* New York: J. J. Little & Ives, 1909; Austin: Eakin, 1986.

Pancoast, Josiah. *Sketches of Life on the Western Frontier and in the Army in Mexico during the '40s.* Woodstown, NJ: First National Bank, 1911.

Paredes, Américo. *With His Pistol in His Hand: A Border Ballad and Its Hero.* Austin: University of Texas Press, 1958.

Parsons, Chuck. *The Capture of John Wesley Hardin.* College Station, Texas: Creative, 1978.

——. "Pidge," a Texas Ranger from Virginia: The Life and Letters of Lieutenant T. C. Robinson.* South Wayne, Wis.: C. Parsons, 1985.

Parsons, Chuck, and Marianne E. Hall Little. *Captain L. H. McNelly, Texas Ranger: The Life and Times of a Fighting Man.* Austin: State House, 2001.

Parsons, Chuck, Gary Fitter, and Charles C. McKinney. *Captain C. B. McKinney: The Law in South Texas.* Austin: State House, 1993.

Parsons, John E. *Samuel Colt's Own Record of Transactions with Captain Walker and Eli Whitney, Jr.* Hartford: Connecticut Historical Society, 1949.

Peskin, Allan, ed. *Volunteers: The Mexican War Journals of Private Richard Coulter and Sergeant Thomas Barclay, Company E, Second Pennsylvania Infantry.* Kent, Ohio: Kent State University Press, 1991.

Pool, William C. "The Battle of Dove Creek [1865]." *Southwestern Historical Quarterly* 53 (April 1950): 367–85.

Prassel, Frank R. *The Western Peace Officer: A Legacy of Law and Order.* Norman: University of Oklahoma Press, 1972.

Preece, Harold. *Lone Star Man: Ira Aten, Last of the Old Texas Rangers.* New York: Hastings, 1960.

Procter, Ben. *Just One Riot: Episodes of Texas Rangers in the 20th Century.* Austin: Eakin, 1991.

Rathjen, Frederick W. *The Texas Panhandle Frontier*. Austin: University of Texas Press, 1973.

——. "The Texas State House: A Study of the Building of the Texas Capitol Based on the Reports of the Capitol Building Commissioners." *Southwestern Historical Quarterly* 60 (April 1957): 433–62.

Raymond, Dora. *Captain Lee Hall of Texas*. Norman: University of Oklahoma Press, 1940.

Reid, Samuel C., Jr. *The Scouting Expeditions of McCulloch's Texas Rangers; or, The Summer and Fall Campaign of the Army of the United States in Mexico–1846; Including Skirmishes with the Mexicans, and an Accurate Detail of the Storming of Monterey; also, the Daring Scouts at Buena Vista; Together with Anecdotes, Incident, Descriptions of Country, and Sketches of the Lives of the Celebrated Partisan Chiefs, Hays, McCulloch, and Walker*. Philadelphia: G. B. Zieber, 1847; Austin: Steck, 1935.

Remington, Frederic. *How the Law Got into the Chaparral: Conversations with Old Texas Rangers*. Edited by John Holmes Jenkins. Austin: Jenkins, 1987.

Richardson, Albert D. *Beyond the Mississippi: From the Great River to the Great Ocean. . . . 1857–1867*. Hartford: American, 1867.

Richardson, Rupert N. *The Comanche Barrier to South Plains Settlement*. Rev. ed. Edited by Kenneth R. Jacobs. Austin: Eakin, 1996. Originally published in 1933.

——. *The Frontier of Northwest Texas, 1846 to 1876*. Glendale: Arthur H. Clark, 1963.

Richter, William L. *The Army in Texas during Reconstruction, 1865–1870*. College Station: Texas A&M Press, 1987.

Rigler, Erik. "Frontier Justice: In the Days before NCIC [National Crime Information Center]." *FBI Law Enforcement Bulletin* 54 (July 1985): 16–22.

Rippy, J. Fred. "Border Troubles along the Rio Grande, 1846–60." *Southwestern Historical Quarterly* 23 (October 1919): 91–111.

——. "Some Precedents of the Pershing Expedition into Mexico." *Southwestern Historical Quarterly* 24 (April 1921): 292–316.

——. *The United States and Mexico*. New York: Alfred A. Knopf, 1926.

Rister, C. C. "The Significance of the Jacksboro Indian Affair of 1871." *Southwestern Historical Quarterly* 29 (January 1926): 181–200.

Roberts, Daniel W. *Rangers and Sovereignty*. San Antonio: Wood Printing and Engraving, 1914.

Roberts, Lou Conway. *A Woman's Reminiscences of Six Years in Camp with the Texas Rangers, by Mrs. D. W. Roberts*. Austin: Von Boeckmann-Jones, 1928.

Robinson, Charles M., III. *The Indian Trial: The Complete Story of the Warren Wagon Train Massacre and the Fall of the Kiowa Nation*. Spokane: Arthur H. Clark, 1997.

——. *The Men Who Wear the Star: The Story of the Texas Rangers*. New York: Random, 2000.

——. *Satanta: The Life and Death of a War Chief*. Austin: State House, 1997.

Roland, Charles P. *Albert Sidney Johnston*. Austin: University of Texas Press, 1987.

Romero, Mary. "El Paso Salt War: Mob Action or Political Struggle?" *Aztlan* 16 (1985): 119–43.

Romero, Matias. "The Garza Raid and Its Lessons." *North American Review* 155 (September 1892): 324–37.

Rose, Victor M. *The Life and Services of Gen. Ben McCulloch*. Philadelphia: Pictorial Bureau of the Press, 1888.

——. *Texas Vendetta: or, The Sutton-Taylor Feud*. New York: J. J. Little, 1880; Houston: Frontier Press of Texas, 1956.

Rosenbaum, Robert J. *Mexicano Resistance in the Southwest: "The Sacred Right of Self-Preservation."* Austin: University of Texas Press, 1981.

Samora, Julian, Joe Bërnal, and Albert Peña. *Gunpowder Justice: A Reassessment of the Texas Rangers*. Notre Dame, Ind.: University of Notre Dame Press, 1979.

Shearer, Ernest C. "The Callahan Expedition, 1855." *Southwestern Historical Quarterly* 54 (April 1951): 430–51.

Sheffy, L. F. "Old Mobeetie–The Capital of the Panhandle." *West Texas Historical Association Year Book* 6 (June 1930): 3–16.

——, ed. "The Arrington Papers." *Panhandle-Plains Historical Review* 1 (1928): 30–66.

Sinise, Jerry. *George Washington Arrington: Civil War Spy, Texas Ranger, Sheriff and Rancher: A Biography*. Burnet, Texas: Eakin, 1979.

——. *Pink Higgins: The Reluctant Gunfighter and Other Tales of the Panhandle*. Quanah, Texas: Nortex, 1973.

Smith, David Paul. *Frontier Defense in the Civil War: Texas Rangers and Rebels*. College Station: Texas A&M Press, 1992.

Smith, E. Kirby. *To Mexico with Scott: Letters of E. Kirby Smith to His Wife*. Edited by Emma Jerome Blackwood. Cambridge: Harvard University Press, 1917.

Smith, Franklin. *The Mexican War Journal of Captain Franklin Smith*. Edited by Joseph E. Chance. Jackson: University Press of Mississippi, 1991.

Smith, George Winston. *Chronicles of the Gringos: The U.S. Army in the Mexican War, 1846-48; Accounts of Eyewitnesses and Combatants*. Albuquerque: University of New Mexico Press, 1968.

Smith, Justin H. *The War with Mexico*. 2 vols. New York: Macmillan, 1919.

Smith, S. Compton. *Chili con Carne: or, The Camp and the Field*. New York: Miller and Curtiss, 1857.

Smithwick, Noah. *The Evolution of a State: Or, Recollections of Old Texas Days*. Austin: H.P.M. Gammel, 1900; Austin: University of Texas Press, 1983.

Sneed, Edgar P. "A Historiography of Reconstruction in Texas: Some Myths and Problems." *Southwestern Historical Quarterly* 72 (April 1969): 435–48.

Sonnichsen, C. L. *I'll Die before I'll Run: The Story of the Great Feuds of Texas*. New York: Devin-Adair, 1962; Lincoln: University of Nebraska Press, 1988.

——. *Pass of the North: Four Centuries on the Rio Grande*. El Paso: Texas Western Press, 1968.

——. *Ten Texas Feuds*. Albuquerque: University of New Mexico Press, 1957.

Sowell, Andrew J. *Early Settlers and Indian Fighters of Southwest Texas . . . Facts Gathered from Survivors of Frontier Days*. 2 vols. Austin: Ben C. Jones, 1900; New York: Argosy-Antiquarian, 1964.

——. *Life of "Big Foot" Wallace: The Great Ranger Captain*. Austin: State House, 1989.

——. *Rangers and Pioneers of Texas, with a Concise Account of the Early Settlements, Hardships, Massacres, Battles, and Wars by Which Texas was Rescued from the Rule of the Savage and Consecrated to the Empire of Civilization*. San Antonio: Shepard Bros., 1884; New York: Argosy-Antiquarian, 1964.

Speed, Jonathan Gilmer. "The Hunt for Garza." *Harper's Weekly*, January 30, 1892; 103–4.

Spratt, John S. *The Road to Spindletop: Economic Changes in Texas, 1875-1901*. Dallas: Southern Methodist University Press, 1955.

Spurlin, Charles. "Ranger Walker in the Mexican War." *Military History of Texas and the Southwest* 9 (1971): 259–79.

——. *Texas Volunteers in the Mexican War*. Austin: Eakin, 1990.

Spurlin, Charles D., comp. *Texas Veterans in the Mexican War: Muster Rolls of Texas Military Units*. Victoria, Texas: privately printed, 1984.

Stephens, Robert W. *Texas Ranger Indian War Pensions*. Quanah, Texas: Nortex, 1975.

——. *Texas Ranger Sketches*. Dallas: privately printed, 1972.

——. *Walter Durbin: Texas Ranger and Sheriff*. Clarendon, Texas; Clarendon, 1970.

Sterling, William W. *Trails and Trials of a Texas Ranger*. Norman: University of Oklahoma Press, 1959.

Sullivan, W. John L. *Twelve Years in the Saddle for Law and Order on the Frontiers of Texas*. Austin: Von Boeckmann-Jones, 1909; New York: Buffalo-Head, 1966; Lincoln: University of Nebraska Press, 2001.

Sweet, Alexander Edwin, and John Armory Knox. *On a Mexican Mustang, through Texas, from the Gulf to the Rio Grande*. Hartford: S. S. Scranton, 1883.

Taylor, Paul S. *An American-Mexican Frontier: Nueces County, Texas*. Chapel Hill: University of North Carolina Press, 1934; New York: Russell and Russell, 1971.

Taylor, Zachary. *Letters of Zachary Taylor from the Battle-Fields of the Mexican War, Reprinted from the Originals in the Collection of Mr. William K. Bixby of St. Louis, Mo.* Edited by William H. Samson. Rochester, N.Y.: Genesee, 1908.

Texas Adjutant General. *Annual Reports*.

Texas Congress. *Secret Journals of the Senate of the Republic of Texas, 1836–45*. Edited by Ernest W. Winkler. Austin: Austin Printing, 1911.

——. *Senate Journals*, 1st to 9th Congress, 1836–1845. Edited by Harriet Smither. 2 vols. Austin: Texas Library and Historical Commission, 1929–40.

Texas Governor. *Legislative Messages of the Chief Executives of Texas*. 3 vols. Austin, 1972.

Texas State Historical Association. *The New Handbook of Texas*. 6 vols. Austin: Texas State Historical Association, 1995.

Texas War Department. *Report of the Secretary of War and Marine*, 1839–40 through 1843–44. n.p. 1840–1844.

Thompson, Jerry D. *A Wild and Vivid Land: An Illustrated History of the South Texas Border*. Austin: Texas State Historical Association, 1997.

——, ed. *Fifty Miles and a Fight: Major Samuel Peter Heintzelman's Journal of Texas and the Cortina War*. Austin: Texas State Historical Association, 1998.

——. *Juan Cortina and the Texas-Mexico Frontier, 1859–1877*. El Paso: Texas Western Press, 1994.

Thorpe, Thomas B. *Our Army at Monterey*. Philadelphia: Carey & Hart, 1847.

——. *Our Army on the Rio Grande*. Philadelphia: Carey and Hart, 1846. Also in House Executive Document 209, 29th Congress, 1st session (Serial 486), 1846.

Thrapp, Dan L. *Victorio and the Mimbres Apaches*. Norman: University of Oklahoma Press, 1974.

Tijerina, Andres. *Tejano Empire: Life on the South Texas Ranchos*. College Station: Texas A&M Press, 1998.

Tyler, Ronnie C. "The Callahan Expedition of 1855: Indians or Negroes?" *Southwestern Historical Quarterly* 70 (April 1967): 574–85.

——. "The Rangers at Zacualtipan." *Texana* 4 (Winter 1966): 343–45.

U.S. Commissioner of Indian Affairs. *Annual Reports*, 1847–1880.

U.S. Congress. *Claims of the State of Texas*. Senate Executive Document 19, 45th Congress, 2nd Session (Serial 1780), 1878.

——. *Congressional Globe*. 35th Congress, 1st Session (1857–1858).

——. *Difficulties on the Southwestern Frontier*. House Executive Document 52, 36th Congress, 1st Session (Serial 1050), 1860.

——. *El Paso Troubles in Texas*. House Executive Document 93, 45th Congress, 2nd Session (Serial 1809), 1878.

——. *Mexican War Correspondence*. House Executive Document 60, 30th Congress, 1st Session (Serial 520), 1848.

——. *Relations of the United States with Mexico*. House Executive Document 701, 45th Congress, 2nd Session (Serial 1824), 1878.

——. *Report on Texas Frontier Troubles*. House Report 343, 44th Congress, 1st Session (Serial 1709), 1876.

——. *Texas Border Troubles*. House Executive Document 64, 45th Congress, 2nd Session (Serial 1820), 1878.

——. *Troubles on the Texas Frontier*. House Executive Document 81, 36th Congress, 1st Session (Serial 1056), 1860.

——. *United States and Mexican Claims*. Senate Executive Document 31, 44th Congress, 2nd Session (Serial 1720), 1877.

——. *U.S. Relations with Mexico*. House Report 701, 45th Congress, 2nd Session (Serial 1824), 1878.

U.S. Secretary of War. *Annual Reports*, 1846–1890. Published as House Executive Documents in the U.S. Serial Set.

Utley, Robert M. *Changing Course: The International Boundary, United States and Mexico, 1848–1963*. Tucson: Southwest Parks and Monuments Association, 1996.

——. *Frontier Regulars: The United States Army and the Indian, 1866–1890*. New York: Macmillan, 1973; Lincoln: University of Nebraska Press, 1984.

——. *Frontiersmen in Blue: The United States Army and the Indian, 1848–1865*. New York: Macmillan, 1967; Lincoln: University of Nebraska Press, 1981.

——. *The Indian Frontier of the American West, 1846–1890*. Albuquerque: University of New Mexico Press, 1984.

Van Oden, Alonso. *Texas Ranger's Scrapbook*. Edited by Ann Jenson. Dallas: Kaleidograph, 1936.

Walker, Samuel. *Popular Justice: A History of American Criminal Justice*. New York: Oxford University Press, 1980.

Wallace, Ernest, and E. Adamson Hoebel. *The Comanches: Lords of the South Plains*. Norman: University of Oklahoma Press, 1952.

Weaver, John D. *The Brownsville Raid*. New York: W. W. Norton, 1970.

——. *The Senator and the Sharecropper's Son: Exoneration of the Brownsville Soldiers*. College Station: Texas A&M Press, 1997.

Webb, Walter Prescott. *The Texas Rangers: A Century of Frontier Defense*. Boston: Houghton Mifflin, 1935; Austin: University of Texas Press, 1965.

Weber, David J. *The Mexican Frontier, 1821–1846: The American Southwest under Mexico*. Albuquerque: University of New Mexico Press, 1982.

Weiss, Harold J., Jr. "Organized Constabularies: The Texas Rangers and the Early State Police Movement in the American Southwest." *Journal of the West* 34 (January 1995): 29–30.

——. "The Texas Rangers Revisited: Old Themes and New Viewpoints." *Southwestern Historical Quarterly* 97 (April 1994): 621–40.

——. "'Yours to Command': Captain William J. 'Bill' McDonald and the Panhandle Rangers of Texas." Ph.D diss., Indiana University, 1982.

Whittington, Robert D. *The Colt Whitneyville-Walker Pistol: A Study of the Pistol and Associated Characters, 1846–1851*. Hooks, Texas: Brownlee, 1984.

Wilbarger, John W. *Indian Depredations in Texas: Reliable Accounts of Battles, Wars, Adventures, Forays, Murders, Massacres, Etc. Etc., Together with Biographical Sketches of Many of the Most Noted Indian Fighters and Frontiersmen of Texas*. Austin: Hutchings, 1889; Austin: Pemberton, 1967.

Wilcox, Seb S. "The Laredo City Election and Riot of April, 1886." *Southwestern Historical Quarterly* 45 (July 1941): 1–23.

Wilkins, Frederick. *The Highly Irregular Irregulars: The Texas Rangers in the Mexican War*. Austin: Eakin, 1990.

——. *The Law Comes to Texas: The Texas Rangers, 1870–1901.* Austin: State House Press, 1999.

——. *The Legend Begins: The Texas Rangers, 1823–1845.* Austin: State House Press, 1996.

Williams, Robert H. "The Case for Peta Nocona." *Texana* 10 (1972): 55–72.

Winders, Richard B. *Mr. Polk's Army: The American Military Experience in the Mexican War.* College Station: Texas A&M Press, 1997.

Winfrey, Dorman H., and James M. Day, eds. *The Indian Papers of Texas and the Southwest, 1825–1916.* 5 vols. Austin: Texas State Historical Association, 1995.

Winkler, E. E., ed. "The Bexar and Dawson Prisoners." *Texas State Historical Association Quarterly* 13 (1909–1910): 294–95.

Woodman, Lyman I. *Cortina: The Rogue of the Rio Grande.* San Antonio: Naylor, 1950.

Wooster, Ralph A. "Texas Military Operations against Mexico, 1842–1843." *Southwestern Historical Quarterly* 67 (April 1964): 465–84.

Wooten, Dudley G., ed. *A Comprehensive History of Texas, 1685 to 1897.* 2 vols. Dallas: William G. Scharff, 1898.

Yoakum, Henderson K. *History of Texas from Its First Settlement in 1685 to Its Annexation to the United States in 1846.* 2 vols. New York: Redfield, 1855; Austin: Steck, 1935.

INDEX

Abilene, Texas, 235
Acklin, Kit, 332 n. 24
Affleck, J. D., 322 n. 1
Agua Nueva, Mexico, 76–77
Alabama,14, 121, 172, 174, 175
Alamo, 30, 37, 38, 41, 44, 52, 55, 56, 94, 294, 299
Albany, Texas, 217
Alexander, Andrew J., 165–67, 346 n. 13
Allison, W. M., 261–63
Alpine, Texas, 229, 264, 268
Alston, Fielding, 76–77
Amarillo, Texas, 257; prohibition in, 283–85
American Railway Union, 259–60
Ampudia, Pedro, 55, 67, 68, 73, 74
Anadarko Indians, 98, 100–01
Anglo Texans, 3, 4, 13, 287; attitudes toward
  blacks, 133, 134, 142, 239, 246, 260–61, 279–83;
  attitudes toward Indians, 18, 94, 288, 294; atti-
  tudes toward Mexicans, 18, 38, 41, 49, 555–56, 94,
  164, 245–46, 279, 288, 294; characterized, 14–15;
  national composition of, xii; origins of, 14; vio-
  lence of, 154–55
Antelope Hills, battle of, 101–2, 121, 122, 133, 299
Apache Indians, 179, 188, 192, 294, 299. See also
  specific tribes
Appalachian Mountains, 17, 153
Arizona Rangers, 302
Arizona Territory, 212, 237
Arkansas, 14, 125
Arkansas River, 6, 9, 22, 27, 89, 91, 102
Armstrong, John B., 170, 176; capture of John Wesley
  Hardin, 173–75, 347 n. 29; characterized, 171
Arrington, George W.: characterized, 217, 220, 221;
  explorations of, 220–21; feud of with Davidson,
  219–20
Arrington, William A., 20

Aten, Ira, 244–45, 247–48, 290, 356 n. 41; fence-cutters
  and, 236–37
Atkinson, John, 198, 199–200, 351 n. 27
Austin City Gazette, 32
Austin, Stephen F., 5, 13, 14, 15, 19, 94
Austin, Texas, 23, 28, 33, 35, 39, 43, 90, 100, 116, 126,
  134, 144, 146, 155, 170, 174, 177, 185, 188, 191, 204, 209,
  216, 219, 222, 248, 261, 269, 271, 274, 277, 278, 286;
  description of, 106

Bailey, David, 150
Baker, A. Y., 276–77, 279
Baker, David P., 140
Balcones Escarpment, 6, 22, 38
Ballowe, Samuel, 335 n. 24
Baltimore, Maryland, 74
Bancroft, Hubert H., 321 n. 1
Band of Brothers, 39
Bandera Pass, 139
barbed wire, 225, 233–39
Barela, Bernal, 217
Barela, Francisco (Chico), 191–92, 197, 198–201,
  205–06, 267, 349 n. 6
Barela, Tranquilino, 267
Barnes, Seaborn, 185–87, 349 n. 17
Barry, James B., 126–27, 129, 130–31, 133
Bass, Sam, 183–87, 295, 349 n. 17; characterized, 183
Bastrop, Texas, 19, 21
Batson oil field , 278
Baylor, George W., 207–9, 226, 251–52, 264, 349 n. 6;
  Apache campaigns of, 212–16; characterized, 208–9,
  216; fence-cutters and, 235–36
Baylor, John R., 103–4, 208
Bean, Roy, 229, 269
Beaumont, Texas, 278
Bee County, Texas, 243